Philosophical Practice

Philosophical Practice

LOU MARINOFF

City College
The City University of New York

Academic Press
San Diego New York Boston London Sydney Tokyo Toronto

Academic Press
a division of Harcourt, Inc.
525 B Street, Suite 1900, San Diego, California 92101-4495
http://www.academicpress.com

Academic Press
Harcourt Place, 32 Jamestown Road, London NW1 7BY, UK
http://www.academicpress.com

Library of Congress Control Number: 2001094342

International Standard Book Number: 0-12-471555-9

PRINTED IN UNITED STATES OF AMERICA
01 02 03 04 05 06 SB 9 8 7 6 5 4 3 2 1

Where Tao is, equilibrium is. When Tao is lost, out come all the differences of things.

Lao Tzu

It is impossible to believe something which is not the case—one can only believe what one is experiencing, and this is always true. What is possible, however, in my opinion, is that someone who is in an unsound mental state and whose beliefs are cognate with it can be made to think differently.

Plato

Men are not disturbed by things, but by the views which they take of things.

Epictetus

Many also (perhaps most men) either through defect of mind, or want of education, remain unfit during the whole course of their lives; yet have they, infants as well as those of riper years, a human nature; wherefore man is made fit for society not by nature, but by education.

Thomas Hobbes

The whole function of philosophy ought to be to find out what definite difference it will make to you and me, at definite instants of our life, if this world-formula or that world-formula be the true one.

William James

My purpose is to suggest a cure for the ordinary day-to-day unhappiness from which most people in civilized countries suffer, and which is all the more unbearable because, having no obvious external cause, it appears inescapable. I believe this unhappiness to be very largely due to mistaken views of the world, mistaken ethics, mistaken habits of life.

Bertrand Russell

I do not deny the fact that there is a widely prevalent sense of philosophy's bankruptcy in the twentieth century. But I would offer a different explanation of it—not that philosophy is at the end of the road, but that it is on the wrong road, that it is not dealing with the right problems in the right way. The appearance that philosophy gives of being bankrupt does not mean that it is really barren, but only that it is temporarily insolvent. That is a remediable condition.

Mortimer Adler

Having understood how human lives are diseased, a philosopher worthy of the name—like a doctor worthy of that name—will proceed to try to cure them. The whole point of medical research is cure. So, too, the whole point of philosophy is human flourishing.

Martha Nussbaum

Nemo veritatem regit [Nobody rules truth]

*motto of the American Philosophical
Practitioners Association*

CONTENTS

Acknowledgments   xiii

Foreword
Paul Sharkey   xv

Author's Preface   xix

PART **I**

Foundations of Philosophical Practice

1 Stand-Up Philosophy.   3
    Notes.   16

2 Is Philosophy a Way of Life?   21
    2.1. What Makes Philosophy Special as a Way of Life?   21
    2.2. What Makes Philosophy Special as a Discipline?   26
    Notes.   34

3 Why Is Philosophy Regaining Popularity?   37
    Notes.   52

PART **II**

Modes of Philosophical Practice

4   **Two Meanings of Meditation** 57
       Notes. 64

5   **Client Counseling** 67
    5.1. Some Formative Names 67
    5.2. How I Became a Philosophical Counselor 68
    5.3. The Geometry of Philosophical Counseling 72
    5.4. The Modality of Dialogue. 79
    5.5. A Typology of Philosophical Counseling Dialogue 87
    5.6. The Golden Triangle. 94
       Notes. 105

6   **Philosophy with Groups—and Groupies**. 109
    6.1. Is "Group Philosophy" an Oxymoron? 109
    6.2. The Philosopher's Café 112
    6.3. Nelsonian Socratic Dialogue. 125
    6.4. Philosophy With Other Groups 136
       Notes. 137

7   **The Corporate Philosopher** 139
    7.1. Origins of Philosophical Consulting 139
    7.2. General Services. 153
    7.3. Substance, Form, and Artistry 159
         Motivational Speaking 160
         Ethics Code-Building. 161
         Ethics Compliance. 162
         Moral Self-Defense 163
         Short Socratic Dialogue 164
         Dilemma Training. 165
         The PEACE Process 167
         Leadership and Governance. 168
         Artistry 168
    7.4. The Summit of Practice 170
       Notes. 172

PART **III**

Professionalization of Philosophical Practice

8 Pioneering Versus Pedagogy 177

    Notes. 196

9 The Making of a Profession 199

    9.1. Programs of Training at Universities or Institutes
         Chartered by the State and Accredited by Professional
         Accrediting Bodies 200
    9.2. Established Criteria (Including an Examination)
         for Certification of Practitioners. 212
         APPA Certification Standards. 213
         Certification Standards for Client Counselors. 215
         Certification Standards for Group Facilitators. 216
         Certification Standards for Organizational Consultants 217
    9.3. Established Body of Knowledge as Reflected in the
         Publication of Reference Books and Professional
         Journals and Regularly Scheduled Scientific
         [sic: Read "Learned"] Meetings 220
    9.4. Established Code of Ethics. 221
         Standards of Professional Ethical Practice. 222
         Notes. 227

10 Recognition Versus Regulation. 229

    10.1. The Political Economy of Regulation 229
    10.2. Licensure 231
    10.3. Certification. 239
    10.4. Registration 241
    10.5. Recognition qua Politics 242
         Notes 244

PART **IV**

Marketing of Philosophical Practice

11   IRB Approval of Research Programs   249

    11.1.   Commodities and Public Service.   249
    11.2.   Research Involving Human Subjects   250
        1.   Evidence that You Are a Qualified Philosophical
           Counselor.   251
        2.   A Description of Your Scope of Practice   252
        3.   A Script (i.e., Advertisement) that You Will
           Use to Recruit Potential Subjects   254
        4.   A Contingency Plan and Referral List to Other
           Counseling Professions   254
        5.   Instrument of Informed Consent and Relevant
           Procedural Details   257
    11.3.   Bridging Necessity and Sufficiency   259
    11.4.   Post-hoc Speculations   261
        Notes   262

12   Hanging Out a Counseling Shingle   263

    Key #1: Publicity.   279
    Key #2: Promotion   283
    Key #3: Packaging.   284
        Notes.   286

13   Opportunities for Facilitators.   289

    13.1.   Informal Facilitation: The Philosopher's Café Revisited   289
    13.2.   Formal Facilitation: Socratic Dialogue Revisited   290
    13.3.   Philosophy for Children   291
    13.4.   Philosophy for Undergraduates.   295
    13.5.   Philosophy for Seniors.   298
    13.6.   Philosophy for Felons   299
    13.7.   Philosophy for the Otherwise Challenged.   301
        Notes   302

14 Opportunities for Consultants 305

The Modularity of Practice 306
The General Nature of Conflict in
    the Workplace 306
Special Effects of Diversity on Conflict in
    the Workplace 310
Inability of Political Correctness and Other
    Oppressive Ideological Mechanisms to
    Manage Such Conflicts Equitably 315
The Rising Importance of Ethics Compliance,
    and the Ethical Unpreparedness of Generic
    Management Consultants 317
Notes 320

PART **V**

Politics of Philosophical Practice

15 Friends and Foes of Philosophical Practice 325

15.1. Psychiatry 326
15.2. Psychology 328
15.3. Philosophy 334
    Coffeehouse Mentality 337
    Sophistry 339
    Fraud 344
    Ambivalence 345
    Concealing Personal Problems Behind
        Philosophical Facades 346
    Academic Vanity, Fear of Change or Appearance
        of Inadequacy 347
    Notes 349

16 International and Interprofessional Relations 351

16.1.   National and International Relations 351
16.2.   Interprofessional Relations 353
    Notes 358

17   Making and Breaking News   359

   17.1.   Parting Shots   359
   17.2.   *Plato not Prozac* Goes Global   360
   17.3.   Surf and Turf at City College: Making Waves
         and Defending Territory   362
   17.4.   Philosophy and the World Economic Forum   366
   17.5.   Last Word.   367
         Notes   367

References   369

Appendices

   A   APPA Membership Information   377
   B   Directory of APPA-Certified Practitioners   381
   C   Directory of Organizations   393
   D   Select Bibliography on Philosophical Practice   397
   E   Scholarly Journals   399

Index   401

ACKNOWLEDGMENTS

I gratefully acknowledge the encouragement and advice of many acquaintances, friends and supporters of philosophical practice, including Steven Balch, Paul Bennett, Joelle Delbourgo, Moshe Denburg, Ruben Diaz Jr., Paul del Duca, Mary Lou Edmondson, Lawrence Fleischer, John Greenwood, Mahin Hassibi, Merle Hoffman, Katie Layman, Thomas Morales, Ron Perowne, Christian Perring, Ernesto Spinelli, Tanis Salant, Jeremy Stangroom, Jennifer Stark, and Edwin Villenova.

I am also grateful for the help and advice of many colleagues in the movement, including Lydia Amir, Dries Boele, Stanley Chan, Vaughana Feary, Jess Fleming, Pierre Grimes, Will Heutz, Alex Howard, Ida Jongsma, Peter Koestenbaum, Ran Lahav, Mark du Mas, Christopher McCullough, Tom Morris, Ron Nahser, Anette Prins, J. Michael Russell, and especially Paul Sharkey.

I am profoundly grateful to four friends and colleagues in particular, who troubled to read the manuscript and offer constructive criticisms and helpful suggestions that greatly conduced to its amelioration and final preparation. Moshe Denburg contributed sound diplomatic advice, even if I didn't always follow it. Vaughana Feary helped me to be more conciliatory in tone, or at least less unconciliatory. Alex Howard hunted every hare; no utterance or implication eluded his meticulous scrutiny. Paul Sharkey not only wrote the Foreword, but also encouraged me to express myself both creatively and candidly, and reminded me of my philosophical entitlement—if not duty—to defy political fashion in order to rescue some flotsam of rhyme or jetsam of reason from the shipwreck of contemporary American culture.

Thanks also if not essentially to Mark Zadrozny of Academic Press, who invited this book to begin with, and to Tim Oliver, who copy-edited the manuscript and typeset and designed the final product.

I bear sole responsibility for any errors, whether of fact or of judgment.

The views expressed herein are mine. Although I am a founder of the APPA, I do not speak for it—only for myself, as a philosopher.

FOREWORD

This is a book I wish did not have to be written, yet one which I hope will not be the last of its kind. The plain, simple, and sad fact of the matter is that the central relation of philosophy and of philosophers to the foundations of virtually every important institution of western civilization (not to mention their effects upon our personal and professional lives) has been largely ignored, unappreciated, and even disparaged—all too often by philosophers themselves.

Like many of our profession, I did not set out to be a philosopher. I thought I was going to be a doctor of a different kind, certainly one for whom there would be a better income and more social recognition. Yet also like many of our profession, once I was introduced to it I could not leave philosophy alone, nor would it leave me alone. To put this a bit more positively, I have not found myself alone since entering the wonder-filled world of thought and ideas of those who preceded and coexist with me in the love of wisdom—a constant and ongoing dialogue with men and women of every time and every culture, seeking answers to life's biggest questions, the wonders of the universe, the meaning and purpose of life. Yet in the course of becoming formally educated in this most ancient and noble of disciplines, the paradox of its practical importance to virtually every aspect of my life became increasingly and abundantly clear. Virtually everything I believed and every institution of the world in which I lived—from religion to science, health to politics, economics to education, and ethics to art—had its foundations in the thought of one or another of those individuals the world calls "philosophers"; and yet that very world seemed to view philosophy as irrelevant, impractical, and worthless. It seemed to have been taken over by educators who were uneducated, counselors who needed counsel, moralists who were unethical, healers who were unhealthy, and politicians who were unjust. Something seemed clearly wrong—a wrong which needed to be righted.

This book is one of the many necessary steps in that direction. It not only provides an account of philosophy's current renaissance as a discipline of applied practice, but also does so in the context of a penetrating critique of the historical, social, and cultural forces which have contributed to its recent descent into relative obscurity. *Plato Not Prozac*, by the same author, also called attention to this renaissance, but it was written (and coauthored) for a popular audience. *Philosophical Practice* is a book about philosophy, by a philosopher, for philosophers. It represents a long-ignored and undervalued meta-philosophical viewpoint: the heretical idea that philosophy might actually be put to practical use, that it might have something useful to say about the events and issues of our time, that it might actually make a difference in our lives. For this reason alone it is bound to be controversial and anathema to some, inspirational and gospel to others.

We all practice philosophy. The only question is whether we do so self-consciously and well, or unconsciously and poorly. Our beliefs shape the course of our actions, policies forge the future of businesses, and a culture's philosophy determines the character of its civilization. As long as these remain unconscious and unexamined, they control us. By becoming aware of them, their origins, nature, conflicts and consequences, we gain control of them and thereby our lives. In other words, when Socrates said, "the unexamined life is not worth living," he was not just expressing an abstract principle of personal introspection but a practical necessity underlying all human freedom and the course of human destiny. Philosophy is neither irrelevant, impractical, nor worthless. It is ultimately the ruler, both as destiny and measure, of our lives. Not every philosopher of the twentieth century has been blind to this fact. In his concluding remarks to *Science and The Modern World*, Alfred North Whitehead poignantly observed that

> the great conquerors, from Alexander to Caesar, and from Caesar to Napoleon, influenced profoundly the lives of subsequent generations. But the total effect of this influence shrinks to insignificance, if compared to the entire transformation of human habits and human mentality produced by the long line of men of thought from Thales to the present day, men individually powerless, but ultimately the rulers of the world.

And yet, the world doesn't know it. *Philosophical Practice* is here to change that.

Contrary to popular belief, philosophers and their philosophies are not creatures confined to Ivory Towers. Their thoughts and ideas are woven into the very fabric in which we clothe our lives. We are not and cannot be "emperors in new clothes," going forth naked while pretending to be dressed in the finest of garments. No, ours is the opposite folly. We pretend to be naked, all the while oblivious to the fact that we are dressed in rags because of our failure to attend to our wardrobe. It is not a question of whether we practice philosophies; it is only a question of whether we are aware of them, whether they fit comfortably, clash, or are appropriate for the occasion. This book draws our attention back to this fact and offers both a chronicle and a critique of philosophy's recent descent into obscurity. It is an invitation for philosophy and philosophers to come out of the closet.

In the West at least, philosophy was conceived within the ever-changing influences of conflict, commerce, and communication. Were it not for the multicultural exchange of ideas and worldviews piggybacked on the wars and commerce of the peoples of the ancient Aegean and Mediterranean cultures, western philosophy (and with it western civilization) might never have been born. Yet never before in history was there such a time as now, in which the forces of commerce and communication have become so globally immense, instantaneous, and multiculturally diverse. Neither has there been a time in which philosophical insight and skill were more urgent or important—or more scarce in their practical application. Again, *Philosophical Practice* is here to change that.

There was once a time when a classical education—even a classical professional education—not only included but was also founded upon the philosophical insights, principles, and traditions of one's culture and its heritage. This is unfortunately no longer the case. Philosophy—the very mother of the academy—is more and more finding itself either entirely excluded from or at least pushed to the furthest fringes of academic curricula. The profession that once provided counsel to kings and comfort to peasants now finds itself on the endangered species list of professional disciplines. Once thought to be indispensable for the practical integration of one's talents, virtue, and character, philosophy now finds itself characterized as abstract, frivolous, and impractical. Yet nothing could be further from the truth nor more dangerous in its blindness.

Philosophical Practice is dedicated to examining the philosophical myopia, and its consequences, of the last century and to correcting it by encouraging those who still have eyes to see to become the visionaries and guides for those who haven't. It is not, however, a philosophical eye-chart. It should not be read as asserting the only *correct* way of seeing all the issues with which it deals. To paraphrase the typical disclaimer, "The views expressed in *Philosophical Practice* are those of its author and do not necessarily represent those of ..." Nor would the author have it any other way. The point of philosophical practice is not to tell anyone how or what to think. It is rather to encourage them to think for themselves: philosophically, practically, and responsibly. That is what this book encourages, and, whether it does so by provoking debate or inspiring assent, it will have accomplished that task at least. At its heart, *Philosophical Practice* is a rallying cry, a motivational speech, a provocation to action.

It is not, I think, the place of a writer of a foreword to a book to summarize its contents, criticize its arguments, or challenge either its or its readers' perspectives on the various issues it addresses. I have complete trust and confidence in the intelligence and philosophical skill of its author, Lou Marinoff, and you, its reader, as being more than adequate to those tasks. However, having had the privilege of reading the manuscript before you, I cannot help but make a few remarks about my own reactions to at least some of its content and style.

Lou Marinoff is a talented writer. His skill at word crafting is sometimes brilliant, never dull, and usually insightful. Like many of his other works, and Lou himself, *Philosophical Practice* has its moments of acerbic wit, if not downright caustic critique. Some may think its treatment of this or that particular issue to be "over-done," but in most cases, and upon careful review, I have found them to be generally accurate, entertainingly advanced, and reflectively profound. Upon my first reading, I thought its treatment of university administrators to be perhaps a bit harsh and overstated. But after reflecting on my own thirty-plus years acquaintance with them (and even having been one myself), I had to admit that the characterization was generally true to my experience—similarly so its treatment of what has happened to education in this country. I will not here comment on the many other provocative issues encompassed in the content of this volume. They include examinations of "political correctness," "equal opportunity," and "the new world order," to name but a few. Despite its forays into social and political critique, however, the reader needs to keep in mind its central purpose: the annunciation of philosophy's return to the practical concerns of living in the quest for a life well-lived.

Finally and in conclusion, a word about style. Composing prose, I think, is not entirely unlike performing music. Each has its timbre, cadence, accent, and melody. I know Lou Marinoff to be a talented musician and accomplished classical guitarist. I believe this talent is also manifest in the compositional style of this volume. Enjoy the performance!

Paul W. Sharkey, PhD, MPH
Los Angeles, 2001

AUTHOR'S PREFACE

The phenomenon of philosophical practice is proliferating and evolving around the globe. The purpose of this book is to describe the field as it currently stands, from a practitioner's point of view. Yet these two assertions are somewhat contradictory. Since the field is dynamic, not static, it hardly stands in any place; it continually gains—and therefore regularly shifts—its ground. So the description this book affords is more akin to a quick snapshot, or a rough-and-ready portrait, rather than a photographic retrospective or extensive exhibition of the subject.

This book is also intended to complement my popular self-help book, *Plato Not Prozac*, which at this writing continues to fare remarkably well, both in the United States and internationally.[1] *Plato Not Prozac* looks at philosophical practice from the outside-in, that is, from the client's perspective. It illustrates how philosophical counseling in particular (and other forms of philosophical practice in general) can help one resolve or manage a host of everyday problems—ranging from interpersonal conflicts to mid-life crises, from moral dilemmas to existential angst, from coping with loss to leading a meaningful life, and so forth. Most such problems are neither symptoms of brain diseases nor resultants of emotional traumas, and are therefore best treated neither by psychiatry nor psychology. Rather, the manifestation of difficulties in life is indicative of the human condition, and of life itself. Such problems being the norm, they are best addressed by examining neither one's brain chemistry nor one's childhood traumas; rather, by examining one's present intentions, volitions, desires, attachments, beliefs, and aspirations. This is quintessentially a philosophical task. *Plato Not Prozac* offers laypersons a new way to conceptualize their quotidian difficulties, and a new language in which to articulate and manage them: neither a pseudo-medical diagnosis, nor a political dialectic, rather a philosophical dialogue.

By contrast, this book looks at philosophical practice from the inside-out, from the viewpoint of the practitioner or prospective practitioner, rather than that of the client or prospective client. What exactly is entailed by philosophical practice? What are its aims and methods? How does philosophical counseling differ from psychological counseling and other forms of psychotherapy? How are philosophical practitioners educated and trained? How do philosophical practitioners relate to other professions? What are the politics of philosophical practice? How does one become a practitioner? How does one avoid becoming a practitioner? What is APPA Certification? What are the prospects for philosophical practice in the USA and elsewhere? This book answers these and similar questions. Inasmuch as *Plato Not Prozac* fosters and fuels a growing consumer demand for philosophical services, this book fosters and fuels the supply of practitioners.

Given its "snapshot" characterization of the field, this book is also a kind of instant history. William Shirer observed that there are primarily two good occasions on which to write a history of anything.[2] The first is while the salient events themselves are yet unfolding, or have lately unfolded, with the writer thus positioned in their immediate wake. The advantages of this way are currency and authenticity of viewpoint; its disadvantages, subjective preoccupation, and incompleteness of perspective. This way was adopted by Shirer himself, in his *Rise and Fall of the Third Reich*. It was earlier adopted by Thucydides, in his *History of the Peloponnesian War*. Both are magnificent works. The second is long after the salient events and their significant repercussions have abated, with the writer thus ensconced in the unaffected observatory of hindsight. The advantages of this way are detachment and objectivity; its disadvantages, subjective preoccupation and over-completeness of perspective. This way was (necessarily) adopted by Gibbon, in his *Decline and Fall of the Roman Empire*, and by Toynbee, in *A Study of History*. Again, both are magnificent works. Human history—writ large or small, during or after—is largely the history of struggle, conflict, revolution, and warfare of various kinds.

The history of philosophy is not too different, save that its associated wars are far less sanguinary but much more protracted. We philosophers argue across centuries for or against this or that notion in Plato, or Hobbes, or Nietzsche, as if they were present among us, which of course they are noetically. Their ideas cannot be slain, only made more or less fashionable according to the contingencies and exigencies of the day, and of the patchwork quilt of other histories or narratives that inform, epitomize, and ultimately define the day. Although philosophy is not flesh-and-blood, it animates and governs flesh-and-blood, and does so either for the betterment or to the detriment of flesh-and-blood. Quoth Trotsky: "You may not be interested in the Dialectic, but the Dialectic is interested in you."[3] Quoth Bagehot: "It is often said that men are ruled by their imaginations, but it would be truer to say they are governed by the weakness of their imaginations."[4] Quoth Buddha: "All that we are is a creation of our thoughts."[5] We philosophers are neither buried under the mountain of rent flesh nor drowned in the sea of shed blood that is human history writ large; rather, we are wanderers through the labyrinth of human ideas, explorers of the galaxy of human mentation, pilgrims in the wilderness of human potential. We forge or conquer empires of the mind.

To write an insider's account of philosophical practice is, at this juncture in the history of the movement, to perform a recursive function: writing a book on philosophical practice is itself a form of philosophical practice. It entails both the responsibility of introducing the field to those who want to know more about it, and the occupational hazard of characterizing and reshaping the field by way of introduction. If badly done, it could degenerate into a self-serving exercise in onanistic bathos, like that of the unaccomplished academician who updates his CV every week, by the expedient of listing on it the dates on which he updated it. So his CV contains entries such as "September 15: updated CV," etcetera.[6]

To me, philosophical practice represents both a revolution and a renaissance. It is revolutionary in that it offers alternative (and highly effective) ways of dealing with common problems, ways that appear to fly in the face of not one but many powerfully entrenched establishments. Some psychiatrists claim we are practicing medicine without a license; some psychologists claim we are untrained and can't recognize severe emotional dysfunction; some academic philosophers claim that "true philosophy" can't be practiced at all. Beyond them, some anti-academics claim that "true philosophy" can't be practiced by anyone with a PhD or a Professorship. Thus we practitioners are clearly revolutionaries, not so much on account of what we do, but on account of the reactions to what we do, from self-identifying reactionaries and radicals of many stripes.

And just what do we do? We simply utilize philosophy to help people. While those psychiatrists and psychologists who oppose us are not necessarily opposed to helping people, they are understandably opposed to us exposing them as unable to help everyone, or unable to help some whom we can help, or willing to harm some people by offering them inappropriate help. They see us as trespassers on their turf. Bear in mind that "their turf" is *your* noetic discomfort. Given that there are tens of thousands of them and only dozens of us, and that behind them stand the deep pockets of the pharmaceutical industry and the monopolistic laws on psychotherapy, we certainly appear as a band of revolutionaries—or more precisely, Davids to their Goliath. Behind us stands one small item, immune to capital and Capitol alike: namely, the truth about the power of the mind. Part of that truth is that philosophy can and does help people solve or manage many everyday problems. And as that truth comes to be experienced by increasing numbers of people, our turf wars are won, our cultural revolution is accomplished, and our philosophical Renaissance blossoms.

I believe that writing books is analogous to bearing children. I have done the former myself, and at least have been a party to the latter. Both require conception, gestation, and labor. But with books, the conception is not necessarily or altogether pleasurable; the gestation, indefinitely protractable; and the labor, painstakingly prolongable. A writer can conceive, gestate and also abort a book wherever he finds himself, but the labor of bringing one forth often calls for an accustomed surrounding, a patterned routine, a measured exertion. It is my preferred mode to write every and all morning, to imbibe exactly two cups of coffee brewed from freshly ground beans, to take in a peripheral view from a window onto a landscape or cityscape, to be surrounded by quietude and motionlessness in and around my sunlit study, and to hear nothing more than the sounds of the sea and sea-birds, or the sibilant rustle and muted chatter of the forest, or the swishing, grinding, and hooting of urban traffic from afar. Thus ensconced in my chair, gazing at my monitor, tapping on my keyboard and dancing in my mind, I catalyze thoughts into books.

Alas, such was not the case with this one. The opportunities and demands of philosophical practice keep me traveling year-round, with a laptop computer as my constant companion and an internet connection as my daily destination. Plucked from my familiar surroundings by a flood-tide of events, I have written this book on the fly. I have written it on planes and trains; in airports and railway stations; over hill and dale; high in the Rocky Mountains and under the English Channel. I have written it in two dozen American states and a dozen foreign countries. I have written it in hotels, motels, inns, and guest-houses, sometimes waking up in the morning not knowing exactly where I was, but knowing precisely what I had to write. I have written it at all hours, from unpredictable vistas with unpotable coffee. In sum, I have penned it from pillar to post. Some days I would rather have written it ten years hence, with the usual benefits of hindsight, in an unchanging place, in an unhurried frame of mind. Then again, my peregrinations have also conduced to my understanding of philosophical practice—in terms of who practices what, which clients contract what services, and how the movement evolves in light of local or national ethos. Thus, Lao Tzu was wrong for once: "The more one travels, the less one knows"[7] is happily falsified by wearying counterexample.

If you dislike polemicism, stop reading now. I evidently have some natural talent for it, which I have taken few pains to suppress. Some years ago, in England, one of my PhD thesis examiners was so appalled by my excavation of the philosophical foundations of human conflict that he was moved to call me "the Thomas Hobbes of the twentieth century." This being the twenty-first, I obviously have a reputation to maintain. So do not take undue umbrage at my criticisms of the academy herein. They are motivated by my love and esteem of all that can be right with it, in the face of much that has gone wrong with it. There are really only two ways to irritate people: by telling lies about them, or truths about them. Irritating truths are sometimes called "polemics," with a view to dismissing their veracity by disparaging their attire. This book emanates from my heart as well as my mind; it is therefore reflection infused with passion. Such is the exercise of philosophical license. You are free to dislike it, but not to revoke it.

I also penned this book during lulls in various battles, and from the eyes of several storms. As our movement gathers strength and force, and restores a semblance of cosmos to a civilization flirting with chaos, it also seethes and swirls within, and encounters tumultuousness without. Dear reader: Be neither overstimulated by the effects, nor intoxicated by the success, nor corrupted by the power, nor disgusted by the faction, nor distracted by the possibilities of this movement. All great movements require stillness at their cores. The stiller we become, the more we can move. And by moving minds, we move the very world.

NOTES

1. For some details, see Chapter 17 herein, "Making and Breaking News."
2. See the Foreword in W. Shirer, *The Rise and Fall of the Third Reich* (London: Book Club Associates, 1985; original work published 1959).
3. Paraphrased by M. Walzer, *Just and Unjust Wars* (London: Allen Lane, 1978), p. 29.
4. W. Bagehot, *The English Constitution* (London: C.A. Watts & Co., 1964; original work published 1867), p. 82.

5. Cited by C. Humphreys, *Karma and Rebirth* (London: Curzon Press, 1983), p. 29: "All that we are is the result of what we have thought; it is founded on our thoughts, it is made up of our thoughts." See also Buddha's *Dhammapada*, trans. H. Kaviratna (Pasadena: Theosophical University Press, 1980), p. 5: "All the phenomena of existence have mind as their precursor, mind as their supreme leader, and of mind are they made."

6. Mark Glouberman acquainted me with this form of mockery, by private communication, 1993.

7. Lao Tzu, *Tao Te Ching*, trans. Ch'u Ta-Kao (London: George Allen & Unwin, 1959), p. 62.

Lou Marinoff
New York City, 2001

PART I

Foundations of Philosophical Practice

CHAPTER 1

Stand-Up Philosophy

J meet a lot of well-educated people these days, erudite at least by postmodern standards. But since "postmodern standard" is an oxymoron, erudition has become largely synonymous with functional literacy at the level of a contextless teleprompter. A sizeable proportion of these nouveau-erudite managed to avoid philosophy courses altogether during what passed for their higher educations. Some eschewed it because they heard it was too difficult—in other words, they could not get an "A" merely by showing up regularly, chewing gum earnestly, and highlighting every sentence of the text assiduously. Others took the odd philosophy course, but either recall nothing of it (save the meta-recollection that it was unmemorable), or say that it disappointed them greatly, owing to its complete lack of relevance to their lives. A few fortunate ones had inspiring philosophy professors, who awakened in them all the wonder of the world. Now philosophy professors cannot take sole credit for putting students to sleep in lecture-halls; any professor worth his salt can accomplish this task with any subject-matter. Nor can philosophy professors take sole credit for giving unmemorable courses; the visual tradition that has replaced the written tradition in American culture begins by eroding attention span instead of developing it, and ends by attenuating memory instead of expanding it—or, after T. S. Eliot, of mixing it with desire.

But professors of philosophy must assume responsibility for having managed to reduce their subject to irrelevancy in the larger community. Philosophy forms the foundation of all rational inquiry—whether scientific, theological, ethical, axiological, aesthetic—and is the wellspring even of idle speculation. People hold strong beliefs about themselves and others and the world, and whether these are well- or ill-founded is a matter of philosophical examination. People make daily inferences about themselves and others and the world, and whether these are sound or unsound is a matter of philosophical rigor. People obey or break laws, and follow or defy customs, according to their philosophical interpretations of justice, liberty, and right. People seek, find, or deny meaning and purpose in their lives and deaths, according to their philosophical conceptions of these very things. People make myriad choices on a daily basis, guided by their philosophical deliberations, or blinded by a conspicuous lack thereof. People constantly wonder who and where they are, how they came to be who and where they are, and who they shall become and in what place and by what means and to what end they shall become it. These are quintessentially philosophical questions. So how in Heaven's name has philosophy managed to make itself irrelevant in the larger community? Even university students who cannot read, write, reckon, or reason, who cannot say whether the earth orbits the sun or the sun the earth, who have never heard of plane geometry, the periodic table, or natural selection, who cannot explain the terms "social democracy" or "cold war," who do not know how to convert a raw test score into a percentage—even these nouveau-erudite students somehow know that philosophy plays, or ought to play, a central role in their lives.

By the late twentieth century, philosophy had all but ceased to be a mode of active engagement with oneself and the world—as it was in antiquity and throughout the ages—and had become too frequently a drab and deficient mind-game, with no apparent purpose other than to grapple with concepts about concepts about concepts, ad nauseam if not ad infinitum. Instead of attracting students, it repelled them. University administrators began to down-size philosophy departments and merge them with two other endangered academic species: classics and religious studies.

The demise of classics and religious studies has been gradual but relentless. When a civilization acquires and transmits a primary (i.e., "first") language, it can then afford the luxury of studying the languages, and thereby the cultures, of other civilizations. Since Western civilization was built on the foundations of Hellenic and Roman civilizations, and also of Judaeo-Christian religions (liberally admixed with paganism), it behooved the torch-bearers to study Greek, Latin, and Scripture. In the 1960s, I was a beneficiary, at Lower Canada College, of an excellent secondary Canadian education—which would have been a superlative education in America, and an above-average one in Britain at the time. Because we studied formal English grammar and composition (two separate subjects aside from literature!), and thus acquired sufficient command of a first language, we were able to learn Latin and—since we lived in the Province of Quebec—French as well. We had six or seven years of Latin, and slightly more than a token amount of Scripture (Old and New Testament). Years later, when I met more senior university colleagues whose secondary educations had also included Greek and copious amounts of Scripture, I felt positively cheated by comparison. America, still spearheading the decline, has now reached a stage in which English is taught as a second language to immigrants, but no longer as a first language to citizens. Many Americans have no formal first language at all (grunts, hoots, profanities, vernacular, and monosyllables notwithstanding); English, if acquired, is therefore their informal second language. That being the case, it is increasingly pointless to teach classics in the universities.

Religious studies have suffered a similar fate: the Statist abdication of moral authority, and its deconstruction of and prohibition on moral instruction, has turned out a generation of assorted hedonists, barbarians, vulgarians, yahoos, sociopaths, and juvenile mass-murderers. Secularization of education by the political left, and its concomitant relativization of ethics and New Age return to pantheism, has been the naive prelude to this dismal fugue. Instead of truly diversifying and enriching the moral curriculum by studying the Koran, the Talmud, the Upanishads, the Pali Canon, and the Tao Te Ching in addition to the Books of Moses and the Gospels of Jesus, religious studies have been made illegal in public schools, and replaced instead by mandatory and vindictive propagandizations that attempt to normalize moral relativism, social depravity, and sexual aberration. The result is polarization: half the American populace has no conception of morality whatsoever, and therefore declines unchecked into ignorance, barbarism, and eventually savagery; the other half embraces religious fundamentalisms, and so imbibes with their moral teachings the ineluctable toxins of intolerance, zealotry, dogma, anti-science, and a return to the worst aspects of Dark Age superstition—or else New Age pantheism. That being the case, it is increasingly pointless to teach religious studies in the universities.

The foundations of Western civilization having partially rotted through apathetic political neglect, and having been weakened by parasitic gnawings of neo-Marxists, bureaucrats, militant racialist, and feminist proto-fascists,[1] bureaucrats, deconstructionists, bureaucrats, social constructivists, bureaucrats, and other verminous pests (not to mention bureaucrats), the academic edifice of Western civilization seems ready to collapse. In a final act of supreme irony, those who have failed to maintain it, and those who have sought to demolish it, are conspiring to blame their defects on those who built it. Meanwhile, the poor citizens who merely inhabit it, and who aspire to eke out some kind of existence within it, having been made systematically incognizant of its builders and therefore incognizant too of the distinction between appearance and reality, mistakenly cheer when the demolition team arrives to evict them and plant the charges. "We're here to improve your home," they say to the hapless citizens. "We're here to make you homeless" is what they mean.

To all this I say "WHOA!" acronymically. The acronym is a conjunction of Whorf–Hobbes–Orwell–Ayer; its components together serve to characterize the current predicament of the West, and the role of philosophical practice in ameliorating the situation. In the twentieth century, Benjamin Whorf (along with Sapir) observed that natural language is neither value-neutral nor flawlessly objectively descriptive, that the way we view the world is partly (or largely) determined by our idiomatic conventions, our linguistic structures, our semantic functions.[2] Take, for example, the meaning of "addiction." We speak of a heroin addict as someone whose body needs regularly to metabolize this drug in order to function. Given a sufficient presence of this drug, the addict experiences pleasurable narcotic intoxication, and remains quasi-functional in other ways. But given a sufficient absence of the drug, the addict's body exhibits severely unpleasant symptoms of withdrawal, and his mind becomes accordingly dysfunctional. The addict is therefore a literal slave of the addictive substance, in so far as his labor is devoted chiefly to its procurement, and his state of "addicted well-being" depends entirely on its regular imbibement. When we speak of a drug-addict, we know whereof we speak.

But lately the word "addiction" is used (or abused) with increasing breadth by psychologists, which results in increasing imprecision in its meaning, particularly as such usage (or misusage) is rapidly mimicked by the public. For example, people with greater-than-average appetites for sexual congress are called "sex-addicts"; and people who spend longer-than-average periods surfing the worldwide web are called "internet-addicts." The absurdity of such misusage becomes apparent if one protracts it to a further extreme. Most people sleep every night; are they therefore "sleep-addicts"? Most people eat every day; are they therefore "food-addicts"? Are professional tennis players, who practice several hours per day, "tennis-addicts"? Similarly, are musicians "music-addicts"? Are people who practice zazen every morning "zen addicts"? Ultimately, are people who persist in remaining alive by refusing to commit suicide "life-addicts"?

A short exercise in critical thinking (i.e., informal logic), which "postmodern education" oxymoronically neglects, clarifies this confusion. While all addictions entail appetites, not all appetites entail addictions. For example, while all heroin addicts have a periodic appetite for heroin, a periodic appetite for sex does not make one a sex addict. In sum, while all heroin addicts crave heroin regularly, not all persons who crave a given thing regularly are necessarily addicted to that thing. While craving is not usually good for one, it is not the same as addiction.

A heroin addict who needs money for heroin will rob or steal or sell himself in order to satisfy his craving. But a person who craves sex will not necessarily or even usually rape in order to satisfy that craving. Similarly, a person who craves the internet, but whose gateway is temporarily shut, will not necessarily or usually break into someone else's home to gain access. A person habituated to watching too much TV, when traveling in a foreign land without cable service, or during a power outage in his own region, will not go through debilitating physical withdrawal from his habit: he will simply either find something else to do, or will experience boredom. There are no "TV addicts"; there is only misuse of language.

It really amounts to conflating figurative with literal speech. We speak literally of a heroin addict; figuratively of a "television addict." But when psychologists ignorantly or negligently drop the diacritical quotes, and imagine they are really diagnosing "the disease" of television addiction, we experience the full sociological force of the Whorf–Sapir hypothesis: what begins by misusing language to reify putative entities that have no existence in extra-mental reality, continues by elaborating social and professional structures that purport to diagnose, research, and treat the nonexisting condition. The surest and quickest way to eliminate bogus "diseases" would be to eliminate those who reify them. Teaching the reifiers critical thinking would be more compassionate, but also much more laborious.

Psychologists did not invent this trick; they merely copied it from psychiatrists. Thomas Szasz has done legion work in exposing the psychiatric myth of "mental illness," but that myth is so deeply embedded in the remnants of collective American consciousness that no one man's life work—even that of an extraordinary man like Szasz—can possibly excise it merely by publishing insightful books.[3] Re-education, as always, is the key. But since we are in the process of destroying our civilization by de-education, we are not yet ready for re-education. That will come, as usual, once it is too late.

The Hobbesian contribution to the WHOA conglomerate is brief, pointed, and salient. In the bifurcation of logos into speech and reason, Hobbes's nominalism compels him to assign causal primacy (and his empiricism, epistemological primacy) to the former. He asserts, in other words, not that we can speak because we can reason; rather, that we can reason because we can speak. Thus spoken words are the very tokens of reason, not its byproducts. Hobbes's hypothesis is well-supported by the few but horrifying documented cases of feral children;[4] and particularly well-supported by some the gibberish that passes, oxymoronically, for "postmodern scholarship."[5] Though Hobbes's criticisms were directed at the Schoolmen who employed such nonsensical phrases as "incorporeal substance" in their post-peripatetic ramblings—which passed for "philosophy" during the Dark Ages (which is precisely why they were "Dark," and why Bacon and Hobbes precipitated the Enlightenment)—they may just as acutely be redirected at the reified disease, or the deconstructed gobbledygook, or the New Age psychobabble, that passes for the reasoned speech of the current Endarkenment.[6]

Hobbes's thesis is simple and demonstrable: precision of speech fosters precision of reasoning; imprecision of speech fosters imprecision of reasoning.

The implications of his thesis are also evident and chilling in contemporary America: imprecise reasonings about matters of illness, immorality or injustice, having initially been fostered by imprecise speech, themselves proceed to foster inappropriate social structures, inappropriate economic policies, inappropriate legislative measures, inappropriate judicial remedies, and ultimately inappropriate political sanctions.

Another pervasive consequence of the Whorf–Hobbes component of our current linguistic and semantic malaise is "fuzzy speech," wherein even the most literal meanings of words and acronyms are obscured by a haze of blurred mentation. We are subjected to a constant barrage of postmodern malapropisms that derive not from confused phonemes, but from confused meanings. From the ubiquitous misusage of superfluous prepositions—as in "focus in on," "circle around," and "continue on"—it is clear that the speakers have no conception of the denotations of the verbs respectively employed. Similarly, from the ubiquitous but woefully redundant phraseology "ATM Machine" (i.e., "automated teller machine machine"), it is abundantly clear that the speakers have no idea what the acronym "ATM" stands for. Instead of using language as a precise tool, Americans and others now employ it as a blunt instrument.

Synonymic and homonymic confusions also abound as a result of fuzzy speech; one prime example of each will suffice to illustrate the point. The term "African-American" has become, in certain contexts, a synonym for "black." Employing Frege's classic distinction between sense and reference, one would assert that while "the greatest African-American tennis player of the 1970s" and "the greatest black tennis player of the 1970s" make identical reference to the late Arthur Ashe, they nonetheless are not identical in sense.[7] The former modifier is more formal; the latter, more informal. In contemporary parlance, the sense of "African-American" bestows a kind of fundamental dignity upon the referent so described—as do "Irish-American," "German-American," "Italian-American," etc., in their respective senses. These are geopolitical denotations, devoid of pejorative connotation. By contrast, the generic denotation "black" is much more variable in connotation: black markets, the Black Death, and black magic are but three among many pejorative examples, which have nothing to do with race, but which utilize the word "black" in unsalutary contexts. Of course, there are also salutary contexts (e.g., Black Beauty) and value-neutral ones (e.g., black hole). However, when fuzzy speech conflates reference with sense, it produces nonsense. A television "talking head" read the following text from a teleprompter during a national news broadcast: "Nelson Mandela, the first African-American [sic] President of South Africa." We understand that the producers meant to say "the first black President." In my classroom, I occasionally write on the blackboard. I never write on the "African-American board."

Homonymic confusions abound because there are homonyms. I leave aside the commonest students' errors (e.g., confusing "their" and "there") as well as the commonest writers' ones (e.g., confusing "principle" and "principal"). My pet homonymic peeve—again symptomatic of a culture rendered senseless by fuzzy speech—is named "sound-bite." You think you know what this means, don't you? If so, then you probably understand its reference, but not its sense. That's because "sound-bite" is nonsense. The proper name, whose reference bears the intended sense, is the homonym "sound-byte." In the technical language of digital computing, a "byte" is a chunk (or word) of data, typically eight bits in length, which is processed as a single unit of information. "Bit" itself is a contraction of "binary digit," i.e., either a 1 or a 0. It follows that a chunk of audible data, when elicited as a unit of auditory information, especially as an encapsulated commentary, is called a "sound-byte." The sense of the term "sound-byte" has nothing whatsoever to do with any of the dozens of standard and colloquial meanings of "bite" as enumerated in any decent dictionary—unless dictionaries are now being edited by the cultural illiterates who disseminated the malapropism in the first place. Moreover, I am adamant on this point because my popular book, *Plato Not Prozac*, unfortunately embodies the hideous neologism. After that publisher's copy-editor had reflexively changed my "sound-byte" to "sound-bite," thus bringing it into conformity with universal error, I managed to persuade my editor, by dint of the foregoing argument, that I was probably right and everyone else was probably wrong. Although he astutely conceded my point about sense, he also deferred pragmatically to received nonsense for the purposes of publication. If you are reading these words, then the editor of this book is deferring to sense, and is thereby helping shear the sheep of fuzzy speech.

The blunting of reason with fuzzy speech, however, is only a prelude to the attenuation and suppression of reason with euphemistic speech. With this we move beyond the Whorf–Hobbes contribution to "WHOA," in which our experience is misinformed, and our reason misguided, by misleading language and imprecise speech, and into the Orwellian realm, in which pure political process itself is driven by imprecise speech and misguided reason. The slippery slope, as Orwell knew too well, begins with the substitution of value-neutral descriptions of phenomena by pejorative, distorted, or inflammatory—in other words, value-laden—descriptions of those phenomena.[8] The substitution is made by agitators in order to instil or mobilize public sentiment against a particular phenomenon, with agitators' intention of reaping political gain thereby. It is also made by despots, and their minions, to align public sentiment for like reasons.

Suppose that Smith employs Jones. No one minds this (and most, including Smith and Jones, deem it moreover a good thing), until Baker begins to agitate that Smith exploits Jones. Since exploitation is deemed "bad," everyone thinks this is a bad thing. Eventually, so do Smith and Jones, although nothing material has altered in their mutual relation. Employment becomes conflated with exploitation—and employers with exploiters—by the stirring up of sentiment via imprecise speech. And now that an economic ill has been reified, a political remedy appears justified.

Similarly, "Smith offended Jones" becomes politically transmuted to "Smith harmed Jones"; "Smith made a sexual advance that Jones rebuffed" becomes politically transmuted to "Smith sexually harassed Jones"; "Smith made a sexual advance that Jones accepted but later regretted" becomes politically transmuted to "Smith date-raped Jones"; "Smith married Jones, and they jointly decided that he would keep his job while she would stay home and mother their children" becomes politically transmuted to "Smith enslaved Jones"; "Smith dominates Jones in the context of their primatological hierarchy" be-comes politically transmuted to "Smith maintains oppressive hegemony over Jones"; "Smith relinquishes to Jones a position which Smith merits but Jones doesn't, authority which Smith can command but Jones can't, and privileges which Smith earned but Jones didn't" becomes politically transmuted to "Smith empowered Jones"; "Smith prefers that his children not be taught explicit homosexual practices in grade school" becomes politically transmuted to "Smith is homophobic"; "Smith observes various kinds of differences between races" becomes politically transmuted to "Smith is a racist"; "Smith observes that many women would prefer to stay home and raise their children" becomes politically transmuted to "Smith is a sexist"; and "Smith believes that people should assume a reasonable measure of personal responsibility for the conse-quences of their choices in life" becomes politically transmuted to "Smith is right-wing." Ultimately, when politico-linguistic agitators become policy-mak-ers, the state begins to manifest markedly totalitarian features—as we see in social democracies such as Sweden and Canada,[9] and in ever-increasing meas-ure in the Republic of America.

But, as Orwell knew too well, this is only the beginning. The substitution of value-laden for value-neutral language in order to arouse and misdirect public sentiment for the political gain of agitators at public expense is still dependent on universal semantics. Economic "employment" has near-ubiqui-tous probative connotations; economic "exploitation," near-ubiquitous pejora-tive ones. The substitution works politically because, although the public has been duped by linguistic sleight-of-mind, it still knows the meanings of words. But Orwell presciently envisioned that the slippery slope of linguistic substi-tution slides into the abyss of semantic inversion: a stage at which meanings of words themselves are lost, so that any word can signify any concept—and in particular (and most politically useful), its opposite. Imprecision of speech results in fuzziness of reason, but further impairments of speech operating on already impaired reason lead to the arbitrariness of speech and the attenuation of reason. At this stage noises stimulate emotions, slogans animate mobs, and the political transformation from a statehood of free and thoughtful individuals to one of slavish and thoughtless masses is complete. At this stage they can be told that "Freedom is Slavery," "War is Peace," "Genius is Idiocy," "Bounty is Dearth," "Life is Death," or anything else that suits the agitators, who are by now the dictators.

Do you think America is not approaching this stage? Think again. Have you received any "courtesy calls" lately? A "courtesy call" is an unsolicited invasion of your privacy, by telephone, usually during the evenings or weekends, by a goods- or service-provider that wants your business. Some marketing "genius" (or possibly "idiot") had the Orwellian inspiration that by calling a detriment a benefit, or a disservice a service, potential customers would actually be grateful for the intrusion merely on account of its misnomer. I usually attempt to explain to such callers that what they are labeling a "courtesy" is in fact a gross discourtesy—but most of them, whose reason is already atrophied by arbitrary speech, really believe that they are rendering a courteous service simply because they are labeling it this way. The meaning of courtesy is obliterated. One may as well open a restaurant, serve garbage, and call it "gourmet cuisine"; if a diner's palate is far enough atrophied, his gustatory experience of garbage will be overruled by a linguistic suggestion of fine victuals. And even if he tastes the garbage, he will be loath to complain as long as everyone else seems to be relishing it. Gustatory correctness demands that we do not call garbage "garbage"; rather, "gourmetically challenged cuisine" or "alternative cuisine" at the euphemistic stage, and "gourmet cuisine" if we can get away with it politically.[10]

So the bottom of one slippery slope becomes the top of another. Rudeness on a massive scale, labeled as courtesy, becomes accepted as courtesy. As we slide down that slope in America, suppression of individual liberties on a massive scale, labeled as social progress, becomes accepted as social progress. Remember Nazi Germany, in which genocide on a massive scale, labeled as conducive to emergence of the Master Race, becomes accepted as conducive to emergence of the Master Race. Remember Stalin's Soviet Union, in which mass murder ("liquidation") of this-or-that group, labeled historically necessary for the success of the utopian revolution, becomes accepted as historically necessary for the success of the utopian revolution. Whoever objects to the idea of historical necessity, or to the choice of group, is next to be liquidated. And in the American academy, whoever objects to neo-totalitarian suppressions of the canons of learning and their replacement by political indoctrination, or defies the suppressions with free speech and libertarian deeds, is liquidated economically or professionally, that is, summarily fired or institutionally ostracized. Totalitarian states and the North American universities have come to differ only in degree, not in kind.

And the universities are chiefly responsible (in theory) for the exercise of reason—and therefore must also accept responsibility for its widespread atrophy and attenuation. Philosophy, which more than any discipline exercises and upholds reason, is radicalized or marginalized by administrators to whose visions of "social progress" reason is anathema, and is avoided at all costs by students whose "higher education" consists largely in political indoctrination and vacuous pretense to self-esteem. Or philosophy departments are simply allowed to waste away by attrition, until they are small and weak enough to be merged with classics and religious studies—and by implication regarded as the last waning vestige of "white heterosexual patriarchal hegemony over the exploited, abused, oppressed, and enslaved masses, globally victimized by reason." In too many universities, this vestige is all that stands between our civilization's high culture and its destruction by fanatical feminists, militant ethnocentrists, assorted neo-Marxists, postmodernists, deconstructionists, social constructivists, and the camp-followers of these tenured legions of boorish misologists and venomous misanthropes.[11] Yet this vestige also makes itself irrelevant, by removing philosophy from the purview of the ordinary citizen and the average student alike, thus playing unwittingly into the hands of reason's executioners.

This is precisely where philosophical practice comes in. By offering philosophy directly to the masses, through client counseling, group facilitation, organizational consulting, and educational programs, we practitioners transcend the radicalized and fanaticized academy, where arbitrary speech and atrophy of reason reign supreme. Instead, we return philosophy to the marketplace whence it came, to ordinary citizens who are sincerely concerned about the meanings of words and the exercise of reason.

And here is the fourth component of "WHOA," which consists in a repudiation of Ayer's version of the naturalistic fallacy.[12] Ayer famously and contentiously asserted that, while one could ask an art historian about a painting's authenticity, and expect to receive an objectively true or instrumentally accurate answer, one could not (and by implication, should not) ask a moral philosopher about the rightness of an action, and expect to receive anything remotely true or accurate in response. Ayer's unfortunate utterance signaled the clarion and full retreat of philosophy from its Socratic tradition of leading the examined life, to its analytic preoccupation with footnoting the examined examination. Societal secularization and technological prowess neither obviate nor solve moral problems, which are experienced as natural outgrowths of man's moral consciousness. Secularized technological man is at least as needful of moral guidance as any of his predecessors, and is arguably more needful than all of them; accelerated technological progress potentiates hitherto unimaginable social possibilities, yet remains mute on their moral permissibilities. By abandoning the normative ethical field wholesale, analytic philosophy created a moral vacuum, which has been opportunistically filled by relativists, nihilists, and anarchists of every stripe. This leaves ordinary people—who intuitively disagree with Ayer—both profoundly dissatisfied and bereft of moral guidance. If philosophers will not stand up and defend what they hold to be right, and attack what they hold to be wrong, then either it will not be done, or it will be done badly. Neither your doctor, nor your lawyer, nor your psychologist, nor your psychiatrist, nor your social worker, nor your accountant, nor your psychic, nor your insurance agent, nor your congressman is educated or equipped to offer you moral guidance. Your priest, minister, rabbi, imam, or guru is educated and trained to offer you moral guidance, but at a price: they want your soul, or at least your subscription to their religious doctrine. Many people need moral guidance, but are unwilling to pay that price.

Your stereotypical academic professor of philosophy is educated, but not trained, to offer you moral guidance. He is educated to tell you what Aristotle's moral theory is, or Kant's, or Nietzsche's, but he is not trained to help you apply their insights—or your own—to your problem. That is because, in the wake of Ayer's pronouncement, academic philosophers are educated as theoreticians only. They know the history of philosophical ideas surpassingly well, but do not understand the process of applying philosophical ideas to everyday concerns. That is what we philosophical practitioners do. We, the pioneering generation, have trained ourselves in the time-honored academy of practical experience, or the school of life, and are now enlisting that experience to train the next generation of practitioners—under the very auspices of the foundering academy itself: on its besieged towers, within its assaulted keeps, behind its crumbling battlements, and in its clogged moats.

Ayer was mistaken. While a philosophical counselor does not normally tell a client what he ought to do, or make moral decisions for him, a philosophical counselor can indeed help a client ascertain whether a proposed action is consistent or inconsistent with respect to the client's own belief system or worldview, and, in the case of a moral dilemma, can help the client deliberate whether resolving the dilemma mandates configuring a necessarily imperfect choice against a fixed ethical or axiological background, or whether a resolution can be more propitiously effected by unfixing and modifying the ethical or axiological worldview itself, hence configuring a more perfect choice against a more malleable background. While this kind of moral counseling is therefore subtended by a species of meta-ethical relativism, it allows the client to alleviate his "decision-paralysis" and exercise first-order moral reasoning himself.[13]

Moreover, since APPA-certified philosophical practitioners are bound by a Code of Professional Ethical Standards[14] which explicitly proscribe both harmful acts by counselor and the counselor's condonement of harmful acts by the client, the meta-ethical relativistic stance of the counselor is itself circumscribed by widely accepted and strongly defended deontological norms. I could not, do not, and would not counsel my clients to commit murder, rape, robbery, perjury, retaliatory violence, or other harmful acts.

Given that no pragmatically workable deontology is absolute, there are always tolerable exceptions. I do not myself believe in capital punishment, yet I believe that a given district attorney might find philosophical justification for seeking it in a given case, and might, as a hypothetical client, even find such justification from me. But such justification would always be tempered by countervailing arguments, of which I would be remiss in not making my hypothetical client aware. I do not impose my beliefs on my client; I only ask that he consider and weigh arguments both for and against his proposed action, whatever it may be. Yet there is a signal difference between a client who, in his capacity as a district attorney, experiences a moral dilemma about seeking the death penalty in a given case and, after philosophical counseling, decides to seek it; and a client who, in his capacity as a potential vigilante, experiences a moral dilemma about whether to take justice into his own hands and murder an accused murderer, or else rely on the justice system to do it. While I believe that, on balance, it might be justifiable for the D.A. to seek the death penalty in some cases (although I am opposed to the death penalty myself), I also believe that, on balance, vigilantism is almost always wrong.

I am not asserting that the moral distinction between a state-sanctioned execution and a mafia-style execution lies in the legality of the former and the illegality of the latter; on the contrary, I eschew and repudiate legal moralism. Legislated laws should be reflections of our morals, or at least of their shadows. Morals and laws are not coextensive. In cases of gross injustice, civil or even criminal disobedience may be warranted in order to recast laws as reflections of morals. That they are not coextensive is demonstrable across the spectrum of contemporary issues. Even though abortion is decriminalized, many still believe it is immoral. Even though possession of cannabis is still criminalized, many believe it is not immoral. Intensive animal husbandry is big legal business, but some consider it immoral. The manufacture and sale of arms is even bigger legal business, and some consider it even more immoral. Prostitution and euthanasia—two perennial supply-side aspects of sex and death—are still largely illegal, yet many consider them morally justifiable. When life-and-death issues are involved, and when these entail political repercussions, then divergent moral evaluations may be dictated by divergent political sensibilities. The signatories of the American Declaration of Independence were considered patriots in the Thirteen Colonies, but traitors in England. While the winners of wars, revolutions, and elections write the laws, there is no unequivocal or universal justification for war, revolution, or election, and no guarantee that the prevailing laws will be unequivocally or universally susceptible to either moral opprobrium or approbation.

Would a philosophical counselor be inconsistent to condone the American revolution and condemn the Bolshevik revolution? Not necessarily. Would it be inconsistent to condemn the American revolution and condone the Bolshevik one? Not necessarily. What about condemning both, or condoning both? Again, either position can be made consistent with an appropriately selected set of background assumptions.

However, a philosophical counselor should identify himself as either willing to work within a given legal and political framework (even if this means practicing civil disobedience at times, in order to stimulate legislative change), or unwilling to work within it; in other words, as either conciliatory or revolutionary. Philosophical counselors who seek professional recognition in America are therefore implicitly conciliatory; they maintain what Socrates understood as an implicit contract with the state.[15] It follows that while they may agree or disagree with the death penalty, and counsel or not counsel a D.A. to seek it accordingly, they may not counsel an ordinary citizen to murder an accused murderer. While Americans are and should remain free to change laws by due democratic process, we are not and should not become free to take criminal justice arbitrarily into our own hands. Then again, a philosophical counselor who identifies himself as a revolutionary is neither bound by existing laws, nor seeks to be recognized by incumbent governments themselves bound by those laws. Revolutionaries do not seek political sanction; they seek to topple and replace the sanctioning system, and become themselves the arbiters of political sanction.

So for now, I subsume the moral question not under the legal one, but under the political one. I have lived, worked, and philosophized in assorted constitutional democracies, social democracies, ancient monarchies, and modern republics. In my experience, America is the freest of these nations, because it tolerates the greatest diversity and divergence of opinion. Having won a revolutionary war against colonialism, a civil war against feudalism, two world wars against imperialism and fascism, and lately a cold war against communism, America is now ironically losing the peace. The rampant abuse of hard-won freedom has seen the emergence, nurture, and entrenchment of domestic subcultures which embody the very evils that America fought so long and hard to extirpate abroad. Large, unresponsive, inefficient, and bureaucratic government is an evil. Political correctness and its neo-Bolshevization of the universities, the justice system, and the workplace is an evil. To the extent that it contributes to illiteracy, the postmodern deconstruction of high culture is an evil. The medicalization and psychologization of every human discontent is an evil. The fatuous expectation that equal opportunities lead to equal outcomes, and the socially engineered monstrosities that the camp-followers of this expectation impose, is an evil. The philosophical ignorance, cultural bigotry, and entrenched intolerance of political and religious fundamentalism alike is an evil. The unremitting celebration of physicality at the constant expense of mentality is an evil. The abuse of liberty is an evil. The decline of America is an evil.

Lest you have forgotten what prompted this disquisition on morality: it is the deeper meaning of the merger of Philosophy with Classics and Religious Studies. University administrators who ordain and attain such mergers think, perhaps constructively, that they are merely economizing on a secretary's salary; whereas I have endeavored to illustrate that they are actually driving nails into the coffin of our civilization. Such—as the twentieth century has taught—is the banality of evil.[16]

So in my view, philosophical practice is here to say "WHOA!" to America's precipitous decline. The lessons of Whorf, Hobbes, Orwell, and Ayer must be heeded, lest this ship of state founder on the reefs of the unexamined political life. Philosophical practitioners do not lie down, roll over, or play dead on command. We are our own masters; we command ourselves. We also help our clients—individuals, groups and organizations—achieve self-mastery; not by ephemeral theory, but thorough concrete practice. This is "stand-up" philosophy.

NOTES

1. I support programs of ethnic studies and women's studies that are rigorous and scholarly; I oppose those which foment fanaticism, intolerance and misology.

2. This is known conventionally as the Sapir–Whorf hypothesis. E.g., E. Sapir, "The Nature of Language," in *Selected Writings of Edward Sapir*, ed. D. Mandelbaum (Berkeley and Los Angeles: University of California Press, 1949), p. 10: "It is highly important to realize that once the form of a language is established it can discover meanings for its speakers which are not simply traceable to the given quality of experience itself but must be explained to a large extent as the projection of potential meanings into the raw material of experience." E.g., B. Whorf, "Science and Linguistics," in *Language, Thought and Reality: Selected Writings of Benjamin Lee Whorf*, ed. J. Carroll (Cambridge: Technology Press of MIT, 1956, New York: Wiley, 1959), p. 212: "It was found that the background linguistic system (in other words, the grammar) of each language is not merely a reproducing instrument for voicing ideas but rather is itself the shaper of ideas, the program and guide for the

individual's mental activity, for his analysis of impressions, for his synthesis of his mental stock in trade. Formulation of ideas is not an independent process, strictly rational in the old sense, but is part of a particular grammar, and differs, from slightly to greatly, between different grammars."

3. Among dozen of books by Thomas S. Szasz, see, e.g., *The Myth of Mental Illness: Foundations of a Theory of Personal Conduct* (New York: HarperCollins, 1984), and *Cruel Compassion: Psychiatric Control of Society's Unwanted*, (New York: Wiley 1994). His main premise is that "Mental illness is a metaphor (metaphorical disease). The word 'disease' denotes a demonstrable biological process that affects the bodies of living organisms (plants, animals, and humans). The term 'mental illness' refers to the undesirable thoughts, feelings, and behaviors of persons. Classifying thoughts, feelings, and behaviors as diseases is a logical and semantic error, like classifying the whale as a fish. As the whale is not a fish, mental illness is not a disease. Individuals with brain diseases (bad brains) or kidney diseases (bad kidneys) are literally sick. Individuals with mental diseases (bad behaviors), like societies with economic diseases (bad fiscal policies), are metaphorically sick. The classification of (mis)behavior as illness provides an ideological justification for state-sponsored social control as medical treatment" (Szasz Cybercenter, 1998). For this and inferences from it, see Thomas S. Szasz Cybercenter for Liberty and Responsibility, <http://www.enabling.org/ia/szasz/>.

4. See, e.g., J. Itard, *The Wild Boy of Aveyron*, and L. Malson, *Wolf Children*, trans. E. Fawcett, P. Ayrton, and J. White (London: NLB, 1972).

5. E.g., see *Philosophy and Literature's* (ed. D. Dutton) "Bad Writing Contest," whose 1998 "winner" was this extract from J. Butler's "Further Reflections on the Conversations of Our Time" (*Diacritics*, 1997): "The move from a structuralist account in which capital is understood to structure social relations in relatively homologous ways to a view of hegemony in which power relations are subject to repetition, convergence, and rearticulation brought the question of temporality into the thinking of structure, and marked a shift from a form of Althusserian theory that takes structural totalities as theoretical objects to one in which the insights into the contingent possibility of structure inaugurate a renewed conception of hegemony as bound up with the contingent sites and strategies of the rearticulation of power." Other winning extracts are archived at <http://www.cybereditions.com/aldaily/bwc.htm>. See also Alan Sokal's deliberately contrived gibberish, published by a leading postmodern journal, to its subsequent mortification: "Transgressing the Boundaries: Toward a Transformative Hermeneutics of Quantum Gravity," *Social Text*, 46/47 (Spring/Summer), 217–252, 1996. That scandal is catalogued at <http://www.physics.nyu.edu/faculty/sokal/>.

6. E.g., "And in wrong, or no definitions, lies the first abuse [of speech]; from which proceed all false and senseless tenets; which makes those men that take their instruction from the authority of books, and not from their own meditation, to be as much below the condition of ignorant men, as men endued with true science are above it." T. Hobbes, *Leviathan*, ed. R. Tuck (Cambridge: Cambridge University Press, chap. 4). "All other names, are but insignificant sounds ...

whereof there have been abundance coined by schoolmen, and puzzled philosophers" (ibid.).

7. G. Frege, "Über Sinn und Bedeutung," *Zeitschrift für Philosophie und philosophische Kritik*, C (1892), pp. 25–50. Reprinted in *Translations from the Philosophical Writings of Gottlob Frege*, trans. and ed. P. Geach and M. Black (Oxford: Blackwell, 1952).

8. See G. Orwell, "Politics and the English Language," *Horizon*, April 1946. It has been reprinted in many editions of his works: "Now, it is clear that the decline of a language must ultimately have political and economic causes: it is not due simply to the bad influence of this or that individual writer. But an effect can become a cause, reinforcing the original cause and producing the same effect in an intensified form, and so on indefinitely. A man may take to drink because he feels himself to be a failure, and then fail all the more completely because he drinks. It is rather the same thing that is happening to the English language. It becomes ugly and inaccurate because our thoughts are foolish, but the slovenliness of our language makes it easier for us to have foolish thoughts. The point is that the process is reversible."

9. For a broad-spectrum societal account, see, e.g., W. Gairdner, *The War Against the Family* (Toronto: Stoddart, 1992); for a narrower account of the academy, see L. Marinoff, "Equal Opportunity versus Employment Equity," *Sexuality and Culture*, 4, Fall 2000a, 23–44.

10. Sometime after writing these words, I stumbled across a trendy bistro in Hollywood. It was called "La Poubelle," which means "The Garbage Can." It was packed with patrons, and presided over by a smirking Parisian. Given the sign and the smirk, I ate elsewhere.

11. I repeat that I do not oppose any of the foregoing studies or schools per se. I do oppose the fanaticism without which some of them appear incapable of functioning. Unfortunately, academic fanatics arrogate to themselves the authority to speak for everyone, even though they represent only a tiny minority viewpoint. If unopposed, they can certainly terrorize and politicize academic institutions. The Nazis terrorized and politicized Germany; the Bolsheviks, Russia. Terror and politicization were the hallmarks of the Inquisition, the Salem witch-hunts, and McCarthyism. They are also the hallmarks of the postmodern academy.

12. Moore's thesis that "the good" is unanalyzable and indefinable does not repudiate the rightness or wrongness of actions; see G. Moore, *Principia Ethica* (1903) (Cambridge: Cambridge University Press, 1959). However, Ayer claims that "The common belief that 'it is the business of the philosopher to tell men how to live,' although it has the authority of Plato, is based upon a fallacy. The mistake is that of supposing that morality is a subject like geology, or art-history, in which there are degrees of expertise, so that just as one can look to an art-historian, in virtue of his training, to determine whether some picture is a forgery, one can look to a philosopher to determine whether some action is wrong." A. Ayer, *Philosophy in the Twentieth Century* (London: Unwin, 1984), p. 15.

13. See L. Marinoff, "On the Emergence of Ethical Counseling: Considerations and Two Case Studies," in R. Lahav and M. Tillmanns, eds., *Essays on Philosophical Counseling* (Lanham, MD: University Press of America, 1995), pp. 171–191.

14. See Chapter 9 herein.

15. See *Crito*, in *Dialogues of Plato*, trans. B. Jowett (Oxford: Oxford University Press, 1895), passim.

16. This is Arendt's oft-repeated phrase. See Hannah Arendt, *Eichmann in Jerusalem: A Report of the Banality of Evil*, rev. and enlarged ed. (New York: Penguin, 1977). I am manifestly not comparing the gaffes of university administrators to the crimes of Adolph Eichmann. I am merely pointing out that annihilations of cultures, and annihilations of persons, can both be overseen by banal bureaucrats.

CHAPTER 2

Is Philosophy a Way of Life?

2.1. What Makes Philosophy Special as a Way of Life?
2.2. What Makes Philosophy Special as a Discipline?

2.1. WHAT MAKES PHILOSOPHY SPECIAL AS A WAY OF LIFE?

There is strong evidence, both in the historical record and in the continuum of culture, which suggests that philosophical traditions of antiquity were primarily concerned with ways of leading a good life, with understanding proper versus improper conduct of life, not only for the sake of solitary man but also for the sake of the family, the community, the state, and posterity. Philosophy, as love of wisdom, meant inculcating and practicing virtues, identifying and eschewing vices, thinking thoughts and examining arguments for the sake of their applicability to life, and not only as inapplicable intellectual exercises, which sharpen the blades of mind but sever none of life's knotty problems.

What is perhaps most remarkable about philosophy is that it emerged at all. As the great civilizations of Athens, Indus, and China grew industrious and prosperous enough to produce periods of relative economic stability, and waxed powerful and civilized enough to export warfare as far as possible from their respective palace gates, the neo-cortex of man found sufficient leisure at last to begin speculating and experimenting systematically on life's imponderables, and sufficient culture to record, preserve, and further his speculations and experiments. The geographical explorations, the military expeditions, the political conquests, the rise and fall of warlords, city-states and empires, and the emergent neolithic technologies of weaponry, agronomy, and animal husbandry that made permanent settlements and their expansion possible could have continued unabated without philosophy. While Alexander was tutored by Aristotle, Alexander—not Aristotle—conquered the immediate temporal world. Alexander's father, Philip of Macedonia, who paved the way for his son's illustrious conquests, was tutored sufficiently by his ambition. The role of philosophy here is that of handmaiden; a servant, a diversion, pleasant to look on and perhaps amusing to trifle with, but occupying a replaceable and ultimately dispensable position. Only through history's cumulative lens, after the short-lived triumphs and long-rued disasters of mortal Ozymandian men, however great or terrible for a day, have reverted to hearsay, have been captured in legend or art, or are simply forgotten and returned to dust, do we notice that ideas possess greater longevity than genes and deeds. Although Aristotle's ideas had arguably little to do with Alexander's conquests, they reached much further and lived far longer. Alexander is an icon, and his empire an artifact, of history; that, along with the ongoing usage of his namesake, is his only relevance to daily life. A few people named Alex, and an apocryphal epithet about tears shed over lack of worlds to conquer, is the sum of his contemporary legacy. "The rest," as we finely say when relegating something to the cold storage of the causal nexus, "is history."

Aristotle's politics, poetics, rhetoric, virtue ethics, and syllogistic logic percolated through and came to exert enormous influence on Western civilization entire. They are still taught today, are still germane to a university curriculum (at least in universities whose students can read), and are useful in philosophical counseling. His scientific speculations and teleological aetiology were also, more unfortunately, coopted by Augustine and ossified by Aquinas in Roman Catholic doctrine, and so became irrefutable by association, even though demonstrably absurd. Not until the sixteenth century, when Peter Ramus took for his thesis in the University of Paris "Whatever is in Aristotle is false"[1] did the peripatetic tree of science begin to receive a proper shaking. In the seventeenth century, it was felled by Galileo and Hobbes, who reduced Aristotelian physics to absurdity.[2] For two millennia, Aristotle had been known as "the philosopher." Finally, Thomas Hobbes found sufficient refutation and ample temerity both to supplant him—and to mock schoolmen, transubstantiationists, and alchemists in the process—by writing his own witty epitaph: "This is the true philosopher's stone."[3] One could add that Hobbes killed several birds with that stone.

Hobbes was also a philosophical practitioner. His *Leviathan* became the seminal text of two great fields of social study: political science and empirical psychology. It was Hobbes, not Marx or Spencer, who first endeavored to articulate social and political philosophy as logical appendages of materialism (not of theology)—and he arrived at a design for commonwealth, not universal poverty. And it was Hobbes again, not Freud, who first articulated the thesis that civilization hinges upon man's voluntary renunciation of natural desires and appetites, and transfer of power to a higher authority, in exchange for necessities of life and securities of livelihood.[4] And as we saw in the previous chapter, Hobbes moreover inveighed against the "insignificant speech" produced by the Schools, which were the equivalents of the postmodern academy, only stultified by theological dogmas instead of political ones.

It is no coincidence that the finest minds of the early modern period and subsequent Enlightenment, including Bacon, Hobbes, Descartes, Spinoza, Galileo—and later Newton, Hume, and Locke—had little or nothing to do with the universities of their day. (The same applies still later to the likes of Kant, Gauss, Darwin, and Einstein.) The medieval and early modern academy was an extension of the Church, committed to dogma and not to reason. When, in 1619, the Savile Chairs of Geometry and Astronomy were established at Oxford, the townsfolk soon became terrified. Rumor and ignorance jointly proclaimed that the algebraic symbols which John Wallis penned were "spells" and "art diabolical," and that he must be a sorcerer or wizard.[5] We have come full circle in the West: most of my Philosophy 101 students, beneficiaries of a deconstructed, politically correct but otherwise contentless education, ask with earnest mystification how I convert their raw test scores into percentages. I reply that I use Magic (a.k.a. Arithmetic, Algebra, Sorcery, Wizardry, etc.). Thanks in some measure to Hobbes's unrelieved Erastianism, which eventually culminated in the separation of Church from State in America, these students have inherited no theological bias against Wizardry, only an ideological bias against erudition. Such is the price of social progress.

In fact, even in a rational as opposed to a politicized academy, the seminal ideas and works that define and shape a given generation, independent of discipline, emanate from perhaps 5% of the professorate.[6] These are the ground breakers, mavericks, and luminaries. The remaining 95% are essentially drones, who produce secondary, tertiary, ... and n-ary interpretations, interpolations, and extrapolations of the seminal works.

Published philosophical papers often take the form "A rebuttal of Smith's attack on Jones's defense of Brown's interpretation of Parker's repudiation of White's thesis on Jackson's philosophy of X" (where X is some celebrated dead philosopher, usually Wittgenstein). This is what I call "theoretical philosophy." I am hardly disparaging it; I happily engage in it myself. It requires long attention span, adroit thinking, skillful exegesis, and competent technical writing just to produce such a paper—one must then run a gauntlet of peer review to see it published. But is such theoretical philosophizing a way of life? Well, it is at least a way of livelihood, in that ritual publication of such pieces is demanded of those who would draw tenured salaries. But is such a paper directly or immediately applicable to any of life's pressing practical problems? Obviously not. Moreover, if such a paper merits publication in a good scholarly journal, it will be read and grasped in its entirety and nicety (if any) by some fraction of one percent of the philosophical community. Mountains of such literature have accumulated exponentially during this century, not only in philosophy but also across the spectrum of disciplines, neo-disciplines, and pseudo-disciplines that populate (and perforce imperil) the contemporary academy. While such knowledge is hardly proprietary—anyone can walk into a good public library, or obtain permission to use a good research library, and begin to ascend any face of any mountain in this range—the intelligent layman is at best an endangered species, and at worst a fiction. The level of comprehension and erudition required even to follow the thread of a theoretical philosophical debate, let alone contribute to it, is as far above common parlance as common parlance is above birdsong. Yet birdsong serves some immediate purpose, and conduces in some direct way to a bird's survival. Ritual scholarly publication serves no comparable purpose; neither in immediacy, nor in directness.

So philosophy is not necessarily a way of life for professors of philosophy, who are beset by the same assortment of human problems as everyone else, but whose inclination toward theoretical thinking and hypothetical reasoning does not dispose them to apply much of their philosophical expertise to the resolution or management of such problems. They establish little or no connection between professing "love of wisdom" and leading life wisely. They flounder about like everyone else. Some academic philosophers, in fact, deny that philosophy can be so applied: their conception of it is strictly theoretical and hypothetical, and also guardedly proprietary. Just as some devout people attenuate religious experience at the level of ritual observance, so do some erudite professors attenuate philosophical experience at the level of ritual publication.

While philosophy as a way of life may sound glamorous, romantic, or adventurous compared with philosophy as an academic livelihood, it is fraught with all kinds of potential hardships and perils. The authentic and exemplary lives led by Socrates, Buddha, Confucius, and Seneca in antiquity, and by the likes of Hobbes, Hume, Russell, and Sartre in more modern times, also entailed disillusionments, deprivations, dangers, and a willingness to stare down death. Some who applied philosophy toward well-defined political ends, such as Gandhi and King, were assassinated even in the attainment of those ends. Being true to oneself and one's philosophy can also banish one to the very margins of social existence, and cause one to lead a life characterized by poetic eccentricity (e.g., Diogenes), unjust persecution (e.g., Spinoza), psychological torment (e.g., Schopenhauer), or prophetic madness (e.g., Nietzsche). Most practitioners prefer that philosophy be a way of examining and improving lives; but one must remain cognizant that one's philosophical beliefs, however plainly asserted and sincerely practiced, may attract detractors and culminate in public execution (e.g., Bruno), or may attract admirers and culminate in untimely death (e.g., Descartes).

The human being is manifestly capable of faith and doubt, which are Taoistic (i.e., dualistic) complements. The whole which they comprise is the reach of human mentation, which perennially exceeds its grasp. There is no pure or perfect faith, because all faith is tinged with doubt. Likewise, there is no pure or perfect doubt, because all doubt is tinged with faith. For those who incline to the profession of faith, the world offers myriad religions; to the profession of doubt, myriad philosophies. Reason is the antithesis of neither, but the instrument of both. Religion reasons from the ground of faith; philosophy, from that of doubt. What religion and philosophy hold in common is therefore the metaphysical complementarity of their respective grounds.

The empirical unity of this complementarity can be appreciated in the literal history of Western philosophy, which saw the unification of theology (then called "divinity") and philosophy in the Schools, or rather the appropriation of the latter by the former. One studied Classics and Divinity explicitly, and (thereby) philosophy implicitly. It is no coincidence that three of the four great British Empiricists—Hobbes, Hume, and Locke—never became professors, because that required ordination (and philosophical stagnation) in the Anglican Church. Hobbes was a heretic; Hume, an infidel; Locke, a liberal: they eschewed priesthood in favor of philosophy. The fourth Horseman of this Empirical Apocalypse, namely Berkeley, was an Anglican Bishop, who wrote philosophy to rescue the learned world from impinging and impending materialism—and its familiar traveling companion, atheism—which he feared and presaged would erode and ultimately eradicate moral sensibility.

Yet even in societies which have separated Church and State, the complementarity of religion and philosophy is plain. The modern academy resembles a medieval monastery in respects too numerous to name. Among the more conspicuous resemblances are: academic tenure, whose monastic equivalent is the taking of final vows; ritual publication, whose monastic equivalent is ritual observance; and reverence for a canon of literature, whose monastic equivalent is reverence for a canon of scripture. Stronger than mere resemblances is the catalog of congruencies between the two, which include: learned helplessness, atrophied initiative, and dependence on others' resources that result from long-term institutionalization; protraction of deep-seated grievances, intrapersonal conflicts, and festering hatreds that result from coerced long-term relations; egotism, pettiness, viciousness, small-mindedness, and mean-spiritedness that result from grandiose quests for pathetic spoils or political victories for empty gains. In these and similar unsalutary senses, philosophy is no more a way of life for professors relegated entirely to the academy than is Christianity a way of life for monks relegated entirely to the monastery. As Christianity is well-learned in the seminary but best practiced outside the monastery, so is philosophy well-learned in the seminar but best practiced outside the academy.

2.2. WHAT MAKES PHILOSOPHY SPECIAL AS A DISCIPLINE?

Anyone who has spent ten or fifteen years as a student in institutions of higher learning, and who has subsequently taught thousands of university students dozens of different courses over several decades has—if not too dogmatic, bombastic, or inattentive—learned some valuable lessons himself. One discovers that some students are able to learn more, more quickly, and more thoroughly than others. Some are made by nature fleeter of foot than others; some, cleaner of limb; some, kinder of heart; some, deeper of understanding. With patient, careful, and effective instruction, most students can improve at almost anything; yet some always remain more gifted than others. I am not here addressing the extrema of this spectrum: feral children, like the wild boy of Aveyron, can learn virtually nothing; while mathematical prodigies such as Ramanujan, or musical ones like Mozart, apparently need learn little to contribute momentous things.

Ferality vindicates empiricist epistemology in a brutal but poignant fashion: there is clearly a period of plasticity in human children, during which any number of languages may be learned, and any set of social conventions (including moral rules) imparted. More that is learned and imparted during this period, more that can be learned and imparted thereafter. But less during also leads to less later. Prodigy likewise vindicates rationalist epistemology; some children appear almost born to play a given instrument or sport, to furrow a given field or discover one outright. Having acquired the same basic cultural tools as everyone else in their generation, prodigies erect ingenious or amazing edifices with them.

But most people are neither feral nor prodigious; that is to say, we depend more keenly upon a subtle interplay of nature and nurture to chart our courses through life. To what kinds of pursuits does one most broadly incline in terms of nature's gifts? And to what particular careers or callings will one gravitate under the influence of nurtural heritage? Speaking in the main, university undergraduates constitute an undifferentiated horde, which by fits and starts gradually distributes itself across the curriculum according to natural inclination and acquired interest. Even so, this broad spectrum is never uniformly distributed according to performance. Nature appears to adore a Gaussian distribution of qualities,[7] and this is not an accident. Rather, it may be overdetermined by a series of "accidents" themselves. One begins with a random walk in one dimension: choose a starting point, toss a coin, and step right if it lands heads, or left if it lands tails. Continue this process indefinitely. If you chart, in a second dimension, the probability (i.e., relative frequency of occasions) of your proximity to the starting point, you will see the Gaussian distribution emerge. The more times you toss the coin, the smoother the curve you will obtain.

This function is also called the "normal distribution" and, with more notorious connotations of late, the "bell-shaped curve." Gauss, the mathematical prodigy who first derived it, also discovered non-Euclidean geometry well in advance of Riemann, Bolya, and Lobachevsky, but refrained from publishing this finding because he feared "the clamor of the Boeotians." Had he anticipated the clamor lately caused by his curve, it too might bear another's name. The current tempest lies in the teapot of intelligence quotient, which is precisely what I must enlist in this section. Given that our course inadvertently brings us through the heart of this storm, we will reef the sails, batten the hatches, and trust to the seaworthiness of our vessel, philosophy (qua love of wisdom), to ride out the rough weather stirred up by the vituperative debate (qua misguided opinion) over IQ.

If we randomly assemble a group of people and measure their heights, we find height to be normally distributed. The height one attains at adulthood is almost entirely dependent on one's genes, and is partly dependent on one's childhood diet, one's habitual posture, and other extragenetic factors. No one finds this proposition difficult or objectionable, primarily because no one correlates moral worthiness (or unworthiness) with height. Knowledge that a person is shorter than average, or taller than average, conveys no information whatsoever about that person's ethical precepts, or moral behaviors.

Similarly, if we randomly assemble a group of people and measure their IQs (i.e., the "G" factor), we find intelligence to be normally distributed. The intelligence one attains at adulthood is partly dependent on one's genes, and is partly dependent on one's upbringing, education, socialization, environment, diet and other extragenetic factors.[8] Many find this proposition difficult or objectionable, primarily because many people intuitively or misinformedly correlate moral worthiness with high intelligence, and moral unworthiness with low intelligence. This, I own, is a desperately mistaken view.[9] It is simply not the case that a person is more likely to be good if intelligent, and more likely to be bad if unintelligent. The issue is further compounded, and clouded almost to opacity, by the introduction of a non-spurious correlation between IQ and socioeconomic standing. The unfortunate and utterly misguided syllogism naively drawn from daisy-chaining these two correlations is: that since upper-middle-class Americans tend to be more intelligent, on average, than lower-middle-class Americans (an apparently true but hotly disputed correlation),[10] and since more intelligent people tend to be morally superior, on average, to less intelligent ones (an utterly false correlation, I claim),[11] therefore it follows (fallaciously, I claim) that upper-middle-class Americans are more morally worthy than lower-middle-class ones. In plain speech, the thesis asserts unsoundly that: the rich are better—i.e., more deserving—than the poor, and that's exactly why they're rich. Neither social Darwinism nor human sociobiology have properly formulated their thesis; I will correct their fundamental error as soon as I can find more time.

The three reflexive objections to this thesis, which I term "denial," "displacement," and "de-Occamization," are just as patently flawed. Objection one simplistically denies that intelligence exists, and thereby seeks to preempt its putative correlation with moral worthiness. Objection two acknowledges that intelligence exists, but displaces its primary ground from nature to nurture, and thereby reframes the putative correlation: people can "learn" to be intelligent and thus can "learn" to be good. Objection three also acknowledges that intelligence exists, but proceeds to multiply the entity needfully, recognizing "emotional intelligence," "musical intelligence," "athletic intelligence," "social intelligence," "political intelligence," "sexual intelligence," "criminal intelligence," "moral intelligence," and so forth, in addition to the generic "intelligent intelligence." Ultimately, from this perspective, everyone turns out to be intelligent in some way or other, and thus by putative correlation also good in some way or other.

My point about the IQ debate is both simple yet compelling. Like Plato among other philosophers, I cannot say precisely what "good" means, but like Gautama I can attempt to equate it with non-harm.[12] Thus, if one can measure the amount of harm done by a given word or deed, one can say something about the extent to which it lacks goodness. Every day in America, petty but violent criminals hold up convenience stores at gunpoint, and sometimes even shoot the cashiers, even when compliant. The net "take" from such a crime may amount to only a few dollars, and may cost lives in the bargain. The average IQ of such petty criminals is no doubt below that of the general population, and of course such armed robbers are violent and often harmful characters, and therefore bad. Hence, one forges an apparent empirical link between low intelligence and immoral behavior.

However, it is also the case that non-petty and non-violent criminals are capable of inflicting great harms. Swindlers and other charlatans bilk innocent but gullible people out of enormous sums of hard-earned savings. Lawyers legally defraud clients; insurance companies legally cheat policyholders, banks legally gouge depositors; states legally rob citizens. These and similar activities are non-violent, but nonetheless harmful. Their perpetrators are therefore immoral, yet also of above average intelligence. As Socrates implied to Crito, with greater intelligence comes a capacity to do greater evil—as well as greater good.[13] Intelligence alone does not entail morality, for the smartest people are capable of behaving in the most immoral ways. Serial killers are undoubtedly of above-average intelligence, which allows them to gull their intended victims and elude arrest.

Intelligence means ability to learn, and is always distributed normally. In the universities, where the most intelligent learners are gathered to be taught by the most intelligent instructors, intelligence is also normally distributed. Again, in passing, we note that harms, cruelties, incivilities, and injustices of all kinds are inflicted by denizens of the academy on one another. Although their speech is more refined than that of the general populace, their structural violence is not less harmful than that inflicted by organizations of far less intelligent people. But my main point concerning intelligence is not simply that it does not, in and of itself, entail morality—even though this minor observation may cause consternation to some. My main point is that some subjects require more intelligence to master than do others; and in so far as that is true, the subjects that demand the greatest intelligence to master also confer the profoundest understanding of the things studied.

As far as students are concerned, their abilities to learn, being synonymous with their IQs, are normally distributed in any class. But that distribution is likely to become skewed as the difficulty of the subject matter increases. And is there a recognizable order of difficulty in the catalog of academic disciplines? Certainly so. The rudimentary hierarchy was known in antiquity, and has scarcely changed since; it only has become more highly incremented. Since the universities have by and large bifurcated along the lines of Snow's characterization of the "two cultures," namely, humanities and science, I will bifurcate the hierarchy accordingly.[14] The most difficult subjects of all are formal logic and mathematics, followed by the applications to which they give rise: philosophy and physics. Only the most intelligent students are undaunted by these subjects, and study them as ends in themselves. Although logic and mathematics can be regarded in certain respects as largely equivalent formal systems, and although arithmetic as well as digital computing are famously reducible to logic (for those who seek ancestral primacy), their respective applications are significantly different indeed. Logical structures (deductive, inductive, and ampliative) undergird cogent argumentation in the humanities, while mathematical structures constitute the very language of science itself.

IQ means ability to learn, which at the apex means ability to understand logical and mathematical structures. Again, this has nothing to do with having a good spirit or kind heart, and may have little or nothing to do with leading a fulfilled social or professional life. But in the academy, which is the repository of nonproprietary knowledge, the depth of a student's understanding thereof is nothing but the height of his IQ. And the ordering of the disciplines themselves ranges similarly, according to the intelligence required to grasp their regnant paradigms. The natural sciences are more difficult than the social; that is, they require more raw intelligence to digest. And within the natural sciences, physics is more difficult than chemistry, and chemistry more difficult than biology. And within physics, the theoretical stream is more difficult than the experimental (although many experimentalists, like Eddington and Fermi, were able theoreticians). Of course, a genius like Darwin may have been as intelligent as any number of contemporary rank-and-file physicists, but Darwin's intelligence pales before that of Newton, Maxwell, Einstein, Dirac, or any physicist who made a comparable paradigmatic contribution to his respective field. Of course, there are geniuses in every field, and arguably a field cannot exist unless some genius first clears the ground. But the difficulty of a field is gauged not by the IQ of its founders, but by the intelligence necessary to understand the ritual publications of its rank and file.

Spencer, who coined and founded Sociology (although his learned friends shuddered at the half-Latin, half-Greek neologism and urged him not to use it, to no avail), was evidently a brilliant man, as was Durkheim, whereas contemporary rank-and-file sociology is far beneath that standard. Similarly, those who helped found psychology (e.g., William James) and those who work at its contemporary edges of excellence (e.g., Damasio in neuropsychology) were and are undoubtedly brilliant, whereas one is continually amazed by the almost willful stupidity of many rank-and-file psychologists. But worst of all in its rank and file is Education, founded (ironically) in America by the philosopher Dewey. Individually, I know many intelligent, ethical, and accomplished academicians who hold PhDs in Education. Collectively, however, they too often remind one of Goethe's lament about his fellow Germans: "so estimable in the individual and so wretched in the generality." At worst, Education has sunk to such an abysmal depth that its instructors and students alike cannot grasp the fundamentals of any other discipline in the academy, so they busy themselves with contentless "studies" that purport to address the continuous spectrum of learning, but which appear incognizant of any discrete portion thereof. Education is the Academy's Trojan Horse; trying to improve it, moreover, is like flogging a dead one. Here are extracts from two published criticisms spanning more than twenty years:

> Occupying a vast area far below the professors in any other category are the professors of that branch of study and training that we might wish to merit very great respect. The lowest of the low in academic life are the educationalists, the professors in the schools or departments of education, whose job is to prepare those who will teach in the nation's primary and secondary schools.... The educationalists never read anything except their own pious literature, which revolts all other academics.... The resulting books and articles ... are almost always devoid of substance.[15]

> Although I am affiliated with Harvard's Graduate School of Education, that is usually not enough to redeem me in the eyes of scholars in the arts and sciences or in other professional schools, at Harvard, as well as at other universities. Indeed, education schools have always been at the low end of the academic totem pole because their courses, their research, and their ideas on pedagogy and curriculum have not been viewed as warranting intellectual respect. Regrettably, there is good reason for this judgement. Education schools have not tended to promote pedagogical ideas that result in the qualities that college faculty have traditionally sought in their students: disciplined study habits, a knowledge base that enables them to study the subject matter of their courses in its mature form, a capacity for analytical thinking, and the ability to write clearly and cogently about the substance of their courses. That many students enter college with these qualities is usually not a result of the training their teachers received in schools of education.[16]

Just so. And owing to the native component of intelligence, intelligent students attend intelligent teachers, and ignore unintelligent ones. Thus, intelligent students cannot be made stupid by mere exposure to dull educators. However, I reiterate that the moral characters of education professors, like everyone else's moral character, cannot be determined from their IQs alone. A low IQ does not make a person bad; neither does a high IQ make one good.

In contrast to Education, Philosophy both provides the foundation for and stands at the summit of all knowledge, learning, and rational inquiry. For every field of study in the academy—whether humanities or sciences—there is a philosophy of that field. One can study philosophy of mathematics, physics, computing, biology, psychology, sociology, economics, religion, art, literature, music, sports, education, and all subjects in between, as well as philosophy of the practical technical professions like law, medicine, and engineering. Note that the converse does not generally hold: there is philosophy of psychology, but no psychology of philosophy. There is philosophy of psychiatry, but no psychiatry of philosophy. There is philosophy of biology, but no biology of philosophy. There is philosophy of science, but no science of philosophy. There is philosophy of religion, but no religion of philosophy.

History is a noteworthy exception to this rule: one can study both philosophy of history and history of philosophy. The difference between history and philosophy, however, is twofold. First, there is a body of knowledge intrinsic to philosophy—logic, metaphysics, ontology, epistemology, ethics, aesthetics—which does not depend on the study of anything external to its concerns. While one can study philosophy of x-ology or history of x-ology, history is always history of something external to itself; it has no internality. Second, one can write an acceptable history of x-ology without necessarily understanding the inner workings of x-ology itself. While historians of, say, mathematics usually know some mathematics, one could always approach such history from a political, sociological, or ideological perspective, and thereby eschew technicalities. One could conceivably write a history of the Pythagorean abhorrence of irrational numbers, and the apocryphal drowning at sea of Hippasus of Metapontem for his discovery that the square root of two is irrational, without understanding either that proof or anything about number theory itself. One cannot, however, write any meaningful philosophy of mathematics without understanding something about proofs, numbers, and the like.

Philosophizing about science presents similar challenges. To undertake the philosophy of x-ology without grasping at least the technical fundamentals of x-ology is at best to waffle in meta-theory, and at worst to wallow in ignorance. We encounter both scenarios in the academy. First, when analytic philosophy endeavors to encompass philosophy of science, and when such philosophizing is attempted by people who have studied logic but not science, they can only revert to meta-theory. Second, when deconstructionist or feminist philosophy endeavors to encompass philosophy of science, and when such philosophizing is attempted by persons who have studied nothing but political indoctrination, they revert either to hysteria or to nonsense. The former is epitomized by Sandra Harding's charge that Newton's *Principia* is a "rape manual,"[17] while the latter is typified by terminology such as "social epistemology." For example, a well-known social epistemologist delights in informing audiences that Newton's laws are wrong. She neither knows Newton's laws, nor knows the Galilean transformations upon which they represent improvements, nor knows how to derive Kepler's laws from them, nor understands the constraints upon the domain in which they function approximately enough, nor grasps the physical transitions and mathematical niceties that differentiate Newtonian from quantum and relativistic domains, respectively. Yet she boldly declares that Newton's laws are "wrong."[18]

By contrast, the best uses of philosophy allow one in the first place to conduct a general inquiry—and by degrees an increasingly specialized one—into any field whatsoever: for philosophy stands at the origin of all rational inquiry, and generates the axes thereof in any direction, and as far as anyone cares to extend them. In the second place, the best uses of philosophy allow one to function when such axes be extended beyond the bounds of reliable knowledge—as they are both at the frontiers of science and in ordinary daily life. When inferences need be drawn, extrapolations made, speculations indulged, intuitions consulted, there is nothing for it but to employ heuristics; and there is no better guide to their useful employment than philosophy.

The corpus of reliable knowledge can be likened to a sphere, which continuously grows in volume and surface area. The expanding volume represents the sheer amount of knowledge that has accumulated (thanks to the written tradition coupled with the scientific revolution, backed by laissez-faire economics and democratic politics). The expanding surface represents both new and recombinant areas of knowledge open to study and research: from molecular anthropology to genetic engineering, from garbology to neuroendocrinology, from Dylanology to queer studies, from multimedia communications to psychoclimatology. The surface of the sphere also represents the limits of reliable knowledge. Man stands on what he knows, reaches into the unknown, grasps of it what he can, and by so doing makes it knowable. Then he stands on that, and reaches further. Not only is there no end to knowing, there is no end to unknowing. For as the surface area of the sphere of reliable knowledge increases, so does that with which it interfaces, namely, the unknown. Hence the more we know, the more we also know we don't know. This is not social epistemology—which pretends that no knowledge is reliable, seeks to learn the social implications of putative falsehoods accepted as truths (itself, as usual, excepted)—rather, is the geometry of epistemology, which centers on reliable knowledge and builds outward in all directions, increasingly making the unknown known, and by so doing encountering (or perhaps engendering) ever-more unknown. This is why science always raises more questions than it answers, and why the proliferation of science has, in last few centuries and exponentially in the twentieth, given rise not to a completion of knowledge, but to greater knowledge and a greater vista onto the unknown. And cognizantly or not, one's philosophy—and in particular, one's set of metaphysical presuppositions—guides one at this interface.

So this is how philosophy differs from all the other disciplines, whether in the academy or outside its precincts. Formal logic, pure mathematics, and the ability to apply and ampliate them by means of rational inquiry, accumulated experience, and reasonable inference (i.e., via theory, experiment, and interpretation), lie at the center of the sphere of reliable knowledge, and make all other reliable knowledge possible—up to and including normative inquiries about leading a good life. This was called "philosophy" in antiquity, "natural philosophy" or "experimental philosophy" in early modern times, "applied philosophy" in the late twentieth century, and "philosophical practice" in this new millennium.

NOTES

1. See, e.g., A. Koestler, *The Sleepwalkers* (London: Hutchinson, 1959), p. 198: "At the Sorbonne in 1536, Peter Ramus received an ovation when he took as his thesis 'Whatever is in Aristotle is false.' Erasmus called Aristotelian science sterile pedantry, 'looking in utter darkness for that which has no existence whatever.'" Similarly, Milton had called his scholastic education at Oxford's Magdalen Hall "an asinine feast of sow-thistles and brambles," cited by S. Mintz, *The Hunting of the Leviathan* (Cambridge: Cambridge University Press, 1962).

2. Galileo landed himself in enormous political trouble by refuting both Aristotelian astronomy, which erroneously asserted (among other things) that the moon is a perfect sphere, and Aristotelian physics, which erroneously asserted (among other things) that the velocity of a falling body is proportional to its weight. See, e.g., P. MacHamer, ed., *The Cambridge Companion to Galileo* (Cambridge: Cambridge University Press, 1998). Hobbes likewise identified the circularity of Aristotle's teleological physics: "If you desire to know why some kinds of bodies sink naturally downwards towards the earth, and others go naturally from it; the Schools will tell you out of Aristotle, that the bodies that sink downwards, are heavy; and that this heaviness is it that causes them to descend. But if you ask what they mean by heaviness, they will define it to be an endeavor to be below: which is as much to say, that bodies descend, or ascend, because they do" (Hobbes, chap. 46).

3. See W. Kennet, *Memoirs of a Cavendish Family*: Hobbes was "best pleased with this humour for a gravestone: This is the true Philosopher's Stone," in A. Wood, *Athenae Oxonienses*, ed. Philip Bliss (London: Rivington, 1817), Vol. 3, p. 1218. Thanks to Peter Snell for providing this citation.

4. Compare Chapter 13 of the *Leviathan* to S. Freud, *Civilization and Its Discontents*, in J. Strachey, ed. and trans., *The Standard Edition of the Complete Psychological Works of Sigmund Freud*, Vol. 21 (London: Hogarth; original work published 1930). See also J. Roy, *Hobbes and Freud*, trans. T. Osler (Toronto: Canadian Philosophical Monographs, 1984).

5. See G. Robertson, *Hobbes* (Edinburgh: William Blackwood and Sons, 1886), p. 32. The professors of mathematics themselves were called "limbs of the devil."

6. This estimate was provided by the late Thomas Kuhn, by private communication (1993). He said this casually to me over coffee; he presumably made no secret of it.

7. The basic function is $f(x) = e^{-x^2}$.

8. The questions both of measuring intelligence (IQ or "G"), and of implications of such measurements, have engendered passionate but also (I claim) somewhat misguided political debates. The twentieth-century "liberal" position is represented by S. Gould, *The Mismeasure of Man* (New York: Norton, 1981). The twentieth-century "conservative" position is represented by R. Herrnstein and C. Murray, *The Bell Curve* (New York: The Free Press, 1994). An oblique position, namely, that there are other kinds of intelligences other than "G," is represented by D. Golman, *Emotional Intelligence* (New York: Bantam, 1995). The extent of heritability of IQ is by no means agreed on; heritability estimates in the literature range from about 50 to 80%. My colleague Michael Levin has remarked (private communication, 1995) that many very intelligent people appear to suffer substantial instantaneous drops in their IQs as soon as they begin discussing the politics of intelligence.

9. I own it to be mistaken on its face (i.e., as a matter of fact), and not because of its unsalutary axiological–political implications (e.g., valuing more intelligent people, and by implication devaluing less intelligent ones). I am working on ways to test my hypothesis: that if one could find a reasonable way of quantifying moral behavior, that is, of measuring a person's "moral index," and if one then averaged the moral indices in each of the five quintiles of IQ and connected the dots, one would obtain a horizontal line—the moral line. This would demonstrate the independence of morality and intelligence, and put an end to much unnecessary strife.

10. See Herrnstein & Murray (1994).

11. This correlation is upheld or implied by Social Darwinists (e.g., Spencer, 1969; Haeckel, 1916), by eugenicists (e.g., Jordan, 1907; Cattell, 1937), and by contemporary social scientists (e.g., Herrnstein & Murray, 1994; Brand, 1996). While IQ is but one of a constellation of human properties in which there seem to be, on coarse average, demonstrable racial, ethnic, and sex differences, it is the only one that foments serious political strife, mostly because of its ostensible correlation with morality. Black people demonstrate superior athletic abilities to white people, on coarse average, but no one concludes from this that blacks are therefore morally superior to whites. Men demonstrate superior mathematical skills to women, on coarse average, but no one concludes from this that men are therefore morally superior to women. Ashkenazi Jews demonstrate superior IQs to everyone else— including Caucasians and Asians—on coarse average, but no one concludes from this that Ashkenazi Jews are morally superior to everyone else. (E.g., lawyers are of relatively high intelligence—on coarse average—yet some of them demonstrate no cognizance whatsoever of ethicity, and so are arguably morally inferior to many less intelligent persons.) Serial killers are apparently of relatively high average intelligence, but are evidently altogether incapable of moral sentiment. How then can one draw inferences about morality from IQ alone? Why then should one seek to draw moral inferences from average IQs of black people, or anyone else?

12. By "non-harm" I mean: minimally, abstinence from unprovoked violence against fellow humans; maximally, *ahimsa* (non-harm). Jains and Buddhists, along with older schools of Indian philosophy and religion, tend to eschew harming any sentient being.

13. "I only wish it were so, Crito; that the many could do the greatest evil; for then they would also be able to do the greatest good—and what a fine thing this would be! But in reality they can do neither" (Plato, *Crito*).

14. C. Snow, *The Two Cultures and the Scientific Revolution*, The Rede Lecture, 1959 (Cambridge: Cambridge University Press, 1993), and *Corridors of Power* (New York: Scribner, 1964).

15. R. Mandell, *The Professor Game* (Garden City, NY: Doubleday, New York, 1977), pp. 82–83.

16. S. Stotsky, "Pedagogical Advocacy," *Academic Questions*, 13, Spring 2000, 27–38.

17. Cited, for example, by P. Gross and N. Levitt, *Higher Superstition* (Baltimore: Johns Hopkins University Press, 1994), p. 131.

18. Public lecture by Professor Miriam Solomon at the CUNY Graduate Center, 1998.

CHAPTER 3

Why Is Philosophy Regaining Popularity?

I am asked this question frequently, and in many forms. In some respects, I would be the last person to know the answer. Although I seem to have become a popularizer of philosophy, a purveyor of popular philosophy, or simply a "pop" philosopher, this role bequeaths no special insight into the whys and wherefores of its own emergence. In somewhat coarsely stated economic terms, I am merely one among several contemporary producers of an ancient yet perennially innovative product (philosophical practice), which can function either as a commodity (e.g., a book) or as a service (e.g., a consultation). In a free-market economy, the popularity of a product is determined ultimately by the consumers, not the producers. But given that marketing is also a notoriously two-edged sword, publicity and advertising can obviously create or inflate a demand, at least in the short run. Beyond that, political coercion can compel the universal popularity of a product—an infamous example being Hitler's *Mein Kampf*, which became required reading for all Germans.[1] Similarly, Mao Tse Tung's *Little Red Book* probably sold millions of copies by fear and force in Red China—even more than it sold by naivete in Berkeley. All-time best-sellers include Euclid's *Elements*, the *Bible*, and Agatha Christie's novels. From a Platonic viewpoint, an ideal measure of potential popularity is intrinsic worth. Philosophy itself has enormous intrinsic worth, and is therefore potentially enormously popular. It may require a philosophical agent, however, to catalyze the reaction that results in the actualization of said potential. As a catalyst, I am by definition and in practice unchanged by the reaction that I help catalyze. If this makes my opinion more credible, so be it. But my opinion as to why philosophy is regaining popularity may be completely mistaken. The most popular cultural heroes of my adolescence—notably Bob Dylan and The Beatles—were possibly among the least well-qualified to explain their popularity. Since mine is much less than theirs, perhaps I am that much better-qualified. But at all events I am a philosopher, and therefore can be relied upon to harbor an opinion on everything.

I might also add that popularity is not itself ubiquitously popular. There are sprinklings of academics in every discipline, not just in philosophy, who variously loath, abhor, and sneer at popularizations of their respective subjects-matter. When some academic philosophers hear about the success of *Plato Not Prozac*, which (among other things) makes philosophy accessible to a very general readership, and which *ab initio* was designed for and aimed at the self-help market, they recoil in horror. Some of these academic philosophers believe that philosophy is an exclusive preserve of professors or scholars, and not meant for the masses at all. To these I reply, "On what priggish or proprietary authority do you remove *love of wisdom* from the purview, or deem it beyond the capacity, of ordinary people? If you take your whiskey neat, it has alcoholic content and will intoxicate you; if you take your whiskey with water, it has alcoholic content and will intoxicate you. At what point does watered-down whiskey cease to have alcoholic content? (This is a Sorites paradox.) Similarly, at what point does popularized philosophy cease to have noetic content? And among you purists who would permanently incarcerate philosophy in the ivory tower, and allow her no visitors from without, how many are purely original thinkers, and how many mere book-learners, mouthing the watered-down thoughts of others?"[2] Still other professors may castigate popular works simply because they are envious of the popularizers, in which case they might benefit from philosophical counseling themselves.

Mostly I frame the question at hand the other way around: How (in Heaven's name) did philosophy ever manage to make itself so *unpopular* that people deem its current popularity newsworthy, or worthy of any special consideration? The answer to this is also ancient and philosophical: things change; pendula oscillate; fashions vacillate.

There has been a continuous presence of philosophers in Western culture since the era of the pre-Socratics, dating back at least to 600 BCE; in Hindu culture since the Vedas and Upanishads, dating back to 600 BCE or earlier; in Chinese culture since the authorship of the *I Ching*, which apparently influenced both Lao Tzu and Confucius, dating back once again to roughly 600 BCE. Philosophy once entailed and unified medicine, psychology, law, science, and embodied the general quest for knowledge, value, meaning, purpose, truth, justice, and progress. Philosophy was therefore central to human existence and endeavor. How did it manage to become relegated to the periphery?

In the West, philosophers and philosophy have been variously lionized, ostracized, monasticized, politicized, patronized, radicalized, academized, organized, and professionalized. Philosophers have tutored emperors (e.g., Epictetus), administered empires (e.g., Seneca), and have been expelled from cities (e.g., Rousseau). They have leapt into volcanoes to prove their godhood (e.g., Empedocles) and have withdrawn from society to improve their personhood (e.g., Thoreau). They have been accused of every heresy extant (e.g., Hobbes), have been excommunicated (e.g., Spinoza), and burned at the stake (e.g., Bruno). They have served as physicians (e.g., Locke), diplomats (e.g., Hume), parliamentarians (e.g., Mill), and foot-soldiers (e.g., Wittgenstein). Some lived opulently as aristocrats (e.g., Bacon); others were unemployable aristocrats (e.g., Russell). Some accepted money as stone-masons but philosophized freely in public (e.g., Socrates); others accepted money as historians but philosophized clandestinely in private (e.g., Leibniz). Philosophers have fomented revolution (e.g., Marx); rejected morality (e.g., Nietzsche); resisted tyranny (e.g., Sartre). In short, philosophers have often led interesting, astounding, and sometimes quite unenviable lives. Their philosophies have explored, shaped, and populated the vast mindscape of thought; have invented, discovered, and examined all manner of thinkable things; and have contemplated, forged, and interpreted intricate relations between and among such things. Philosophers have been as vital, and at times even more celebrated or reviled, as poets and prophets.

So how did this extravagantly variegated zoo of bold thinkers and daring doers deteriorate into the pathetic stereotype of *homo academicus*: impractical, incomprehensible, irrelevant, institutionalized, eccentric, absent-minded, and ultimately incapable of incisive thought or decisive deed? While all stereotypes hyperbolize some truths, they also obscure other truths. Great philosophers are neither born nor made, nor have great philosophy thrust upon them, with any apparent uniformity, regularity, periodicity, or other regard for recurrent needs of the human race. Moreover, for every outstanding philosopher—as for every outstanding athlete, actor, artist, architect, and any other kind of person—there will be ten good and a hundred middling ones, as well as ten mediocre ones and an abysmal one. Philosophical ability is normally distributed too. Great philosophers cannot flourish in an academy which celebrates bureaucracy and rewards mediocrity, any more than saints can flower in such a monastery. The vocation of a great philosopher, as that of a saint, unfolds in the public square, not in the cloister.

The twentieth-century academy performed another function, too: it gave shelter and succor to noetically dominant but otherwise (i.e., physically, emo-

tionally, socially, economically, politically) subordinate types, who were and are
not constituted to make their ways much in the "outside" world. Outside what?
Outside mind. But do not commit the error of supposing that the arena of high
mind is less competitive, combative, avaricious, egoistic, vainglorious, sanguinary, unforgiving, and gain-driven than the arena of big business or the arena
of *realpolitik*. On the contrary, it is well-known that the politics of the academy
(like those of the monastery) are much more vituperative than those of business
or *realpolitik*, ironically because there is so much less at stake. But academic
conflicts are played out, and its wars waged, silently, secretly, spinelessly,
cravenly, and in slow-motion; behind closed doors, within closed minds, and
between the lines of closeted publications. This has probably always been so,
from Plato's Academy to the present. Quoth Erasmus, of scholars and philosophers, in 1517:

> Here also I find war of another kind, less bloody indeed, but not less furious
> ... if they do not proceed to use real swords and spears, they stab one
> another with pens dipt in the venom of malice; they tear one another with
> biting labels, and dart the deadly arrows of their tongues against their
> opponents' reputations.[3]

Moreover, what Erasmus wrote of medieval courts is also true of academic
administrations:

> But I leave the common people, who are tossed about like the waves, by
> the winds of passion. I enter the courts of kings.... I see every outward sign
> of the highest offices and humanity.... It is all paint and varnish. Everything
> is corrupted by open faction, or by secret grudges and animosities.[4]

The "currency" of academic philosophy is ideas, not money. The "conquests" of academic philosophy consist of producing primary ideas, about
which other academics reproduce secondary ideas, about which other academics reproduce tertiary ideas, and so forth. This is a life of mind, and is a
wonderful life—as far as it goes. For most of the twentieth century, however,
philosophy went no further, ironically because of the very successes of early
modern and enlightenment philosophy itself. Bacon's epiphany of knowledge
as power, and Hobbes's liberation of politics from its bondage to theology,
together unleashed a conception of man that engendered both British empiricism and the scientific revolution. At its early modern inception, there was no
word for "science"; Boyle and his contemporaries, founders of the Royal Society, conceived their enterprise as "experimental philosophy." This meant love
of wisdom pursued by conducting experiments in the world. Attaining knowledge through the sheer exercise of unaided reason soon became a fruitless

engagement with "armchair metaphysics," comparable to later nineteenth-century "desk anthropology" in its potentiation of every kind of wrongheadedness. Plato's compelling form of dialogue endured, and was used by the likes of Galileo to disseminate scientific argument. But the youthful enthusiasm of nascent science may be forgiven its implicit naivete for assuming that the sum total of reliable knowledge amounts to wisdom, and that successful pursuit of the former leads to love of the latter. Knowledge alone does not make us wise, only arrogant (if we think we know much), or humble (if we realize how little we know). Similarly, pursuing reliable knowledge alone does not make one a lover of wisdom, and that is why scientists are not necessarily, and not usually, philosophers. Even so, they cannot operate beyond the pale of metaphysical presupposition—which obliges them either to become more philosophical, or to employ philosophers themselves.

This is exactly what transpired in quantum physics. While the Vienna Circle, composed of logical positivist philosophers, was busily carrying out Hume's injunction to consign all metaphysics to the flames, physicists themselves rediscovered that metaphysical presupposition, at least in the quantum world, is indispensable. What one discovers about quantum phenomena depends upon what sort of experimental apparatus one constructs, which in turn depends upon what one chooses to measure, which itself depends upon what one presupposes about the phenomena themselves. Einstein, Bohr, and the other great physicists of the early twentieth century became entangled in deep philosophical debate about the fundamental nature of the world, and its knowability by us—classic questions of ontology and epistemology—even as the great contemporary philosophers eschewed such discussions, and charted the impossible course of reducing the world and our knowledge of it to formal (i.e., logical) structures.

Russell characterized this situation most aptly in his metaphor of twentieth-century philosophy in "no-man's land," caught in a cross-fire between religion and science.[5] The philosophical survivors of this furious fusillade, which pitted fire and brimstone against fusion and fallout, immortal souls against transient subatomic particles, omniscient Gods against indeterminate quantum fluctuations, moral rules against genetic codes, and divine love against mundane biochemistry, retreated fully and ignominiously from the field. Love of wisdom, which began with a bang in Athens, ended with a whimper in Cambridge. After Russell, Moore, and Ayer in Britain, and Frege, Schlick, and Carnap on the continent, post-enlightenment philosophy rapidly divorced itself from the empirical, moral, social, and political world, and became entirely self-referential. Wittgenstein, however revered by some academic philosophers, epitomizes its debilitation and institutionalization. A towering academic cult-figure of twentieth-century philosophy, indeed regarded by many as the most influential philosopher of that century, he said little either intelligible to non-academic humanity, or applicable to its concerns. Regarding language as a kind of game, Wittgenstein precipitated an avalanche of language games about language games. Following his example, mainstream philosophy became almost relegated to self-referential and inconsequential realms. Philosophy of language purported but failed to extract meaning from formal syntax; philosophy of mind purported but failed to explain consciousness by conscious deliberation; philosophy of science purported but failed to explain the accrual of reliable knowledge via logical theories of confirmation. Tarski, when he first arrived in New York City, gave courses at City College to assuage his impecuniosity. While he willingly taught logic, he refused to teach ethics, on the grounds that ethics is not axiomatizable.

Worse still, the large-scale political revolutions and totalitarian regimes of the twentieth century required no Aristotles, Confucii, Senecas, or Bacons to tutor their leaders or influence their fortunes; philosophical consultants were replaced by ideologues, zealots, propagandists, and mass-murderers. Similarly, the global world wars of the twentieth century required no Sun Tzus or Von Clausewitzes to philosophize about their proper conduct; even generals themselves were replaced by mathematicians and physicists. Beyond that, behavioral psychology and game-theoretic economics became the applied social sciences of choice. What was a mere philosopher to do? Apparently, he could profess philosophical vows of poverty (i.e., trading only in abstractions), chastity (i.e., refusing to be wedded to the world), and obedience (i.e., adhering to approved academic cults). This rapidly made philosophy incomprehensible, irrelevant and insignificant in the eyes of the world, and reduced the philosopher himself to a hapless creature of the institution, a kind of intellectual holy fool at best, an absent-minded professor more commonly, or Pozzo's Lucky with a PhD at worst. Philosophy lectures in the universities put students to sleep instead of keeping them on their toes, or drove them to despair instead of inspiring them. Once a preparation for any worthy endeavor, philosophy became what one endeavored to avoid while preparing for anything else.

The institutionalization of philosophy during the first three-quarters of the twentieth century, and its concomitant divorce from the world, are ultimately paying dividends for philosophical practice. Academic philosophy as I have characterized it can also be termed "theoretical philosophy"—which is by no means a bad thing, only an incomplete thing. It is a part that gets mistaken for the whole. The noetic rigors and complexities of theoretical philosophy have always attracted astute and acute minds; nowhere in the humanities wing of the academy is so much raw intelligence and analytical acumen concentrated than in philosophy departments. The problem is not that philosophy became over-theoretical and self-referential in its orientation; rather, that (until the mid

1970s) its practical applications neglected to keep pace with the enormity and variety of its theoretical developments. The proliferation of universities and colleges required to serve the baby-boomer generation entailed a proportionate proliferation of philosophy departments, mostly under the aegis of theoretical (mostly analytic) philosophy. The recent popularity of philosophical practice can be attributed partly to a widespread, accumulated, and lingering sense, on the part of generic college graduates who either struggled through theoretical philosophy courses or avoided them altogether, that something profoundly important is missing from their lives. This invariably turns out to be the possibility of leading the examined life itself, which theoretical philosophy eschews but which practical philosophy (qua philosophical practice) engenders. That philosophy is not only an esoteric and theoretical pursuit of erudite academics, but is also an exoteric and practical guide to leading ordinary lives, is a revelation currently celebrated by increasing numbers of practitioners and clients alike. The richness, depth, and variety of twenty-five centuries of theoretical philosophical systems, insights, and methods potentiates an equally rich, deep, and diverse renaissance of philosophical practice.

Two other philosophical traditions bear mention here; namely, existentialism and pragmatism. Existential and phenomenological perspectives contributed largely to what is generally termed "continental" philosophy, as distinguished from the analytic variety. Philosophers still needed to discuss ethics and aesthetics, social and political philosophy, as well as issues of meaning and purpose. Existentialism fared much better than most attempts at resuscitating secular morality, although in the main it is a philosophy that can depress normal people and drive depressives to the brink of despair. But existentialism provided powerful remedies to the egregious anti-Hobbesian romanticism that permeated European thought thanks to Rousseau, and the anti-realism that pervades American thought thanks to the likes of Rorty. For three-quarters of the twentieth century, students of philosophy identified themselves either with the "analytic" or the "continental" traditions. Philosophy departments became mildly to acerbically divided between these two camps. Although the division is somewhat arbitrary, and makes for peculiar bedfellows especially on the continental side (e.g., the Christian existentialist Kierkegaard and the God-slayer Nietzsche, the Nazi-sympathizing Heidegger, and his student, the communistic Sartre), it was a comprehensible division and it stood for some time. Continental philosophy at least endeavored to provide an accounting for the unprecedented technological, military, and political horrors of the twentieth century, on which analytic philosophy was necessarily mute (with noteworthy exceptions like Russell). Classically trained philosophers who tried to re-extend its boundaries to cover momentous human strife, like Joad and Collingwood in Britain, became casualties of the false dichotomy. Neither fish nor

fowl, that is neither conspicuously analytic nor continental, their works virtually perished from inattention.

Pragmatism is an originally American contribution to modern philosophy,
and perhaps it is no coincidence that the works of Peirce, James, and Dewey
lend themselves vastly to philosophical practice. Their respective applications
represent unploughed fields, which will be furrowed in the course of time. As
philosophical practice unfolds in America, it will be natural for American
practitioners to explore their own roots more deeply. Pragmatism of the original
kind (not of Rorty's specious kind) bootstrapped itself into viability, just as
philosophical practice is doing. In many ways, that original triumvirate of
pragmatists formed the first wave of American practitioners—albeit a wave
without a sea. The relevance of original pragmatism to philosophical practice
deserves a volume of its own, and I shall say no more about it here.

The continental tree of philosophy was transformed beyond recognition by
the cultural revolution of the sixties, because upon its radical trunk was most
readily grafted the fanatical and militant branches of philosophy, ideology, and
political indoctrination that—within one generation—infiltrated, undermined,
and ultimately all but eradicated erudition and rational inquiry in the humanities canopy of the academy. Intolerant anti-realists, in the various garbs of
feminism, ethnocentrism, neo-Marxism, postmodernism, deconstructionism,
social constructivism, and the like, which first debased standards and next
destroyed curricula, then set their aberrated sights on the sciences themselves—but proved unequal to the task of toppling reliable knowledge and
method with predictable inanity and cupidity—ironically helped prepare the
ground for philosophical practice. A classical philosophical education reflected
both the analytic and continental traditions: it cultivated noetic rigor on the
one hand, yet contemplated unaxiomatizable notions of the good and the just
on the other. A postmodern philosophical education—an oxymoron of the first
stripe—inculcated the doctrine that "white male patriarchal hegemony" was
solely and completely responsible for all the world's ills, and that by eliminating
its representation and eradicating its canon the Emperor's New Academy would
lead the world into enlightened utopian bliss. Proponents of this doctrine have
Stalinized the academy—not the world, which has endured horror enough—
into a retrograde totalitarian state of political correctness and noetic rectitude
that lies beyond the imagination and comprehension of ordinary Americans.
That the ideologically motivated and bureaucratically monitored regulation of
thought, speech, and act should become the workaday standard in American
institutions of so-called "higher learning," that the exercise of First Amendment
rights should be proscribed on their campuses, that open debate and rational
inquiry should become crimes against university administrations, is a tragedy
that cannot be compassed in this work. Suffice to say that the American

academy has succumbed to a hyperbolic abuse of its own liberties, which has entailed their utter repudiation. The implications for philosophical practice are immediate: some wings of the academy, having molted their pinions of noetic flight, have become so derelict in their duty to educate, that people must seek higher education elsewhere. Thus, many are turning to philosophical practitioners.

At the same time, precisely because of its noetic rigor, analytic philosophy has staunchly resisted postmodern predation and debilitation. Like mathematics and the natural sciences—but unlike the humanities and social sciences—analytic philosophy cannot be perverted from the inside, only attacked and possibly suppressed from without. Its rabidly politicized opponents are incapable of the sustained erudition, objectivity, and rationality necessary to defeat analytic philosophy on its own ground, and so must resort to replacing it on purely political grounds. The continental school is not so intrinsically defensible, since it is grounded from the outset in phenomenology and hermeneutics, and so on its coattails have ridden, wittingly or not, all the neo-Marxist and other postmodernist revolutionaries who have subverted, radicalized, and ruined the academy. This bifurcation became most literally enacted at the University of Sydney, whose philosophy department underwent a division into the analytic (called "traditional") and the radical (called "modern"). They remain separate but unequal: one assiduously educating its charges; the other, sedulously politicizing them.

The distinction between analytic rigor and political indoctrination has a direct bearing on philosophical practice, which can be tasted immediately from the fruits of these respective schools. Graduates of K-through-12 systems and university programs whose curricula have been dictated by political agendas—which means the majority of graduates in humanities and social sciences, except for those who study analytic philosophy—are either functional illiterates or dysfunctional aculturates. Simply stated, they can neither read, nor write, nor reason; nor have they but dim conceptions of culture. What happens when they are hired by some corporation? They can neither comprehend their jobs, nor can they communicate effectively with others. The dumbing-down of American culture, which was once very good for politics, has become excruciatingly bad for business. As a result, the *Wall Street Journal* discovered that philosophy majors make superior entry-level hires in the corporate world, even though have not studied economics, marketing, communications, business, law, or any other relevant subject.[6] Why? Because alone in the humanities and social science wing of the academy, philosophy majors are obliged to read, write, and reason. They can therefore comprehend their jobs and communicate effectively with others. Whereas graduates of programs in political indoctrination comprehend little beyond the ideologies with which they have been brainwashed, and communicate little beyond the slogans, euphemisms, and jargon with which their washed brains have been infused.

The irony is that the Professors of Theoretical Philosophy who have thus far developed, preserved, and transmitted the analytic blueprints for Western civilization have had no idea how to reconstruct the edifice itself. Although they are largely immune from deconstruction themselves, and although their students can be of immediate and vital use to a disintegrating culture, they represent only so many fingers in a crumbling dike. Philosophical practitioners, by contrast, can both understand the blueprints and undertake the reconstruction. The more our academy and civilization are deconstructed, the more work the deconstructionists provide for philosophical practitioners.

This general method of countering destructive political forces, not by opposing them directly but by repairing the damage they do, I call "social judo." It is informed by ancient Chinese philosophy in general, and by the Chinese philosophy of the martial arts in particular (although judo itself is Japanese). Social judo has many applications in my philosophical practice, both large- and small-scale. One does not waste energy opposing a hurricane, which is violent and destructive but which blows over quickly: one weathers it and then rebuilds one's edifice. Similarly, a violent ideological storm does not long endure; one weathers it and then reconstructs one's polity. Analytic philosophy weathers barbarization by preserving and transmitting reading, writing, and reasoning in its most developed forms; philosophical practice does not resist the barbarians, but brings cultural relief to the victims of barbarism. Moreover, we practitioners thank the barbarians for affording us such opportunities. Those who have lost their dwellings to hurricanes have unprecedented opportunities for home improvement. If they are wise, and as far as they are able, they take advantage of the tempest.

If you understand from this argument that philosophical practice owes its current popularity to the overall denouement of western civilization, and to the desperate needs of citizens caught in the decline and swept into the abyss, you have understood correctly. It may well be that philosophical practice is a kind of last straw at which our civilization can grasp. Thus the real world (as contrasted with the academic one) and the urgent needs of people in it (as opposed to the deferrable needs of academics) is completely at odds with the marginalization of philosophy.

I will also offer an explanation grounded not in politics, but in historical metaphysics. It would appear that any movement or inspiration, to be successful, requires two things: first, an intrinsic idea, objective, mission, or vision; second, an extrinsic means to actualize or carry it out. It is not generally appreciated that the extrinsic thing is not, strictly speaking, confined to material realms. With art, one needs the manuscript, the paintings, the score, the screenplay; but then one requires the publisher, the gallery, the orchestra, the production company. The successful artistic actualization that results in the book, the exhibition, the performance, or the film is not just a matter of money spent concentrating material resources: it is also, crucially, a matter of timing. Even a brilliantly conceived and impeccably produced artistic endeavor will flop if it is not well-received by the public. Its reception or rejection are determined by the propitiousness of the timing. "Propitiousness" is a somewhat ineffable yet palpably operative term. A successful cultural movement, like a successful comedy routine, depends as much on timing as on content. Short-term success depends more on timing than content; long-term success, more on content than timing. Yet timing does not always lend itself to algorithmic or scientific precision; timing a movement or a vernissage is not like timing an engine or a rocket-launch.

This holds for enterprises good or ill. Hume's *Treatise* "fell dead-born from the press"; reissued as the *Enquiry*, it met with broad acclaim. This was about timing, not philosophical content. Hitler's "Beer-Hall Putsch" failed miserably in 1923, and landed him in a prison (where he dictated *Mein Kampf*); his Reichstag fire succeeded perfectly in 1933, and landed him in the Chancellory (where he carried out *Mein Kampf*). This was about timing, not political content. Norman Lear, who produced the legendary television sitcom *All in the Family* (adapted from the British counterpart *Til Death Do Us Part*), required two years to sell the concept to the incumbent "geniuses" running the major networks; but by the time he did so, the issues both addressed and addressable in the controversial program were even more poignant in American consciousness. This was about timing, not social content. Similarly, I am near-convinced that there have been philosophical practitioners in every generation—just as there have been theoretical philosophers—but whether they were afforded substantive opportunities for the emergence and ensconcement of their practices depended not only (or not so much) on their intrinsic abilities and volitions, but also (or greatly) on the extrinsic propitiousness of their times.

Clearly, the current times very much favor philosophical practice, and not only because the ground had been laid (or eroded) by the entrenchment of deconstruction, and allied barbarisms, in postmodern western civilization. A constellation of forces external to the attempted supplantation of analytic philosophy by political indoctrination has contributed formatively to the propitiousness of the times. Foremost among these are: growing public disenchantment with received modalities of counseling; growing public dissatisfaction with the inadequacies of psychopharmacology; growing public discontent with the chronic inabilities of religion, science, economics, law, and politics alike meaningfully to address problems that are and always have been fundamentally philosophical; and growing public awareness that practical philosophers (i.e., applied ethicists) are indispensable to the professional ethical concerns of medical practice and research, engineering, environmental science, business, computing, journalism, and public policy-making. I will briefly address each of these in turn.

First, people are not such fools as P. T. Barnum believed. Biological mechanisms of self-preservation (in acute circumstances) and psychological self-assessments of overall wellness (in general circumstances) have functioned since the dawn of man, and have not been eroded by technological intervention. Most people know perfectly well when they need help; their real difficulty lies in determining what kind of help is most appropriate. If they are hornswoggled by pseudo-diagnoses of non-illnesses, they will endeavor to accept the entailed treatment, but this does not mean that they will be made well. In fact, they are sometimes made more ill. I have seen many clients who are refugees from psychiatric and psychological camps, who have simply not been helped by these modalities because, self-evidently, their problems were neither psychiatric nor psychological. If you have a psychiatric problem, consult a psychiatrist. If you have a psychological problem, consult a psychologist. If you have a legal problem, consult a lawyer. If you have a philosophical problem, consult a philosopher. This is nothing more than theoretical common-sense.

In practice, however, the boundaries among these disciplines can become blurred, owing to factors ranging from honest scientific error, to dishonest professional territorialism, to disreputable individual misconduct. The State of New York used to require job applicants to undergo phrenology examinations, but no longer does so. This honest scientific mistake was corrected by the very system that made it. Ongoing self-correction—and hence verisimilitude—are hallmarks of an open society, and of the unpoliticized science that an open society embraces. Dishonest professional territorialism is more difficult to combat, because it plays new tunes on evolutionarily entrenched survival and reproductive instruments. For example, the Chair of the Human Subjects Committee of the Institutional Review Board at City College, to which I had applied for approval of my *pro bono publico* research protocol in philosophical counseling, deliberately obstructed my application for three years. A psychologist (not even of the counseling variety), he declared to the committee, in my presence, that he viewed philosophical counselors as trespassers and poachers on psychological turf. Any applied ethicist (and anyone with common sense) would recognize a clear conflict of interest here: blinded by personal prejudice, he was in no position to make a competent professional judgment, and should have disqualified himself from presiding over this case. *He* needed philosophical counseling. Similarly, when the President of the American Psychiatric Association accused me, in print, of "practicing medicine without a license" because I dispense ethics counseling, he was acting to protect what he (erroneously) viewed as his turf. People experiencing moral dilemmas are not therefore "mentally ill," and anyone who believes they are needs philosophical counseling. The extraordinary hubris of some psychologists and psychiatrists disenchants their patients, and drives them to philosophical counselors. Disreputability is impossible to eliminate from the professions. Predation on clients is a prevailing norm among lawyers, many of whom have no conception whatsoever of professional ethics. In medicine, fraudulent diagnoses and treatments are used to milk health insurance plans dry, to the tune of billions of dollars per annum—which, as usual, the honest consumer subsidizes via increased premiums and reduced services. There are disreputable philosophical practitioners too, but fortunately the damage they do is insignificant at present.

Second, there is growing public awareness of, and horrified reaction to, the hyperbolic abuse of prescription drugs. One of the least salutary aspects of residing on the leading edge of scientific progress and technological affluence, as Americans do, is the temptation to view science as a prosthetic deity, and imbue it with omniscience. This erroneous view entails the mistaken corollary that every human problem has a technological "quick-fix." The new litany of "chemical imbalance in the brain" becomes the rationale for attempted mood-enhancement and behavior modification by monkeying with neurochemical transmitters and their mechanisms of uptake. Any cook can treat the brain as a soup, sample it, and declare that it needs a little more salt. But as important popular works like Breggin's and Damasio's show, this is a science exploring the mere foothills of explanation, while pretending to stand at the summit.[7] Even people who are legitimately helped by neuropharmacology need dialogue, once their "chemical imbalances" are equilibrated. They do not cease thinking at that point; rather, they are just beginning to exercise their abilities to be rational, and can therefore benefit from philosophical guidance. Pharmacology is no more a panacea than faith-healing. It may be necessary at times in abetting emotional stability, but is rarely sufficient for leading an examined or fulfilled life. Remember Cicero's vital question concerning accusations: "Cui bono?"[8] One must ask the same questions about gratuitous pharmacological prescriptions. "Cui bono? Who benefits from the prescription?" The patient, or the pharmaceutical industry? America has not only lost the so-called "war" on illicit drugs; it is also losing the "peace" on licit ones. In fact, people who self-medicate judiciously with illicit herbs (such as cannabis) may be sometimes better off than people who allow themselves to be medicated injudiciously with licit drugs (like Prozac).

Third, most problems involving ethics, values, meaning, purpose, truth, justice, and the like, are primarily neither medical nor psychological, and cannot be resolved or even competently managed by diagnosis, medication, and interminable validation of emotion. One who is suffering from a philosophical problem may as well visit a faith-healer as a physician or psychologist. A vast variety of dissatisfactions with life, and discontents within it, have nothing to do with one's physical condition, psychological conditioning, socioeconomic standing, legal status, scientific understanding, ethnic heritage, professional vocation, political affiliation, or religious persuasion: fundamental philosophical problems both underscore and transcend these and other facets of human necessity. Moreover, life in the modern world is increasingly complex; and while specialists over-abound, generalists are in short supply.[9] People need more help than ever in reassembling the micro-laser-jigsawed fragments of their lives into intelligible wholes. Philosophical practitioners, who are specialists in conducting general inquiries, can render such assistance. We help people make sense of their lives through the integration of the parts that comes with cultivating a philosophical perspective; whereas further fragmentation can lead to nonsense, confusion, pointlessness, despair, and ultimately to spurious diagnosis, unnecessary medication—or to recruitment by a cult, or any other religious or political faction that preys on confusion, unhappiness, and despair. If you have a philosophical problem, see a philosopher; you'll save yourself a lot of trouble. This option has not always been readily available, but it is now.

Fourth, applied ethics helped paved the way for philosophical practice. Applied ethics, as distinguished from theoretical ethics, began proliferating in the 1970s, as an academic approach to framing and addressing secular ethical issues in business and the professions. Applied ethics quickly became a growth industry, with an identifiable subject matter, a corpus of textbooks and scholarly literature, a calendar of conferences, a locus of attraction for graduate students, and a funding of centers and programs across North America and Europe. Well-defined specialized subjects within the applied ethics stream, each with its own set of ongoing concerns, include biomedical ethics, business ethics, computing ethics, engineering ethics, environmental ethics, journalism ethics, legal ethics, and professional ethics. As the professions become more susceptible and sensitive to ethical issues that inevitably arise within them, and as legal liabilities wax more lucrative, it behooves the professionals-in-training to come to grips at least with fundamental ethical frameworks and precepts, and the moral arguments that flow from them and that undergird the perennial conflicts in their respective fields. For some professionals-in-training, an applied ethics course is their only exposure to philosophy during their entire university careers. I have taught many such courses, and have seen deep philosophical interests awaken in these students. As usual, an overspecialized technical curriculum had preempted their awareness of the philosophical foundations of their professions.

Beyond that, applied ethicists assume important reactive positions with regard to controversial legislative issues (e.g., abortion and euthanasia), man-made disasters (e.g., the *Exxon Valdez* wreck and the Bhopal catastrophe), conflicts of interest in business and the professions (e.g., the Air Force Brake and the Challenger explosion), extrapolation of moral reasoning into new technological territories (e.g., issues of privacy and free speech in cyberspace), and many other less-publicized but ethically significant domains. In so far as laws are but the shadows of morals, it is vital that a secular polity's legislation be informed by cogent moral reasoning. Beyond the academy, applied ethicists began to act as consultants to various professions and industries, and as such pioneered the inception of philosophical practice with organizations.

Philosophical practice overlaps with applied ethics as far as organizational consulting is concerned. From the APPA's perspective, philosophical consultants to businesses and the professions are obviously practitioners. But in other respects, philosophical practice is more proactive than applied ethics. Assessing ethical accountability after the fact in a given case is reactive philosophical practice—in a sense, theoretical philosophical practice. Counseling individual clients and facilitating groups, as well as engaging in corporate training, is proactive philosophical practice: practical practice, if you like.[10] That is the broader mandate of APPA-certified practitioners.

This brings me to the final point of this chapter. A good many seminal Western philosophical classics have been highly reactive, and embody *a posteriori* preventive intentions; they are responses to and explanations of political or cultural catastrophe, as experienced firsthand by the philosopher in question, and offer preventive remedies against a recrudescence. Plato's *Republic*, for example, is his reaction to the destruction of Athenian high culture by the Peloponnesian War, and the martyrdom of Socrates by a Spartan puppet government. The *Republic* offers a model of a state that would not endure such a downfall. Similarly, Augustine's *City of God* is his reaction to the Visigoth sacking of Rome, a supposedly Christian empire (at that point) which ought therefore to have enjoyed God's protection against barbarians. It offers permanent and secure refuge in the spiritual City of God, as opposed to transient and uncertain shelter in the temporal City of Man. Similarly, Hobbes's *Leviathan* is a reaction to the vicissitudes of the English Civil War, and offers a contractarian remedy, backed by strong central government. Similarly, Kant's *Perpetual Peace* is a reaction to unremitting European conflict, and attempts to structure an enduring diplomacy (although Kant may have had tongue in cheek: his title is taken from an inn adjacent to a cemetery). Similarly, Marx's *Communist Manifesto* is a reaction to the iniquities and inequities of nineteenth-century English capitalism, and to how well that system served his own capacity for social isolation and economic deprivation; it offers a prescription for dismantling class structure, capitalism, and organized religion at one stroke, and instituting in their place the most repressive form of central economy and crass ideology the world has yet endured—thus preventing anyone from having a better life than Marx had, when he was unknown and impoverished in London. Similarly, Ayn Rand's *Atlas Shrugged* is a reaction to the anticipated horror of neo-Marxian collectivism encroaching on the West, after it had swallowed the East; it offers a clarion reminder that an ethos of enlightened self-interest is the only reliable and justifiable way conducive both to the celebration of civil liberty and to the generation of economic wealth.

Similarly, this book has thus far been highly reactive, necessarily in this introductory section, for the purpose of setting an appropriate historical and political stage for the play of philosophical practice. I will also embark on a preventive course, but on a much reduced scale, at least compared with the grandiosity of my predecessors' visions. While an ounce of philosophical pre-vention is worth a pound of political cure, one's ability to alter the past presently awaits the future. Philosophical practice itself is primarily neither reactive (toward the past) nor preventive (toward the future); rather, proactive in the present. It follows that a practical philosophical mind need be neither afflicted by past remembrance, nor infected by future anticipation. Rather, a practical philosophical mind attends to the present alone, knowing that such attendance entails past and future together, only undistractedly so. Many are loath to give the present the attention it deserves, perhaps because there seems to be so little of it at a given time—while the past and future appear inex-haustible. I see things just the other way around: the past and future, although conceivably infinite in extent, are both illusions of a kind; whereas the present, although of no extent whatsoever, is really inexhaustible. Perhaps philosophical practice is regaining popularity because people are tired of living in illusory pasts and imaginary futures—guides to which abound in this age as in no other—and would fain try living in the present for a change, if they only knew how. Perhaps this book may also be a guide, not only to the art of loving wisdom, but also to living in the present, whenever that may be.

NOTES

1. It was a required purchase, at any rate. Its turgid prose probably discouraged most readers.

2. Schopenhauer wrote, "For the man who thinks for himself becomes acquainted with the authorities for his opinions only after he has acquired them and merely as a confirmation of them, while the book-philosopher starts with his authorities,

in that he constructs his opinions by collecting together the opinions of others: his mind then compares with that of the former as an automaton compares with a living man." "On Thinking for Yourself," in *Essays and Aphorisms*, trans. R. Hollingdale (Middlesex: Penguin, 1985), p. 91.

3. Erasmus, *The Complaint of Peace* (London: Headley Brothers, 1917), p. 14 (original work published 1517).

4. Ibid., pp. 12–13.

5. B. Russell, *History of Western Philosophy* (London: Allen & Unwin 1961), p. 13. (original work published 1946).

6. *The Wall Street Journal*, Tuesday, 25 October 1995, p. B1: "On just about everybody's list of hot skills for the 90s are communications and analysis. So who has these skills? How about philosophy majors? Philosophy majors who took the Graduate Record Examination between 1990 and 1993 finished first among all fields in verbal skills and third in analytical skills, the American Philosophical Association notes."

7. Among Breggin's many expository books, see, e.g., *Toxic Psychiatry* (New York: St. Martin's Press, New York, 1991). A. Damasio, *Descartes' Error* (New York: Avon Books, 1994), p. 258: "I hasten to add that the lack of definitive answers on mind/brain matters is not a cause for despair." In that case, it cannot be a cause for taking antidepressants, or for rejecting noetic agency.

8. "Cicero maketh honorable mention of one of the Caseii, a severe judge amongst the Romans, for a custom he had, in criminal causes, (when the testimony of the witnesses was not sufficient,) to ask the accusers, *Cui bono*; that is to say, what profit, honor, or other contentment, the accuser obtained, or expected by the fact" (Hobbes, chap. 47).

9. While attending a specialist philosophy conference on logic, a logician asked me to identify my field. I replied that I was a generalist, whereupon he became visibly puzzled, and began to rack his brains. After a few searching seconds he asked "What is generalism? I can't recall hearing about it." He had mistaken generalism for a new specialty!

10. I started counseling individual clients inadvertently, precisely because of media exposure of applied ethics. I will relate how this happened in Chapter 5.

PART **II**

Modes of
Philosophical Practice

CHAPTER 4

Two Meanings of Meditation

*I*f Jesse Jackson were to write a slogan for philosophical practice, it might run, "Mediation means meditation, not medication." You are in a sense the mediator of your fortunes, the arbiter of your destiny, the captain of your soul. You are powerless to alter your past, which includes everything from the DNA you inherited from your biological parents (i.e., your nature) to the language, culture, and experiences foisted on you involuntarily or non-voluntarily during your formative years (i.e., your primary nurture), to the events that you causally manifested by conscious or unconscious choice (i.e., voluntary or involuntary volition—karma in the Buddhist sense),[1] to their repercussions on you, whether foreseen or unforeseen (i.e., karma in the Vedic sense).[2] Similarly, you are powerless to know the future, which you can only anticipate with Hobbesian prudence, or extrapolate from experience with Humean expectation, or predict in theory from scientific laws and statistical correlations, or prophesy from divine revelation or mundane delusion, or speculate from calculated risk. Your influence over your life, if you have any, is exerted in the infinitesimal, fleeting instant between the determined past and the undetermined future, and is manifest sometimes through some combination of your nature, conditioning, and habit (if you are on "auto-pilot"); at other times, through your spontaneity (which is the antipode of conditioning and habit); or else through your volition (which is neither predetermined, nor conditioned, nor habituated, nor unplanned; rather, is *premeditated*).

If indeed you can mediate your life by exerting volition in the moment, with the effect of intervening between the fixed past and actuating one of myriad unfixed futures, it certainly behooves you to meditate upon the choice you will make. Situations regarding fairly inconsequential or routine decisions, such as what flavor of ice cream to eat at the local parlor, can be left to spontaneity or habit. But in situations regarding momentous or unprecedented choice—whether involving careers, relationships, duties, conflicts of interest, or the expression of strong emotion—you will surely wish to meditate as deeply and wisely as possible before making a decision. This is independent of whether you subscribe to deontological or teleological ethics, or virtue ethics, or some admixture of them. For if you are a deontologist, you will still need to consult your ethical rules, and more importantly consider acceptable exceptions. Most conflicts between deontologists are not over the rules at all; rather, are over the exceptions.[3] And if you are a consequentialist, of course you will need to deliberate among the envisioned outcomes of your choices, in order to choose what seems best. And if you subscribe to some version of virtue ethics, your particular list of virtues (and vices), as well the best ways to inculcate (or not to inculcate) them, may be subject to change over time and may conflict with other such lists at any time. I am neither an absolutist nor a relativist in these matters. In some situations I prefer deontology; in others, teleology; in others still, virtue ethics. My meta-ethical preferences are themselves guided by no fixed rule or even heuristic, other than a sense of justice applied to each case on its merits. What ethical approach is most just in a given case is itself part of the meditation.

Your practical meditations are also independent of the issue of free will, in which they are nonetheless theoretically grounded. The point is most simply illustrated thus: when you go into a restaurant, do you read the menu and choose your victuals, or do you leave it up to fate? Do you request that the server bring you the meal you have chosen, or do you merely say "bring me whatever I'm fated to receive"? The fact that you and millions of others do the former and not the latter is practically independent of whether your choice of meal is itself determined by you or predetermined by fate. That you do behave as though you exercised volition is reason enough to think before you act. Whether or not you are be fated to meditate in a certain way, or fated to eschew meditation, cannot be settled by meditating or eschewing meditation.

Accepting the acausal freedom and causal efficacy of the will, as a practical working assumption, also entails the further difficulty of distinguishing between willing and wishing. The former denotes what one can attain or persist in striving to attain; the latter denotes fantasizing over the unattainable. Thus an imprisoned man may will to be free, and plan an appeal, a parole, or an escape accordingly. His fellow-prisoner may simply wish to be free, and (freely) indulge his imagination in freedom for an arbitrarily long time, without acting in any way to attain the object of his wishes. However, the distinction is fraught with complication. For failure to attain an end does not always entail lack of willing the means—one's appeal may be rejected; one's parole, denied; one's escape attempt, thwarted. Moreover, one's apparent attainment of an end does not always entail willing the means—one may be automatically paroled, or have one's sentence reduced for good behavior that was not intended toward that end. Nonetheless, by examining the relevant causal nexus, one may ascertain to what degree an end was attained voluntarily, involuntarily or non-voluntarily. Except in cases of involuntarism, one can declare the will to be involved. And note that a man who voluntarily commits a capital crime may later be non-voluntarily executed by the state. I am not here debating the issue of capital punishment; rather, asserting that if we choose certain actions, and those actions entail unpalatable consequences for us, we may be powerless to avoid them. This is true of physical laws, which operate sufficiently if not necessarily: I may freely choose to jump off a roof, but am then powerless to avoid the conversion of my potential gravitational energy into the kinetic variety. And this is true contingently of manmade laws: I may freely choose to defy them, but am then powerless to avoid the consequences of defiance, even though I may wish and even will such avoidance later on. This only serves to emphasize the importance of meditation prior to action. Thoughts need not be enacted, but deeds cannot be undone.

Nonetheless, the empirical effects of harboring a given set of beliefs, inculcated by and through one's meditations (and manifested as one's philosophy), and the empirical differences between different belief systems (and manifested as one's sociopolitical ethos), vary drastically as a function of those beliefs. It is well-known that philosophers are by nature disputatious beings, capable of disagreeing on almost any point, however large or small. The human brain is an organ of staggering complexity, an explanation of whose precise functioning, particularly in relation to conscious mentation itself, has thus far eluded even those who mentate most effectively about it. We know less about our brains, and the noetic functions to which they apparently give rise, than about almost any other palpable object of study. Even some of the most advanced contemporary works in this area, by leading experts, fall far short of explanations.[4] We cannot yet distinguish a philosopher, who supposedly thinks deeply about everything, from an ordinary layperson, who supposedly thinks deeply about nothing, merely by examining their brains. Since no one has yet the foggiest notion how neurons, synapses, biochemical transmitters, and electrochemical brain states actually give rise to consciousness—if indeed they alone do—and to associated ideas, beliefs, states of mind, and their contents, no one can say anything substantive about the biological basis of mentation in normally functioning brains. Thus we are thrown back time and again, on recurrently futile attempts to mentate mentation, to rationalize rationality, and to understand understanding.

The upshot is that, since philosophers think more deeply than most people, their disagreements run deeper too. But since philosophers make emotional commitments to their beliefs, just like everyone else, they have even more to be committed to. Moreover, since philosophers are perhaps more prone to absurdity than ordinary people, the potential depth of their absurdities, as well as the strength of their emotional commitment to absurdities, are correspondingly greater than average as well. Russell once characterized philosophy as "an exceptionally ingenious attempt to reason fallaciously." And Cicero famously said, "There can be nothing so absurd, but may be found in the books of philosophers."[5] But when absurd philosophical beliefs are put into practice, as social policy or political agency, the results can be catastrophic. Therefore quality control becomes a vexed question for philosophical practice, for while the free play of thought is essential, and the freedom of speech desirable, yet not everything thinkable or sayable is, or ought to be, doable.

In sum, we cannot assert that intelligence alone, or range or complexity or profundity of thought alone, guarantees the emergence of a workable set of beliefs about the world. But just as with science, the child of philosophy, empirical confirmations or falsifications of beliefs are the best complements of beliefs themselves. But instead of asking, as a scientist would, "To what extent does a given experiment corroborate or vitiate a given hypothesis about the nature of the world?" a philosophical practitioner asks "To what extent does a given personal lifestyle, social fabric, or political ethos corroborate or vitiate the workability of the beliefs that underlie it?" Some answers are forthcoming. While we can conceive no experiment to test the scientific hypothesis that man can exercise free will, we have ample empirical evidence that a philosophical belief in the causal efficacy of free will produces an ethos that is itself far freer (both in individual liberty and from shared prejudice) and also far more productive (both in individual attainment and in aggregate wealth) than that which emanates from a philosophical belief in fate as the sole arbiter of men's fortunes. While we cannot determine empirically whether some individuals and societies adopt fatalism freely or are fated to adopt it, we can determine empirically that those who reject fatalistic beliefs and assert volitional ones (either freely or because they are fated to) live more freely, more productively, and more purposely than those who freely embrace (or are fated to be embraced by) doctrines that preempt their freedom, productivity, and purpose.

But a life of liberty and fulfillment does not arise from philosophical meditation alone, nor from the doctrinaire implementation (e.g., by disaffected activists) of half-baked meditations (e.g., by disaffected philosophers). The singular implication of this line of argument is the impossibility, in the sense of inadvisability, of applying a given philosophy as though it were a brute fact of nature, as opposed to an artefact of consciousness, and therefore also of nurture. In other words, it is impossible, in the sense of inadvisable, to isolate the profound beliefs of any philosopher from the emotional and therefore also the psychological commitment required to produce and sustain them. A raving lunatic may write a perfectly coherent book on logic, but any attempted repudiation of the logic based on the lunacy commits the fallacy of *ad hominem*: just because so-and-so is a raving lunatic, it does not follow that so-and-so's logical skills are impaired. But whatever gives rise to the attribution of raving lunacy may well manifest itself in value-laden writings, if not in value-neutral ones. Hence, societies would do well to consider the psychology—and, where appropriate, psychopathology—of the philosophers by whose value-laden beliefs they, the societies, are most profoundly influenced. To suppose that some principle or other should be applied simply because some celebrated philosopher or other deemed it a good idea is to chart a course through treacherous waters using tea leaves, goat entrails, peasant superstition, Panglossian idealism, New Age solipsism, or feminist critiques of navigation—instead of sextants, compasses, computers, and maps. While the facts of science, and their utility to man, stand independent of the psychology of the scientists who discover them, the artifacts of philosophy (aside from deductive logic) are dependent upon the psychology of the philosophers who produce them. Those who would take small pains to study the psychology of philosophy might spare inflicting greater pains upon themselves and others, as they do when they wheel some Trojan horse of prescriptive axiology into the inner keep of their ethos, and out springs an army of psychological troubles, concealed, transported and smuggled in by an ostensive philosophical construct. Needless to say, the psychology of philosophy is a course currently offered nowhere by no one. I will be pleased to teach it if the opportunity arises. It forms an implicit component of APPA certification training, and will form an explicit component of an accredited degree program in philosophical practice, once that becomes established.

How then should one meditate? This is the very rudiment of philosophy, among whose catalog of works we find at least two classics bearing literally that name: the *Meditations* of Marcus Aurelius, and the *Meditations* of René Descartes. They bear little mutual philosophical resemblance—one being a work of Roman stoicism, the other of Gallic rationalism—because the perspectives of their authors, being particular functions of unique world-lines through Minkowski space-time, have no intersection and bear no relation. Said a different way, active meditation of this kind produces fruits that taste uniquely of the particular character and experience of the meditator, which are functions of his place, time, ethos, nurture, perspective, *zeitgeist*, *weltanschauung*, gestalt, and—ineluctably—psychology. Active meditations of this kind have always produced, and will continue to produce, a wildly prolific, richly diverse (and sometimes noetically cloned) philosophical literature. Guides to the efficacies and effects of applying these doctrines are, however, contrastingly few and far between.

It follows that active meditations, which are trains of thought pulled and pushed by varieties of engines (e.g., logical, ontological, epistemological, axiological) can begin anywhere and lead anywhere. Philosophers are at least willing and able to think extensively and systemically about human problems, although their prescriptive solutions may diverge widely, and can range from salient to irrelevant, from priceless to worthless, from enlightening to enslaving. Philosophers meditate actively with themselves, in monologues, and do so with their clients, in dialogues or polylogues. Active meditation is the mind's second-best way, in my view, of maintaining its equilibrium in the face of constant change, of integrating past and future seamlessly in the present, and of generating a kind of ataraxia. Leisurely yet exhaustive contemplation is one of life's greatest joys, but is restricted to those who have the capacity to engage in it, which is definitely not everyone. Then again, many people close enough to the threshold of active philosophical meditation, who cannot quite manage it on their own, are without doubt able to engage in it usefully, with a little assistance from a philosophical counselor.

If active meditation, which entails all the thoughts of all the great philosophers, a mighty sum of mentation indeed, is only second-best, then what is possibly better? The answer is easy to give, but difficult to justify, in words: inactive meditation, or bringing the mind to a quiescent state. If one wishes to speak and act from the deepest clarity, to function both precisely and spontaneously, the surest and swiftest way to instantaneous exactitude is inactive meditation. Active meditation, by contrast, allows the mind to ruminate, but not necessarily to concentrate. It encourages the mind to wander, but not always to focus. It grapples pugnaciously with ideas, but does not readily acquiesce in their flows or perceive their patterns. It can be rooted in subjective judgment and mired in personal prejudice while claiming utter objectivity. It can exacerbate arrogance, but rarely engender compassion. The actively meditating mind does not always solve problems; rather, it endeavors to force solutions by generating kinetic energy of thought. Inactive meditation doesn't solve problems either; rather, it endeavors to coax forth solutions by accruing potential energy of quiescence. Yet a funny thing often happens on the way to senescent mindfulness: many problems, once deprived of thoughts on which to feed and flourish in one's active mind, starve and shrivel in one's quiescent mind.

While theoretical philosophers will never prosper in the academy by dint of publishing lengthy papers replete with blank pages, reflecting the fully refined verbal output of inactive meditation, philosophical practitioners will always prosper outside the academy by emptying their minds of preconception and distortion, thus allowing clients to articulate their concerns on the practitioners' *tabulae rasae*. In order to render the best service, practitioners must not only listen to, but also hear their clients. How can you hear clearly if your meeting place is noisy? But your mind is the ultimate meeting place. How can you hear clearly if your mind is noisy? Noetic noise is best attenuated by inactive meditation. As Lao Tzu said, "the Sage carries on his business without action, and gives his teaching without words.... He governs by non-action; consequently there is nothing ungoverned."[6]

To those who have no idea what I am talking about, it is really a very simple matter. While self-government is man's ideal estate, those incapable of self-government need to be governed. Those who would govern others should also be self-governing, and the best way to govern oneself, and one's actions (including the government of others), is through inactive meditation. Sitting still and paying attention to one's breath is one of the most ancient and efficacious philosophical practices known to man. There are dozens if not hundreds of specific techniques that one can employ thus to empty and quiet the mind, and thousands of teachers who convey such techniques in widely varying contexts. They are all variations on a single theme: bringing the mind to rest, and remaining without judgment. In order for your body to function properly, it needs periodic sleep. In order for your mind to function properly, it needs periodic repose. We do not have to learn how to make or practice making the body sleep, but we do need to learn how to bring and practice bringing the mind to alert repose. To that end, it hardly matters whether you learn and practice yoga, martial arts, Buddhism, transcendental meditation, biofeedback, or any of dozens of other endeavors that bring the mind to alert repose. The contexts of such practice vary widely, as do their avowed purposes, but their noetic byproduct is unitary: a state of alert repose. While philosophical practitioners need harbor no vested interests in these manifold systems' ultimate purposes—mental control of bodily functions toward ends ranging from crossing the sea of samsara to mastering self-defense, from inculcating compassion for sentient beings to dissipating physiological tensions—philosophical practitioners can always benefit their clients and themselves from active insights which rise from the depths of inactive clarity. Still waters run deep; still minds think deeply.

Inactive meditation improves active meditation. The two are complements, not opposites. In fact, the two are not necessarily two, but one. It has long been known that inaction is superior to action in many instances, and that more can be accomplished by inaction than by action. It is perhaps only a superficial quirk of language that "inflammable" and "flammable" are synonymous, but it is a profound insight that inaction can be superior to action. For activity does not always entail accomplishment, and is counterproductive when abetting inappropriate or wasteful processes. Similarly, inactivity does not always entail sloth, and is productive when abetting appropriate or efficient processes already unfolding of their own accord.

Part of wisdom is knowing not whether to act, but when to act. One usually acts best from a state of alert repose; one does not usually repose alertly from a state of action. Only those advanced enough in inactive meditation have attained a state in which there is no longer a distinction between action and inaction. Though they act, their actions leave no trace; though they refrain from acting, yet they leave nothing undone. But this state too is attained through expansive inactive meditation, and not through the strutting and fretting of endless trains of thought across the crowded stage and shunting-yard of active mind.

If you would be a philosophical practitioner, then practice first and foremost on yourself. Meditate actively and inactively both. Sharpen and clarify your mind before shedding its light, and you will help yourself and others. A dull and obfuscated mind helps no one, and may do harm by shedding darkness. Whether you meditate to invigorate or quiet your thoughts, you do so ultimately in solitude. You cogitate by yourself; you breathe by yourself. You alone formulate judgments; you alone remain without them. Either way, meditation is a solitary practice. In my view, clarity of cogitation is enhanced by stillness of reflection, and vice versa. One form of meditation improves the other.

By nature, I am an energetic person. Less active people often ask how I "fill the unforgiving minute" to overflowing. I tell them that useful activity, which stems from attending to one's cogitations, is predicated on useful inactivity, which flows from attending to one's respirations. Hence I begin by practicing what I preach, in order to continue preaching what I practice. I have always had the audacity to voice my thoughts, and while time has not diminished my natural temerity, it has augmented my acquired concern over the substance of the voicings themselves. Since I cannot shut my mouth, I would that the noises emanating ineluctably therefrom be first filtered, and so somewhat purified, by periods of silence.

NOTES

1. According to Buddha, karma is will: "It is volition that I call 'karma.' Having willed, one acts by body, speech and mind." Buddha, *The Word of the Buddha*, trans. Nyantiloka (Kandy, Sri Lanka: Buddhist Publication Society, 1981), p. 19.

2. According to Vedic teachings, karma is the ripening fruit of action, and pejoratively of the bond of attachment, broken by right renunciation: "Having surrendered all claim to the results of his actions, always contented and independent, in reality he does nothing, even though he is apparently acting. Expecting nothing, his mind and personality controlled, without greed, doing bodily actions only; though he acts, yet he remains untainted. Content with what comes to him without effort of his own, mounting above the pairs of opposites, free from envy, his mind balanced both in success and failure, though he act, yet the consequences do not bind him. He who is without attachment, free, his mind centered in wisdom, his actions, being done as a sacrifice, leave no trace behind." *Bhagavad-Gita*, trans. S. Purohit (London: Faber & Faber, 1969), chap. 4, v. 20–23.

3. Classically, for example, Jews and Christians uphold the commandment "thou shalt not kill." But some favor abortion or euthanasia, while others do not. Some kill in self-defense or in just war; others do not. And some kill others to defend the sanctity of life!

4. For example, Damasio's engaging book, *Descartes' Error* (New York: Avon, 1994), can be read as a neuropsychological admission of dualism (in the guise of epiphenomenalism), not a repudiation thereof. And, for example, Dennett's rather pretentiously entitled book, *Consciousness Explained* (Boston: Little, Brown, 1991), appears to explain quite well that consciousness cannot explain itself. Similarly, Churchland's eliminative materialism (e.g., Churchland, 1986) eagerly advocates the day when thoughts will be reduced to electrochemical brain states, but does not itself effect this reduction. See Searle (1980) and Penrose (1989) for good holistic accounts of the irreducibility of mind to brain.

5. Cited by Hobbes (chap. 5).

6. Lao Tzu, *Tao Te Ching*, trans. Ch'u Ta-Kao (London: Allen & Unwin, 1959), chaps. 2 and 3.

CHAPTER 5

Client Counseling

5.1. Some Formative Names
5.2. How I Became a Philosophical Counselor
5.3. The Geometry of Philosophical Counseling
5.4. The Modality of Dialogue
5.5. A Typology of Philosophical Counseling Dialogue
5.6. The Golden Triangle

5.1. SOME FORMATIVE NAMES

With this chapter, we move into the area that put philosophical practice "on the map" of American and global awareness, although it is only the second of four concentric modes of practice addressed in this book. The first mode, as we have just seen, is the meditative. As with the other modes, philosophical counseling has been done intermittently or sporadically for centuries. It is lately being portrayed as something new, but that portrayal is inaccurate: it is really something quite ancient, which has been rediscovered and is being reformulated in contemporary contexts.

Even this benign account assumes a fairly recent and important precedent, namely, the professionalization of twentieth-century talk therapy itself. It began with Freudian analysis early in that century, developed with a branching of psychoanalytic variations on or rejections of Freudian themes, continued with a vast proliferation of psychological versions of counseling (generically called "psychotherapy"), and culminated with the rediscovery of philosophical counseling in the last twenty years of that century. That rediscovery was earlier presaged by Bertrand Russell in *The Conquest of Happiness*,[1] and by Mortimer Adler in several works, most notably *The Conditions of Philosophy*.[2] But Russell, like Aristotle, did not suppose that ordinary people were fit to philosophize;

while Adler, although he ably fingered the deficiencies and shortcomings of theoretical philosophy, did not quite envision what to do with it in practice.

Jungian synchronicity perhaps plays a role in the (re)emergence of the phenomenon as we recognize it today. In the late 1970s and early 1980s, a number of independent events heralded the current philosophical Renaissance. In 1979, Paul Sharkey was appointed "Philosopher in Residence" at a county hospital, and wrote a paper calling for a renewal of philosophy as a helping profession.[3] In 1980, Seymon Hersh published a paper entitled "The Counseling Philosopher."[4] In 1981, Gerd Achenbach founded the German Society for Philosophical Practice, and hung out his counseling shingle in Bergisch Gladbach. Other philosophers, particularly in America, had already begun either to practice or to theorize seriously about practice. Maurice Friedman, Pierre Grimes, Peter Koestenbaum, Matthew Lipman, and J. Michael Russell are other names to conjure by in this formative period.[5] There was no ethos to support them, no surging demand for their services, and no general awareness that philosophy was a service at all.

The aforementioned people were the early pioneers and visionaries of contemporary philosophical practice, and labored long in darkness just to conceive it. Although their labors (and ours) now bear fruit in the light of day, such fruits are hardly spontaneously generated. One plants olive trees for one's grandchildren; perhaps one does philosophical practice for them too.

5.2. HOW I BECAME A PHILOSOPHICAL COUNSELOR

Since I am often asked how I became a philosophical counselor, this is as relevant a place as any to offer a brief autobiographical account. I have written a rather lengthier literary one in my first novel—*Return To Eden: A Fantasy of Redemption*—which I am not quite prepared to reveal to the world. Here, then, is the tip of that iceberg. In 1991, a decade and it seems a lifetime removed from this writing, I took up a position in the Center for Applied Ethics at the University of British Columbia. I was not at that time an applied ethicist; rather, had just finished writing my second PhD thesis, in the philosophy of science, for my examiners at University College London. My first PhD thesis, a massive tome on the philosophical foundations of human conflict, was not entirely to my examiners' taste, so they neither passed nor failed it; rather, invited me to write a completely different thesis instead. This I did, along with my second unpublished novel (*Eloquent Sinking: A Gaspesian Tragicomedy*)—during two marvelous years ensconced in the fastness of maritime Quebec. My second PhD thesis, a computer-simulated breeding experiment that engendered a family of robust strategies for the iterated Prisoner's Dilemma,[6] which did convenient double-duty as a metaphoric resolution of the earlier conflict with my examiners themselves (while engendering a fresh conflict with Anatol Rapoport, because my leading strategy outperformed his Tit-For-Tat), eventually passed muster as a doctoral dissertation.

So I took up a position at UBC, apparently through a succession as well as an iteration of PDs. I was living in the town of Port Daniel, had just completed a thesis on the Prisoner's Dilemma, and then made the acquaintance of Peter Danielson, a senior research fellow at UBC's Center for Applied Ethics.[7] On behalf of Michael McDonald, the Center's Director, Danielson was looking to recruit a Moderator for the Canadian Business and Professional Ethics Network (CBPENET), a well-conceived meta-research project designed to link applied ethicists, primarily via e-mail, from across the country. I knew little enough at the time about applied ethics, but did have considerable computing skills for a philosopher, plus the further asset of bilingualism—indispensable for Federally funded projects in Canada. Nowadays one can define and set up an e-mail discussion list in a few minutes, and maintain it for free on a remote server, but in the early 1990s cyberspace was more primitively confined to unix-based text without a worldwide web, so setting up a high-end research list meant pioneering work in the humanities. Within three years, the CBPENET had spawned sibling networks for accounting ethics, biomedical ethics, and environmental ethics, all under the aegis of Canadian Applied Ethics Research Networks (CAERNETS), of which I became Executive Moderator.

While this was transpiring in-house at the Center, applied ethics was also being factored regularly into news reporting. Vancouver afforded a fertile field for clashes between left-wing activism and right-wing conservatism, played out across the usual spectrum of local "push-button" issues that also make national news: abortion, euthanasia, logging, insider trading, political scandal, and so forth. The media had all the applied ethicists at the Center—and I soon become one myself—on their Rolodexes, and they regularly elicited sound-bytes from us. Hardly a week went by when one of us wasn't on radio or TV, or quoted in a newspaper. We offered fairly standard and reliably sober ethical commentary on these issues and others, and did so from a standpoint of academic public service. Thus the public, not surprisingly, became aware of the existence of applied ethicists. More surprisingly, individual members of that public began to approach the Center, seeking ethics counseling for their personal or professional problems. They seemed to be reasoning quite consistently: having heard a philosopher make some relatively objective, evidently thoughtful, and not completely uncompassionate pronouncement on an ethical issue of general social concern; they supposed that said philosopher, or one of his colleagues, might have something useful to say on an ethical issue of particular personal concern.

Most clients simply telephoned, asking to speak to a philosopher, and the secretary at the Center soon became adept at screening their problems and streaming their calls to the appropriate specialist. In other words, she reinvented "intake." For less specialized problems, she merely asked "Who wants to field this call?" A few clients walked into the Center right off the campus street, demanding to see a philosopher. They were screened in person and given appointments. That's how I got my first two clients: one by phone, one by walk-in. Naturally, we had no official mandate to be offering ethics counseling to individuals on this basis, but we turned no one away whom we felt able to help, regarded our counseling as a somewhat idiosyncratic but altogether justifiable extension of public service, and offered it to all who requested it on a strictly *pro bono publico* basis. (The latter is perhaps not as altruistic as it appears; we had in fact no means to recover fees for such services in any case.) Nonetheless, I saw fit to suggest to my colleagues a few informal protocols for seeing people on this basis, and I began to write up case studies accordingly. This marked my entry into a field of whose existence I remained entirely unaware for some time henceforth; and considering all that has transpired since, given that that entry is less than one decade removed from this writing, I am frankly awed at the extent of the developments. My astonishment quickly yields to resolve, however, in the face of what remains undeveloped.

What followed was merely an exercise in habitual secular deontology: with neither anticipation nor expectation of consequences, I did only what seemed to be the right thing at the time.

Thus, when Ran Lahav e-mailed a primary philosophical discussion list, requesting academic referees for an anthology of essays on philosophical counseling, I responded that I'd be happy to referee one or more of the essays, or (inclusively) to submit an essay on ethics counseling. Ran correctly pointed out that being both a referee and a contributor might constitute conflict of interest, and he expressed the preference that I submit rather than referee an essay. My (then Canadian) contribution rounded out an international field of leading practitioners, to which I was at that time a newcomer. Ran's revised and edited volume, *Essays on Philosophical Counseling*, received sufficiently favorable reviews from referees to convince the University of California Press to accept it for publication—only to reject it at the eleventh hour, when it was in imminent danger of actually being printed and sold. According to Ran, the publications board came down with a case of academic cold feet, or administrative spinelessness, or some similar occupational affliction that regularly yanks *homo academicus* back from the brink of decisive action, and compels him instead to convene a subcommittee to study either the feasibility of convening a sub-subcommittee to report to the committee on why it convened a subcommittee in the first place, or some equally burning question. Instead of publishing the *Essays*, the daring university press undoubtedly brought out yet another earthshaking book on Aristotle, or perhaps Foucault, endorsed with the expected profusion of superlatives that guarantees it will sell at least one hundred copies, and perhaps one hundred and fifty. Rather than resubmit the manuscript to another university press, and jump through similar hoops for another year, and face anew the possibility of ultimate rejection owing to academic fear of the unknown idea, Ran decided to publish the *Essays* with University Press of America. UPA is essentially an academic vanity publisher, slightly better-disguised than Mellen Press, which maintains no apparent backlist and sustains no evident interest in marketing. The *Essays* went through three editions in three years, variously bankrolled but always selling out. It is both perennially sought-after, and mostly out-of-print.

Ran Lahav rendered another service to philosophical practice, perhaps even more vital than compiling and editing the *Essays*. He came to visit me at the University of British Columbia in 1993, toured the premises, and proposed that we co-organize the first-ever international conference on philosophical counseling. Ran was then in the late stages of a limited-term contract at a southern American university, which he had originally mistaken for a tenure-track position. By this time he harbored no delusions: notwithstanding his ability to do analytic philosophy as well as philosophical counseling, his strictly analytic colleagues were horrified by any thought of "as well as." Bound and determined to shop him, they were certainly not about to aid or abet an international conference on "as well as." The ethos at UBC was very different, and Ran sensed this immediately. My superiors at the Center for Applied Ethics were academic philosophers nonetheless accustomed to raising money. And while we had our political differences, we never let them obstruct individual progress or the common good. With help from the Center, the University and the usual Governmental resources, I raised the necessary funds and saw to the logistics. Ran, for his part, knew most of the key European and North American practitioners, and persuaded them to attend. The conference was a great success, and spawned an internal consciousness of an international movement among the practitioners. (The New York conference, three years later, would spawn an external consciousness of the movement among the general international populace, one rarified effect of which is this book itself.)

I am recalling these salad days not for sentimental, historical, or autobiographical purposes, but to illustrate that each philosophical practitioner, during these formative years, came to practice via an original and perforce unforeseen route. Becoming a philosophical counselor was not the same, and is still not the same, as deliberately choosing some well-defined profession—say, dentistry. People don't become dentists inadvertently; they first choose to become dentists, and then follow a prescribed course of study and practice to become dentists. If able, they become certified and licensed to practice dentistry, whereupon their careers are furthered by a well-established professional infrastructure. But some dentists, at some point, had to pioneer all this. There were no dentists in the Garden of Eden, and by all accounts Adam and Eve didn't reside there long enough to develop dental caries. The first dentist was not created from Adam's wisdom tooth; the profession of dentistry was pioneered by professionals long out of Eden. It is my professional interest, and duty, to help pioneer the professional of philosophical practice, by building an infrastructure through which future practitioners may progress on well-paved avenues toward well-illumined stations, rather than hack through dense bush toward uncertain makeshift camps. Once born, every profession suffers periodic growing pains and is subject to myriad vicissitudes of survival, but no profession need be born twice.

If philosophical counseling is indeed a profession, what characterizes it as such? I believe that such a fundamentally necessary yet dauntingly broad question can be compassed peripatetically at the outset, by addressing two features pertinent to the form of philosophical counseling, prior to considering its substance. These features are, first, an elliptical (as opposed to a medical) account of some typical human problems, and second, a therapeutic conception of dialogue, as contrasted with monologue and polylogue, but not as opposed to any particular modality of discourse.

5.3. THE GEOMETRY OF PHILOSOPHICAL COUNSELING

Normally, man is both a biological and a cultural being. If human children are accidentally or otherwise deprived of all enculturation, they become feral, and indistinguishable from wild animals. And if human children were reared as laboratory "brains in vats," they would be no more empathic, and no better socialized, than our desktop computers. Attempts to reduce nurture to nature, or to adduce nature from nurture, are all incomplete at the core and tend to be unwholesome at the edges. Our understanding of biological evolution is developing well, thanks to a cluster of sciences operating within the neo-Darwinian paradigm. Our understanding of cultural evolution lags behind, owing partly or largely to the lack of a corresponding regnant paradigm. I have elsewhere described the bare outline of a possible paradigm, but this is not the place to elaborate it.[8] Suffice that the phenomenon of natural selection has its cultural analogue in what I term "synthetic selection," but that the latter operates in strictly cultural domains.

The cultural entities that compete and cooperate for survival, and which undergo "descent with modification" (to borrow Darwin's actual words: he eschewed "evolution") are of two interacting kinds: symbolic structures and technological products—i.e., symbols and tools. No one's DNA contains information about the myths to which he subscribes, the language he speaks, the customs he observes, or the instruments he uses. All these things are artefacts of cultural evolution and—unlike DNA—are not transmitted by any means internal to the organism. They are invented, discovered, acquired, or lost via extra-somatic processes, which by definition are themselves culturally generated. Cultural evolution therefore unfolds *sui generis*, is fundamentally Lamarckian in character, and thus not Darwinian at all.

The geometric figure that most simply and arguably best metaphorizes this state of affairs is the ellipse, a conic section closely related to the circle, but

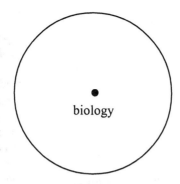

For plants and most animals, an individual's locus of possible action emanates from a biological center, and serves biological purposes only.

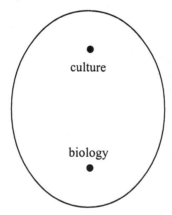

For humans, an individual's locus of possible action emanates from both biological and cultural foci, and serves either biological or cultural purposes.

FIGURE 5.1   Spheres and Ellipses of Action.

with one key difference. A circle is defined as a locus of points (the circumference) equidistant from a given fixed point (the center). Beings that appear to be biological but acultural (i.e., the amoeba) have all and only biological concerns at the center of their existence, and are thus metaphorized by the circle. An ellipse, by contrast, is defined as a locus of points (again the circumference) at which the sum of the distance from two given fixed points (the foci) is constant. Human beings have both biological and cultural concerns at the respective foci of their existence, and are thus metaphorized by the ellipse. One's emphasis may shift from one focus to another at different times in one's daily routine, and in different periods overall during one's lifetime. In keeping with this figure, I will offer an elliptical, but hardly circumlocutory, view of philosophical counseling.

Purely biological creatures are at the mercy of the interaction between their phenotypes and their environments. For every species on this earth save man, environment uniquely determines whether given phenotypes constitute successful or unsuccessful adaptations, and hence environment exerts indirect yet decisive selective or deselective pressures on the underlying genotypes. This much we have from Darwin's brilliant albeit skeletal hypothesis, amply fleshed out by subsequent biological sciences. Humans excepted, neither flora nor fauna choose among possible worlds; rather, the world chooses among possible flora and fauna. The lingula, the ant, and the shark are examples of creatures that have endured virtually unchanged for untold millions of years; they are biologically stable in geological time. The mammals and their latest family—the primates—are far more complex but also far less stable. The large primate brain has yet to show itself to be a successful adaptation, if we measure biological success by the yardstick of geological time. Beginning from the alleged Dryopithecine divergence (wherever located in time by calibrations of immunological distancing, DNA sequencing, and other manifestations of molecular anthropology), the life expectancy of a hominid species has been inversely proportional to the meaningful measure of its brain size.[9] The bigger the brain, the shorter the duration of the species. Inductively, this does not augur well for man.

Unlike all other terrestrial species, man is not at the mercy of external nature; rather, is at the mercy of the very internal forces that grant him mastery over nature. *Homo sapiens* is something of a misnomer; man is as at least as rapacious as he is sagacious, hence *homo rapiens* is surely a more accurate taxonomic depiction of the broad spectrum of human history. Among other species, wants are synonymous with needs; territory and hierarchy are the sole biological imperatives, and they determine access to nutritive and reproductive resources. Other animals either solve their problems quickly, or quickly cease to be other animals. Man alone protracts his problems, and compounds them, and exacerbates them, and moreover discovers or invents problems he cannot or will not solve, and proves he cannot or will not solve them, and sometimes he implements solutions that are worse than the problems themselves.

This is because man is not a purely biological creature, whose genotype is not indirectly selected or deselected primarily by environmental forces, beyond his control, that act on the phenotype. Man shapes and reshapes his environment to suit his liking; his wants are not synonymous with his needs; and although still strongly subject to territorial and hierarchical imperatives formerly grounded in biology, man's access to nutritive and reproductive resources are filtered and gated by cultural conventions, artifices, and processes that function *sui generis* and independent of Darwinian natural selection. Cultural evolution is a human complement of biological evolution, and supersedes it in salient respects. Some humans live for art; no animals do. Some humans die for ideals; no animals do. Some human females form pair-bonds with sterile or condemned males; no female animals do. Many human couples bear offspring that they cannot properly care for; in nature such offspring would die, but cultural institutions often intervene to save them, or at least to prolong their agonies. Most humans use sexual energy for additional purposes entirely unconnected with reproduction, and moreover commingle sexuality with dominance and violence; no animals other than primates do. All other animals have foolproof intra-specifically recognized gestures of submission and appeasement, "lock-and-key" mechanisms which prevent ritualized conflict from escalating into counterproductive wounding, maiming and death; no humans do. No animals form ethical conceptions, face moral dilemmas, fight for just causes; only humans do.

The gulf that separates us from other animals is cultural. Culture is a product of our big brains, to be sure, but is not reducible to electrochemical brain states any more than computer software is reducible to computer hardware. Hardware is designed to run software, but doesn't write it. Software moreover determines what hardware will produce, within its architectural capacities of course. Similarly, man's culture determines what man's nature will produce, within its biological capacities. There must be compatibility between hardware and software for a given computer to be functional and productive; similarly, there must be compatibility between human nature and human nurture for a given human being to be functional and productive. A computer can be pointlessly functional in a tight infinite loop, consuming energy without producing anything useful. So can a human being.

If something goes wrong with a computer, one needs to know whether the root problem lies with hardware or software. Faulty hardware cannot be repaired by reloading software; faulty software cannot be remedied by replacing hardware. If something goes wrong with a human being, one similarly needs to know whether the root problem lies with the body (including the brain) or with the mind (including the beliefs). A lesion in the brain cannot be repaired solely by changing one's beliefs about it. Further, strongly ingrained emotional attachments to unwarranted, obstructive, or destructive beliefs and behaviors cannot necessarily be relinquished without their lengthy and arduous replacement, *through lived experience*, with warranted, instructive, and constructive beliefs and behaviors; or else via a more rapid dissolution, *also through lived experience*, of the attachments themselves.

Psychiatry, as a branch of medical science, is concerned with cerebral chemistry; psychology, as a branch of behavioral and cognitive sciences, is concerned with emotional affect; philosophy, as the parent discipline of both siblings, is concerned with effective thought. Most people are troubled by something sometimes, but most troubles are caused neither by brain disease nor by affective dysfunction; rather, are effects of ineffective thought. In so far as philosophy helps people think effectively about their problems, it helps them cultivate effective beliefs and engage in effective behaviors. Relatively few people are too far gone for that, although ineffective thinking can make them believe they are.

Purely biological beings must face and solve purely biological problems; viz., "What will I eat?" "Where will I sleep?" In the case of social animals, one adds "With whom will I associate?" and (in the case of sexual dimorphism) "With whom will I mate?" Brute force answers the first two existential questions by replacing them with empirical ones: "What can I kill?—That is what I will eat" and "What can I occupy and defend?—That is where I will sleep." Beyond that, dominance hierarchies and pheromones are nature's ways of resolving, respectively, the related social and sexual questions. These are not simply questions to be answered abstractly; they are problems to be solved concretely, on whose solutions hinge life itself.

In biocultural beings, all of these problems are initiated by biological imperatives, but are mediated by cultural processes. Someone wrongs you; your biology says, "Retreat or retaliate now"; your affect says "Exact revenge or elicit apology later"; your prudence asks "What is the wisest thing to do now, and later, in this particular case and in similar general cases? What is the most foolish thing? How can I reliably discern the difference?" If your culture supplies you with a gun, your biology may impel you to shoot your foe; if your culture supplies you with a lawyer, your affect may impel you to sue your foe; if your culture provides you with a philosophy, your thoughts may impel you to transcend your foe. You are usually best served by the latter.

The transactions of biocultural beings involve, among other things, the solution of biological problems in cultural terms. Your nature bequeaths you a periodic appetite for food; your culture initially determines which foods you will eat, and how they will be procured and prepared. Your nature bequeaths you a longing to call some place "home"; your culture initially determines where it is situated, and how constructed and furnished. Your nature bequeaths you a need to associate with (or dissociate from) others of your kind; your culture determines the myriad complex structures and conventions that mediate social, economic, educational, religious, and political relations. Your nature bequeaths you an intermittent desire for sexual congress; your culture determines the propriety or impropriety of contexts for and objects of erotic expression.

To abet the satisfaction of this minimalist menu of human biological requirements, and to reinforce and retransmit the medium of cultural transaction through which they must be satisfied in human terms, your nature further bequeaths you the ability to acquire a language; your culture, as usual, determines what the tokens and syntax of that language shall be. Although you provide the semantics yourself, through the awakening of your understanding, a manipulative culture (and they are all manipulative) will endeavor to appropriate and attenuate your semantic capacities, and subsume your understanding under a latticework of emotional attachment to the received superstitions (i.e., religion), inherited allegiances (i.e., politics), and personal prejudices (i.e., unexamined opinions) of your tribe. You will also be tempted or even misguided to generalize falsely from particular experiences.[10] As symbolic structures develop and technologies progress, then geopolitics may permit and psychoclimatology afford a prevailing ethos that unifies many such tribes under a larger totem without necessarily homogenizing them (e.g., America). Your search for personal identity, as well as meaning and purpose in your life—in other words, the growth of your understanding of what it is to be you—may entail your successive captivation by or emancipation from any number of ideas which, when codified and preferably accompanied by theme-music and ceremonial dress, we call "doctrines."

Your first indoctrination (i.e., enculturation) was imposed upon you, involuntarily, as a child; and if you were fortunate, then it also came bundled with a modicum of love, affection, discipline, play, education, and encouragement. If you were unfortunate, then you were unloved, or neglected, or perhaps even tormented, beaten, tortured, or sexually abused. (The term "abuse" itself has been so subjected to abuse that I use it cautiously.) Nonetheless, even an unfortunate enculturation is better than none at all, for ferality appears one hundred percent irreversible, whereas any number of extraordinarily miserable children (e.g., Isaac Newton, Bertrand Russell, Herman Hesse) have become admirably fulfilled adults, and noteworthy contributors to culture.[11]

If you live in an undemocratic state, or under a repressive regime, or on the campus of a politically correct university, then your involuntary childhood indoctrination is continued as non-voluntary political rectitude, and God help you if you object or rebel.

If you live in a democratic state, under a tolerant government, or on the campus of a university that still supports literacy, numeracy, and reasoned inquiry, then your remaining indoctrinations (i.e., enculturations) are imposed upon you by your leave, voluntarily accepted, as you seek to renovate and refurbish whatever cultural edifice you originally inhabited, to accommodate your maturity, its increased responsibility, and its changing tastes.

To recapitulate: unlike other animals, humans satisfy their basic biological needs through superpositions of cultural media. To attain their biological goals, humans must traverse cultural domains. The satisfaction of human biological needs is inevitably subject to cultural transaction costs. Every fundamental biological problem relating to food, shelter, social relations, and procreation, that arises regularly and must be regularly solved to continue survival, is refracted through cultural media and must thus be reformulated and resolved in cultural terms. The definitive (or underlying) terms of any culture are not explained by its appurtenance of conventions; rather, are entailed by its codified ideas. The highest level of problem-solving is therefore neither biological nor behavioral; rather, is noetic. Even the most basic activities in which humans, as animals, must engage, are instantaneously, ineluctably, and inextricably woven with ethical, aesthetic, and axiological threads, which form a cultural tapestry whose patterns represent not what we must do as biological beings—but rather the deeper meaning, higher purpose, transcendent value, and inherent virtue of what we do as cultural beings.

Therefore every ordinary human problem, which arises from biology but which is resolved through culture, raises myriad philosophical questions in its resolution. Resolving the complex cultural refractions of ordinary biological problems is an activity of the normal human being. Most people do this on a daily basis, and become neither physically incapacitated nor emotionally unhinged because of it. Most have neither any lesions, nor any "chemical imbalance" in their brains; their brains, in fact, are doing exactly what they evolved to do. Mind, not brain, is the regulator of cultural life, and if the cultural refractions of ordinary biological problems impose insuperable difficulties on biologically functional beings, then they must look to the noetic sources of their dysfunctionality. The keenest instrument for doing that is philosophy, and philosophical counselors help clients wield that instrument.

In its simpler elliptical (but not circumlocutory) formulation, then, philosophical counseling helps people solve or manage everyday problems whose biological focus is not primarily at issue but whose cultural focus requires illumination or elaboration. This is a goal-oriented formulation, because there is a specific, identifiable problem that needs to be addressed as a prominent figure against a contextual background that is deemed essentially or relatively stable. Thus a client with a pressing moral dilemma does not normally require either a brain-scan or a psychological exploration of his childhood: he requires a philosophical inquiry into the nature of the dilemma, the scope of its possible resolutions, and their ethical implications. Even a client who is furious with or frustrated by a given state of affairs, and whose problem therefore has some biological purchase, can benefit from philosophical counseling, provided he is rational enough to rein in his emotions long enough to deliberate how best to channel or express them constructively. When facing ordinary provocations in life—and life is full of them—do you lose your mind entirely and let loose what Freud called the Draconian unconscious, which kills in return for any slight;[12] or do you hire a hit-man, or a lawyer, or a psychiatrist, or a philosophical counselor? The question is meant to be rhetorical, but judging from the daily news it is hardly even asked, let alone understood rhetorically. If it were, this book would not be necessary.

In its more complex elliptical formulation, philosophical counseling is process- (rather than goal-) oriented, because the client's problem may not be readily configurable against a relatively stable ground, and its resolution or management may thus require a reexamination of the ground itself. This is most obviously the case when the major focus of the ellipse is biological (i.e., medical or emotional), and the client needs to incorporate the prospect or reality of drastic change into his worldview. Someone who has just been diagnosed with a life-threatening illness should obviously maintain a major focus on medicine, but can still benefit from a minor focus on the philosophy of medicine, and of life and death. Someone whose marriage is conspicuously failing may experience a tremendous churning of emotions, whether endeavoring to salvage the marriage or save himself, and may even benefit from short-term antianxiety medication to assuage the emotional crisis. But the resolution of this problem (as opposed to the crisis itself) is likely to be longer-term and therefore process-oriented, and can be compassed by philosophical counseling.

In its most complex elliptical formulation, philosophical counseling can consist of an examination of the doctrines that were once imposed upon you, of those you presently impose upon yourself, and of those you are contemplating imposing upon yourself in the future. What constellations of biological and cultural forces compelled you to embrace and apply ideas you didn't savor, or that proved detrimental to your progress? What ideas do you now embrace, or find beneficial to your progress? What ideas can you further embrace and apply that disperse yet reconcile the constellation of biological and cultural forces that once compelled you? These are the substantive questions of philosophical counseling, addressed from the cultural focus of the human ellipse.

5.4. THE MODALITY OF DIALOGUE

Verbal language mediates daily transactions and interactions, both with the self and with others. While extraordinary individual creations, particularly in the arts and sciences, may be forged by representational states of brain or mind that are pre-linguistic or non-linguistic, verbalism is a mainstay of ordinary human communication. One normally thinks in one's first language, and indeed true proficiency in a second or further tongue is gauged by one's ability not only to speak it, but also to formulate thoughts in it. Language is the vessel of our beliefs, the vehicle of our intentions, the crucible of our volitions. It is also a primary, though woefully inadequate, mode for the expression of feelings. While much theoretical philosophy is given these days to studying formal properties of languages, often with the hope of explicating semantics in terms of syntax, practical philosophy is concerned, as usual, not with formalizing language, but with utilizing it.

Most people engage in ongoing, silent conversations with themselves. Occasionally, these conversations may become advertently or inadvertently audible to others. Whispering or talking aloud to oneself in public is usually viewed with amusement, suspicion, or trepidation. (Singing aloud to oneself is a generally accepted practice, provided it is done in the shower.) A conversation with oneself is called a "monologue," which is also the name given to any usurpation through monopolization of a dialogue, or indeed of any dictation or lecture imposed upon a passive group. Thus most connotations of monologue are not particularly salutary or wholesome. The equivalents of monologues in the performing arts, e.g., the solo in a concerto, or the soliloquy in a play, stand in incomparably better odor with the public, because at best they become showcases for virtuosity, of creator and performer alike. An eloquent and charismatic orator—whether actor, comedian, poet, politician, or philosopher—can work that magic with words. This is a far cry from the monotonous monologician who waylays victims at open bars, and sobers them with tedium; or from the prosaic professor whose dreaded drone is more dormitive (if less addictive) than opiates. On the whole, the monologue's ill reputation is well-deserved.

More to my point, monologue is a linguistic mode that generally furthers neither one's understanding nor one's progress. Meditating on a problem is one thing, as we have already seen, while muttering to oneself is quite another. The proliferation of psychology as a profession of personal counsel lends more than ample evidence to this claim: that if people could resolve their difficulties in life merely by talking to themselves, at their own convenience, without having to visit someone else's office, without the limitations of a fifty-minute hour, and without having to pay for the service, then they would talk to themselves more often, and to others less. That they have instead hired psychologists in such abundant numbers, and lately philosophers in more modest ones, suggests that most people require far more than monologue even to maintain themselves in unstable equilibrium, let alone to further their understanding or their progress. Only in the most ossified of institutions—the monastery, the asylum, and the academy—does one encounter throngs of isolated individuals, muttering to themselves in cells and corridors; each called, condemned, or tenured to perpetual monologuery.

The inadequacy of monologue results in its modal complication: a movement from one to two. Surprisingly, this tiniest of integral increments on the number-line, when applied to verbalizing ideas, gives rise to an infinitude of possibility for understanding and progress. Talking to oneself is stale; talking with another, fresh. Debating with oneself is unenlightening; debating with another, illuminating. Gossiping to oneself is boring; gossiping with another, exciting. Expressing views to oneself makes one dull; expressing them to another, sharp. Monologue retards thinking; dialogue advances it.

It is therefore not a coincidence that the most celebrated philosophical teachings of antiquity were recorded not as monologues or narratives, but as dialogues. If not for Plato, the dramatist and dialogician par excellence, who today would revere, or could even study, Socrates the philosopher? That gem of orthodox Indian philosophy and theology, the *Bhagavad-Gita*, presents a dialogue between an avatar and a man. The unorthodox teachings of Siddhartha Gautama—the sutras of Buddha—are recorded by his disciples as dialogues. The most ancient philosophical wisdom of China, the *I Ching*, offers dialogue (in the form of question-and-answer) between the reader and itself. Closer to our time, Shakespeare's dialogues explore pervasive psychological and philosophical themes. The Talmud, compiled of painstakingly accumulated argument and counter-argument on interpretations of Judaic laws, contains dialogues that span centuries. Important early modern philosophers like Hume and Berkeley, as well as experimental philosophers like Galileo, used dialogue in addition to narrative to convey their significant thoughts and discoveries. Ayn Rand and Jean-Paul Sartre conveyed their respective philosophies through plays as well as prose. Although the art of dialogue is mostly lost on twentieth-century theoretical philosophy, some artful contemporary philosophers have found creative ways of using it.[13]

But the special indispensability of dialogue to philosophy is only one facet of its general indispensability to humanity. Social, familial, economic, professional, corporate, and political interactions rely upon it too. In social terms, the verb "socialize" itself denotes indulgence in informal dialogue. An "anti-social" person is merely aloof, one who does not talk to others: not necessarily a sociopath. Familial dialogue is vital to maintaining healthy relationships between husband and wife, as well as permitting guidance from parent to child. Economic dialogue involves barter or negotiation, and is the vehicle of commercial exchange. Professional dialogue assumes many forms. In medicine, the physician–patient dialogue is a vehicle for diagnosis. In the courtroom, the lawyer–witness dialogue is a vehicle for adversarial justice. In the academy, the professor–graduate student dialogue is a vehicle for advanced learning. Corporate dialogue between the CEO and the directors is a vehicle for defining and fulfilling organizational missions. Political dialogue between leaders and advisors is a vehicle for shaping both strategy and policy.

Philosophical dialogue between counselor and client is a vehicle for exploring the client's noetic world, with a view to developing a philosophical disposition that enables the client to resolve or manage his problem. It is mostly educational in intent and content, and is neither adversarial nor diagnostic. The philosophical counselor is an advocate for his client, not his adversary. Then again, being a responsible advocate sometimes entails encouraging a client to reexamine his assumptions or inferences, which can itself entail the client's critical reappraisal of certain values or strongly held beliefs. Yet even a relentless counseling exercise need not be conducted from an adversarial perspective; after all, it is a reexamination, not a cross-examination.[14] The counselor is not a critic, not even a constructive one; rather, is a guide who awakens or instills in the client the capacity to philosophize for himself. This will eventually entail more than enough critical thinking on the client's part.

Neither is philosophical dialogue diagnostic, for everyday human problems are not regarded as illnesses by philosophical counselors. In fact, the opposite is the case: people who recognize their everyday problems and seek to manage or resolve them are regarded as fundamentally (and mentally) well, not ill. Surely it is a sign of wellness to seek appropriate help when one needs it, and a sign of unwellness only to seek inappropriate help or not to seek help at all. This idea is immediately and intuitively grasped by many people, as soon as they hear about philosophical counseling, and it has resulted in the proliferation of Peter March's epithet of philosophical counseling as "therapy for the sane." This makes perfect sense to everyone except—predictably—one or two philosophers, who happen to be counselors and whose conceptions of "therapy" and "sanity" differ radically from mine.[15] Every philosophical counselor I know regards his clients as sane, and engages in philosophical dialogue with them. If a client is not sane, or cannot engage in a philosophical dialogue, then obviously that client is not a good candidate for philosophical counseling.

Those who object most strenuously to March's epithet are also the most zealous adherents of Thomas Szasz's doctrine that no one is really insane, and consequently that "mental illness" is a myth. They also interpret "therapy" in the narrowest possible sense, equating it strictly with medical treatment. So on this view, since no one is mentally ill, no one requires medical treatment for noetic problems. This view wilfully misinterprets the phrase "therapy for the sane" as harnessing philosophical counseling to a medical model, which is both bizarre and ironic—bizarre because it is, and ironic because this view is otherwise espoused only by the second-worst enemies of philosophical counseling, namely, a very small contingent of obstructive psychiatrists and psychologists.

When these latter repudiate us publicly, they do us a service, because the public is much wiser than they realize, and rightly understands their inter-professional warfare as personal cries of anguish. But when a small contingent of fanatical philosophical counselors repudiates other philosophical counselors publicly, they do us, themselves, and the nascent profession an initial disservice, because the public becomes understandably confused by intra-professional warfare. The public needs to bear in mind that some philosophers are their own worst enemies; they are sometimes chronically troubled people, constitutionally unable either to cooperate or compete productively with others, or even to abide in themselves. Philosophers are often favorably compared with poets—presumably for their eccentricity, insight, candor, power of expression, and their impudent and imprudent disregard for convention. Such a philosopher could make an interesting philosophical counselor. Then again, philosophers are also often arrogant, quarrelsome, impetuous, impenitent, vindictive, unrealistic, irrational, capable of drawing sublime inferences from ridiculous premises, and as overburdened as anyone else with affective problems. If such a philosopher also becomes a philosophical counselor, she is likely to give philosophical counseling a very bad name indeed. However diplomatic or egalitarian one might like to be, one cannot escape the issue of professional quality control.

Such internecine warfare has already been waged all out, both famously and infamously, in the fields of psychoanalysis and counseling psychology. When Freud's disciples split with him, one by one, the variations in that field left it richer but also mined with acrimony. Psychologists of different schools are similarly on non-speaking terms; many are unable or unwilling to communicate except by exchanging venomous or explosive verbal salvos. This fragmentation is so far gone that literally hundreds of psychological "sects" exist, each distinguished primarily by its repudiation of or enmity toward the rest. And as one insider reminded me, outside observers of these ceaseless psychological wars are privy only to the tip of that bitter iceberg.

Nor are natural scientists immune from this kind of conflict, even though their observables—and often their wits—are incomparably sharper than those of their social scientific counterparts. A celebrated example is Newton, who fashioned the much-quoted epigram that he had seen so far because he stood on the shoulders of giants. Far from a self-effacing tribute to his allegedly illustrious forebears, the utterance is also a clever but caustic and surprisingly mean-spirited jibe at Newton's chief rival in England, Robert Hooke. Physics students know Hooke's name because he studied elasticity, and discovered among other things that the extension or compression of a spring is directly proportional to the extending or compressing force. This is Hooke's law: $F = kx$. What physics students don't generally learn is that Hooke and Newton disagreed publicly and vituperatively about theories of optics among other things, and that Hooke—notwithstanding his high IQ—was a congenital dwarf. Hence Newton's *double-entendre* about giants. If one seeks a good-natured example of verbal dueling between scientists, consider Niels Bohr's remarks to Wolfgang Pauli, whose freshly hypothesized Exclusion Principle had precipitated heated debate among the world's leading quantum physicists: "We are all agreed that your hypothesis is crazy. The issue that divides us is whether it is crazy enough to stand a chance of being correct."

Evidently, natural scientists are quite capable of engaging in sharp-witted verbal duels, and social scientists are equally capable of indulging in truculent displays of temper and protracted fits of pique. "He attacked my pet thesis" is a *causus belli* among academics, who rule empires of the mind. No emperor can suffer his seat to be sacked; no scientist can permit his hypothesis to be vilified; no academic can allow his thesis to be criticized. My point, however, is that philosophers are capable of far worse. Philosophy is the parent discipline of science, but philosophers can behave much more childishly than scientists. No verbal blade is better tempered than a philosopher's wit, yet no verbal dispute can be more intemperate than a philosopher's duel. Among many who profess love of wisdom, some are also wedded to folly. When these become philosophical counselors, their follies may confound the public and discredit the practice. Yet this too shall pass.

So what's the problem with philosophy as therapy? Broadly construed, none at all. That the allopathic medical connotation of the word "therapy" appropriates it to allopathic medicine is merely a tautological observation, which exerts no compelling semantic restraints but merely reflects outmoded semantic conventions. In homeopathic contexts, it is perfectly germane to speak of aromatherapy or massage therapy, which may be efficacious although not administered by physicians. Art therapy, music therapy, occupational therapy, and physiotherapy can also be effective treatments for certain problems, although not administered by physicians. Human beings can be so negligently uncritical of semantic conventions that they fail to consider this glaring inconsistency in the relation between medicine and counseling psychology: psychologists aren't physicians either, yet they have enjoyed a virtual non-medical monopoly over the talk-therapy referral system. If your physician can refer you to a non-physician (i.e., a psychologist) for talk-therapy of a psychological kind, and have your health-care insurance foot the bill, then your physician should also be able to refer you to a non-physician (i.e., a philosopher) for talk-therapy of a philosophical kind, and have your health-care insurance foot the bill.[16]

As I indicated in *Plato, Not Prozac*, the etymology of "therapy" provides ample justification for breaking the psychological monopolization of dialogue as health-care, long maintained through a selectively pseudo-medical connotation. In Greek, a "theraps" is merely an attendant, of an unspecified kind. The verb "therapuein" means, generically, "to attend to something." Parking attendants and flight attendants are therefore therapists in this generic etymological sense, although they usually attend to non-medical aspects of well-being rather than to medical health. However, it should be noted that wellness is not always a function of health. A medically healthy person can feel quite unwell in other respects, such as when a parking attendant accidentally dents his new car or a flight attendant accidentally spills red wine on his white shirt. In our broad etymological sense, this kind of accident through inattentiveness is actually bad therapy.

Vaseline is currently being marketed as "Lip Therapy"; while an in-flight magazine bears the title "Retail Therapy." These usages are perfectly consistent with the etymology. Evidently a philosopher was required to point this out.

Very well, I have done so. Without a doubt, some other philosopher will immediately take indignant exception to this point, and write an impassioned polemic against the use of philosophy, or etymology, or marketing, or petroleum jelly—or lips. If some philosophers didn't tilt at windmills, philosophy would be that much less endearing and entertaining. Then again, if fewer philosophers tilted at windmills, more would be usefully employed.

A larger stumbling block, made reflexive by habit, obtrudes over the term "psychotherapy," because it has been misappropriated by psychologists and psychiatrists alike. Another appeal to etymology is in order: the Greek "psukhé" means, variously, "breath," or "soul," or "character." The English equivalent, "psyche," can designate any of the following things at least: mind, soul, id, ego, self, nature, spirit, subconscious. Thus "psychotherapy" means attending to any of the foregoing. Needless to say, psychology and psychiatry not only exert no functional monopoly over attending to these things, they do not always provide the most appropriate ways of attending to these things. In the ancient world, philosophy was regarded as the "cure of souls"; philosophers were predominantly and uniquely psychotherapists. At present, twenty-five centuries of accumulated philosophical insights on all the foregoing synonyms of "psyche" are vast, vastly applicable, and at times vastly more appropriate than psychological or psychiatric ones. Philosophy remains psychotherapeutic, only no longer uniquely so.

In addition, many state laws inadvertently support this nonexclusive interpretation of psychotherapy. In New York, for example, the term "psychological counselor" is protected by title license; it is a felony for an unlicensed psychologist (or any other person) to use that term. At the same time, the term "psychotherapist" is completely unprotected: anyone may hang out a shingle describing himself as such, and charge fees for dispensing the service.[17]

In sum, if you have a problem whose focus is ethics, values, meaning, purpose, moral dilemmas, resolving conflicts, coping with change, searching for identity, seeking fulfillment, dealing with injustice, managing adversity, or a host of other issues related to these, then philosophical counseling may be exactly what you require, and moreover psychology and psychiatry may have little or nothing relevant to offer. People with the foregoing problems are in general neither physically ill nor emotionally incapacitated nor socially dysfunctional. In other words, they are sane. Yet their problems may still require urgent attention. Thus philosophical counseling provides therapy for the sane. I repeat that the only people who object hypercritically to this terminology are certain philosophers, who possibly require some other kind of therapy themselves.

Philosophical counseling therefore proceeds by attending to certain kinds of problems through the medium of dialogue. There is nothing mystical or medical about it. Philosophers are trained in the rigors of valid argumentation and the exposure faulty inference; in the heuristics of ampliative logic and the grounds for holding beliefs; in the exercise of moral reasoning and formation of aesthetic judgment; in the theory of making decisions and the justification for acting on them; in the method of resolving conflicts through the building of consensus; in the juxtaposition of scientific knowledge with skeptical challenge; in the maintenance of humanity in the face of dehumanizing aspects of technological change; in the acceptance of personal, professional, and social responsibility; in the acquiescence to conditions imposed by birth and death; in seeking to understand the meaning, realize the purpose, and fulfill the potential of sentient being in a universe replete with mystery, uncertainty, and unknowability.

The medium of dialogue is well-suited to the accomplishment of such commonplace yet vital tasks. The order of difficulty in the mental processing of language clearly increases from speaking to reading to writing. While all babies babble naturally, as a prelude to mouthing intelligible phonemes, none read or write without instruction. We speak before we read, and read before we write. Speaking and writing convey one's thoughts to others; reading conveys others' thoughts to one. Yet independent of directionality, each mode of linguistic expression of thought can serve to sharpen (as well as to dull) one's own thinking. To speak intelligibly is to focus one's immediate thoughts; to read comprehendingly is to accommodate another's ideas in one's thoughts; to write lucidly is to direct one's thoughts toward sculpting one's ideas. The most highly crafted technical writing is found in reputable, peer-reviewed scholarly publications, in which well-directed thought is not only sculpted into profoundly shaped ideas, but whose shapes themselves are further refined and polished via constructive criticism of other sculptors (i.e., referees). At its profoundest, this kind of expression is inaccessible to all but the deepest thinkers. Simulacra of such profundity abound in jargon-laden, fashionable frauds of the kind exposed by Alan Sokal's quantum parody,[18] but mimicry of profound writing no more passes for profundity than a chimpanzee's paintings pass for Dutch Mastery. At its most creative, literary writing is aesthetically more titillating and also more accessible than scholarly publication, yet still can be profound. Scholarly writing is a slow-motion dialogue with one's peers, in which the author can learn from their ideas; creative writing is a monological gallery open to one's readers, in which the author exhibits his own ideas.

Most people cannot write great prose of either kind, but can engage in great conversations of many kinds. Philosophical counseling utilizes dialogue as a vehicle of exploration. The terrain is provided by the client—it consists of his background mindscape and its prominent ideas.[19] The dialogue, as vehicle, is necessarily provided by client and counselor together. The exploration is conducted jointly, but is led by the counselor, for whom the client's mind and its workings are initially unknown territory (which he explores by questioning), but to whom the leading of noetic expeditions and the philosophical mapping of mindscapes is a routine though adventurous undertaking. The client knows his own mind all too well in narrowly accustomed ways—familiarly, habitually, affectively, cognitively—but may not know it at all philosophically. Yet the client's common problems could often be resolved or managed in philosophical domains, had he but access to them. Dialogical exploration grants that access.

5.5. A TYPOLOGY OF PHILOSOPHICAL COUNSELING DIALOGUE

Dialogue is neither a zealous clash of opposing views, nor a superficial exchange of sophomoric opinions, nor a feigned compromise of irreconcilable beliefs. The counselor suggests philosophical ways of interpreting, understanding, managing, or solving a problem without necessarily imposing his own philosophical prejudices or even preferences. Since dialogue is not diagnostic, outcomes are not usually prescriptive. We can identify at least three types of dialogue utilized by philosophical counselors. In order to delay if not deter their entrenchment in some "grand theory" of philosophical practice, which would hamstring the practice's artistic aspects in direct proportion to the misplaced seriousness with which any typology is likely to be taken and, in due course, idolatrized and schismatized, I will not label these types of dialogue beyond A, B, and C.

Type A dialogue is one in which most philosophical counselors whom I know, including myself, engaged routinely with most of their clients, at least until August 1997, when philosophical counseling began to gain substantial media attention in America—after which Type B became expected in certain quarters and emerged to satisfy that demand. Type A dialogue is simply a generic philosophical inquiry into a problem, in which the client carries on a conversation with the counselor. The fact that the counselor is also a philosopher, and therefore thinks like a philosopher and talks like a philosopher—or as Wittgenstein might have said, quacks like a philosopher—but does so in terms the client can both understand and apply, is precisely what makes the conversation philosophical. Thus Type A dialogue is a salutary and, *pace* the odd philosopher's Quixotic reflex, therapeutic example of *déformation professionel.*[20] If you want to discuss the medical implications of a problem, do so with a physician; the legal implications, with a lawyer; the psychological implications, with a psychologist; the theological implications, with a theologian; the political implications, with a politician; the sociological implications, with a sociologist; the historical implications, with an historian; the philosophical implications, with a philosopher. Type A dialogue is generic but also philosophical either because it assumes the form of a general inquiry, or because its orientation is by definition philosophical, or because the client believes that generic advice is worth more from a philosopher, or even because the client finds some other way of utilizing philosophy to suit her purpose.

An example of a hypothetical generic inquiry, peculiar to philosophy because it involves ampliative logic, is provided by my colleague Harriet Chamberlain. Consider the Hale–Bopp Comet cult which, prior to its mass-suicide, purchased an expensive telescope which they returned to the shop, claiming it was defective. Its defect was that it failed to reveal the putative spaceship parked behind the comet. An elementary exercise in critical thinking suggests that one should merely exchange the telescope, not return it. After trying every telescope in the shop, and failing to observe the putative spaceship parked behind the comet, one might reasonably infer that there is no spaceship. Of course, that is not the sole conceivable inference. It might also be the case that the putative spaceship is invisible at optical wavelengths. Any number of possibilities can be dreamed up as to why the putative spaceship cannot be observed, but none of them provides evidence for the premise that it is there at all. One may as well believe in Santa Claus or the Tooth Fairy. But people do retain powerful emotional commitments to beliefs in such entities, no matter how unsupported by evidence, or no matter how patently false.[21] Such beliefs are irrational yet compelling for apparently deeply seated psychological reasons, and thus persons incapable of being disabused of them by rational intervention are probably not good candidates for philosophical counseling.

Since this is a hypothetical case, it is a matter of sheer speculation whether any of the Hale–Bopp cultists would have been dissuaded from suicide by rational inquiry. The human being is almost alone among animals in its propensity for self-destruction. The so-called "mass-suicides" of lemmings are apocryphal; their blind herd-movement sometimes leads them over precipices—which accounts rather ironically, if metaphorically, for the anthropomorphism. Whales and other cetaceans appear to beach themselves from time to time, but again this behavior is not necessarily suicidal. The hymenopterans sacrifice themselves as individuals for the sake of the hive, nest, or formicary to which they belong, but here sociobiology provides a reasonable neo-Darwinian account: such behavior is neither altruistic nor defiant of individual selection, because the degree of genetic relatedness among members of a given colony of ants, bees, or wasps is such that the individual member has no identity—whether genetic, pheromonic, psychological, or teleological—distinct from the group. Each dies for the "super-self" it serves, just as individual cells of our body die for us. We shed dead skin cells daily; they died for us, but were not altruists. Which returns us to us.

Some humans are, at times, definitively and unequivocally suicidal beings, precisely because humans alone form and maintain elaborate belief systems, which at times prescribe or impel actions. The content of beliefs can vary wildly, and their prescriptions or impulsions can be self-preservative or self-destructive, other-preservative or other-destructive. Beliefs, moreover, can vary over time; and this is precisely what makes philosophical counseling both possible and practicable. While counseling cannot make the leopard change its spots, it can make the client change his beliefs. What do we believe? What grounds do we have for believing as we do? What inferences do we draw from our beliefs? Are they valid? To what acts are we committed or impelled by our beliefs and inferences? What are conceivable consequences of these acts, for ourselves and others? Are they likely? Are they desirable? These questions bear weight only for fully or mostly self-preservative beings. Sometimes, perhaps too often, we also need to fight and even die for our beliefs, but then that is self-preservative for one's culture in the same way that an ant's death is self-preservative for its nest.

In the absence of warfare, or other external mortal threats to one's culture or tribe which call for heroic self-sacrifice, self-destruction can be impelled by nurture or nature alike. Culture sometimes transcends biology in the service of suicide, in that a biologically healthy person may find reasons to self-destruct. Biology sometimes transcends culture in the service of suicide, in that deep emotional disturbances may translate into sufferings that make living unpalatable. At the very brink of suicide, perhaps the two become one. Suicide may even be a rational option, as the current debate over euthanasia, and the practice of euthanasia, attest. Death with dignity can become preferable to life with indignity, in which case philosophical counseling might be its advocate too. In any case, this is precisely the generic kind of inquiry that Type A philosophical counseling conducts.

Similarly, for a host of other common problems, many people would rather engage in generic dialogue with philosophers rather than with other counseling professionals, and many can benefit from doing so. Type A counseling has no predefined methodology, and therefore potentiates a kind of spontaneity which many clients find refreshing or attractive. This is the basis of Gerd Achenbach's practice, among many others. Furthermore, the education and training of philosophers equips them far better than most to approach, analyze, and reinterpret the problems to which flesh and fantasy alike are heir.[22] What most theoretical philosophers lack, of course, are the interpersonal skills and professional (as opposed to academic) expertise necessary to practice philosophy as a discipline of personal counsel. Those deficiencies are precisely what this book addresses, and what APPA Certification Training Programs remedy.

Type B counseling was always practiced in certain situations by certain philosophical counselors, but was not necessarily their bread-and-butter methodology. Petra von Morstein championed Nietzsche's thought in counseling, while Stanley Chan discovered a therapeutic use of McTaggart's B series. Many resort to Buddha's four Noble Truths and some parts of the Eightfold Path. Counselors often bring one or another insight from a particular philosopher to light in a session, from the allegory of Plato's cave to Mill's conception of liberty. From my perspective, however, Type B counseling provided an occasional reference or idiosyncratic allusion rather than a workaday methodology, that is, until the media got hold of us, and began to recast us in their own light. My early Type A orientation was so much like Achenbach's in this regard—viz., a counseling session is philosophical primarily because it is conducted with a philosopher—that I resisted Type B methodology when goaded into it by media representatives, who assumed that was all we did.

I recall being on an open-line National Public Radio program out of Boston, whose callers presented the usual range of problems, and whose operating constraints afforded about one minute's worth of counseling, if that much. There was no time even to think about conducting a general inquiry with any phone-in client, so I merely tried to extrapolate and summarize an anticipated conclusion of such an inquiry, were it to have taken place, based on what the client told me during his half-minute allotment. This seemed to satisfy the callers, but not the host, who kept prompting me with questions like "Lou, what philosopher said that?" or "Lou, give us the name of the philosopher whose idea you just suggested." I wanted to reply with the plain truth: "I'm the philosopher who said that; I just said it now," or "Dammit, why can't I be the philosopher who just said that?"

But I had already intuited that this wasn't what he sought. He apparently needed a dead philosopher's name pronounced as kind of sanction, benediction, or incantation to authenticate or legitimize (in their eyes) the counseling process. This expectation initially struck me as gratuitous, misleading, or perverse, until I gradually began to experience its pervasiveness in the culture, and better understood it as the Moorean hangover of mass intoxication by a perennial cocktail mixed from equal parts herd-instinct, idolatry, and superstition. This cocktail is served during "Unhappy Hour"—i.e., at any time of the day or night. The associated Moorean sentence is "I know this is a good idea, but I won't believe it until I learn the name of the dead philosopher who thought it up." Buddhists may recognize this as an equivalent of that famous sutra, "The Perfect Net,"[23] in which Buddha describes a man shot with a poisoned arrow, who will not consent to have it removed until he learns the name of the archer, the kind of wood of which the bow was fashioned, and so forth.

The herd-instinct, extrapolated to humanity, causes people to become "the masses." Groups coalesce around and follow leaders, whose authority sanctions or proscribes ideas and behaviors. Though many leading medical practices of the nineteenth century would constitute gross malpractice today, leading philosophical ideas of that time are still beneficial to contemporary philosophical practice. But their relevance is scarcely predicated on their age; rather, on their pragmatic efficacy.[24] But in the common conception of philosophy, art, religion, and politics alike, works that somehow survive a test of time are thereby deemed authoritative on that basis alone. (The other side of that coin is postmodernism, which rejects them precisely on that basis.) Though this tendency is brilliantly parodied in Miller's *A Canticle for Leibowitz*, it operates ubiquitously. Thus an unidentified philosophical insight may strike someone as having intrinsic value or immediate applicability, but it is still regarded with hesitation or suspicion until extrinsically labeled with a renowned name, which lends it authoritative sanction. Such sanction is of course entirely chimerical, in the sense that Aristotle's conception of the Golden Mean as virtue's compass is an effective guide to temperance without the least mention of Aristotle's name. Similarly, Ohm's law ($E = IR$) can be used to calculate resistance in a circuit without the least mention of Ohm. But such sanction appears to have the philosophical equivalent of a placebo effect upon the media, and upon the kind of clients they engender in this fashion: the principle that one applies is both efficacious and not functionally inert, and is therefore not a placebo, while pronouncing the name of its primogenitor is efficacious but functionally inert, and is therefore a true placebo.

Clients who have abandoned religious faith for philosophical doubt, or who maintain the former in tandem with the latter, are sometimes still susceptible to the elevation or inflation of philosophical wisdom to the stature of benediction, which is why they need a name pronounced. Whereas "I commend the principle of moderation to you" may suffice for an agnostic or atheist, "I commend the principle of moderation to you in the name of Aristotle" is the philosophical version of a blessing to which lapsed religionists or practicing theists are more accustomed. Nonetheless, it may strike philosophical counselors as bizarre, as it did this one, at least until they reflect upon the ground of such expectations. But with the passage of time, and the human need for myth, legend, and glorification, the name of an authoritative philosopher (or poet, or politician) can become an artefact of secular benediction. The greater the emphasis on name, the lesser the attention to idea.

The transition from benediction to incantation is equally smooth, and marks a return to superstition and supernaturalism. I have little doubt about the efficacy of prayer, the importance of individual communion with one's Godhead, or the intoxicating effects of mass-worship. I am not an enemy of organized religions— only irritated by the aggressive proselytization, doxastic myopia, and flagrant intolerance that characterizes so many of them. But I would not see philosophical counseling conflated with religious devotion. Type B counseling provides many potential paths to that conflation. Historically, philosophy became appropriated by theology at so many junctures that many contemporary theologians still consider themselves philosophers (and some apply for APPA Certification as Philosophical Counselors, armed with nothing more than degrees in theology). While it may be true that some people's acute sufferings are temporarily assuaged (more likely, anaesthetized) by accepting Jesus Christ as their Lord and Savior, the preaching of a gospel is not philosophical counseling: it is pastoral counseling, or spiritual counseling, or proselytization.

One need not even declare oneself the offspring of a deity in order to achieve apotheosis. On the contrary, Siddhartha Gautama eschewed theological and metaphysical speculation both, on his way to becoming enlightened (i.e., discovering his "Buddha-nature"), yet no purely secular and pragmatic practice has been more amenable to supernaturalism and idolatry than Buddhism. Without skipping a beat, humanity turned even this consummate idol-smasher into an idol. Jews understand this irony particularly well, since Abraham himself was the son of a craftsman who fabricated idols for a living—possibly made-to-order, whether retail or wholesale we no longer know. Abraham's patriarchy of the Jewish people begins with the smashing of his father's idols, and his worship of the author of this world, and not of the world's artifacts. Much later, Moses encountered a recrudescence of idolatry while receiving or conceiving the fundamental Law of this people: he descended from Mount Sinai with the Ten Commandments, the first of which is "Thou shalt have no other Gods before Me," only to find his tribe worshipping a golden calf. Jews are forbidden even to pronounce the name of Yahweh in prayer, let alone to worship graven images. More ironically, since Buddha embraced agnosticism, idols of Buddha are worshipped throughout the world. These worshippers are often heedless of the practice in which he himself engaged, and which he taught, and which definitively eschewed worship.

I had the following exchange with a young Chinese Buddhist in gift shop in San Francisco's Chinatown. She was a salesgirl, evidently earning commissions, and she followed me politely but hopefully around the store, at a discrete distance. It contained the largest collection of Buddha likenesses I have ever seen. There were statues and busts of Buddha fashioned of every conceivable material, from a great many countries, filling what seemed like miles of shelves. I also noticed, behind the counter, an altar enshrining an idol of Buddha, gilded with incense and candles.

> "So many Buddhas!" I remarked to her.
> "There is only *one* Buddha!" she corrected.
> "There is *no* Buddha!" I replied.

Philosophical practice can entail sitting as Siddhartha Gautama sat, to achieve clear-minded compassion without the affirmation or denial of supernatural being; whereas idolatry and incantation led to the religion of monotheistic Buddhism—a sublime contradiction in terms.

At its worst extreme, the incantative aspect of Type B counseling removes attention entirely from the substance of a given philosophical insight, and fixes it instead on the recitation of a name—which is effectively the replacement of reason with spell-casting. If you walked into my office and presented a problem amenable to philosophical evaluation, and if I listened carefully then replied "Plato!" or "Nietzsche!" would that help you in any way? "Take two aphorisms and call me in the morning" is not philosophical counseling; it is the casting of philosophical spells. Yet this is precisely how some mainstream media conceive and represent us.

Yet between the extremes of superfluous sanction and supernatural incantation lies a sensible and functional bandwidth of Type B counseling. Here the philosophical counselor toils as a kind of glorified switchboard operator, or noetic catalyst, connecting needy clients to helpful insights. Most clients on their own cannot negotiate effective passage through a philosophy library, nor even through the philosophy section of their local bookstore, yet could benefit from some of the ideas contained therein, if they only had experienced guides. This kind of Type B counseling works admirably well, and we practitioners owe the more perspicacious media representatives thanks for having reinvented us in this capacity. *Plato Not Prozac* illustrates the efficacy of this bandwidth of Type B counseling, both for its readers (i.e., consumers of philosophical counseling) and its readers-between-the-lines (i.e., producers of philosophical counseling).

Type C is an outgrowth of either Type A or B, although it most commonly proceeds from the latter. Clients who are especially literate and thoughtful, who find a given philosophical idea helpful in their problematic situation, may seek to explore the context of that idea—either as elaborated by a particular philosopher or as descended though the history of philosophical thought. In such cases, the counselor recommends an appropriate reading or readings, and the client may return at intervals for discussion. For obvious reasons, this is called "bibliotherapy." I conducted it with myself for many years, and settled time and again on certain texts (notably *Nicomachean Ethics*, the *Bhagavad-Gita*, the *I Ching*, and the *Tao Te Ching*) which contain invaluable advice for charting a course through life's hidden reefs and stormy latitudes.

Bibliotherapy also illustrates the salient distinction between theoretical and practical philosophy. One can pursue a theoretical philosophy course, assimilate and regurgitate its ideas, and earn academic credit thereby, without ever giving a thought to practical applications. One can pursue a bibliotherapeutic philosophy course, assimilate and apply its ideas, and resolve or manage some of life's problems thereby, without ever giving a thought to academic credit. Both processes are equally educational: the philosophy professor and the philosophical counselor are both educators. The contemporary difference, not drawn by the ancients, is between theoretical love of wisdom, literally *philosophy*, and practical applications of wisdom, literally *phronesis*. The philosophical counselor is therefore properly a phroneticist, although this term does not exactly glide off the tongue, and would not be an attractive word to print on a shingle or business card. Nonetheless, bibliotherapy is a valuable type of philosophical counseling for those with the temperament to pursue it. However, it should never be foisted on a client who does not explicitly request it.

Bibliotherapy can also be a relatively cost-effective form of education. Consider that a university student pays hundreds of dollars for perhaps thirty hours of instruction in a given course, and that the personally applicable portions of that course, which are inevitably and only what he recalls of it in the longer run, consume no more than a few hours. Those same few hours could be better spent with a philosophical counselor, at less overall cost to the student and with far more purposive philosophical focus on his concerns.

So much, for now, on this primitive and adumbrated typology of philosophical counseling. If intelligible types ever proliferate to the end of the English alphabet, the profession will be both well-ensconced and thoroughly corrupted. If it takes a hundred more years to define Types X, Y, and Z, then we are probably moving too quickly.

5.6. THE GOLDEN TRIANGLE

In the final section of this chapter, I characterize and contextualize philosophical counseling within a triadic relation, whose components are: biology, affect, and thought. These may be conveniently represented as a triangle, with a component at each vertex. Before elucidating this model, it is mete to make a few remarks on its ontology.

Monism, dualism, and pluralism are philosophically fascinating topics, to which ontologists devote entire lifetimes of reflection, and among which there are no ubiquitously recognized demarcations. Monotheistic religions, e.g., Judaism, assert that one God created the universe, yet remains apart from it—thus there is from the beginning a dualistic cosmology. Christianity's trinity raises the perennial ontological question: are the Father, the Son, and the Holy Spirit three manifestations of one thing, or three different things? I have never detected a consensus among Christians. Classical Hinduism is even more exquisitely complicated: since Atman (the individual soul) is really Brahman (the Godhead), the apparent multiplicity of beings is actually one. This sounds like monism, until one learns that Brahman subtends a trinity—the *Trimurti*—of fundamental Gods (Vishnu, Shiva, Brahma), and moreover that the world itself is composed of two kinds of things: matter and spirit. Add to this the five gunas and the pantheon of other deities, and one has a superposition of monistic, dualistic, and pluralistic states. This is almost as ontologically intractable as modern particle physics.

Intractable ontological questions are grounded in metaphysics, and philosophical arguments are inevitably shaped by metaphysical presuppositions. The mind–brain problem persists, and its ontological dualism is dispelled neither by Berkeleyan adductions of matter to mind, nor by posited Churchlandish reductions of mind to brain. Consciousness is not explained by *Consciousness Explained*. Hand-waving references to electrochemical states of the brain do not explicate volition. Earnest but vague narratives about representational brain-states do not account for the efficacy of mathematical thought, or its powerful connection to physical process. The Neckar cube metaphorically illustrates the irreducibility of this duality: any open-minded person can perfectly well understand the eliminative materialist (or any equivalently reductive) position; after all, it makes sense. Then again, the same open-mindedness compels one to recognize the Cartesian (or Popperian–Ecclesian, or equivalently interactionist) position, which also makes sense. Our eyes and brains (or eyes and brains and minds) are constructed by nature to view the two-dimensional Neckar cube in strictly alternating three-dimensional orientations. Only a philosopher would be rash enough to claim that the "real" 3D orientation of the cube is one or the other of the orientations; whereas in fact the plane figure is not a cube, and therefore has no 3D spatial orientation at all. It is our brains (or brains and minds) which create the unresolvable duality. Based on current evidence, I see no reason to regard the mind–brain duality as different in kind, except that it is self-referential and thus far more prone to entanglement from the beginning.

A degree of difference is manifest in the non-contradictoriness of the two alternating perspectives on the Neckar cube. Viewing one orientation at one time does not negate the possibility of viewing the other at another time; it merely negates the possibility of viewing both simultaneously. However, subscribing to a reductionist view of mind at one time might appear to negate the possibility of subscribing consistently to an interactionist view of mind at another time, at least until one recognizes the metaphoric projection of the Neckar cube, in which case there are merely alternating states of mind (or brain) concerning the ontological status of mind (or brain). There is perplexity, but no contradiction.

The mind–brain dyad is but one of three dyads, relationally sustained by the triangular model presented herein. As mentioned, biology occupies one vertex of the triangle; affect, a second; thought, a third. Each relates to itself and to the others pairwise, in reciprocating ways. Within this triangle, and its dyadic pairs, we will locate and better apprehend the function of philosophical counseling.

The biological vertex is given by nature. From this vertex, the human being, like every other organism, is viewed as a manifestation of its DNA, which is the blueprint for "constructing" the organism itself. The coarse features of your physical being, such as potential height, normal weight, eye-color, hair-color, and so forth, are predetermined at the genetic level. A good deal more than that is predetermined too, including the anatomy, physiology, and morphology

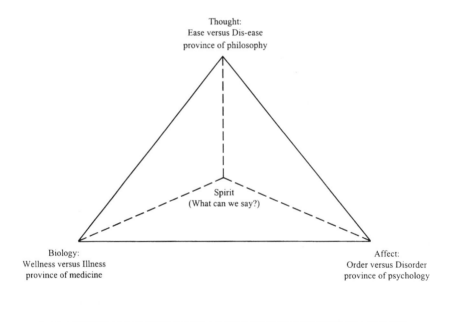

Thought:
Ease versus Dis-ease
province of philosophy

Spirit
(What can we say?)

Biology:
Wellness versus Illness
province of medicine

Affect:
Order versus Disorder
province of psychology

Biology   Affect

Twentieth-century man was reduced to this. His philosophy and
his spirituality alike collapsed, and his humanity all but vanished.

FIGURE 5.2 Vertices and Human Problematics,

of your body, sexual differentiation of various systems and organs—including the brain itself—and the regulation of the host of systems that need to function properly and in concert for you to survive a minute or a lifetime. Medical textbooks are full of graphic photos depicting the phenotypic effects of abnormal genotypes. All kind of debilitating or even fatal conditions can result from abnormal gene sequences—from spinal bifida to cystic fibrosis to Down syndrome, from hemophilia to lactose intolerance to malformed organs. The autonomic nervous system, which is not normally (if ever) under conscious control, oversees tasks ranging from cardiac and respiratory function to spinal reflexes. The oldest portion of the brain, namely the limbic system, is also not under conscious control, and its responsibilities include the mediation of powerful emotions such as rage or terror, and the physiological changes our bodies undergo when preparing for fight or flight.

But even at this early stage of identifying purely biological facets of being, we see plainly how activity at this vertex will mesh seamlessly with activities at the other vertices. When you are walking down the jungle path and you suddenly encounter a tiger, the biology of fight or flight may lie beyond your conscious control, but it is not independent of your affective and noetic processes. How did you recognize the tiger, and how did you know that the tiger is a dangerous animal? That knowledge is not inborn; it had to be acquired. Perhaps one of your parents taught you that tigers on jungle paths are best avoided, and perhaps your culture provided you with weapons for fighting and techniques for fleeing. These are behavioral extensions, acquired extra-somatically, and they illustrate the relation between biology and affect. Moreover, you need not only recognize a particular tiger—the one your parents pointed out—as dangerous, but need also be able to generalize about tigers, lest the one you next encounter is not the same one you previously encountered with your parents. Hence you are able to reason, informally but validly: "All tigers are potentially dangerous. This animal is a tiger. Therefore this animal is potentially dangerous." Even small and untutored children are able to cope well with such syllogistic reasoning, which, in the absence of definitive reduction, can be ascribed to the logical engine of the mind. Our senses, which are interfaces with extra-mental and extra-somatic reality, and which are biological couriers of external data to the processing centers of the brain, make, as Berkeley said, "no inferences" about the data they transmit. Conclusions are drawn by the mind, in consultation with its catalog of lived experienced, rumor, hearsay, feeling, and such reasoning as can be brought to bear.

Thus even if your senses accurately detect the tiger in your path, and even if old instinctive survival mechanisms induce strong emotions and concomitant physiological change, what you do next depends chiefly upon your affect and your reason. Your feelings, your conditioning and your habits contribute to the affective component of your action, while your symbolic structures, your tools, and your reasoning contribute to its noetic component. You may be carrying an AK-47 assault rifle, but your animal rights ethics may restrain you from firing it, and so you take to your heels. You may be carrying a "tiger fork,"[25] and have considerable practice in its use, and so you stand your ground. You may be weaponless, but decide to adopt the tactic of many defenseless prey animals, and remain motionless. Perhaps you will climb a tree, or simply panic and flee headlong. Biology is not the sole arbiter of these behaviors; custom and thought—the other two vertices—play decisive roles in action.

What is true of spontaneous action is truer of actions pertinent to carrying out plans, and truer still of formulating plans pertaining to careers, relationships, hobbies, vacations, investments, risks—including decisions about what path to take through the jungle, and who or what to bring along. Our biological foundations give us the capacities for actions of all kinds, but it is our affect mediately and thought ultimately that determine what many of those actions shall be. No matter which literal pathways we pursue, we are always on the figurative path of action. It behooves you to choose your path as wisely as possible, and to this means, as to its end, such choices are best governed not by the senses allured to action, and not by habits accustomed to action, but by principles applied to action.

One's environment, which includes factors ranging from parental to climatological influence, is the crucible in which raw biological material—i.e., the human neonate—is forged into a problem-laden being. The brain itself is incompletely grown at birth, and so experiences of infancy and early childhood are preconsciously but somehow profoundly registered; undoubtedly many traumas (or even mild disturbances) of this period do manifest themselves in later life. For this reason psychology and psychoanalysis are warranted in revealing and unraveling early experience as a key to understanding later conflict—but are by the same token misguided in asserting either the primacy of innate psychosexuality, or the ascendancy of acquired trauma, as the ultimate causes or final determinants of difficulties in adulthood. The Tibetans are fond of saying that there are but two kinds of misery: that of having, and that of not having.[26] Children who have families, no matter how loving, will be disturbed, abused, or traumatized by them. Children who have no families will be equally disturbed, abused, or traumatized in their absence, or else by their surrogates. Children who have siblings suffer in some ways; children who don't suffer in others—but suffering is a unitary experience.[27] Children whose parents are alcoholics or drug-addicts will suffer potentially many ill effects of their parents' substance abuse; yet children whose parents are perfectly normal will suffer potentially many ill effects of their parents' normalcy. Children born to poverty may suffer and strive to overcome its disadvantages; children born to wealth may likewise suffer and strive to overcome its disadvantages. Children born into any race, class, or gender may suffer because of it. Anything in one's environment may become a link in the chain of suffering. Thus the particularities of one's suffering may bind one to it, but these particularities are also incidental causes. The meta-cause of suffering is the human form and function, which carries with it the propensity not only to suffer, but also to mistake the appurtenances of environment for causes of suffering. We suffer primarily because we are human—and as such can always find something we lack, and crave it—and not normally because of a surfeit or dearth of anything in our environments. This is Buddha's First Noble Truth.

One's nurture can complement or abrogate one's biological promise. Your nature ordains that you may attain a certain potential height at maturity, but your nurture—in this case, your nutrition and your posture—determine the degree to which that potential is actually attained. Similarly, the purely genetic component of your life expectancy—the rate at which cells age, their capacity to be repaired or replaced, and your ability to ward off infectious disease via your immune system—is radically complementable by cultural interventions. These begin with the ingestion of mother's milk, which provides invaluable antibodies to the infant's immature immune system. Note that, although mother's milk is nature's partial solution to the problem of immunization, it is overridable by cultural conventions which may regard breast-feeding as unfashionable, unnecessary, or inconvenient. Such cultural supersession over biology attained a drastic form in Africa, with Nestlé Corporation's scandalous marketing of synthetic infant formula in wanton disregard of the unavailability of safe drinking water, and in culpable neglect of instructions for the boiling of impure water, and via crude disinformation implying that babies fed synthetic formula would be healthier than babies fed mother's milk.[28] An epidemic of infant deaths followed the irresponsible and inappropriate marketing of this product. On the whole, however, responsible medical practices—including infant vaccination—allied with appropriately hygienic technologies and reliable infrastructures for the delivery of clean water and the concomitant filtration of human waste have resulted in the virtual doubling of life expectancy, in the developed nations, during twentieth century.

Viewed in retrospect, this dramatic extension of life expectancy via technological intervention illustrates not only the power of affect over biology, but also their complementarity. People who lead active and healthy lives into their seventies and eighties are not said to be cheating death; they are understood to be fulfilling a natural potential that nonetheless requires nurture to bring about its fulfillment. Yet those who remain in a state more purely of nature itself, who have implemented less technology, and who therefore rely on superstition or shamanism instead of empirically sound allopathic and homeopathic remedies to cure disease, are held captive in that state by neither nature nor custom; rather, by the very belief-systems that prevent them from adopting the technologies that could prolong their lives. Thus thought can hold sway over affect, just as affect can over biology.

That we are conditionable beings has been amply demonstrated by the behaviorists, but the conditions of a given conditioning are not themselves conditioned to the extent of infinite regress. Sooner or later one strikes noetic bedrock, and discovers a meta-condition: a system of beliefs voluntarily maintained and inferences volitionally drawn, which premeditate and endeavor to justify a given stimulus, and which anticipate and desire a given response. Thus one cannot intelligibly explicate the affective–biological dyad without taking account of thought. Phobias and their proper treatment illustrate this indecomposability of the triangular model. A phobia is an affective disorder with unpleasant biological consequences. Fear of a given class of things—be it snakes, spiders, heights, lawyers, or reasoned arguments—might serve some evolutionary purpose, but on the whole phobias, as opposed to prudent concerns, are debilitating rather than empowering behaviors. Exposure to the psychologically feared stimulus produces physical responses ranging from anxiety to panic to hysteria, and mere awareness that one has a phobia is almost never sufficient to assuage or dispel it; on the contrary, active consciousness of a phobia is itself a kind of cognitive reinforcement of it. Two empirically viable solutions present themselves: the affective and the noetic. The former is accomplished by gradual behavioral reconditioning; the latter, by discrete hypnotic suggestion. Evidence suggests that phobias are more rapidly dispelled by noetic rather than by behavioral interventions.[29]

Then again, there are many other disorders against which noesis is not particularly proof, such as within the family of obsessive-compulsive disorders (OCDs). It turns out that behavioral modification therapy can be effective, for example, in mild to moderate cases of hoarding disorder—a behavioral condition whose affectees are unable to throw away garbage, wrappers, junk mail, or any other disposable items. They inhabit chaos, yet imbue their detritus with extraordinary significance. Moreover they know something is wrong with them, yet are unable to rectify it by cognition alone. But behavioral modification diminishes in efficacy as the disorder increases in severity. In extreme cases, perhaps the best thing to be done is to recover some useful noetic function, independent of the behavioral dysfunction. I had a client like this: an intellectually capable man who had nonetheless hoarded himself out of his own home—had literally filled the place so full of junk that he could no longer maintain himself there, and lived in a kind of hotel, where he ran the same risk. While he had not been able to find behavioral help with his hoarding problem, and whereas ten or twelve years of psychological talk-therapy had produced no change in him, at least with some philosophical counseling he was able to take stock of his professional and creative aspirations, and reevaluate his ethical and aesthetic dispositions, independently of hoarding junk.

There are also many instances in which behavioral modification is simply inadequate or inappropriate to the task at hand, particularly in matters regarding ethics or aesthetics. This is amply illustrated in *A Clockwork Orange*,[30] in which the antihero is behaviorally conditioned to be "good", that is, to refrain from behaviors undesirable to his society at large. Of course this fails dismally, since our ethical (and hence legal) understanding of criminality is predicated on presumption of autonomy and therefore also choice. In an open society, one can be considered culpable only if one is deemed reasonably able to distinguish between right and wrong, relatively free to choose between them, and guilty of an error in moral judgment that leads to some wrongdoing. Since conditioning is the antithesis of choice, one conditioned to refrain from wrongdoing is not a moral being; rather, a socially programmed automaton. Morality flows from noetic function, not behavioral conditioning.

And as we earlier saw in a different context, one must exercise considerable caution in making attributions about affect, lest one reflexively reduce affect to biology in cases when it plainly adducible to noesis. Only by careless use of language, and underlying thoughtlessness, does any and every affect become reduced to a putative biological disorder. This is psychologism at its worst. Not all affected behaviors are addictions; some are simply habits. Literal habits are affects maintained volitionally, not metabolically, and are broken volitionally, not metabolically. Habits are acquired by indulging in repeated and similarly motivated actions. Bad habits are broken by indulging in voluntary or coerced substitution of other, presumably less detrimental or more beneficial, repeated and similarly motivated actions. Benign behaviors motivated by the satisfaction of natural appetites may indeed become habits, but they are not therefore addictions. Life is not a disease. Life-sustaining pursuits are neither illnesses nor symptoms of illnesses, and to assert that they are is preposterous. Through the acquisition of bad noetic habits, some social and behavioral scientists have mistaken bad affective habits for physical addictions.

Successes of institutionalization in general also entail unfortunate pitfalls, such as the systemic or structural inculcation of predetermined judgments of their wards. We have already commented on the average university student's common conception of the philosopher as an incomprehensible professor of an irrelevant subject. Now consider this phenomenon in the context of correctional institutions. One expects and encounters denial from convicted felons, who mostly assert that they are innocent and were framed. While it is nonetheless true that some *are* innocent and *were* framed, it is understandable that guards and wardens can more easily perform their functions if they believe that all inmates are guilty and deserve to be incarcerated. If you deem this a rather oppressive assumption which ordinary people would never make, ponder Milgram's classic experiment, which within a matter of hours transformed average university students into sadistic warders.[31]

Contemplate this phenomenon in the context of psychiatric institutions. One expects and encounters a much smaller percentage of denial among such inmates, some of whom nonetheless insist that they are there for golf lessons, or for a vacation, or for some other clearly implausible purpose. What is true of prison guards and wardens is even truer of psychiatric nurses and doctors; namely, that they can more easily perform their functions if they believe that all their charges are "mentally ill." Now consider the Rosenhan study,[32] recounted by James Rachels:[33]

> A few years ago a group of investigators led by Dr. David Rosenhan, professor of psychology and law at Stanford University, had themselves admitted as patients to various mental institutions. The hospital staffs did not know there was anything special about them; the investigators were thought to be simply patients. The investigators' purpose was to see how they would be treated.
>
> The investigators were perfectly sane, whatever that means, but their very presence in the hospitals created the assumption that they were mentally disturbed. Although they behaved normally—they did nothing to feign illness—they soon discovered that everything they did was interpreted as a sign of some sort of mental problem. When some of them were found to be taking notes on their experience, entries were made in their records such as "patient engages in writing behavior." During one interview, one "patient" confessed that although he was closer to his mother as a small child, he became more attached to his father as he grew older—a perfectly normal turn of events. But this was taken as evidence of "unstable relationships in childhood." ...
>
> No one on the hospital staffs caught on to the hoax. The real patients, however, did see through it. One of them told an investigator, "You're not crazy. You're checking up on the hospital." And so he was.[34]

If you took you car into a garage and asked that it be looked at, an honest mechanic would not find anything "wrong" with it necessarily, merely by virtue of its being there. A dishonest mechanic, by contrast, would diagnose all kinds of problems, and replace all kinds of parts unnecessarily. His motive would be profit. However, dishonest mechanics still know that they are dishonest, and have misidentified working parts for a defective ones. The Rosenhan experiment illustrates something far more serious; namely, that some psychiatric nurses and doctors regard patients who fall into their hands as necessarily "mentally ill," merely by virtue of their being there. They then treat them as though they were mentally ill—not out of dishonesty, but out of something far worse: the inability to distinguish sanity from insanity, other than by uncritical inference from circumstantial evidence—in other words, out of hubris, dogmatism, professional deformation, failure of imagination, preponderance of ends over means, incompetence, malpractice, and the like. Their dual motives would be profit as usual, plus the maintenance of power. Like those in Milgram's experiment, these were once average students, too. Now they are licensed by states to enact bad comedy.

This kind of psychiatry, as well as some of clinical psychology, does not passively await patients, as mechanics await vehicles. Rather, psychiatry and psychology have colonized not only the health care system, but also the education system, the legislative system, the justice system, the corrections system, the military, and other branches of state and federal government. They are, among other things, marines sent in by the generals of the pharmaceutical industry. My point is that, where normal affective states are reified as behavioral disorders, or erroneously reduced to putative biological illnesses, the root cause is not the presence of something; rather, the absence of recognition of the noetic vertex our triangular model, and its subsequent collapse and disappearance into the affect–biology axis.

Moving from the behavioral to the cognitive side of the affective vertex, one can plainly appreciate recent attempts of psychologists, psychiatrists, and physicians themselves to return to their philosophical roots. Under the aegis of cognitive psychology, one sees a variety of late modern attempts to demedicalize ordinary human problems, and reintroduce autonomous deliberation and rational mentation into psychological intervention. Carl Rogers's client-centered therapy, Albert Ellis's rational emotive therapy, Victor Frankl's logotherapy, Eric Fromm's biophilic ethics, and Ernesto Spinelli's existential analysis all represent reunions of psychology with philosophy. Similarly, psychiatrists such as R. D. Laing, Thomas Szasz, and Peter Breggin have, in their several ways, similarly repudiated the over-medicalization of affect, and advocated a return to reason. If only more physicians were as actively philosophical about their professions as Alfred Tauber,[35] and if only more psychiatrists were as wise and compassionate as Scott Peck,[36] then many more patients would be far better-served, as human beings, even in the absence of philosophical practice.

Beyond cognition of one's problems' proper origins, recognition of one's own ideation and mentation as efficacious in their resolution or management, just in case they are rooted in noetic domains, relocates the arena of appropriate

intervention from psychology into philosophy. Competent philosophical counselors do not discount the importance of feeling and behavior any more than
competent psychological or psychiatric counselors discount the importance of
noesis; rather, we tend to meet them halfway along the axis between affect and
thought. The mid-region of this axis is perhaps demarcated by the work of
Pierre Grimes and his Academy of Philosophical Midwifery, which saliently
applies Plato's theory of identifying and dispelling one's false beliefs, as spelled
out in the *Thaetetus*,[37] to the resolution of problems whose roots are ultimately
noetic, even though they have cognitive and affective manifestations.

From the vantage of the noetic vertex of our triangle, one clearly recognizes
the powers of thought in both dyadic directions, over biology and affect alike.
Just as one's thoughts may be formed habitually, one's habits may be formed
thoughtfully: this is a two-way street. And just as one's brain-states influence
the mind's function, so too does one's mental function influence one's brain-
states: this is another two-way street. Efficacious and beneficial mental regulation of bodily process is demonstrable in many ways, including biofeedback
mechanisms of stress reduction, yogic and martial arts practices that ameliorate
physical function, the allopathic rediscovery of visualization techniques that
combat cancers, the therapeutic uses of hypnosis, and the placebo effect itself.

Beyond these, in the long run philosophical contemplation (or lack thereof)
governs both the affective and the biological being. Thought (or lack thereof)
determines what beliefs we shall defend and what habits we shall inculcate;
proper mentation can thus override many cognitive and behavioral facets of
affect. Again, thought (or lack thereof) similarly determines what we shall
ingest and how we shall otherwise maintain our physical vitality; proper
mentation can thus govern its own province of bodily function, and can also
discriminate vitally between appropriate and inappropriate remedies for bodily
dysfunction. Notwithstanding ineluctable biological and affective constraints,
the optimization of one's quality of life is at least as much a noetic task as it is
a medical or psychological one. Thought and its powers were sorely neglected
in the twentieth century, and marginalized as passive echoes or shadowy
epiphenomena of biological and affective phenomena. The noetic vertex was
projected onto the biology–affect axis; the triangle collapsed into a straight
line. As the three dyads were reduced to one, mentation was reduced to
nothing. Twentieth-century man scurried back and forth along the remaining
axis—a tight corridor with a psychiatrist's office at one end, and a psychology's
at the other—trying vainly to solve or manage his noetic problems with inappropriate biological or affective remedies, thus making them and himself only
worse in the process.

Philosophical practice through its primary appendage, namely, counseling,
reconstitutes the triangle, redefines the three dyads, revivifies the mind, re-

stores the balance of powers, and thus refreshes the being. We are born fresh, but require constant refreshment. Philosophical practice provides refreshment of the highest order.

Those who wish to extend our triangular model could well project a fourth vertex, into a third dimension. That vertex would represent man's spiritual, theological, or mythological being, and would transform our triangle into a tetrahedron. Instead of one face and three distinct axes (i.e., sides), one would encounter four faces and six distinct axes. I defer the elaboration of this tetrahedral model to a future undertaking.

NOTES

1. Championing philosophy as a conduit to eudamonia, Russell had written, "The man capable of greatness of soul will open wide the windows of his mind, letting the winds blow freely upon it from every portion of the universe. He will see himself and life and the world as truly as our human limitations will permit; realizing the brevity and minuteness of human life, he will realize also that in individual minds is concentrated whatever of value the known universe contains. And he will see that the man whose mind mirrors the world becomes in a sense as great as the world. In emancipation from the fears that beset the slave of circumstance, he will experience a profound joy, and through all the vicissitudes of his outward life he will remain in the depths of his being a happy man." B. Russell, *The Conquest of Happiness* (New York: Horace Liveright, 1930), pp. 227–228.

2. Adler wrote, "Understanding the human enterprise as a whole—in which science and technology, as well as history, religion, the various arts, and the institutions of the state and of the church are component parts—is a task that calls for philosophizing of a high order, yet philosophizing of a kind that everyone engages in to some degree. It is a task that no other discipline, no other part of our culture, is able to discharge. It is a task that academic philosophy, as currently constituted and practiced, either turns away from or fails to measure up to." M. Adler, *The Conditions of Philosophy: Its Checkered Past, Its Present Disorder, and Its Future Promise* (New York: Atheneum, 1965), p. 13.

3. Paul Sharkey started giving philosophical counseling in 1974, and was appointed "Philosopher in Residence" at Forrest County General Hospital in 1979. See P. Sharkey, "When?—The Philosophical Revolution," *Contemporary Philosophy*, 11, No. 3, 1986.

4. Seymon Hersh, "The Counseling Philosopher," *The Humanist*, May/June, 1980, pp. 32–33.

5. Notwithstanding the European myth that Achenbach was the first philosophical counselor—he may well have been so in Europe—it is now clear that several American philosophers had begun to practice such counseling either previously or contemporaneously.

6. L. Marinoff, *Strategic Interaction in the Prisoner's Dilemma: A Game-Theoretic Dimension of Conflict Research*, unpublished doctoral dissertation, University of London, 1992a. This gave rise to ongoing publications in that area, e.g., Marinoff (1990, 1992a, 1993, 1994b, 1996a,b, 1998b,c).

7. Danielson does interesting work on the iterated PD; see, e.g., P. Danielson, *Artificial Morality* (London: Routledge, 1992).

8. In L. Marinoff, *On Human Conflict*, unpublished manuscript, 1987–88.

9. This is neither raw cranial capacity nor individual brain-to-bodyweight ratio; rather, is the logarithm of the ratio of brain-weight to body-weight averaged across a given species. E.g., G. von Bonin, "Toward an Anthropology of the Brain," *Annals of the New York Academy of Sciences*, 63, 1955–56, pp. 505–509.

10. Generalization has indubitable survival value in a state of nature. For example, if a particular snake or tiger is dangerous, then all animals resembling that snake or that tiger should be construed as dangerous. But when this becomes transmuted into cultural terms, it produces one kind of stereotyping through over-generalization, whose survival value (as well as truth value) is much more questionable.

11. In becoming enculturated, we all receive what Korzybski called a "lubricant with emery," by which he meant an identification with (and emotional commitment to) semantic structures that render "general sanity and complete adjustment impossible." A. Korzybski, *Science and Sanity* (Lancaster, PA: International Non-Aristotelian Library Publishing, 1933), pp. ii–iii.

12. See Freud (1955), *Thoughts for the Times on War and Death*, in J. Strachey, ed. and Trans., *The Standard Edition of the Complete Psychological Works of Sigmund Freud*, Vol. 14 (London: Hogarth, original work published 1914–16), p. 297: "Our unconscious does not carry out the killing; it merely thinks it and wishes it.... In our unconscious impulses we daily and hourly get rid of anyone who stands in our way, of anyone who has offended or injured us.... Indeed, our unconscious will murder even for trifles; like the ancient Athenian code of Draco, it knows no other punishment for crime than death."

13. For example, epistemologist Susan Haack reconstitutes a delightful imaginary dialogue between Charles Pierce and Richard Rorty, culled from their actual writings, which utilizes Pierce's scientific pragmaticism to expose and refute Rorty's postmodern neo-pragmatism. See S. Haack, *Manifesto of a Passionate Moderate* (Chicago: University of Chicago Press, 1998), pp. 31–47.

14. Then again, one of my counseling sessions with a journalist was subsequently described as a verbal boxing match: "Unlike psychotherapists, whose conversations

are dotted with anodyne 'is that so's?' and 'why do you think that was?' Marinoff does not hold back. Keeping up with his arguments is like fending off a vicious left hook." H. Kirwan-Taylor, "No Brain No Gain," *Financial Times Magazine*, March 1999, pp. 69–70.

15. This issue will be taken up in more detail in Chapter 12.

16. We will return to this in Chapter 15, on the politics of practice.

17. We will take up legislative matters in more detail in Chapter 10.

18. See note 5, Chapter 1.

19. Ran Lahav calls this the client's "worldview." See R. Lahav, "A Conceptual Framework for Philosophical Counseling: Worldview Interpretation," in R. Lahav and M. Tillmanns, eds., *Essays on Philosophical Counseling* (Lanham, MD: University Press of America, 1995), pp. 3–24.

20. That is, the phenomenon of interpreting the world (and thus "deforming" it) according to one's professional orientation. See the "Introduction" in W. Barrett, *Irrational Man* (Garden City, NY: Doubleday, 1962).

21. See W. James (1956), *The Will to Believe, and Other Essays in Popular Philosophy* (New York: Dover, original work published 1897).

22. See J. Michael Russell, *The Philosopher As Personal Consultant*. Archived at <http://www.members.aol.com/jmrussell/philosas.htm>. Also printed in *The Philosophers' Magazine*, archived at <www.philosophers.co.uk>. We will quote from it in Chapter 10.

23. "Brahma-Gala Sutta," one of the "Digha Nikaya" ("Long Dialogues"), in *Dialogues of the Buddha*, trans. T. Rhys Davids (London: Henry Frowde, 1899).

24. E.g., Thoreau's 19th-century theory of civil disobedience was adapted and successfully applied by Gandhi and King in the 20th. In more modest circumstances, Mill's signal distinction between offence and harm (in *On Liberty*) is being adapted and applied by yours truly (see Marinoff 1999a,b). Popper took pains to point out that philosophy should not be venerated on the basis of its antiquity; rather, on its salience: see K. Popper, *The Open Society and Its Enemies* (London: Routledge & Kegan Paul, 1945), Vol. 1 (*The Spell of Plato*), Vol. 2 (*The High Tide of Prophecy*), *passim*.

25. Essentially a trident.

26. By private communication, Sogyal Rinpoche (1986).

27. We distinguish suffering from pain in the usual way: pain is a physical phenomenon, felt somewhere in the body; suffering is an emotional phenomenon, felt in the troubled mind or in the figuratively wounded heart. Thus suffering does not entail pain; yet pain can entail suffering.

28. E.g., see G. Palmer, *The Politics of Breastfeeding* (London: Pandora, 1993).

29. See D. Hammond, ed., *Handbook of Hypnotic Suggestions and Metaphors* (New York: Norton, 1990). The definitive handbook of the American Society of Clinical Hypnosis (ASCH), it is probably the most comprehensive and well-respected book on hypnotherapy.

30. A. Burgess, *A Clockwork Orange* (New York: Norton, 1963).

31. See, e.g., S. Milgram, *Obedience to Authority: An Experimental View* (New York: Harper & Row, 1974).

32. D. Rosenhan, "On Being Sane in Insane Places," in T. Scheff, ed., *Labeling Madness* (Englewood Cliffs, NJ: Prentice-Hall, 1975), pp. 54–74.

33. J. Rachels (1999), *The Elements of Moral Philosophy* (New York: McGraw-Hill, original work published 1993), pp. 79–80.

34. See also Ken Kesey (1989), *One Flew Over the Cuckoo's Nest* New York: New American Library, original work published 1963).

35. A. Tauber, *Confessions of a Medicine Man—An Essay in Popular Philosophy* (Cambridge: MIT Press, 2000).

36. M. Scott Peck, *The Road Less Travelled* (New York: Touchstone, 1980).

37. See Plato, *Thaetetus*, trans. R. Waterfield (London: Penguin 1987), p. 26: "Well, my midwifery has all the standard features, except that I practice it on men instead of women, and supervise the labor of their minds, not their bodies. And the most important aspect of *my* skill is the ability to apply every conceivable test to see whether the young man's mental offspring is illusory and false or viable and true. But I have this in common with midwives—I myself am barren of wisdom." See also P. Grimes and R. Uliana, *Philosophical Midwifery* (Costa Mesa, CA: Hyparxis, 1998).

CHAPTER 6

Philosophy
With Groups —
and Groupies

6.1. Is "Group Philosophy" an Oxymoron?
6.2. The Philosopher's Café
6.3. Nelsonian Socratic Dialogue
6.4. Philosophy With Other Groups

6.1. IS "GROUP PHILOSOPHY" AN OXYMORON?

If you were asked to name the most socially or intellectually dysfunctional group you know, whom would you nominate? Typical responses might include "my relatives," "my in-laws," "families on trash TV," "the cult next door," and "the political party I happen to oppose." While all these may be deserving candidates, by far the most potentially intellectually dysfunctional group in my experience is the academic committee.

Many professors, including some professors of philosophy, are people who long ago stopped listening to others. A professor conducts his lectures as he sees fit, and most of his utterances go unchallenged. Students who challenge professors are usually no match for them anyway. Neither will his colleagues tread too heavily upon a professor's area of special expertise, but will usually cede this ground to him, as he cedes their respective territories to them.

Now convene a committee of professors—each claiming absolute mastery over a few crumbs of knowledge, each exerting total authority over a few students in a lecture hall—and oblige them to discuss an agenda of shared academic concerns. They sometimes behave like either spoiled or neglected children. They can manifest rudeness, pettiness, or vengefulness. They may exchange harsh words, or even come to blows. They can also take hours to resolve some utterly pedestrian matter, that should normally require only minutes.

On the bright side: notwithstanding all its intellectual dysfunctions, an academic committee is preferable to a mob, which is the most socially dysfunctional group I can imagine. People are naturally gregarious; they like to congregate and associate. We generally deem this a wholesome instinct. By contrast, it is the recluse or hermit who more readily arouses suspicions of misanthropy, if not sociopathology. But if the behavior of a group gets out of hand, it becomes a mob—and there is no group more spontaneously evil or consumed by unreason. A rampaging mob is in many respects the antithesis of a meditative philosopher.[1]

The kinds of activities in which human groups can indulge range from sacred to profane, from refined to vulgar, from noble to common. We accept as relatively "normal" groups a community of devout religionists at worship, a horde of adolescents at a rock concert, an assembly of professionals at a conference, a throng of fans at an athletic contest, a jury deliberating a verdict, or a crowd of regulars at a neighborhood bar. We even accept more unusually constituted groups as "normal" in correspondingly unusual circumstances, such as a unit of commandos, a company of actors, a march of protestors, or a gang of criminals. Even at the extremes of human conduct and misconduct, we recognize groups such as the riotous mob, the symphony orchestra, the terrorist gang, the rescue team, the revolutionary party, the drunken orgy.

Of course, this haphazard listing scarcely dents the catalog of groups in which human beings are prone to assemble. Note that a collective of other animals is exhaustively described by a respective singular term—be it a nest of ants, a gaggle of geese, a pride of lions, a troop of baboons, or a pod of whales. Yet despite the immense variety to which human assemblies are subject, the idea that philosophy can be done with groups, or in groups, appears to defy popular imagination.

It is true that philosophers, as thinkers, have a well-deserved reputation for being solitary creatures. This has also been true of poets, painters, and composers—quite possibly for similar reasons—while it has also been less true of actors, musicians, and politicians. Perhaps the crucial distinction lies between the creative and the performing arts. Those who perform are more apt to enjoy professional camaraderie, and to require logistical and therefore also social support; while those who create are more apt to crave quietude, and thus to cultivate solitude. Beyond this, some exceptionally creative souls are also prone to antisocial eccentricities, if not downright social dysfunctionalities. On top of that, quite a number of philosophers appear to pride themselves on being eccentric if not socially dysfunctional, as though that alone were a guarantee of noetic profundity.

Though such impressions may be based on accurate historical accounts and authentic personal experiences, they are by no means comprehensive. It is possible for a philosopher to be both a solitary thinker and a group facilitator. It is once again the false idea that philosophy means only academic (or theoretical) pursuits that fosters the former image at the expense of the latter. Even philosophical counseling has been viewed from this slanted perspective, so that some clients think of it as entering an austere domain and prevailing upon the private thoughts of a cloistered mind, or a brain in a vat. Philosophical practitioners are capable of working with groups in many ways, and in so doing are also working hard to change the prevalent misconception of philosophy as an exclusive and reclusive occupation.

The reconception of philosophy as a group activity also cuts somewhat across the gradient of psychology with groups, which became full-blown in the 1960s as "group therapy," and whose practices as well as residues are still current in both popular conception and corporate culture. There is, however, a big difference between sitting in a circle holding hands, and sitting around a table linking minds.

Some of the earliest, as well as some of the latest forms of philosophy have involved groups. Plato's dialogues themselves could not have emerged from solitary contemplation, but only from Socratic encounters in the agora, the marketplace of ideas as well as commodities. Similarly, one of the Three Jewels of Buddhism is *sangha*, the community, another reminder that philosophical practice does not take place in a vacuum. Even the theoretical philosopher's social if not vocational avatar is that of teacher, who works in the classroom with a group. Most graduate students of philosophy in the twentieth century were preparing hopefully for careers as professors—meaning also teachers—of philosophy. The finest research universities extant, to the extent that they are not wells poisoned by political rectitude, still rank publication as the first criterion of merit when considering candidates for hire, tenure, or promotion. Teaching ability is always second, but still important, in such places. However, the vast majority of universities and colleges do not insist upon publication at all (although they expect it to be done on weekends); rather, they demand teaching ability as their first criterion of merit. Most academicians teach more than they publish, however one compares the two activities, and many are very good teachers indeed. Even so, most academic philosophers probably conceive of teaching in terms of administrative "course load" (i.e., as an imposition on their research and publication time), rather than as a vocation (i.e., as something they set out to do in the first place). Then again, once they find themselves in the classroom, confronted by a captive audience of earnest undergraduates poised to highlight every sentence in their books, most professors warm to the subject at hand, and patiently endeavor to restore a modicum of cosmos to these chaotic young minds. Some professors, it is true, actually come to relish this position of authority; after all, unlike their spouses and children, these students actually listen to them, and even ask them occasional questions. Even professors unenthralled with pedagogy are unlikely to regard themselves as victims of that ancient rabbinical curse: "May you teach other people's children for a living."

Is there an alternative to the chaos of committees and the unruliness of mobs? Can people come together and behave well enough socially to attain something worthwhile intellectually? Of course they can. Teaching is but one way of doing philosophy with groups, and its standard academic methodology is intermediate in formality between the least, and most, formal philosophical practices in this mode. We will revisit pedagogy toward the end of this chapter, but meanwhile we shall look at both the least and the most formal modes of doing philosophy with groups. These are, respectively, the philosopher's café and the Nelsonian Socratic dialogue.

6.2. THE PHILOSOPHER'S CAFÉ

The philosopher's café, or "café-philo" as it is called in France, is a byproduct of neither coffee nor philosophy. Given its rapid propagation through northern Europe and North America, the phenomenon appears to be a manifestation of countercultural backlash against the pervasive dumbings-down produced by globalization, the attendant conformity and tabloidicity of globalized mass-media, and their inadvertent marginalization of the intelligentsia. Many patrons of a philosopher's café are simply diehard intellectual holdouts, who like to read, think, and articulate their views, and who refuse to succumb to the wholesale cultural transition from written to visual tradition. Viewed another way, the philosopher's café is the latest incarnation of the agora, and "Remember the Agora!" has the same appeal to philosophers as "Remember the Alamo!" has to Texans.

Those who ask why the philosopher's café is becoming so popular should ask another question: what does globalized culture do to further the interactions of thoughtful people? The short answer is: not nearly as much as it could. What do I mean by globalization? I mean the emergent transcendence of economic over political power, manifest in myriad ways. The European Union is more akin to a corporate merger than to a political alliance: that is globalization. The widespread importation of capitalist industry into communist China is globalization. The rapid growth of commerce on the worldwide web is globalization. The irritating automated telephone-answering system, which always offers your desired option last and never fails to instruct you that you can hang up when finished, is globalization. The evolution of monolithic multinational corporate structures, and the feeding-frenzy of takeovers that drives the process, is globalization. The uniformity of goods and services one encounters while traveling, whether in airports, hotels, restaurants or bookstores, is globalization. The San Diego symphony orchestra's bankruptcy, for want of less money annually than the San Diego baseball team's monthly payroll, is also globalization.

The phenomenon is welcome because it standardizes goods and services across a huge consumer spectrum (the whole planet!) and, in regularizing so many aspects of life, it renders them more reliable, more predictable, more manageable, more profitable, and often more palatable as well. It allows the Mud-Men of New Guinea to effect the material transition from the late Stone Age to the early post-postmodern period in as little time as it takes to ship them Coca-Cola and Palm Pilots. No religious or political system hitherto conceived can accomplish this so quickly or efficiently. Globalization is egalitarian: it wants everyone's business. Its slogans are about marketing, not ideology. But in the generation of such vastly uniform mass-markets, the quintessential graininess of high culture is often smoothed to the point of bathetic triteness and seamless vacuity. It's like that joke in Rowan Atkinson's *Blackadder*, where the upper-class twit of a World War One General (played perfectly by Stephen Fry) bemoans the map he's reading: "My God, it's a featureless desert out there!" Then his aide informs him that he's looking at the backside of the map. The unwelcome feature of globalization is surely this: its frontside is sometimes barely distinguishable from its backside. Thus fast food tastes much like the box it's served in, and has about the same nutritive value. The relation of philosophical practice to globalization will be addressed in Chapter 7, and updated in Chapter 17.

The intellectual's aesthetic sensibilities have always seemed microcosmic in the macrocosm of popular taste, because they usually are. Nonetheless, intellectuals of bygone ages have always had somewhere to go to express their individuality, and to vivify the distinction between quantity and quality. The salon was a voluntary haven for European intellectuals in the nineteenth century, as was the gulag a non-voluntary one for Soviet intelligentsia in the twentieth. Where do twenty-first century intellectuals go for noetic stimulation? There is nowhere for them to go, and that is why the philosopher's café is gaining popularity. Many intelligent people disenchanted with the overspecialization of higher education, the dogma of organized religion, the inanity of prime-time television, the avarice of casinos, and the bread and circuses of plebeian entertainment, are flocking to philosopher's forums, the only venue where they can walk what mass culture has not yet succeeded in eradicating of their wits.

In general, as we have observed, philosophical practice is shaped by the ethos of the nation-state in which it evolves. This is well-illustrated by the different venues, in different countries, in which philosopher's forums unfold, notwithstanding the globalized thread on which they are strung together, like so many pearls. In France, perhaps the quintessential café-culture, there are about three hundred and fifty café-philos, the majority of which are situated in Paris. This prevalence owes initially to the inspiration of Marc Sautet, who elevated philosophical conversation over coffee to a popular art-form and a business. That he left the academy to do so is perhaps characteristic of old-world European prejudice, which gives rise to the undeniably romantic but often dangerous idea that meaningful change must somehow fly in the face of an *ancien régime*. For whatever reasons, Sautet took his philosophy out of the academy and ensconced it in the coffeehouse. The philosopher-turned-proprietor became something of a media darling, and clearly knew (or quickly learned) how to exploit the perennial double-edged French fascination with serious things done in trivial ways, and with trivial things done in serious ways.

"Café" is a word to conjure by in France, even if it originated in Vienna. The coffeehouse, in certain times and places, is a venue of unrivaled intellectual and unbridled artistic ferment. One imagines the universal Parisian café in which Sartre and Beauvoir huddle in mutual existential admiration at one table, Jacques Prévert scribbles *Paroles* on napkins at another, Picasso doodles on a tablecloth in the corner, Henry Miller cadges cigarettes and ogles women, Django Reinhart and Stephan Grapelli jam on a stage strewn with sawdust, and Ernest Hemingway passes out at the bar. The coffeehouse is also the working-man's salon, so interspersed among these cultural giants are salt-of-the-earth Parisians who came in to swill cheap red wine, chain-smoke Gauloises, and ignore these geniuses in the spirit of the Revolution.

The coffeehouse retained something of this panache even when transplanted to America. For instance, the Café Figaro in Greenwich Village boasted its halcyon seasons of assorted dadaists, beatniks, poets, playwrights, and song-writers—Bob Dylan among many others. Having been graced with bongos, beads and boo, it currently caters to yuppies. True, some frequent the place because it was once "cool" to frequent the place, and they deem old cool better than no cool. Others go there simply because it is there, and they need somewhere to go.

But the coffeehouse is not the venue of choice for philosopher's forums in America, and there are readily ascertainable reasons for that. To begin with, the café is a kind of local community center in France, the default venue for socialization, and thus subserves a function similar to the British pub. (If you now ask whether it follows that philosopher's forums in Britain take place by default in pubs, the answer is that they do.) In America, however, neither the café nor the bar seems the right place for group philosophy; its most natural venue here is the bookstore-café. And since small specialty bookstores are being replaced by mega-bookstore-cafés, we can simply say "the bookstore." Any North American philosopher who wants to start up a forum usually heads to his nearest bookstore. This is globalization again, ironically coming home to roost in ersatz—that is, transient or intermittent—cultural communities.

A word of explanation is probably in order here. To begin with, the great American writers of a century or so ago could not earn a living writing.[2] Edgar Allen Poe, who invented the genre of horror, was impoverished. Today, his successor Stephen King earns perhaps fifteen millions dollars as an advance on a book proposal (though he sincerely admires classic authors, which he humbly admits not being himself). Walt Whitman, America's quintessential poet, cranked out the first edition of *Leaves of Grass* on a Gestetner machine in his Camden basement, and sold it door-to-door. Today, poetess bell hooks earns a hundred-thousand-dollar salary as a Distinguished Scholar at CUNY. Herman Melville, one of America's greatest novelists, required eighteen tortured years to find a publisher for *Moby Dick*. Today, Toni Morrison sees every word rushed into print, and moreover has won a Nobel Prize. Such are the vicissitudes of authorship. If you have it in your heart to write, then write your heart out and may God help you with the rest—because the world of publishing is governed by neither rhyme nor reason, and only an omniscient and supremely ironic intelligence could make sense of it. Almost perversely, one is tempted to assert that the likes of Poe and Whitman and Melville had to endure terrible hardship, precisely because they were so great.

However, great but unknown writers are usually better off than great but unknown painters, because at least they have some reasonable hope of being published and reviewed before they die, as opposed to the hopelessness of being exhibited and collected posthumously. And for precisely this reason, the great and noble publishing houses were once founded, so that the literary heritage could be preserved. In the age of the written tradition, which lasted roughly from the invention of Gutenburg's press to the appearance of the personal computer (at which time the visual tradition began to take over), a culture was nothing but the sum of its published works. But publishers need to make money, too, and so they published perhaps 90% of their titles to satisfy the schlock-market in order to pay for the 10% that constituted literature. As a bibliophile on the cusp of the visual tradition, this is very important to me, for I was reared to love great literature, but have grown to see it and its appreciation largely vanish into the thin but statically charged air surrounding cathode-ray tubes.

Small specialty bookstores, which served a literate public, were a hallmark of the late written tradition. These were generally run by book-lovers, who read every title they stocked and then some, and with whom one discussed literature as a matter of course. One didn't just buy a book; one bought into a tradition and a culture with every purchase, and usually got some kind of lesson, or at least erudite conversation, thrown in for the asking. This model persisted in London until the late 1980s, when the proliferation of specialized bookshops attained a zenith marked by the publication of a guidebook to London bookshops. This guidebook soon saw a rival guidebook published, which briefly held out the delightful prospect of a second-order guidebook—a guidebook to the guidebooks of London bookshops! The beauty of this system at its height was that one could locate and purchase a given artifact of literary culture almost on a whim. As a graduate student, I did so many times: I knew exactly where to find Stcherbatsky's *Buddhist Logic* (at the theosophical bookshop across from the British Museum), or Zinsser's *Rats, Lice and History* (at the medical-historical bookshop near Russell Square), or affordable first editions of great novels (at the antique bookstalls in Chelsea), or very affordable latest editions of anything whatsoever (at the used paperback stalls on Southampton Row). But this literary sun turned out to be in supernova, and it quickly burned out, and went into multinational collapse. In the nineties, mostly the chains remain. The big chains moreover devour the small ones, else spawn them in suburban malls.

The bookstore has become a supermarket, whose employees are no more literati than grocery-baggers are Cordon Bleu chefs. This has occurred in tandem with the globalization of the publishing industry, which has far-reaching consequences for literary culture as well as philosopher's forums. As the noble family-run publishing houses were bought out by faceless multinational corporations, in came the profiteers who observed,

> "We have no problem with your 90% schlock-market, but how come 10% of your titles aren't best-sellers?"
> "Ah, that's our *raison d'être*: that's immortal literature."
> "Well, get rid of it, and replace it with more schlock."

The book-buying public has little idea how this mentality, combined with the supermarket bookstore, has culminated in the retail tail wagging the wholesale dog. When you walk into a bookstore, you notice how everything is categorized and shelved by category. Have you asked yourself what happens to books that don't fit into the established categories? They don't get published, that's what. Did you read my popular book, *Plato Not Prozac*? Where did you find it? Not in the philosophy section (it's too practical), and not in the philosophical counseling section (there's no such section yet—but we're working on it). You found it in self-help or self-improvement (which it is), or possibly in psychology (which it isn't). On that basis, I'd be lucky if it were published at all. But in my case, luck had nothing to do with it—I had a big-time media platform, on which the publishers were salivating to capitalize.

My colleague Barbara Held wasn't so lucky (except that luck has nothing to do with it). She wrote a brilliant little book on the fine art of kvetching,[3] and, as a certifiable Jewish American Princess, she's a real expert in this. Believe me! Here was a book that legitimized and refined the art of complaining. But she couldn't find a major publisher, because the agents all said the same thing:

> "There's no place to shelve your brilliant little book in Barnes and Noble. It's way too funny for the self-help section, and way too helpful for the humor section. Now, if only you had performed fellatio on a President, or married a famous black athlete and murdered him and been acquitted because of a sexist witness, you'd have made the news and we could just pile your book on the floor—category, shmategory. But as it stands there's no place to shelve it."

This is the tail wagging the dog. It is also Western literary culture in full decline, and globalization in full ascendancy. Certainly hundreds and possibly thousands of brilliant little books are not going to appear not because they are unpublishable, but uncategorizable. Thus globalization places the reins of creative culture in the hands of semiliterate stock-mammals, whose sole concern is "Where do I shelve this?" That spells the foreclosure of creativity, and with it, the end of culture. The globalized publishing industry suffers from a category problem, which is therefore also a philosophical problem. Their expectations are accordingly impossible: they require that every book will become both an immediate best-seller, and also a timeless classic. It's a compelling argument for playing computer-games instead of reading.

But the supermarket bookstore serves another vital purpose, aside from consigning creative culture to a literary Yellow Pages. This Procrustean Inn for books also houses overstuffed furniture, sells overdesigned coffee, and keeps overtime hours. In the post-postmodern urban and suburban worlds of secular fragmentation, where every man is an island, where most families are unextended, where many churches are empty, where all communities are ephemeral, where local culture means a shopping mall, the supermarket bookstore serves a vital function: it gives people a place to congregate, where they can come and go as they please, where they can roam about the stacks, where they can carry a pile of books to a comfortable chair and read any but buy none, where they can imbibe designer beverages and talk to their friends, or even field-test books on how to pick up chicks in bookstores. Moreover, there is no mandatory schedule, no admission fee, no costume required, and no dogma imparted.

But the supermarket bookstore does more than offer a richly passive environment for malingerers, free-loaders, and field-testers; it also takes an active stance, by scheduling cultural events. The range of events is quite impressive—from celebrity author signings to live music, from poetry readings to puppet shows. The range of constituencies addressed by these events is equally impressive: classics lovers, psycho-babblers, aficionados of fine cuisine, the gay and lesbian community, stockbrokers, environmental activists, recovering drug addicts, aspiring drug addicts, war heroes, peace activists, misogynists, misandrists, the politically correct, the politically incorrect, children's literati—you name it. The supermarket bookstore takes no political position on any event; it is perfectly egalitarian, and caters to the interests of any group willing to coalesce peacefully and spend time in the store.

In other words, the bookstore functions also as an erstwhile community center, hosting transient communities if not half-spontaneously formed groups, but doing so on a ruthlessly methodical basis. Each store mass produces its monthly broadsheet calendar of events, like a vaudevillian handbill. The only month when the calendar isn't jammed with events is December, when there's hardly room for people amidst the stacks of books. Bookstore patrons may not realize that the two functions—bookstore and community center—are administratively distinct. The person who schedules events, usually called a "community relations representative" on her business card or an "events manager" in parlance, operates autonomously from those who order and reorder stock. Her job is to run successful and popular—meaning well-attended and well-liked—events, and not to sell books directly. Needless to say, the more people who spend time in the store, and the more time they spend there, will be correlated with more book-buying, but the public relations aspect of the events is their primary purpose. A throng of attentive and admiring people, held spellbound by a charismatic reader or entertainer, is itself a kind of a meta-event to be observed and approved by passers-by on other missions in the superstore. It validates their individual presence and social existence too, making them feel they are *somewhere*, instead of nowhere.

Although the community relations manager has relative autonomy in the events she hosts—I say "she" because the overwhelming majority of them are intelligent young women—her potential dictatorial powers are practically reined in by the very community she serves. For one thing, events are informally divided into two broad categories: authorial (consisting of readings and signings), and non-authorial (consisting of other entertainment). It is the ratio of these categories in the ethos of a given neighborhood, more than anything else, that informs the manager's choice of events. For example, I moderate a monthly forum at a Barnes & Noble in Chelsea, a fairly Bohemian quarter of Manhattan. There are authors galore trying to get bookings in this store, and no end of publishers and publicists jockeying with each other to position their authors therein. One might wait months or even years to get one's "fifteen minutes of fame"; although Warhol would have modified his phraseology in this instance, for the event consumes more like ninety than fifteen minutes, while the quality of the celebrity is correspondingly diminished. For although an author is not usually humbled in a library, only irritated if it hasn't collected his book, he soon learns his place in the pecking-order of a bookstore super-market, which is beneath the faceless functional illiterate who bags books at the checkout counter, and beneath even the anonymous schleppers who trun-dle coffee and biscotti through the service entrance. Walking into a supermar-ket bookstore, announcing to the clerk at the information kiosk that you are an author arrived for an evening signing, and asking that the events manager therefore be paged, arouses about as much excitement as a cabin attendant reporting for work in a departure lounge, announcing to the ground-staff that she is ready to enter the jet-way, and asking that the flight supervisor be paged. This is a truly humbling experience.

The point is that authors, in certain localities, are a dime a dozen, whereas entertainers are not. When I walked into the Chelsea bookstore and pitched my Forum cold, it took the events manager less than thirty seconds to size me up and decide to give it a try. But she is awash in authors, and therefore constantly on the lookout for entertainment. When I tried the same cold pitch across the river, in the equivalent Barnes & Noble in Hoboken, I was just as quickly—and almost as politely—rebuffed. Hoboken makes two boasts of consequence: it claims (along with a dozen other places in America) to have held the very first baseball game, and it claims (without any competition whatsoever) to be the birthplace of Frank Sinatra. It also crams about one hundred and fifty bars and restaurants catering to yuppies, pseudo-yuppies, pre-yuppies, and post-yuppies into about ten square blocks; residents do not sleep well on weekends, but their gardens are well-fertilized. The upshot is that no author wants to go to Hoboken, even if it is just across the river from Chelsea. Thus the local Barnes & Noble has a surfeit of jugglers, clowns, and puppet-shows, but a dearth of authors, and no need (so its events manager surmised) of a Philosopher's Forum. The book-juggler was either just there or just coming; an idea-juggler sounded somehow shadowy, intangible or super-fluous.

The moral of this story is that some neighborhoods are "pre-philosophical," and supermarket bookstores will inevitably and nonprejudicially reflect local taste, or lack thereof, in their programming. Not every bank of the Seine was, or could be, the Left. Then again, given the preponderance of philosophical issues with which people grapple in everyday life, and the dearth of overt philosophical discourse and practical philosophical example in the general culture, a great many neighborhoods are potentially very philosophical indeed. Philosopher's forums are preponderating accordingly.

In consequence, any philosopher who seeks to moderate a Forum of this kind can follow a fairly well-beaten path to establishing one. First, you should assemble a folder containing the following four items:

1. Your business card.

2. An 8 x 10 inch glossy photo of you, professionally taken.

3. A covering letter, offering your services (e.g., "Your book-store hosts many important events, but you don't yet have a Philosopher's Forum, or café-philo, or call it what you will. I would be happy to moderate a monthly Philosopher's Forum in your bookstore. These events are very popular in New York, Los Angeles, Paris, London, and many other places; I'm sure they'd be as popular in <your community/town/city> too.... Let's at least give it a try, and see what happens.").

4. A press kit, which in this case consists of a bundle of newspaper articles illustrating how Philosopher's Forums in other cities and countries have met with great success and have generated positive press. If you are a member of the APPA, we will provide you with a press kit and our letter of recommendation. The press kit is probably the most important component of your folder.

Make several copies of this folder, at least as many as the number of bookstores you intend to approach. Then walk into one of the bookstores on your list, and ask to speak to the community relations representative, or events manager. The best time is early to mid-afternoon; they don't usually work mornings and are busy with events in the evenings. You can also phone ahead to ascertain her name and schedule, which is a good idea, but you don't usually need to make an appointment ahead of time, which is too formal for this kind of thing. This is a public relations exercise, not a business deal. The events manager will respond when paged, and may not even, in the first instance, invite you into her office. She expects you to make a thirty-second pitch, and may just stand there while you do it. You, in turn, should be prepared to summarize what you are offering in those thirty seconds. What exactly you say is less important than how you say it. You should be articulate and concise, exude confidence and energy, remain sincere yet uncommitted. You are not selling a product; you are offering a service. She is not doing you a favor by entertaining your pitch; you are doing her a favor by pitching to her. If she doesn't want your service, some other bookstore will. This should not make you arrogant, only benevolently indifferent.

If she says "Yes, let's try it" then and there, you'll set a date. Events are usually booked two or three months in advance. Give her your folder, because she'll use it for promotional purposes. If she says "Maybe," then give her your folder and suggest she read the press. If she says "No, thanks," then she has her reasons. You can ask what they are. You can also ask her to recommend a bookstore that might be more receptive to your proposed event.

When you actually succeed in getting a date, you will enter the real phase of practice: actually doing the thing you have proposed. You can never predict what kind of group you'll encounter on a given night, or what kind of issues it will want to pursue. That makes moderation very interesting and also somewhat risky for the group facilitator, and is thus quite different from teaching a philosophy course, in which one prepares the subject matter in advance and also learns, through teaching, what kinds of questions tend to be asked. One can outline only the form of a Forum, but cannot control its substance in the same way. One can, however, guide the group in certain directions, or down certain avenues, but one is only orchestrating an impromptu score, not composing the music. It's like conducting a jam session, if that makes any sense.

Even so, there are identifiable types of persons who attend these events, and after a while one begins to recognize them. For example, there are regulars who will attend every month—one might be tempted to say "religiously"—and who will be amenable to pursuing almost any issue philosophically. These form the nucleus of the Forum, and you are fortunate if you can attract such a group. They are not necessarily or usually philosophers, of course: some are graduate students; others engineers, physicians, judges, teachers, authors, and thoughtful persons from all walks of life. There are also some who attend for the first time, and who expect a philosophy lecture: such is their conditioning. They sometimes become flustered when they discover that they will be asked to think and speak for themselves, but after a while some grow more accustomed to accepting this responsibility as part of human capacity, if outside social norms. Many will attend who do think and speak for themselves, but as representatives if not proselytizers of a given doctrine or dogma. You will immediately recognize the confirmed nihilist, or the zealous religionist, as they launch into their pre-programmed monologues:

"This meeting is pointless; it will accomplish nothing; the universe is indifferent to man's pathetic yearnings and gropings after nonexistent truths."

"Only by accepting our Lord and Savior Jesus Christ into your hearts can you find real purpose in your life, and love your fellow man, and solve all the world's problems."

The confirmed nihilist usually provokes a response from the New Age psycho-babbler; the zealous religionist, from a neo-Marxist revolutionary:

"Your mind and heart are closed to the metaphysical spirit that animates the cosmos; you need to burn incense, worship crystals, hang wind-chimes and sing along with the whales in order to empower your spiritual wholeness."

"Christianity is a tool of capitalist oppression, which foments conflict and injustice and maintains privileges for an elite based on discrimination by class, race, and gender."

Such pronouncements tend to get chewed up, spat out, and bypassed in favor of discussions about controlling guns, legalizing marijuana, reforming education, and exploring the meaning of "the Good." More than any other of the myriad topics I have seen raised in these Forums is the recurring fundamental question of ethics: "What is Good?" People are often willing to examine questions of justice, of liberty, of tolerance, of duty, of government, of science, and of God, but are always willing to tackle the ethical question above all. The most conspicuous lesson I have learned from my years of facilitating Philosopher's Forums consists of this empirical corroboration of a point I have long pondered in theory: that the most urgent and important question for secular philosophy is an articulation of the good in a way that eschews theological adduction, avoids scientific reduction, evades socioeconomic obfuscation, avoids psychological oversimplification, and transcends political corruption alike, yet which also provides moral guidance. That no philosopher has yet been equal to this task fails to discourage ordinary people from its pursuit. I find this uplifting and heartening. Perhaps the moral journey is only a pursuit. That the hound pursues the fox is indirect evidence that the fox exists; would that the good could be sniffed out and cornered by a pack of reasoning, experienced beings similarly unleashed. That, at least, is the metaphysical spirit which animates my Forums: "Tally ho!"

This characterization of philosophy with groups is thus far reminiscent, by all accounts, of the ancient Hellenic world, and to that extent it squares with public perception of what philosophy used to be about. In reading about Socrates, we reap the benefit of Plato as dramatist par excellence, but also the detriment of the playwright's ineluctable distortions. There is a good chance that many if not most of Socrates' dialogical encounters in the agora were as mundane as many if not most of ours in the supermarket bookstore. Even so, we contemporary facilitators are capable of being gadflies, and of making the odd utterance that scandalizes if not galvanizes people's thoughts. That is undoubtedly why many of them attend. There is something about doing philosophy in public that smacks of intrigue, taboo, and perhaps even danger. It is not inconceivable that some of our most ardent supporters secretly hope to see us imbibe hemlock one day, which would no doubt authenticate their experience and tabloidize ours. But regardless of whether liquid refreshments are dispensed from a coffee bar, an open bar, or a compulsory bar, the return of philosophers to the marketplace stimulates the kind of enthusiasm and awe reserved for poets and prophets.

Two further characterizations of philosophers' forums need be made. One is reasonably favorable; the other, unreasonably favorable. The contemporary resurgence of philosophy in this form is reminiscent of the salons of classical and romantic European capitals. The salon itself is a descendant of the renaissance and baroque patronization of artists by aristocrats. Monarchs and their peers sought to attract the greatest architects, painters, sculptors, composers, and occasionally even thinkers to their courts. They controlled the money and therefore the culture, and probably competed intensely with one another to lure the cream of the crop into their keeps. Undoubtedly their own vanities were inflamed, and their statuses aggrandized, by their commissioning of great works and their command of great artists' time. Many such patrons likely knew nothing whatsoever about the art they patronized—and many of them probably didn't even know what they liked—but they sought to enhance their reputations by association with ostensibly important artists. The gradual emergence of the intelligentsia from the Reformation, mercantilism, the industrial revolution, and the growth of the middle classes eventually relieved monarchs of the burden of pretending to know anything about art, and passed it on to the newly affluent bourgeoisie, who knew just as little but appreciated just enough to emulate the behavior of the ruling classes. Members of so-called "high society" could not afford to build and maintain palaces, replete with courtly cultural accoutrements, but they could afford to host weekly salons in their relatively spacious and well-appointed town houses. Instead of "queen for a day," they played "patron for an hour."

These salons were dedicated largely to recitals of music and readings of literature, and those attending merely to be seen to attend could conceal themselves behind a facade of silent appreciation, or cigar smoke, or feigned boredom. Women, no doubt, used such occasions as excuses to socialize and display their latest fashions. A memorable scene in Davis Lean's movie of *Dr. Zhivago* captures this ambience perfectly. An assembly of well-dressed "art-lovers" takes in a piano recital in a Moscow salon. They overflow the music room itself, and strew themselves on a grand staircase, where one man contentedly dozes. His wife digs him in the ribs and chides "Boris, wake up! This is genius!" "Really? I thought it was Rachmaninoff." The private salon still exists, of course, but no one any longer writes it into novels or builds it into screenplays.

The triumph of economics over politics is apparent in that corporations now control the resources that formerly belonged to monarchs. Corporations are the new grand patrons of the arts, but, unlike their forebears, they also like to turn a profit on their endeavors. Barnes & Noble has effected the corporate synthesis of the grand court and the European salon, by the expedient of hosting semiprivate events in semipublic places. The artists are patronized in a thoroughly neo-Warholian sense: everyone sooner or later enjoys not fifteen minutes of fame, but ninety minutes of celebrity. Most authors wait a very long time to get their books into print, and vie with all the others for those brief ninety minutes, during which their poster is featured, their book is displayed, and they command the attention of the gathered throng.[4] No sooner has their hour and a half of glory faded than their poster is summarily removed from sight, their books vanish from display, and the security staff fails to recognize them on their way out of the store. This is truly revolving-door patronage, but it's better than none. Ironically, I was featured monthly in Barnes & Noble for two and a half years prior to the publication of *Plato Not Prozac*, precisely because I *didn't* have a book to sell. That's philosophical practice for you; it's also show-biz.

The second and less salutary characterization of the philosopher's café is that of "coffeehouse philosophy," which is definitely pejorative in professional contexts. When used as an adjectival modifier, "coffeehouse" connotes an amateurish kind of hustle. Think, for example, of so-called "coffeehouse chess openings": these are cleverly unorthodox but professionally unplayable lines that strand the unwary opponent in strange terrain, wherein the strangeness tends to obscure one's best move. Unrated coffeehouse players can ambush and even defeat rated tournament players by this expedient, just as hyenas can pull down a wounded lion. But clever amateurs cannot defeat wary professionals of the higher ranks, because their traps are sprung by sufficient foresight, and the weaknesses of their unorthodox positions are exploited by superior expertise. In its tritest manifestation, informal group facilitation becomes coffeehouse philosophy in just this sense. And its tritest manifestation is precisely that which misrepresents this small slice of philosophical practice as entire pie.

Informal group facilitation is understood to be part of philosophical practice, but has not been generally (mis)construed as the whole—except notably in France. French culture, as we have mentioned, is the quintessential café culture, and so this form of philosophical practice developed there as in no other country; that is to say, it virtually dominates the landscape. Facilitations range from dialogical moderation to political activism. Interestingly, Sautet himself began to offer a kind of philosophical counseling to some of his coffeehouse clients, in the form of guided readings of texts (i.e., bibliotherapy). A few other French practitioners have lately begun to realize that philosophical counseling and consulting span the broadest part of the professional spectrum, and that the activity taken most seriously in France (coffeehouse philosophy) is taken least seriously everywhere else. While this observation might only serve to persuade the French that the *café-philo* is the therefore most authentic manifestation of philosophical practice, resulting in a doubling or tripling of the number of Gallic coffeehouse philosophers, it also seems possible that counseling and consulting will take root as well. The French are a talkative bunch, and thus should regard philosophical counseling as yet another way of exercising their mouths, if not their minds. Meanwhile, one or two of Sautet's *proteges* have endeavored to market the philosopher's café to Americans as though it were, or should be, the preeminent form of practice here as well, but Americans on the whole have more pressing claims on their time. If one philosopher's forum per month is sufficient for New Yorkers (which it is), then One-A-Day is likely to remain the province of vitamins, not philosophical circuses, in mainstream America.

While informal facilitations render an interesting and important public service, which combines expression, education, and entertainment, there are more formal philosophical methods that can be applied to groups. In the next section, we consider perhaps the most elegant—if not the most important—one.

6.3. NELSONIAN SOCRATIC DIALOGUE

We have reviewed a couple of reliable methodologies applicable to certain kinds of cases in philosophical client counseling; e.g., Pierre Grimes' philosophical midwifery, and my PEACE process. Nelsonian Socratic dialogue is a reliable methodology applicable to certain kinds of philosophical questions, best answered through group-effort. This disclosure will already astonish some readers, whose customary image of the philosopher is that of a solitary beast of noetic prey, a thought-hunter stalking savannahs of imagination and prowling thickets of ideation, relentlessly tracking quarry such as truth, beauty, and justice. The notion of doing philosophy in groups, aside from professors lecturing in classrooms, is alien to many if not most philosophers and their students. Even the models of yore, from Socrates to the Forest Sages to the Confucians, featured philosophical "gurus" ministering in one way or another to their respective flocks of disciples. This model has been replicated in the universities, only more polygamously, as departments entire minister to their respective flocks of graduate students. The culminating feature of graduate studies reverts to a monogamous relation between thesis supervisor and degree candidate. Beyond that, the recognized peaks in the range of academic achievement, namely, the publication of scholarly articles and books, almost always represent individual efforts in the philosophical world. Since experimental scientists necessarily work in groups, with senior professors employing research assistants and laboratory technicians, half a dozen names and more are routinely attached to published lab reports. But theoretical philosophers tend to work alone, or at least tend to take sole credit for their publications. Horror stories abound about well-known philosophers who used PhD students as research assistants, burning the students out while producing *magni opi* to their personal credit. This only reinforces the notion of the philosopher as a soloist.

However, if we examine more closely the structure of Plato's dialogues, and consider the efficacy of the elenchic method employed ubiquitously by Socrates, we gain a preliminary insight into the value of undertaking certain kinds of philosophical inquiry plurally instead of individually. Suppose we wish to inquire "What is justice?"; a perennially important question, among many others, to be sure. A theoretical philosopher's response to this question will assume one of three forms: either he will produce his own book-length answer (as did Plato, Augustine, Hobbes, Rousseau, Marx, Rawls, and many others), or he will produce a book-length critique of someone else's answer (as did many others too numerous to name), or he will edit a volume of condensed answers and/or condensed critiques. The first of these forms is usually a *magnum opus*, which founds a movement or school of thought whose influence may persist for centuries.[5] The second form is usually an exercise in academic journeymanism, which identifies the author as a defender or an offender of a particular philosophical faith. The third form is usually a textbook, which contributes to a burgeoning industry and which, if well-conceived and well-timed, may be utilized by many teachers and students of philosophy. While all the foregoing conduce to the organization of theoretical philosophical activity, and often display scholarship, none conduces overtly to the practice of philosophy with groups, as intended herein. Socrates was a compelling group facilitator partly because he engaged the rationality of participants by appealing to their ordinary experiences, and thus helped them philosophize without referring to a corpus of published works and without dropping names of other philosophers.

When Socrates entertained the question "What is Justice?"[6] he presumed correctly that most members of the group had already some experience of it, or at least of its opposite, injustice, about which they were prepared to advance some tentative, habitual, or provisional conception. Socrates evidently had a great talent for implementing the elenchic method, by which he teased out broader or deeper implications of a given universal, until landing the conceiver in a full contradiction. By this means he revealed to people that their conceptions of universals were flawed, and thus that they did not understand such things nearly as clearly as they had hitherto supposed. Socrates himself never purported to know what justice was, but proved well able to show that any definition of it carelessly advanced was susceptible to refutation in pretty short order.

Plato's epistemology is fairly clearly stated in the *Meno* and the *Thaetetus*; his ontology, in the *Republic*. A supreme rationalist, he believed in the innateness of knowledge and the existence of universals as Ideas or Forms. Education was meant to awaken latent understanding in the student, and not solely or necessarily to impart information. At the same time, Plato insisted that the awakeners themselves be awake: hence his philosopher-kingdom. Could he but witness the corruption of the self-same doctrine in twentieth-century western civilization's bankrupt philosophy of education, descended via Rousseau applied and Dewey misapplied, he would cry that education has become a vehicle for instilling misunderstanding in the student, because too many educators are somnambulists, wandering incognizantly through miasmas of execrable ideologies that further obfuscate, not clarify, opinions.

So Socrates and Plato play "bad cop/good cop" to their groups of students, who are arrested by their healthy appetites for knowledge. Socrates, through relentless elenchic interrogation, shows them that their opinions are flawed with misunderstandings; Plato, through compelling distinction between appearance and reality, and appeal to pure universal Forms, exhorts them to emerge from the cave and, by enlisting understanding, apprehend the illuminated Forms instead of their shadowy representations. But while Socrates' refutations are real enough, Plato's cave is allegorical. How, then, are we to make the transition from darkness to light? Who will the awakened educators be? How can we be sure that they are not somnambulating too?

Enter Leonard Nelson, twenty-four hundred years later, to articulate a theory of "how," which has been refined and applied with considerable success by German, Dutch, and lately American philosophical practitioners.[7] Nelson's method allows one to arrive at an understanding, not of what something *isn't*, but of what it *is*. The method is tolerably simple, and joins Plato's uncompromising rationalism to the most ruthless scientific empiricism—or pragmaticism—producing a wonderful resultant: the articulation of a universal from a small set of particulars. Nelson asserts, like Plato, that you have formed some fuzzy opinion about justice, based on your experiences in the shadowy cave—the mundane human world. He also asserts, like Plato, that you can be led to an apprehension of the Pure Form of Justice, which resides within the recesses of your unawakened understanding (anamnesis). But on Hume's view—to pick one very hard-boiled empiricist—your present idea of justice is copied squarely from your impression of it, which you have formed from perceptions gathered from encounters in extramental reality. Nelson's method reconciles these two apparently irreconcilable views.

For everything idealized, there is by definition but one universal, while there are arbitrarily many particulars. The Pure Form of a (perfect) sphere is easily apprehended: it is described in Cartesian coordinates by the equation $x^2 + y^2 + z^2 = r^2$. By contrast, any representation of a sphere that we discover or construct is bound to admit of imperfections. The more perfect, the more closely it approximates the mathematical representation of the pure form; the less perfect, the less closely. The Earth, like all astronomical bodies, is a rather poor approximation. An oblate spheroid, it has not only flattened poles but also peaks, valleys, and continuously rippling surfaces. Apples and oranges (for once) are comparable in this wise. A beach ball (or any inflatable spheroid) is not much better; it has seams, stitches, and an inevitable nipple or valve. A steel ball-bearing, manufactured to any tolerance whatsoever, looks more perfect to the naked eye but is just as imperfect under suitable magnification: it is a veritable moonscape of microscopic pits, ruts, and scars. Every sphere we experience extramentally is imperfect, yet each can be seen to deviate in quantifiable ways from the pure form of a perfect sphere. Nor does one require much experience with imperfect spheres to awaken one's mathematical understanding of their pure form.

What is obviously true of mathematical ideals (e.g., Platonic solids, conic sections, cycloid curves) is less obviously true of social ideals (e.g., goodness, justice, liberty). That is ostensibly because mathematics is axiomatizable, whereas ethics is apparently not. Perhaps Plato was correct in suggesting that one should study mathematics for ten years before broaching ethics at all. Much of what passes for education in the Western world has "preempted" this problem by eliminating both mathematics and ethics from the curriculum; the bathetic philosophy of education that sanctions this, along with its political philosophical counterparts manifest as social policies, are partly why literate culture is in such precipitous decline.

Nelson suggests that, if you have had a particular experience of justice, then you could not possibly know it was a representation of a universal unless you also had some implicit notion of your innate knowledge of that universal. Nelsonian Socratic dialogue aims to explicitize the implicit. The facilitator of a dialogue elicits from a group of participants their particular experiences of the sought-after universal, which are then used as vehicles for exploring opinions of the universal itself, and for probing the shadows of misunderstanding until an articulation of the form is recognized and illuminated by understanding itself. The facilitator is a trained and skilled philosophical catalyst, who adds nothing to the dialogue itself but who guides its participants through various reactive stages, until the end-product—a clear definition of the universal in question—crystallizes out. Empirically, the method works. Whether it works because Plato and Nelson were correct, or works for some other (underdetermined) reasons, remains to be seen.

Moreover, there are second-order considerations too. If Plato and Nelson were correct, then there is also a pure form of a Nelsonian Socratic dialogue, which all actual dialogues merely approximate, for better or worse. On this hypothesis, what makes them better or worse is the ability of the facilitator to refine his understanding of the method (which he knows in advance of the dialogue), and to weave into its fabric the experiences and ratiocinations of the participants (which he cannot know in advance of the dialogue). So while the substance of the dialogue depends entirely on the participants and not at all on the facilitator, its form depends entirely on the facilitator and not at all on the participants.

I cannot explicitly characterize the pure form of a Nelsonian Socratic dialogue, but I can tell you that it is done differently in different countries. The Germans, who originated it, practice it independently of both theoretical philosophy and philosophical counseling. It is an exercise undertaken unhurriedly, often in conjunction with sojourns in Black Forest resorts or other such places. People hike in the mornings and dialogue in the afternoons. *Mens sana in corpore sano*. A dialogue thus conducted may protract itself for one or two weeks. Moreover, the German version to which I have been mildly exposed is somewhat rule-bound; that is, there are rule-books consisting of fifty or more rules for the conduct of a dialogue, which participants are expected to learn beforehand, and which can take three or more days to ease into practice. The facilitator, whatever else he is, then becomes a kind of procedural adjudicator, who must decide whether or not rules are being properly followed. Naturally, different "schools" have evolved different rules, so there is also plenty of scope for empirical development as well as theoretical debate about the efficacies of various rule-books. At best, the German version of Socratic dialogue could be a kind of Glass Bead Game; at worst, a hopelessly tedious exercise in rule-following.

The Dutch took a different and—typically—much more practical turn. To begin with, they boiled the rules down to a manageable few, which can be learned in minutes instead of hours. They also pared the duration of the dialogue down to days instead of weeks; and, for the corporate world, to hours instead of days. Using the Dutch method, one can facilitate a "complete" dialogue with a private group in two to three days or, at a "forced march" with a corporate team, in a few hours. The word "complete" is quoted in the foregoing sentence because, in some ways, even if the question of a dialogue is satisfactorily answered by the group, ancillary but important issues are inevitably raised that cannot be addressed in the allotted time. Hence a dialogue is terminated, but doesn't really end. Corporate employees are rarely given more than a few hours to indulge their minds on company time, and their dialogues need therefore to be drastically streamlined, goal-oriented, and schedule-driven. This much (or this little!) the Dutch have managed to accomplish, while retaining the essential elements of the dialogue itself. Similarly, most dialogues that I facilitate are completed in two allotted days; I have managed, with an exceptionally good group, to complete one in four hours. I have often jested that if Socratic dialogue is to catch on in Manhattan, we will need to reduce it even further, down to two hours, or preferably a coffee-break. That may prove impossible without taking liberties or short-cuts. It's like sniffing a cork instead of drinking the wine.

And what exactly is the process? In the Dutch method, it is precisely described by the following stages. First, the group chooses its question. Most simply, but not necessarily, this question takes the form "What is X?" where X is a universal (e.g., Justice, Liberty, Integrity, Hope). Second, each member of the group offers an example, from his or her own concrete experience, which purports to embody a particular and first-person instantiation of the sought-after universal. Suppose the question is "What is Integrity?" Each member must have some experience of this. Third, the group selects one example from among the offerings, which it will explore in considerable detail and use as a vehicle for formulating a definition of the universal in question. Fourth, by questioning the exemplar (i.e., the giver of the example), the group telescopes the selected example into a coherent narrative, consisting usually of several dozen chronologically enumerated steps. Fifth, the group decides where, in the enumerated example, the sought-after universal occurs—literally at which step or steps, or between or among which steps, it is located (e.g., "Where, in this example, is Integrity?"). Sixth, the group formulates a definition of precisely what, in the specified location(s) in the selected example, this universal consists (e.g., "What, in this example, is Integrity?"). Seventh, the group returns to the other examples offered earlier but not thoroughly explored, and decides whether this formulation applies to them as well. If not, it modifies the formulation so as to embrace all instantiations offered. Eighth, the group may offer hypothetical examples to test the robustness of its formulation. If the formulation embraces both actual and hypothetical instantiations of the universal, then it indeed captures the essence of that universal, in which case the question of the dialogue is successfully answered. Ninth, the group may, if it has time, pursue other relevant issues that arose during earlier phases of the dialogue. So much for the "anatomy" of the Socratic dialogue.

The "morphology" of the dialogue resembles that of an hourglass: the starting question is very broad; the offered examples narrow the dialogue; the selected example narrows it further; the location of the universal in the selected example nears the waist of the hourglass; the definition of the universal in that example passes the waist of the hourglass; the application of the definition to the other examples further broadens the dialogue; the introduction of hypothetical counter-examples approaches the original breadth, but this time at the other end of the hourglass. The passage is one not only of time, but more importantly of understanding. At the most general top end of the glass, no one could say what the universal meant; at the most general bottom end, everyone can say what it means—and moreover understand what they say.

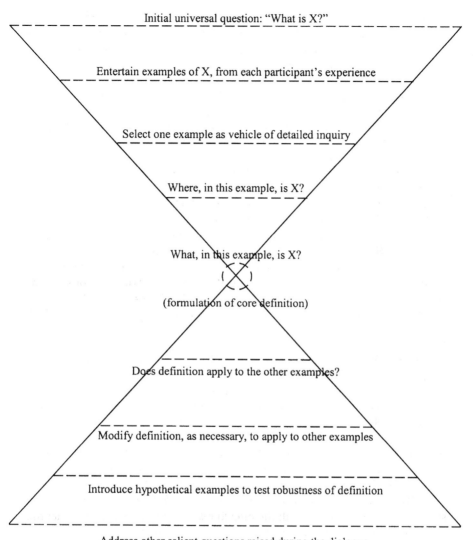

Initial universal question: "What is X?"

Entertain examples of X, from each participant's experience

Select one example as vehicle of detailed inquiry

Where, in this example, is X?

What, in this example, is X?

(X)

(formulation of core definition)

Does definition apply to the other examples?

Modify definition, as necessary, to apply to other examples

Introduce hypothetical examples to test robustness of definition

Address other salient questions raised during the dialogue.

FIGURE 6.1 Schematic of Nelsonian Socratic Dialogue.

So much for "anatomy" and "morphology"; beyond these, it is the "physi-ology" of the Socratic dialogue that potentiates its reliability of method. To articulate a definition of a universal is to formulate a kind of truth. We can analogize this process with deriving a result in deductive logic. Each step of a proof must be justifiable by a truth-preserving rule of inference in order that the proof be valid. Although a Socratic dialogue is obviously ampliative—not deductive—in its contentual argumentation, it is neither inductive nor speculative. As such, it allows the following analogy to be made: at each step of the dialogue, the group must attain complete consensus before proceeding to the next step. In practice, this means that all conceivable doubts must be raised and, through dialogue, dispelled. A failure to attain consensus implies that some doubt remains unresolved, and to proceed to the next phase on that basis is to potentiate a recrudescence of that doubt, usually in a worse manifestation, in some subsequent phase. In other words, just as an unjustifiable inference will, if undetected, not only invalidate a deductive argument but also potentiate other unjustifiable inferences, so will a lack of consensus at each step not only invalidate a Socratic dialogue (by making it impossible to capture the true essence of the universal in question) but also potentiate, if not guarantee, further lack of consensus at other steps. The Socratic dialogue is not a competition, in which some win and others lose; either the group attains consensus at a given stage, in which case everyone wins, or it fails to do so, in which case everyone loses. The explicit "prize," at each stage, is nothing but the privilege of moving on to the next stage, with a Cartesian certitude attained by eliminating doubt. The implicit "prize," at each stage, is the privilege of practicing certain virtues, which in this kind of setting are exercised independently of the universal question or the particular examples.[8]

I almost digress to point out that this model of decision-making—that is, consensuality—is almost unknown in mainstream American culture, and is probably unknown in a great many other cultures too. We are perhaps overfamiliar with the authoritarian model, in which decisions are ordained; the hierarchical model, in which decisions are handed down or delegated; the flat hierarchical model, in which decisions move sideways, like crabs, but have no obligatory force; the academic committee, in which idiosyncrasy, irrelevancy, chaos, and occasionally psychosis drive the decision-making process; the ballot-box, in which qualitative decisions are avoided by quantitative means; and the adversarial model, in which, theoretically, truth emerges via contending theses, but in which, practically, a sophomoric debate between two opposed extremists reveals nothing but their respective distortions. The latter model is favored by justice systems and prime-time television; and in consequence they produce, respectively and often above all, abundant injustice and overabundant controversy. By contrast, the consensus attained in a group, via Socratic dialogue, emerges from initial descensus, is a hard-won and valuable achievement, and—as alluded to in the foregoing footnote on Dries Boele's (1998) paper—promotes all kinds of virtues as opposed to vices.

Foremost among these is hearing and understanding, as opposed to merely listening and responding to, someone else's thoughts. In an ordinary conversation, people do not normally endeavor to place themselves in the mind of another speaker; rather, they exhibit (for the usual evolutionary psychological reasons) a nöocentricity which mandates that they filter out or ignore most of what the other is saying, and respond only to those utterances that bear personal significance for them, or that suggest or are cognate with something personally significant, and moreover that they respond chiefly to utterances with which they can take issue, in whole or in part.[9] Hence the word most often used to describe such interaction is "discussion," whose etymology (as Jos Kessels points out)[10] is shared with that of "concussion" and "percussion." Thus, descensus is provoked by mere selective listening. In contrast, consensus is attained through nonselective hearing. Your biological being does not end with your skin, which rather than an inert sack that contains your body (a "living body-bag") is actually a responsive organ and semipermeable membrane interfacing with your environment, through which are mediated all kinds of physical and chemical transactions. In essence, it is because you have a skin that you cannot demarcate precisely between your body and your extrasomatic environment. Similarly, your cultural being does not end in your mind—and Descartes completely and culpably neglected social ontology with his perversely solipsistic *cogito*. It is equally well true that "Others think of me, therefore I am." When you are interviewed for a job, it is others' thoughts of you, not your own, that determine your social existence. Naturally, their thoughts about you are conditioned by their impressions of you, which in turn are conditioned by your presentation of yourself, which in turn is conditioned by your thoughts about yourself. So while it is true that what others think of you, i.e., your social existence, is conditioned by what you think of yourself, it is conversely true that what you think of yourself is conditioned by what others think of you. As predominantly social creatures by nature—that is, creatures who sustain primary interests in relationships between beings rather than relations between ideas—human females are particularly susceptible to concerns about what others think of them, to the extent that even Rousseau (a supposed champion of egalitarianism) observed that female children could be more readily controlled in this way.[11] Thus, the mind is also a responsive and semipermeable entity, capable of both absorbing and radiating thoughts. A mind is "closed" or "opened" by the assent of its proprietor. A closed mind understands little; an open mind, much. Socratic dialogue obliges one to practice open-mindedness and hence understanding; it obliges one not merely to listen to others, but also to hear them; not merely to filter their utterances through one's nöocentric conceptions, but to conceive of their conceptions too. Thus, the meaning of consensus is neither "let's agree to disagree" nor "let's agree so we can adjourn for lunch," nor "let's agree with the majority"; it is "let's establish the ground of our common understanding."

If you are attempting to articulate a definition of a universal, and you do so with recourse only to your experiences and your conceptions, you are attempting to locate the center of a circle from a single point: literally, from your own point of view. The center might lie in any direction, and at any distance away. Theoretical philosophers think long and hard about universals in this way, in monological isolation, and sometimes they end up very wide of the mark. Introduce another point of view, and you begin to gain a perspective on the circumference of conceivable views, and therefore also a fix on the location and distance of the center. Introduce a third point of view, and you can triangulate that perspective. Empirically, by following Nelson's method, we find the metaphorical center most effectively when five to ten points of view are introduced.

This method, if followed correctly, assures that ordinary but thoughtful people can arrive at profounder understandings of universals than can individual philosophers ratiocinating in isolation. I gave an example of this in *Plato Not Prozac*, recounting a dialogue in which the question "What is Hope?" was answered more fully by the lay group than by either Hobbes or Schopenhauer, who had advanced independent definitions. Thus, Nelsonian Socratic dialogue lends empirical credence to Plato's epistemology. With a philosophical practitioner as midwife, ordinary people can articulate universal truths by consensual means. Moreover, they cannot find such truths by scouring the philosophical literature, in which they will accumulate ineluctably disjointed, often contradictory, and perforce misguided conceptions. They will become theoretical philosophers, knowing what everyone else asserted about a given thing, but possibly understanding little about the thing themselves. I have elsewhere employed the analogy of theoretical bread-baking to describe this state of affairs:[12]

> Imagine an academy of theoretical bread-bakers. Its inhabitants spend their time speculating about every kind of bread, but baking none. They argue over shapes of bread, varieties of bread, recipes for bread, meanings of bread, methods of baking, slicing and bagging bread; and they argue over other foods that can be spread on bread or sandwiched by it. Most of all, they re-deliberate the deliberations of famous bakers past. Novices are told that by deliberating for a dozen years (or a baker's dozen years), they can become expert theoretical bakers themselves. Students who recognize bread as a fundamental and ubiquitous staple of human consumption eagerly pursue these studies, and graduate as expert theoretical bread-bakers. Few have ever tasted bread, and most are incognizant that bread is meant to be eaten. They also find it difficult to gain employment: Most consumers eat fast food and junk food, and will not support sizeable theoretical bakeries.... Eventually a few practically minded graduates of theoretical bread-baking academies reason: "We have such extensive knowledge of bread, perhaps we ought to bake a few loaves." "Heresy!", cry the theoreticians, "Theoretical bread-baking bakes no bread."

Perhaps the outstanding feature of Nelsonian Socratic dialogue is not that it captures elusive universals or inculcates virtues among its participants; rather, that it furnishes ordinary people with the experience of being philosophers for a weekend: philosophers not in the theoretical sense as deplored by Schopenhauer, but in the practical one advocated here. We don't just talk about bread; we bake it and eat it. And this is what will draw people, at least in the United States, to participate in Socratic dialogues. Tell them they can discover the meaning of liberty or justice over a single weekend, and they won't come. Tell them they can practice virtues of patience, tolerance, and attentiveness, and they won't come. Tell them Socratic dialogue is good for them, and they'll make a special effort not to come. But tell them they can be real philosophical warriors for a weekend, and they'll come in droves. As with most things in America, Socratic dialogue needs to be packaged attractively and marketed effectively in order to catch on. This was true of Coca-Cola and NFL football, and will not be false of Socratic dialogue.

Of all its target participants, whether lay or professional groups doing full dialogues, or organizational groups doing short ones, perhaps the most important target group for Socratic dialogue is completely neglected at this stage. I refer to college and university students. I have been a beneficiary of both as good a liberal arts education, and as good a science education, as any college or university student could wish for. Later, as a faculty member, I had the further privilege of teaching in one of the finest undergraduate programs ever conceived or implemented.[13] Yet in retrospect, those programs were all deficient in one important way: they were like a potentially delicious broth needing only a pinch of salt to actualize its delicacy, but wanting the pinch remaining only ordinary. That pinch of salt is a Socratic dialogue. It now seems absurd to me—well-nigh inconceivable—that a college or university education, especially in the liberal arts but across the board as well, could be considered complete in the absence of this experience. Every student, who labors for four years to achieve a "higher" education mostly by enduring lectures, and by reading and reflecting either in isolation or in unguided study groups, and whose active participation is limited to the odd classroom sound-byte, the inevitable essay, or the professor's office-hour, would find a weekend Socratic dialogue the high-point of his or her four-year undergraduate degree. In fact, participation in at least one full Socratic dialogue should be mandatory for every undergraduate. During one weekend in four years, the student would gain an experience of being a philosopher, of practicing virtues, of thinking for himself, of participating in a formal and constructive group dynamic, of striving for consensus, of discovering a universal from a set of particulars, and of understanding the interplay between experience and reason. *This* is an education in the best sense, namely, that which furthers phronesis. The rest is only learning, in which mere knowledge richly embroidered with the vanities of the knowers, or worse, egregious ideologies larded with personal foibles disguised as political causes, degenerate into badly processed, half-corrupted data.

The implementation of Socratic dialogue across college and university curricula will represent a high-water mark of the current Renaissance in philosophical practice, whose inception we are witnessing, and whose development we are now elaborating in this very book. The facilitation of several Socratic dialogues per year in each of hundreds if not thousands of American institutions of higher education will require a like number of trained facilitators. The Dutch had the perspicacity to import Nelsonian Socratic dialogue from Germany, and implement it in Holland, where transplanted and adapted to Dutch society it flourishes like variegated tulips in the fields. We Americans have similarly imported it from Holland, and are implementing it in our society. As it takes root here, the demand for facilitators will multiply accordingly. Ultimately, hundreds if not thousands of facilitators will be required on a regular basis. This will present tremendous opportunities for philosophical practitioners, whose arduous educations in theoretical philosophy need neither condemn them to the vicissitudes of a shrinking and politicized academic job-market nor constrain them to the servitude of permanent part-time adjuncting.

Moreover, many specialized groups of professionals—be they in education, health care, justice, administration, among other sectors—can benefit greatly from abbreviated Socratic dialogues, pursuing questions germane to their special interests.

When Socratic dialogue will have proliferated to a reasonable extent, there will be afforded a vista for an interesting kind of philosophical anthropology. One already finds consistency among answers to the same question by different groups using different examples, at least within a similar ethos. Of course, a universal definition should be independent of particular instantiations, but one is certainly entitled to ask whether a putative universal merely appears universal in the context of a given culture or subculture, or whether human beings across the cultural spectrum will arrive at similar definitions. This is a question which needs to answered empirically.

In sum, although the Socratic dialogue is an activity presently almost unknown in America, it should become as well-known as Socrates himself, and constitute one of the cornerstones of philosophical practice.

6.4. PHILOSOPHY WITH OTHER GROUPS

We have thus far focused on informal and formal facilitation of groups drawn together for the express purpose of philosophical practice. It is also worthwhile mentioning that philosophy can be introduced and practiced with groups constituted for other or larger purposes, to which end we will suggest, in Chapter 13, examples of ways in which philosophy can be practiced with senior citizens, with junior citizens, and with incarcerated citizens, among others. All this goes to show that philosophical practitioners can do much more with groups than lecture them to sleep in a classroom.

If you are wondering why I have not addressed "philosophy with groupies," as this chapter-title advertised, it is because philosophy is not really what one does with groupies, or with groups of them. Although I have attained a station in which I can resist groupies (or groups of them), I simply couldn't resist employing the turn of phrase.

NOTES

1. That is perhaps why philosophers from Seneca to Kierkegaard loathed crowds. E.g., L. Seneca, *Letters from a Stoic*, trans. R. Campbell (Harmondsworth: Penguin Books, 1969), Letter 17: "You ask me to say what you should consider it particularly important to avoid. My answer is this: a mass crowd." Also L. Seneca, *Moral Essays*, trans. J. Basore (London: William Heinemann, 1928), Vol. 2, Book 7: "[L]et us merely separate ourselves from the crowd, and we shall be made whole." See also S. Kierkegaard: "The crowd is untruth." Cited by M. Buber, *Between Man and Man*, trans. R. G. Smith (London: Fontana Library, 1961), p. 81.

2. And neither could one of Canada's greatest writers, Mordecai Richler, earn a living at it in the 1950s. He scathingly indicted Canada's provincialism and cultural juvenility in a classic BBC interview.

3. B. Held, *Stop Smiling, Start Kvetching* (Brunswick, ME: Biddle, 1999). She is also the author of an important scholarly critique of anti-realism in psychotherapy: B. Held, *Back to Reality* (New York: Norton, 1995).

4. A "throng" might be five people, even for a famous author. Thirty is a good turnout. I have drawn hundreds at such events, but that is because people have heard of my popular book—*Plato Not Prozac*—and not necessarily of me at all. This is also a humbling experience: a piece of art can have what is called a "mind-share," without the artist himself being known. I am quite certain that a significant fraction of pedestrians could identify the *Mona Lisa* or *The Thinker* without knowing the names of their respective painter and sculptor. This is equally true of musical themes and their composers. It is even truer of architecture: most New Yorkers would recognize the Empire State Building and the Brooklyn Bridge, but few could name their respective architects.

5. This descent with modification of ideas, their transmission by Lamarckian means, and their adoption or rejection by synthetic selection, is the cultural analogue of biological evolution. Note that one's ideas may have greater longevity than one's genes.

6. The central question of Plato's *Republic*.

7. L. Nelson, *Socratic Method and Critical Philosophy*, trans. T. Brown III (New York: Dover, 1949).

8. See D. Boele (1998), "The 'Benefits' of a Socratic Dialogue, Or, Which Results Can We Promise?" *Inquiry*, *17*, 48–70.

9. "A man hears what he wants to hear, and disregards the rest," sang Paul Simon, in a song appropriately entitled "The Boxer."

10. Jos Kessels is an experienced Dutch practitioner and author (private communication, 1996).

11. J. J. Rousseau, *Émile*, trans. B. Foxley ([London: J.M. Dent, 1762]; Rutland, VT: Tuttle, 1993) Book 5, pp. 392–393: "A man has no one but himself to consider, and so long as he does right he may defy public opinion; but when a woman does right her task is only half finished, and what people think of her matters as much as what she really is. Hence her education must, in this respect, be different from a man's education. 'What will people think' is the grave of a man's virtue and the throne of a woman's.... Even the tiniest little girls love finery; they are not content to be pretty, they must be admired; their little airs and graces show that their heads are full of this idea, and as soon as they can understand are controlled by 'What will people think of you?' If you are foolish enough to try this with boys, it will not have the same effect." For a modern social scientific treatment (by women) that concludes much the same thing, among other things, see, e.g., E. Maccoby and C. Jacklin, *The Psychology of Sex Differences* (Stanford: Stanford University Press, 1975).

12. Marinoff (1998a).

13. Namely, the team-taught "Arts One" program at the University of British Columbia, founded in 1967.

CHAPTER 7

The Corporate Philosopher

7.1. Origins of Philosophical Consulting
7.2. General Services
7.3. Substance, Form, and Artistry
    Motivational Speaking
    Ethics Code-Building
    Ethics Compliance
    Moral Self-Defense
    Short Socratic Dialogue
    Dilemma Training
    The PEACE Process
    Leadership and Governance
    Artistry
7.4. The Summit of Practice

7.1. ORIGINS OF PHILOSOPHICAL CONSULTING

The heyday of American manufacturing, known as the "Golden Era" of capitalism, unfolded between the end of World War Two and the beginning of multinational predation on the American middle class—epitomized by the bogus "energy crisis" of 1973. Children born during that prosperous era are called "baby-boomers." Many of us came of age during the 1960s—a decade of monumental change, whose cultural effects are still palpable and whose delectable philosophical fruits continue to ripen—and in unfortunate cases, to rot.

There was a momentous subcultural revolution in the West during the 1960s, which paradoxically ended almost before it started. Its psychedelic luminaries faded swiftly, and their unprecedented explorations of mind, heart, and soul—the perennial constituents of man's true "final frontier"—became trivialized in the 1970s and obsolete by the 1980s. Most members of the Woodstock generation eventually encountered a fork in the road: Woodstock led them either to Wall Street, or off the wall entirely. That is, these liberal and open-minded youths either evolved into conservative and open-minded adults, who still smoked grass and listened to Canned Heat, but by now drove BMWs and owned mutual funds; or devolved into illiberal and closed-minded radicals, who sired American political correctness and whose progeny now terrorize the emasculated universities, which have become decrepit satrapies of intolerance, ignorance, irrationality, infamy and intellectual ignominy.[1] That's the rotten part.

The ripening came about exactly as it was intended, through expansions of consciousness and infusions of culture. Kipling was falsified; East met West; the two were enriched beyond measure. When major corporations bring in gurus to motivate their employees, they are enacting ancient eastern traditions on postmodern western stages.

That earlier period of unprecedented American prosperity, the Golden Era of capitalism, also witnessed the emergence of an unforseen profession, which contributed to the abundance of the age. Behavioral psychology wedded manufacturing industry and produced a hybrid offspring: the industrial psychologist. While the industrial revolution had concentrated on developing ever more efficient machines and assembly-lines, it unmercifully exploited and cruelly abused its human resources. In the nineteenth century, Charles Dickens immortalized some of these socioeconomic excesses in his novels, while Karl Marx sought to level the system that produced them and replace it with something incalculably worse. Trade-unionism provided a middle way, between literary artistic critique and violent revolutionary reform, for capitalism to thrive. In the twentieth century, enter the industrial psychologist, who answered this question: Given state-of-the-art manufacturing processes, how do we produce state-of-the-art employees? We can build efficient machines and design productive assembly lines, but how do we cost-effectively motivate laborers and managers to their utmost efficacy?

The short answer turned out to be something like: Paint the walls green and pipe in muzak. Even those who dislike green paint and loathe muzak concede that the industrial psychologist achieved symbiosis between the muscle of industry and the science of motivation. In retrospect, he was a primitive precursor of the corporate philosopher.

Owing to multinationalism and emergent global civilization, American (and other "developed") economies are shifting from a base of manufactured goods to one of provided services. Formerly, the vital functional linkage was between human bodies and static machines, and the corresponding operational question was "How do we best mechanize human performance?" You hired an industrial psychologist; he told you how. Philosophers like Henri Bergson and humanists like Lewis Mumford wrote splendid essays explaining why this was reprehensible, before and after the facts, respectively.[2] Currently, the vital functional linkage is between human minds and dynamic structures, so the corresponding operational question becomes "How do we best systematize human performance?" These days one hires a philosophical consultant; he tells you how. (Soon deconstructionists and post-humanists will attempt to write dreadful essays explaining why this is reprehensible.) That's the general picture.

While organizational consulting is hardly new, the philosopher as consultant appears both new and newsworthy. Actually, he is very old indeed, as ancient as philosophy itself. As we have earlier remarked, Confucius was among the first philosophical consultants, seeking to market his services to warlords and instruct them in the arts of government by virtue instead of coercion. Although Confucius was slightly ahead of his time, his contemporary Lao Tzu, if truly a senior civil servant as apocryphally told, undoubtedly applied the Tao to government, although he would not have said he was doing so.[3] In the Athenian agora, Socrates functioned as a kind of anti-consultant, a self-described gadfly, whose stinging criticisms were evidently near enough the mark to warrant his being silenced by legalized assassination. His apt disciple, Plato, became in effect a meta-consultant, endeavoring to turn philosopher-kings wholesale out of his Academy, but producing a bumper crop of tyrants instead. Plato's outstanding legatee, the third and final patriarch of this noble philosophical lineage, namely Aristotle, narrowed but legitimized the primitive consulting enterprise by reverting to the role of private tutor, and having as his pupil no less a figure than Alexander the Great.

In the ancient world, governments and corporations alike were subsumed under monarchy. Other organizations flourished at the pleasure of monarchs, and vanished at their displeasure. Palaces were the seats of money, of power, of commerce, of taxation, of policy, of law, of war, of religion, of intrigue, of ambition, of influence-peddling, of advancement, of undoing. The only worthwhile clientele were bound to be the monarch and his nobles, whose corporate headquarters were ineluctably at court. Therefore, introductions to the rulers were indispensable to aspiring philosophical consultants (and paid considerable dividends to the likes of Hobbes, Descartes, Hume, and Locke), without which they might languish indefinitely in ignominy, or wander indeterminately on the uncertain margins of unsubsidized culture (as with Spinoza, Kant, Rousseau, and Schopenhauer). Their surest form of sinecure lay not in direct consultation either, for monarchs were ever needful of political policy, military strategy, effective diplomacy, and fiscal continuity, but never suffered conspicuously from dearths of, say, epistemology or ethics. This is why Machiavelli caused such a stir, when he merely collected and set down in writing the basic principles, not of despotism (which no one needs to learn), but of enduring despotism. Anyone can be a despot for a day, but endurance as a despot requires the application of some reasonably well-thought-out precepts. Yet from the ancient through the early modern and romantic periods, the philosopher played an indisputably influential role, not as a consultant to monarchs, but as a pre-consultant, that is, as a tutor.

Twixt tit and title lies tutelage. Infant pretenders were suckled by wet-nurses; adult monarchs sucked dry by demands of state; but between helpless infancy and capable reign lay a critical period of education, during which the youth had to learn not how to become a functional adult and useful citizen (a difficult enough lesson for many youths), but a responsible ruler (an insurmountably difficult lesson for many pretenders to thrones). The tutor of choice has almost always been a philosopher. True, in mythological courts he would be a benevolent wizard, as Merlyn was to Arthur; but prior to the advent of science, philosophy was the readiest substitute for wizardry. It is but a passing irony that Thomas Hobbes, who tutored Prince Charles (later Charles II) in geometry at the exiled English court in Paris, was forbidden to impart political instruction to the prince, and that Hobbes's Levianthanesque "blasphemies" (e.g., his advocacy of the separation of state from church, and his repudiation of original sin) would later be cited, by the Bishops of London to Parliament, as "probable causes" of the Great Fire and Great Plague.[4] Like Wallis's algebra, Hobbes's philosophy was mistaken for wizardry.

The connections among philosophy, mathematics, and tutelage run very deep, and will not be undermined by illiteracy cartels that prepare the new American underclass for "careers" under the Golden Arches. The paradigmatic arts of logical deduction and coherent construction alike are epitomized by Euclidean geometry. To the ancient Greeks, who feared the powers of gods but worshipped the powers of reason, mathematics—and in particular its expression through geometry—was the bridge of understanding between man's mind and the cosmos, the universe and its orderliness. (We now know that even chaos, or disorder, can be orderly in its own wondrous way.) From Pythagoras to Plato, it was hoped that the rational character of mathematics would reveal to man not only the deep structures and lawful functions of the natural world he inhabited, but also perhaps a way to govern himself personally and socially, and to build a utopian polity. Thus mathematics reigned not only as the Queen of the Sciences but also, through statistics in the twentieth century, as a way to attempt to legitimize Social Studies as a member of that scientific family. Spencer's friends were emphatic in their warnings against his coinage of "Sociology"; not just because it was a linguistic barbarism, half-Greek and half-Latin, which ridiculed his own education, but because the putative observable suddenly reified and scientized by the neologism—namely, "society"—is *ab initio* condemned to perpetual subjectivity, ephemerality and other imprecisions, thus constituting a manifestly illegitimate extension of the property of observability to conceptual entities distinctly unlike the observables of physics, chemistry, and biology. "Hard" versus "soft" science is the contemporary vocabulary, which applies not only to the relative difficulty of learning physics versus sociology, but also to the extramental substance, and lack thereof, of the very things respectively observed and susceptible to fruitful mathematical modeling. Bentham's "calculus of felicity," by which he vainly hoped to compute the "greatest happiness of the greatest number," predates by several decades Galton's and Pearson's statistical methods for failing to do so, and by a century von Neumann's and Morgenstern's terse but clear explanation of why it is impossible to do so.[5]

Philosophers studied mathematics before the formalization of syllogistic logic by Aristotle, and continued to study mathematics roughly until the formalization of symbolic logic by Frege, and the reduction of arithmetic to logic (or the demonstration of their equivalency) by Russell and Whitehead. The general abandonment of mathematics by philosophers, and their replacement of it with formal logic, did nothing to compromise the philosophical form of rigorous deductive argumentation, but severely curtailed the substance of such argumentation. As far as philosophers understood mathematics, they could understand physics, and from that science gained a window on the other sciences, and on the human world. This is undoubtedly why Plato emphasized the study of geometry as a prerequisite to ethics, why Hobbes could not have written the *Leviathan* prior to his discovery of Euclid's Elements, why Spinoza based the structure of his *Ethics* literally on Euclid, and why, after the replacement of geometry with logic, Tarski refused to teach ethics at City College. If one understands, as apparently Pythagoras did, that the universe is constructed of numbers, or discovers, as Mandelbrot more recently did, that its deep structures are infinitely complex and wondrously beautiful mathematical constructs, or favors, for these reasons, the renewed argument from design, which portrays God not only as architect, but also as mathematician, then one sees the departure of mathematics from philosophy as nothing short of tragedy. While it is true that both mathematics and logic require rigorous thinking, the former also enjoys myriad direct applications to the world; the latter, hardly any directly at all. Logic is about the validity of arguments, not about their soundness. When philosophers jettisoned mathematics, they jettisoned both the real world and their place in it.

Thus the rift between analytic and continental schools opened wide. The analytic school retained "hard" philosophy, namely, logic, but admitted, after Moore, that "the good" is undefinable and unanalyzable. Analytic philosophers still concern themselves with philosophy of mathematics and science, but since many of them have studied no mathematics or science, their philosophizing is substanceless form, dealing with meta-theory only. Analytic philosophers retain their rigor, but have few concrete applications for it. They trade in hypotheticals and counterfactuals, attempting to draw important distinctions and pretending to solve important problems. In fact, many are completely institutionalized, playing esoteric games with language, and understand as little about the world as the world understands about them. They are the ones primarily thanks to whom philosophy has lately earned the reputation of being both incomprehensible and useless. While science is just as incomprehensible to the man on the Clapham omnibus, he knows that it provides him with gadgets and gewgaws, with ointments and organs, with prosthetic limbs and lives alike. He also knows that analytic philosophy provides him with precisely nothing. He does not know, as we have taken pains to mention earlier on, that analytic philosophy has inadvertently safeguarded the noetic building-blocks of our civilization: reading, writing, and reasoning. So monastic orders inadvertently safeguarded literacy during the Dark Ages, as their monks whiled away the centuries illuminating religious myths with gold leaf, allowing their thick stone walls to do the real work, which consisted in keeping out the barbarians, who would have burned their libraries to demonstrate the superiority of barbarism over civilization. Analytic philosophy has no physical walls, but needs none. The universities have already been besieged and sacked by the new barbarians, and are now administered by them. Instead of burning great books, they merely ban them as inegalitarian. Then, to be doubly sure that no one ever discovers the truth about anything, they insist that university graduates be unable to read, write, or reason. These postcultural, postliterate students occasionally wander into philosophy courses, and are lucky to earn Ds. They generally boast that they have A averages—"A" apparently standing for attendance—in all their other courses: deconstructed English, revisionist History, anti-Civilization, dumbed-

down Social Science, feminist Critiques of Everything, and ethno-specific Ideologies-of-the-Month. These sorry students, victims of a sick and
anti-meritocratic cult of victimhood that happens to be governing the
mind-politic, learn more by failing a single philosophy course than by passing
every other excuse for a course in their deconstructed curricula. They
learn not only that they know nothing, but that they are ill-prepared to learn
anything. Ironically, some of them then learn that if only they prepared
themselves accordingly, they could learn philosophy, and thus merit unem-
ployment of an incomparably higher order. Thus, one is drawn into a
love–hate relation with analytic philosophy. One adores its rigor, yet deplores
its irrelevancy.

While the analytic school has erred on the side of saying too little about the
world, the continental school has erred on the other extreme, and has said far
too much. The romantic and idealistic rebellions against the successes of
scientific realism have been played out, in successive generations and centuries,
with increasingly radical amplitude. The more reliable knowledge we accrue,
the more vehement and deranged appears the protest against reality and reliablism. In the seventeenth century, Galileo performed experiments in classical
mechanics, using Euclidean geometry as a calculus, which debunked teleological Aristotelian physics. Hobbes, who met him in Padua and who was immediately impressed and influenced by his methods, invented classical political
science, using Euclidean geometry as a model of argumentation, which rejected
Platonic essentialism in favor of materialism and nominalism, and sought to
perpetuate social order via contractarianism checked by central authority.
Locke and later Rousseau rebelled against the Hobbesian view, because they
wanted human nature to be other than it is. As Cranston says, Rousseau
understood Hobbes's argument—that the human being is an appetitive, egoistic, but short-sighted predator, who needs to be governed for his own good—
but could not stomach his conclusions.[6] So Rousseau reinvented man as a noble
savage, born pristinely good but thoroughly corrupted by civilization. Here is
continentalism at work: let us propagate as formative truths the most palatable
lies we can devise. Who else but Rousseau do we find running the postmodern
academy? This is his philosophy of education, at work across America: children
are born good and wise, but are made bad and foolish by standardized learning.
Therefore we must not teach them anything, especially not grammar, history,
civics, geometry, or ethics. Do away with civilization, and we will return to a
perfect state of nature, claims Rousseau. In fact, we are doing away with it, and
are returning to a perfect state of savagery.

"Man is born free, but everywhere he is in chains"[7]—what consummate
nonsense and sublime folly, even for a romantic Gaul. Man is born in utter
captivity: a captive of his neonatal helplessness and formative phenomenol-

ogy; a captive of his family, and all the idiosyncratic prejudices and inane opinions with which they imbue him; a captive of his tribe and all their myths, superstitions, rituals, and grievances; a captive of his society's language, culture, politics, and religion; a captive of his peers and their fashions; a captive of his own desires in addition to everyone else's; and lately, as we are discovering, a captive of his very genes. What freedom is this? A strange one indeed, that goes more commonly by the name of enslavement. Man is not born free, but in chains. Fettered twice over, by nature and nurture alike, he must learn what freedom means, learn why it is preferable to captivity, learn how to attain it, and learn how to maintain it. That is a tidy sum of learning, not to be afforded much in the contemporary academy.

Romantics, anarchists, idealists, phenomenologists, existentialists, revolutionaries, nihilists—and, ultimately, postmodernists, deconstructionists, and social constructivists—all are grist for the mill of continentalism. Because there is no rigor, one can talk in any way about anything; any proposition seems credible, and, in the absence of rules of inference, any other proposition can be inferred from it. One can ordain the universe according to fancy, or re-ordain multiverses hourly.

Toward the end of the nineteenth century and beginning of the twentieth, we witness the epitome of the bifurcation between analytic and continental schools: while Moore tells us that "the good" is unanalyzable, but that actions can still be classified as right or wrong, Nietzsche tells us that God is dead, and that we must become supermen and transcend ordinary morality. The Nazis will soon take this literally. Nietzsche equates Christian moral decency with slave mentality. Secularized postmodern Americans will later reject moral decency along with Christianity, and the West will furthermore become polarized as secular rejections are counterbalanced by recrudescences of stifling religious fundamentalism and neo-pagan rejectionism, the likes of which have not been seen since the Dark Ages. And Nietzsche was quite wrong about slavery: New Age pagans, social constructivist anti-realists, and theocratic zealots are all equally enslaved: each by the grotesquerie of his ignorance. Philosophers of the continental school can tell us absolutely everything about the world, leaving us with a collective account that is australopithecine in its primitiveness, Babelistic in its incoherence, and hallucinogenic in its self-conception as guide to living. Yet one cannot avoid loving certain aspects of continentalism: its rebelliousness, its artistry, and its romanticism are compelling and enduring, as well as potentially deranged and damaging.

It appears that the analytic and continental schools are really complements. Hobbes is parental; Rousseau, childlike. Kant is sober; Hegel, intoxicated. Frege is grounded; Nietzsche, in orbit. The Vienna Circle tried and failed to philosophize with scientific rigor and exclude metaphysics; the Social Constructivists tried and failed to philosophize with metaphysics and exclude scientific rigor. Tarski's theory of truth has no apparent applicability to problems of living; Rorty's neo-pragmatism is mistakenly applied to problems of living. Analytic philosophy's retreat from mundanity in the over-reverent service of rationality, and continental philosophy's advance on mundanity in the over-reverent service of ferality, are nothing but manifestations of primeval complements: the sacred and the profane. Spengler characterized them as Apollonian versus Dionysian influences, and also as the eternal war between male and female archetypes. The Tao sees them similarly, as yang and yin.

But while rational philosophy tried to remove itself from the world, and passionate philosophy tried to impose itself on the world, the world changed in a fundamental way which disregarded both. And in the light shed by this change, we see that the distinction between analytic and continental philosophy, however sharply drawn in the schools, is a false dichotomy in the world—for both are equally useless in the world. When it comes to real problems of living, one gets no advice from the analytic school, and—which is worse—absurd advice from the continental school; hence twentieth-century philosophy's well-earned reputation as the subject requiring a prodigious intellectual effort but returning a negligible practical result.

The change I allude to is not only momentous in itself; it also resuscitates the utility of philosophy in hitherto unimaginable ways. During the past two centuries or so, from the time of the American and French revolutions to this new millennium, we have witnessed exactly what Hobbes propounded as a necessary condition for the creation of commonwealths; namely, the Erastian separation of church and state. As politics became something other than a branch of theology, and actually began to transcend theology in its exercise of temporal power, its independence stimulated a similar and parallel movement, namely, the separation of state and corporation. The emergence of multinational corporations similarly marks the transcendence of economic over legislative power. Formerly, and for better or worse, governments controlled economies. The twentieth century taught, in excruciatingly painful lessons at times, that laissez-faire capitalism generates the greatest wealth, that centrally planned communism generates the direst poverty, and that socialistic democracies endeavor to sustain high-minded compassionate capitalism, but sooner or later find government-driven compassion unaffordable. In the twenty-first century, it is plain that economies control governments. The price of running for the U.S. presidency is now one hundred million dollars, and only two kinds of candidates can afford that: those who have earned sufficient wealth themselves, or front-men in their pay. Americans are not interested in political issues; they are interested in the economy. The country's prosperity depends increasingly on Wall Street, not the White House. Abroad, all but the most rabid despots are brought to heel by the leash of global economics, and the increasing costs of economic sanctions.

What difference does this make for philosophy? Only a world of difference. When monarchs ruled polities, either by divine right (as in England) or as mortal gods (as in Japan), there existed few or no national organizations independent of their influence. Nationalism itself did not emerge in public consciousness until after Napoleon at the earliest. Philosophers could not be organizational consultants, because there were no organizations, with the vital exception of the monarch and his court, that needed philosophical consultation. The East India Company, the *sine qua non* of colonial corporations, was under orders primarily to send money to the Crown. Macaulay characterized British policy in India as follows:

> "Govern leniently, and send more money; practise strict justice and moderation towards neighboring powers, and send more money"; this is, in truth, the sum of almost all the instructions that Hastings ever received from home.[8]

No need of philosophical consulting here. And more to the point, in the absence of ethical constraint and moral instruction, the East India Company became an economic ally in the Opium Wars, by which England handsomely offset its trade deficit in Chinese tea, and nearly bankrupted the Chinese treasury in the bargain, by creating a sizable population of opium addicts in mainland China. The late eighteenth-century British trade deficit with China, accumulated by imports of tea worth 96 million yuan against exports of woolens and spices worth 17 million yuan, was nicely balanced by the shipment of opium (200 chests in 1787; 2,000 in 1800; 5,147 in 1820; 7,000 in 1821; 12,639 in 1824; 21,785 in 1834; 39,000 in 1837). Large quantities of silver flowed out of China in exchange for the contraband drug.

Meanwhile, the English public was kept in abject ignorance of the drug traffic. James Matheson's detailed treatise of 1836, *British Trade and China*, contained no mention of opium.[9] The parliamentary moral minority, Herbert and Gladstone, accepted junior ministerial posts in Peel's 1841 government in exchange for silence.[10] "Sorcerer's Apprentice" theories seek to absolve the Company and the government of blame; suggesting, for example, that the government had become "addicted" to the revenue in the same way as the Chinese became addicted to the drug.[11] This frivolous simile might lead one to imagine that the former were driven by metabolic necessity to inject molten silver into their veins, or to huddle around vats inhaling argentine vapors. As long as the money followed the flag, which it did throughout the nineteenth century, philosophical consultants were no more in evidence in colonial commerce than they had been in the imperial transactions of Rome—unless, by exception and not by rule, the Emperor happened to be a philosopher, as was Marcus Aurelius.

The twentieth-century independence of economics from politics, and its increasing awareness of ethicity, was achieved in the wakes of the World Wars and the Cold War. The allied victors of World War One imposed severe and inflexible economic burdens on defeated Germany, which hamstrung the nascent Weimar Republic from the outset. Germany experienced hyperinflation that led to economic and thereafter political chaos, and which made Hitler's seizure of absolute political power that much simpler if not surer. While he resuscitated the German economy by purely political means (perhaps the better to destroy the polity and himself in war), the Soviet Union gradually collectivized, centralized, and demolished its economy by purely political means. The British economy, staggered by the costs of the First World War and prostrated by the costs of the Second, its exhaustion exacerbated by the Empire's disintegration, stagnated for decades under an increasingly ossified political system. The United States of America, having weathered the depression without political revolution or regress, merely saw its buccaneer capitalism mildly tempered by the New Deal, and had its industrial might and military resourcefulness awakened by the alarms rung at Pearl Harbor.

The turning point was the Marshall Plan, which saw West Germany become politically stable through massive American economic intervention. Similarly, the forced demilitarization of Japan following its unconditional surrender allowed the pseudo-insectoid organization of its superbly disciplined but extremely insulated populace to be consecrated in the service of economic productivity instead of brutal imperialism. West Germany and Japan became economic giants and therefore political winners, instead of military adventurers and therefore political losers. The same economic forces showered America itself with unprecedented prosperity during the 1950s, which allowed baby-boomers the luxury of not having an economic depression in their collective memory, and which furnished them a basis of political stability and financial security more than equal to the task of supporting civil, social, psychedelic, psychological, and philosophical expeditions into territories unknown but worth knowing and needfully known, in the service of yet grander progress. The American and Western proliferation of civil rights, hippiedom, consciousness-expansion, group-therapy, and eastern philosophical practices—in that magical mystery tour of a decade, the 1960s—made no significant dent in what became known (thanks to Eisenhower's coinage) as the "military–industrial complex," which generated the sufficient wealth to win the space race and the Cold War, to prop up right-wing dictators as hedges against the domino theory, to make conventional (i.e., non-nuclear) weapons into the biggest international business after petroleum, and to manage conflicts well enough to keep both arms and oil flowing. But the counterculture of that decade fomented significant and lasting changes on Madison Avenue—which under the influence of the psychedelic revolution marketed pastel kitchen appliances and tissue products—and on the nöosphere, Teilhard de Chardin's word for the "thinking envelope of earth."[12] These two great success-stories of the 60s—namely world-trade based on a laissez-faire capitalist model backed by U.S. military supremacy, and personal development based on humane, compassionate, and efficacious wisdom traditions ultimately grounded in eastern philosophy but wholly compatible with American pragmatism—gave rise to two fruits which are the subject of our interest here: first, the growth of multinational corporations, with global economic powers that transcend and often define local political influence, and second, the growth of applied ethics as a practical philosophical profession, the only academic discipline extant able effectively to track, study, analyze, and ultimately exert moral influence on the global powers.

This all-too-brief corralling of the main concerted forces allows us to instantiate an important contrast in a significant way. While the East India Company's economic subjugation of Bengal was harnessed to an imperialistic political program that ultimately instigated the Opium Wars—for the sake of money to support the Empire—the British populace was kept in abject ignorance of this business arrangement, was not a beneficiary of the profit-taking, and most likely paid a domestic tea tax to boot. By contrast, in the twentieth century, it has been virtually impossible for corporations and governments alike to cloak their erstwhile clandestine activities indefinitely, especially when these inflict obvious suffering upon ostensibly innocent and defenseless people, either for pure financial gain or for ulterior political motive. Thus, the excesses of Nestlé's marketing of Similac in Africa, which resulted in tens of thousands of unnecessary infant deaths, were brought to light, justly condemned, and arrested by essentially moral forces. Similarly, manmade catastrophes like Bhopal's chemical poisoning, Chernobyl's nuclear meltdown, and the *Exxon Valdez*'s oil spill were at least extensively reported and minutely investigated, with a view both to allocating responsibilities and to preventing recrudescences.

Cynics may hastily charge that the reporting powers of mass media and the evaluative powers of applied ethicists operate only retrospectively, not preventively, and hence that freedom of the press and allocation of moral responsibility are merely reactive but functionally empty gestures—proverbial examples of closing the barn door after the horse has bolted—and not preventive at all. Cynics may further charge that the mass media and applied ethicists alike behave like Wall Street ghouls, because in effect they prey on the victims of these catastrophes, at least in so far as they capitalize on their misfortunes. It is true that many if not most humans have an appetite for bad news (unless it affects them personally), and an aversion to good news (unless it affects them personally), and thus that ghastliness above all sells news in its myriad and lucrative forms. If you acknowledge this in general but at the same time deem yourself outstandingly humane and compassionate, as many do—perhaps just a peccadillo or two removed from sainthood—then pray answer this question: Why can we recite the names of serial killers and mass-murderers, but not of their victims? Name one victim of Jack the Ripper, of Richard Speck, of Jeffrey Dahmer, of Ted Bundy. They murdered dozens: why can't you name one? Or for that matter, name a single victim of Ghengis Kahn, Hitler, Stalin, Mao Tse Tung, Pol Pot, Idi Amin, or Slobodan Milosevic. They murdered millions: why can't you name one? I submit that while the human appetite for news of mass-murder is insatiable, the human capacity to commiserate with its victims is unreliable. By the same somewhat self-contradictory token, most people, upon avidly consuming such news, probably wish sincerely that these tragedies could be averted.

Thus, while I do not assert that unrestricted mass media markets and scholarly case studies in applied ethics will pave the way to world peace, global prosperity, and universal brotherhood, I do assert that these two constituencies serve to dampen, rather than magnify, the pervasively opportunistic forces of harmful exploitation and lethal persecution—provided of course that a moral majority remains intact enough to discern the difference between right and wrong, and influential enough as taxpayers, stockholders, and vote-casters to apply pressure, when necessary and just, on the very institutions that employ and govern them, institutions which, at times, are tempted to cross that moral line merely for the sake of quick profit or political expediency. While public awareness and moral condemnation of war do not necessarily bring an end to war, public awareness and moral condemnation of genocide, among other atrocities and excesses, can at least result in conventions and treaties designed to protect noncombatants, to restrict certain weapons, and to treat prisoners of war humanely. While wars are often fought between some nations which respect such agreements and others which do not, even the most inhumane butchers, when their day of reckoning comes, acknowledge a clear preference for humanity: witness, for example, the legions of Nazis who fled westward and surrendered to the Allies, rather than eastward to the Soviets. While sports may be a moral equivalent of war, conventional warfare is a meta-moral equivalent of aconventional warfare.

So again I rehearse this theme: purely political programs, designed to install or maintain a ruling order, possessing some agenda for subjugating and controlling people, with associated theocratic or atheocratic, military and economic forces under their political sway, have always been and remain potentially impervious to independent and systematic moral influence. Might is, and always has been, its own measure of right in the political arena. Such might has rarely if ever, beyond lip service, cared a fig for the judgment of God, posterity, or applied ethics: but it usually censored the news. However, with the emerging transcendence of global economic over local political sovereignty, and the increasing concentration of wealth in the hands of technocrats rather than theocrats, autocrats, or bureaucrats, we witness not only the supersession of economic sanction over military incursion as the preferred means of effecting political change—reported and abetted by mass media—but also the emergence of the philosophical practitioner in the role of corporate philosopher. The corporate philosopher is not merely a reactive applied ethicist in the employ of the academy, rather a proactive educator and advisor under contract to a corporation itself; a veritable neo-Confucian who finds willing and able organizational clients seeking at a fair market price precisely what more primitive ruling orders eschewed at all possible costs: independent and systematic moral influence.

In sum, then, one witnesses three phases of government, not always or necessarily consecutive, and capable of nested coexistence. The first phase is theocratic. Organized religions first instituted and inculcated moral instruction, from antiquity until the Enlightenment. They continue to do so in fundamentalist *milieux*. While ordained moral codes produce strong social fabrics, perforce with laudable allegiances to family and community, they do not generally conduce to individual liberties, and they perpetuate dogmas that retard development in other spheres. For better and worse, theology regulates the human condition and governs human aspiration.

These shortcomings lead to a second phase, which is political. Where politics ceased to be a branch of theology, i.e., where church and state became constitutionally distinct, moral instruction became accordingly secularized, and flowed increasingly from civics, informed by legislated laws themselves conditioned by scientific discovery, technological development and—ineluctably—political expediency. In this second phase, morality varies with local (i.e., national) political interest. While this phase fosters democratic states that celebrate individual liberties and institute human rights, it tends also to annihilate morality via existentialism, reductionism, or nihilism. Moreover, it also justified imperialism, despotism, and other forces that resulted in catastrophic world wars. For better and worse, politics transcends theology in the City of Man. This has led to greater extremes of individual liberty, as well as of mass enslavement.

The third phase is economic. With the emergence of multinational corporations during the cold war, and the ongoing phenomenon of globalization in the post-cold war era, we are witnessing a separation of corporation and state, analogous to that of church and state in the previous phase. Where economics is no longer a branch of politics, economic forces can no longer be harnessed to serve destructive political ends. In general, local (i.e., national) political interests are becoming increasingly attuned to global economic development. This can engender unprecedented opportunity and globalized commonwealth; but can also lead to localized destabilization, corruption, and exploitation. For better and worse, economics is transcending politics as the governing architectonic feature of the global village.[13]

Interestingly, Thomas Paine presented this very schema in his celebrated pamphlet of 1791, *The Rights of Man*. He wrote that governments "may all be comprehended under three heads. First, superstition. Secondly, power. Thirdly, the common interest of society and the common rights of man. The first was a government of priestcraft, the second of conquerors, the third of reason."[14]

The pivotal role of philosophical practice follows clearly from this third phase. Whereas theocratic leadership ordains moral imperatives, and political leadership legislates them, economic leadership is not intrinsically imbued with them. Hence it must acquire them. Our philosophically ancient and currently cogent premise is that virtue betters vice. Just as virtuous persons lead better lives and make better neighbors than vicious ones, virtuous organizations provide better livelihoods and set better examples than vicious ones. Philosophical practice offers many tools for enhancing virtue at all levels of organizational life. In so far as global economic aspects of leadership transcend local political ones, a meta-moral imperative of leadership in the twenty-first century is therefore the inculcation of a viable morality in the global village. Philosophical practitioners are well-equipped to implement this imperative.

7.2. GENERAL SERVICES

Organizational consulting in the United States, like other forms of philosophical practice, is merely in its inception. Yet from its early vital signs, it has enormous potential for growth. In this domain of practice, as in client counseling and group facilitation, the Dutch have made especially significant strides, and virtually everything they do as philosophical consultants in Holland is applicable either directly or with suitable modification in America. Dutch practicality and American pragmatism continue to be close cousins. Organizational consulting in the U.S.A. also resembles an uneven kind of patchwork quilt, in that prospective clients are seeking but not always finding philosophers, and philosophers are seeking but not always finding prospective clients. Moreover, there is not yet much generalization of approach or standardization of service, so that one doesn't necessarily get a good fit between counselor and client. We can attribute much of this unevenness to the newness of the profession; the field is wide open and scarcely furrowed, but for this reason its contours are not clearly or fully discernible. That fuzziness will sharpen in time, as this mode of practice ripens.

To abet the ripening, I will endeavor to shed some light on the main features of philosophical consulting to organizations, from a practitioner's eye view, in terms of the nature of services rendered. These break down into several intelligible categories, which include building mission statements, inculcating virtues, formulating and implementing codes of ethics, achieving ethics compliance, coaching and providing similar motivational interventions, resolving intra-organizational conflicts, facilitating shortened Socratic dialogues, imparting leadership and governance skills, and delivering all the above services in-house, on a regular basis.

Every organization has a mission, or goal, which is its ostensible *raison d'être*. The bald assertion that a given business organization's mission consists of maximizing profit is tautological in one sense and impoverishing in another. Of course, a business has to turn a profit to remain in business (unless its business is taking losses in the service of greater profits elsewhere), but this is no different than saying that a human being has to ingest more calories than he expends in order to fend off starvation. The salient distinction, whether literal or figurative, is between living to eat versus eating to live. Organizations seeking only to profiteer resemble people living only to eat: they grow unnecessarily fat, subsist unwholesomely on excess, and expire before their time. By contrast, organizations seeking to fulfil missions resemble people eating to live: they remain lean but not hungry, manage wholesomely on moderation, and persist in longevity. Eating to live grants people time and energy to attain loftier goals in life; so too does profiting to thrive grant equivalent gifts to organizations. An organization's purpose, mission, goals, and duties are not what it fulfills to make money; rather, they are what it fulfills to contribute security, prosperity, opportunity, and integrity to its employees, its clients, and its communities and its other constituencies.

You can find out more or less everything you need to know about the character of an organization by reflecting on its mission. This is transparently easier with larger organizations, but it's also true of smaller ones. On the largest scale, it is almost trivial to contrast the mission of, say, the Roman Catholic Church with that of its organizational forerunner, the Roman Empire. The mission of the Roman Catholic Church is to represent the City of God on Earth. Rome qua Empire, as Augustine realized only when it was sacked by the Visigoths, represented the City of Man, which was heir to myriad corruptions and destined ultimately to demolition. Rome qua Church, as we witness it surviving the revolutions of the Ages, appears impervious to this kind of ruin. While representing the City of God on Earth entails proselytizing doctrines to which I myself do not subscribe—and to some which I even harbor powerful aversions—nonetheless it is easy to see that such representation has brought order, comfort, meaning, purpose, goodness, justice, and moral decency to millions of people worldwide. And if one compares successive "CEOs" of these organizations, one gets an immediate sense of how their very different missions are embodied in their respective leaders. Emperors of Rome span a spectrum of human behavior ranging from exemplary, to power-hungry, to bloodthirsty, to utterly depraved. Vicars of Christ, by contrast, tend to be more reliably humane—except when they tacitly collaborate with Nazis, which is an exception and not a norm.

Your local clothing boutique has a mission, too, and so does your bank, bookseller, and beauty salon. While the Roman Empire and the Roman Church both enlisted the labors of eminent philosophical consultants throughout the centuries, corporations large and small are now becoming more willing (thanks to their awakening) and more able (thanks to our availability) to engage our services today. A corporate mission, like any other, involves a conception and articulation of the ultimate purpose, or end, for the which the organization exists. Thus the formulation of a corporate mission statement is an important exercise in teleology, which philosophical consultants are well able to conduct. Goals 'R Us.

Once you know your mission, you can strategize on how best to fulfill it. Assuming your mission is good, it can be better fulfilled by inculcating certain virtues as opposed to vices. If your mission were bad, by contrast, then you'd want to inculcate vices instead. Here, for the first but not the last time, we need to consider the sophists, who have been given a bad name for a number of reasons, some less well-deserved than others. Among other things, the sophists were skilled orators and rhetoricians, who were therefore able verbally to defend or attack any position whatsoever, regardless of its intrinsic merits or demerits. Protagoras and his colleagues were no different than any philosophers of any generation in this regard, for no matter how absurd a position one can ever conceive of taking on any issue, one can always find some philosopher who sincerely espouses it. The sticking point apparently lies with sincerity: one who staunchly defends an absurd position merely because he is a sincere fool is evidently exonerated of ulterior motives and immunized against moral judgment; whereas one who staunchly defends the same absurd position, knowing it is absurd but desirous of earning a living, and having found a client to pay him to defend it, is pejoratively branded a sophist—or a lawyer. In this light, sophists appear culpable only of having trained the first generation of attorneys.

It is perhaps the unabashed relativism of sophistry that attracts so much derision; Protagoras' famous assertion that "Man is the measure of all things" has itself become a thing measured by all men, and been generally interpreted as an absolute declaration of relativism. However, there is more undeniable relativism in the affairs of man than some men are willing to admit. As Aristotle observed, force and fraud are cardinal virtues in time of war. So who would be a more effective consultant to a wartime general: Kant or Machiavelli? Yet this is precisely the kind of charge levied against applied ethicists and philosophical consultants: that they sell seals of ethical approval, much as bishops sold indulgences, and would sell them to the very Devil himself, if he met their asking price. This does not seem quite fair, because it condemns the whole on account of the part. One would not condemn the Roman Catholic Church in its entirety just because of a handful of corrupt priests, bishops, or abbots. And this is precisely where Protagoras' relativism (and Taoistic complementarity) rings true: nothing is absolutely good or bad, for we can always detect the complementary quality or application if we make but a modest effort. For instance, while we may assert that loyalty is often a virtue, the so-called "loyal agent" argument (i.e., "I was only following orders") does not provide exculpation from criminal deeds or immoral acts. But it is also plausible that even loyal agents involved in heinous activities are not bereft of redeeming features. No doubt many ardent Nazis were also loving parents. So while it may be true that some ethics consultants lend their names to unethical organizations with unwholesome missions, it is also true that other ethics consultants may help make unethical organizations more ethical, and unwholesome missions more wholesome. We will deal later with another common proto-sophistic charge—utterly spurious, in my view—that it is somehow meta-ethically wrong to charge money for ethics consulting.

Meanwhile, it is clear that philosophers have increasingly large roles to play in helping organizations attain their goals. On the unquestionable premise that multinational corporations wield enormous economic power, and therefore also political, social, and cultural power, it is also reasonable to assume that they seek to foster constructive competition, engender economic growth, and encourage sustainable development. Those that do not, will not last; those that do, will do better with philosophical consultancy than without it.

When people are assembled under the aegis of an organization, for the purpose of earning livelihoods, pursuing careers or attaining similar goals, they experience problems and difficulties both recognizable in the broader human estate yet manifest in identifiably unique ways. Consider, for example, the complements of competition and cooperation. Social neo-Darwinians, human sociobiologists, and assorted conservatives, laboring on or near one extreme under comparatively neolithic delusions that ignore or blur vital distinctions between biological and cultural evolution,[15] laud the ostensible primacy of intraspecific competition, to the exclusion of cooperation. Neo-Rousseauans, social constructivists, and assorted radical liberals, laboring on or near the other extreme under antirealist delusions that ignore or blur vital distinctions between objective truth and normative fantasy, laud the ostensible primacy of intraspecific cooperation, to the exclusion of competition. The former breed competent bigots; the latter, incompetent empathics. The philosophical consultant's job, in this very general situation, consists in salvaging the virtues of competency and empathy, while sinking the vices of bigotry and incompetence.

Bigotry is a manifestation of a psychological problem, which can be alleviated by philosophical means. People who do not value themselves very much, often because they were not made to feel valued in their childhoods, may seek to compensate their perceived lack of emotional stature by demeaning others socially. By pretending that others are "inferior" to themselves, they gain an illusory measure of "superiority,"—while inflicting palpable harm—which serves as a surrogate for self-esteem. The price of this surrogacy is unworkably high: instead of feeling at ease through loving themselves, they endeavor to feel at ease by hating others. When such bigotry becomes a cultural norm and attracts political sanction, we call it racism or sexism. The philosophical solution to this problem is to teach potential bigots to value and eventually to love themselves, by neither political nor theological nor ideological nor behavioral nor pharmacological interventions (for these will be at best symptomatic), but through lived experiences of accomplishment, in which one's own success does not depend upon another's failure. In other words, bigots need to learn constructive cooperation.

Incompetence is a manifestation of an economic problem, which can be alleviated by philosophical means. Some psychologists, who are conspicuously talented at furnishing empirical corroboration of universally known truths, have recently "discovered" that incompetent people are generally unaware of their incompetence.[16] (This is also unwittingly autological: such psychologists appear generally unaware that everyone else already knows what they are about to "discover.") To know what tasks one can or cannot competently perform is itself a sign of meta-competency; those who are meta-incompetent are therefore dependent upon others to assign to them tasks which they can competently perform. A delegator of authority who is himself meta-incompetent can thus propagate inefficiency (and, if unchecked, catastrophe) of a very high order. Americans have lately enlisted incompetence as attempted remedy against bigotry, with predictably catastrophic results. To exclude persons unfairly from the workplace primarily on account of their race, ethnicity, sex, or age is to encourage bigotry: it is wrongful, harmful, and unjust to all concerned. Moreover, it is economically unproductive. But by the same token, to include persons unfairly in the workplace primarily on account of their race, ethnicity, sex, or age is to encourage incompetence: it is also wrongful, harmful, and unjust to all concerned. Moreover, it is also economically unproductive. The philosophical solution to this problem is to encourage people to discover their talents, to educate them to develop their talents, to employ them to apply their talents, and to promote them to display their talents. In other words, antirealist empathics need to engage in constructive competition.

To integrate and complicate matters, cooperation and competition are concentrically nested. In professional sports, athletes compete against one another to earn a place on a team. Teamwork itself requires cooperation, in order that one team be competitive against another. Competing teams nonetheless cooperate within the conference in which they play, as competing conferences cooperate under the aegis of the league itself. Leagues themselves compete for the patronage of sports fans, and yet they cooperate under the umbrella industry of professional sports. Entertainment industries themselves are in competition, and yet they cooperate within the ethos of market-driven economy. Philosophical consultants can, among other things, help organizations inculcate virtues that enhance competitive performance as well as virtues that enhance cooperative effort. The art lies partly in distinguishing appropriate occasions for each, and in maintaining respect for those against whom we compete, as well as in encouraging expression of individuality among those with whom we cooperate.

Articulating the overall mission of a given organization, and enhancing the particular ways in which it fosters both competition and cooperation in the service of accomplishing that mission, is a principal preoccupation of philosophical consulting. When you bring people together to accomplish a mission, and you organize them in the service of that mission, you also assemble an ineluctable array of individual, interpersonal, and organizational conflicts. Consulting therefore represents the apex of philosophical practice, because it can entail each of the other modes. The consummate corporate philosopher can counsel individuals and facilitate groups within the framework of consulting to the organization. He certainly merits his fee, if hired to implement a particular program; his retainer, if engaged in a troubleshooting capacity; or his reserved parking space, if employed in-house.

Indulging in while not necessarily profiting from an excess of liberty, Americans have managed thoroughly to conflate several distinct concepts, which makes the demand for philosophical consultancy less discretionary and more urgent. Right has been conflated with privilege; equal opportunity with equal outcome; offense with harm; private morality with professional ethic; biological imperative with social construct; objective fact with subjective interpretation; individual liberty with group prerogative—to name the most poignant. These distinctions, vital to the health and prosperity of the American polity, were blurred initially in institutions of higher learning—whose administrations demonstrated unprecedented spinelessness in capitulating to the terrorism of liberal orthodoxy's jihad—and these opportunistic conflationary cancers spread rapidly to justice systems, government agencies and media industries. Corporations in general have proved more resistant to tampering by conflationary social engineering, but federal incentives like "ethics compliance" have opened their pockets for the picking too. Philosophical consultants have more than enough work to do; in their hands lies the reconstruction of a worldview deconstructed to the brink of dysfunctionality.

From my perspective, the singular premise upon which philosophical consulting reposes, is merely the corresponding form of a singular notion taken for granted in any civilized society: that virtuous individuals are more desirable and more functional than vicious ones as members of a community. Similarly, more virtuous organizations are more desirable and more functional than vicious ones as members of a commonwealth. The philosophical consultant helps organizations to be more virtuous. A philosopher can have no higher calling; an organization, no loftier aspiration.

Such services can be provided in executive capacities to CEOs and Boards; provided in open assemblies to rank-and-file employees; provided in small workshops to selected teams. Most organizations need to be ethical, want to be virtuous, aspire to be excellent. Are these things better accomplished by dumb luck, or by philosophical design?

7.3. SUBSTANCE, FORM, AND ARTISTRY

By now you may be convinced of the worthiness of the general idea of philosophical consulting, but are still quite in the dark about the specific kinds of services that such consultants provide. In this section, I will try to explicate a few kinds, via the received peripatetic taxonomy.

I begin with substance, not form. The substance of philosophical consulting is of course philosophy. Although philosophy is neither one thing nor many, nor one way of doing many things nor many ways of doing one thing, yet philosophical deliberations and activities are usually recognizable—even by laypersons—as philosophical, as opposed to something other. When consultants are evaluated by clients, the two main categories at stake are substance and form, which translate evaluatively into subject-matter and presentation, or content and performance. When it comes to content, philosophy is simply unrivaled. Philosophical substance is infinitely diversifiable, endlessly malleable, ubiquitously applicable, and completely inexhaustible. Whatever the concerns of an organization and its employees, they can be examined and reassessed philosophically. Such assessments are at once enduring yet fresh, time-tested yet new, comprehensible yet profound, structured yet spontaneous. Participants in philosophical consulting workshops revel in the realization that they can *be* philosophers, not just be exposed to philosophy. By its very nature and via those aspects of human nature which it stimulates, philosophy far outclasses its competition on providing substantiveness in organizational settings. Our main challenge in this regard is not to be oversubstantive.

The forms of philosophical consulting are many and varied. They are empirically developed frameworks that conduce to the practice of a precept, the inculcation of a virtue, or exploration of an issue. They are field-tested and fine-tuned, to the point where they yield reliable results within specifiable periods. This is particularly important for organizations, which are goal-driven and time-conscious. Most organizations will not allow more than two hours for workshops during the business day, and some philosophical interventions require at least four hours, which need not however be spent consecutively. Some of the principal forms include: motivational speaking, ethics code-building, ethics compliance, moral self-defense, short Socratic dialogue, dilemma training, leadership and governance tools, and the PEACE process for groups. I will say a few words here about each form.

MOTIVATIONAL SPEAKING

This is a well-established and lucrative industry, only sparsely populated by credentialed philosophers—notably Tom Morris, and lately also yours truly. While motivation is correctly understood as a crucial psychological precursor and determinant of both attitudes and actions, the behavioristic outlook that came to dominate so much of psychology during the first half of the twentieth century was empirically well-suited to motivating paramecia and pigeons, not people. The most conspicuously successful motivators of working professionals are neither behavioral nor industrial psychologists, but athletic coaches. The athletic coach is part father-figure, part leader, part confessor, part psychologist, part philosopher, part strategist, part field general, part innovator, and fully a motivator of his charges. Given two more-or-less equally matched teams, the better-coached one usually wins. Moreover, a talented but poorly coached team usually fares less well than even a mediocre but well-coached team. And ultimately, great coaches do not have PhDs in Coaching; they have innate capacities to coach greatly, which are often developed by serving apprenticeships under other great coaches (and sometimes under mediocre ones). Recognition of the importance of coaching is so pervasive that motivational consulting has lately bred a new sub-occupation called, not coincidentally, "Coaching." Not much more need be said here about motivational consulting (or about coaching), for its success depends more upon artistry than upon substance or form. Note, as we have already mentioned, that this is also true of client counseling. The motivational speaker is usually parachuted into a corporate event, such as a banquet or convention, to deliver a "pep-talk" to the troops. The intent is to motivate them—either by persuading them with sound reasons, inspiring them with meaningful parables, infusing them with contagious enthusiasm, galvanizing them with energetic rhetoric, imbuing them with forceful ideas, or mesmerizing them with strong charisma—to perform at or nearer optimal levels, for as long as the spell can last.

ETHICS CODE-BUILDING

Organizations of a growing number of kinds require codes of ethics. Formerly—as epitomized by Hippocrates with medicine—it was solely or primarily the professions that deemed ethical codes essential to their proper function; now we find, for a variety of reasons, that an organization without a code of ethics is like a proverbial meal without wine, day without sunshine, or executive without a corner office: it just doesn't seem right. In this domain, philosophical consulting is congruent with business and professional ethics of the kind that has been practiced since the 1970s. Applied ethics preceded philosophical practice, and to certain extents prepared the ground for it. Applied ethicists initially functioned somewhat reactively, ensconced in the academy, awaiting some incident, scandal, or disaster on which to base a lecture, a publication, or a conference. Soon applied ethicists began to function more proactively, building consulting practices, cultivating contacts, and developing methodologies. Ethics code-building is a prime example of philosophical field-work, because it entails more than a theoretical matching of precepts to professions, or ordinances to organizations.

Management consultants discovered this early on. Most of them have no conception of ethics, but have a clear conception of the corporate world. Academic philosophers, traditionally, have a deep conception of ethics, but no conception of the corporate world. Management consultants therefore prevailed by default, and hawked "knock-off" codes of ethics just as street vendors hawk "knock-off" Breitling or Rolex timepieces. The telling issue here is not how good they look, but rather how reliably they tick. While any intelligent person can formulate a code of ethics, not every intelligent person knows how to implement it in a workplace. Management consultants developed good-looking codes of ethics then faxed them or e-mailed them to employees, and considered their job done. Moses might just as well have faxed the ten commandments from the summit of Sinai; Roman Catholic confessants might just as well phone 1-800-absolvo; Zen acolytes might just as send e-mail to daisan@roshi.com; Muslim pilgrims might just as well visit www.mecca.com— but they don't. The reason they don't is that, while telephonic and virtual media facilitate some kinds of mass communication and data exchange, they don't replace humanity and physicality as essential media for moral reasoning and ethical deliberation. Thus, building a code of ethics for an organization is one thing; implementing it effectively in the workplace, quite another. The art of effective implementation itself reposes on reliable methodology—in this context is a manifestation of *phronesis*—which is precisely what philosophical practitioners have to offer. Ethics codes are best implemented through workshops designed to illustrate to employees how precepts are applied (or contravened) in everyday situations, and how private morality can come into conflict with professional ethicity. An exemplar of this kind of ethics consulting is Kenneth Kipnis (at the University of Hawaii), whose services are much in demand because he not only builds good-looking codes of ethics; he also makes them run well in the workplace.

ETHICS COMPLIANCE

In countries like Holland, where the ethos itself inculcates respect for ethicity in business, professions and government, ethics consulting flourishes on its own merits. In the U.S.A., the prevailing ethos is less idealistic or sophisticated, and is often conditioned by carrot-or-stick scenarios. Many organizations practice ethicity only in so far as they are rewarded for doing so, or punished for not doing so. In America, Federal ethics compliance regulations fuel the engine of ethics consulting. Since organizations are being held increasingly liable for the actions and utterances of their employees, and since judges, juries, and the news media are increasingly inflamed by prevailing liberal orthodoxies toxic to the American Constitution—notably supplantation of individual entitle-ments by group rights (e.g., affirmative action quotas) and suppression of individual freedom of expression by group censorship (e.g., sexual harassment policies and speech codes)—organizations need to protect themselves against collectivist freebooting, which is increasingly pervasive, highly lucrative, mor-ally debased, and blatantly unconstitutional. To the extent that the collective has usurped the individual as the atom of American polity and the beneficiary of rights meant to appertain to the individual (and ironically intended to prevent precisely what has occurred: namely, the coercion of the one by the many), it is a politically consistent corollary of this tragedy that the collective is now deemed legally responsible for the action of any of its members. The countervailing measure is ethics compliance, the only way at present for an organization to sweep minefields dense with frivolous lawsuits, hyperinflated claims, parasitic lawyers, media trials, gerrymandered verdicts, and outrageous awards.

An organization that is ethics-compliant is protected by numbers: a judge may reduce the amount of "damages" awarded against it by up to 95%—a significant amount. This is the "ethical" carrot. By the same token, an organi-zation that is non-compliant is threatened by numbers: a judge may increase the amount of "damages" awarded against it by up to 400%—a likewise sig-nificant amount. This is the "ethical" stick. If you do the math, you will quickly find that a one-million-dollar award—say, to a "victim" who was "offended" by a fellow employee of an organization—could be reduced to $50,000 if the organization is ethics-compliant, or increased to $4,000,000 if it isn't. Even if it costs an organization fifty or a hundred thousand dollars a year to implement and maintain a program of ethics compliance, that's a mighty cheap insurance premium for any medium-sized or large corporation. Ethics compliance is marketed mainly by management consultants (who may know little about ethics) and business ethicists (who usually know a good deal about ethics and have learned something about business).

MORAL SELF-DEFENSE

As an organizational consultant, I deliver a uniquely deconflationary ethical service: moral self-defense (MSD). The net effect of allowing egregious ideolo-gies, incompetent bureaucracies, and avaricious attorneys to manage the ethos of postmodern social and organizational interchange has been to render people powerless to stand their own moral ground, to ignore trivial insults, to defend themselves against verbal offenses, and to transcend common prejudices and similar flaws that can never be legislated or otherwise purged from human interchange. Persons—whether black, brown, white, yellow, male, female, hermaphroditic, gay, lesbian, or other—who are capable of mobilizing their moral worthiness are invulnerable to racism, sexism, and other such manifestations of prejudice. The price of invulnerability, however, also entails that one does not reify, aggravate, or respond to such manifestations for profit. Instead of politically correct workshops in sensitivity training, I conduct politically incorrect workshops in insensitivity training. Instead of politically correct seminars on sexual harassment, I conduct politically incorrect seminars on dealing constructively with sexual issues in the workplace. And so forth. While the ethos that drives ethics compliance rewards people for walking around with their noses permanently out-of-joint, and makes their lives thoroughly miserable in the process, moral self-defense puts people's noses back in joint, and leaves them thoroughly satisfied in the process. Organizations that succumb to the political terrorism ultimately implied by ethics compliance, affirmative action, and regulatory codes that suppress normal utterances and behaviors are bound to become vicious and therefore dysfunctional in key respects. Organizations that resist these intrusions will have happier employees, and will become more virtuous and therefore more functional.

SHORT SOCRATIC DIALOGUE

As we saw in the previous chapter, a full and unhurried Socratic dialogue can take two or three days to unfold. Most organizations cannot or will not allow their employees this much time and, on the other side of that coin, most employees probably deem themselves too busy to take this much time—even for a worthwhile purpose. Needless to say, for a philosophical practitioner nothing is more worthwhile than leading an examined life, and even an entire lifetime seems hardly sufficient for this purpose. Realistically, a philosophical consultant cannot expect a group to be released for more than a couple of hours—perhaps a half-day, or four hours, at most. It is a formidable challenge to compress two days worth of Socratic dialogue to two hours, but it can be approximated with some judicious corner-cutting. The dialogical structure itself is certainly robust enough to withstand temporal compression; the onus to perform efficiently under such constraint will then be borne by the participants and the facilitator. If the group has selected a specific question beforehand, if its members prepare their examples prior to the dialogue, if a preference matrix is used to choose the exemplar, and if the facilitator is able to take a more active role in conducting the dialogue so that it does not become bogged down in the usual places, then a great deal can be accomplished in a few hours. Using this abbreviated and accelerated method, it should be possible to formulate the core statement in such time. Needless to say, at least from the practitioner's viewpoint, a brief taste of Socratic dialogue is better than none at all. From the group's viewpoint, a tangible result is usually required to validate the experience, since the virtues of having participated in the experience may not be immediately apparent. Hence the formulation of a core statement will be the benchmark of a successful short dialogue.

If facilitators can help groups reliably to attain this benchmark in a few hours, then the short Socratic dialogue will become a mainstay of philosophical practice. The sheer number of organizations that could benefit from this activity, and the still larger number of dialogical groups they could form, would cause the demand for short Socratic dialogue to outstrip the supply of facilitators for years to come. This imbalance is not merely a crude outweighing of supply by demand, to be rectified by training more facilitators. It is also a question of skillful practice. One can no more facilitate a successful Socratic dialogue via methodology alone than one can paint a masterpiece by numbers. The qualities of a great facilitator resemble those of a great conductor (or for that matter, a great teacher), and there are many more competent conductors (or teachers) than great ones. If this be true of a full Socratic dialogue, it is even truer of a short one. The demand for greatness will therefore be great, and this bodes well for all concerned.

DILEMMA TRAINING

Business ethicists have developed some useful methodologies in their capacities as consultants; Dilemma Training is an exemplary one. Among many such models, the one developed by Henk van Luijk, Professor Emeritus of Business Ethics at Nijenrode University (Holland's equivalent of the Harvard Business School) is an excellent illustration. It has been taught to and implemented successfully by philosophical consultants in the Netherlands and the U.S.A. The empirically well-founded premise of dilemma training is that people employed by organizations experience particular kinds of moral conflicts in the workplace, which they are usually ill-prepared to manage or resolve. Examples of these include issues of loyalty to the organization itself, conflicts between private morality and professional ethics (or company policy), choices between complicity or honesty in matters of white-collar crime, the question of whistle-blowing, and other issues devolving about doing one's job with integrity. Dilemma Training is a seven-step program for identifying, articulating, and managing such problems in the workplace itself. Since ethics is not axiomatizable, there is no algorithmic or infallibly prescriptive way to solve moral dilemmas; however, the seven steps of dilemma training allow one at least to understand a problem in a way that lends itself to more effective management. The examined problem is not necessarily the solved one, but the solved problem is rarely the unexamined one. The seven steps are:

1. *Formulate the core issue.* What is the moral or ethical conflict about?

2. *Identify the actors.* Whose rights and claims need to be taken into account?

3. *Gather data.* What minimum information is necessary and relevant in this case?

4. *Specify responsibility.* Who is accountable? Who has the dilemma?

5. *Elaborate arguments, both pro and con.* What reasons support possible resolutions? At this stage, plurality is a virtue.

6. *Attempt a decision.* Which arguments are most persuasive, and why?

7. *Justify the decision.* Can you live with this? Would the same reasoning apply again? What would have to change for your decision to change?

While any college instructor or university professor of applied ethics will recognize some of the foregoing steps as typical in pedagogic elaboration of case studies, e.g., in classroom exercises involving business ethics, engineering ethics, biomedical ethics, and the like, there is also a conspicuous difference between the classroom and the workplace, akin to the difference between boot-camp and combat. While many students take casework quite seriously, they are also able to set it aside at the end of a period or the completion of an assignment. By contrast, people who experience moral dilemmas in real-life situations are unable to set them aside, or leave them behind, until or unless they find some way to effect an equilibration or harmonization of the problem. Similarly, the college instructor who competently or even expertly guides his class through an exercise in applied ethical reasoning is not necessarily able to perform the equivalent function outside the groves of academe—where it is often more sorely required. As with all the above-mentioned methodologies, the mere acquisition of a tool does not automatically entail expertise in its utilization. The emphasis in the phrase "philosophical *practice*" is not accidental; effective implementation of the methodology as a practitioner is a matter of training and praxis.

THE PEACE PROCESS

This framework for managing or resolving everyday problems philosophically was introduced in *Plato, Not Prozac*. It met with an interesting reception from both lay readers and fellow practitioners. The process originated with a request from the publisher of this ostensible self-help book for an acronymic characterization of "the methodology" employed in my counseling practice. Like most philosophical counselors, I reflexively eschewed the very notion of a method as antithetical to philosophical inquiry into personal problems, until I began to reflect on what, if anything, distinguishes what we generally do from what psychologists and psychiatrists generally do. This further led me to contemplate the perspective from which we view our clients and their problems—the ground upon which philosophical counseling is configured by the counselor—as well as the way in which the client's perspective changes when the counseling process is fruitful—the way in which the client, as figure, modifies his self-conception. These ratiocinations impelled me to articulate the PEACE schema, which retrospectively described at least two-thirds of the cases I had handled, after eight years of practice at that time, without having preconceived or consciously adhered to any method during those eight years. The PEACE process is therefore a contentless form that suggests some contours of philosophical counseling, without prescribing any particular methodology.

After the publication of *Plato Not Prozac*, I began to receive both real and virtual correspondence from lay readers who more or less successfully applied the process for themselves (as the book ideally intended), and from some lay readers who became stuck in the Contemplative phase (as the book warned might happen) and who sought philosophical counseling from me or my colleagues. I also received correspondence from psychologists and psychiatrists, who said the schema made sense to them and who sought advice in applying it.

Ultimately I heard from some philosophical counselors, who had been initially skeptical about any schema for counseling (skepticism being a workaday facet of a philosopher's occupational stance), but who conducted empirical "trials" and discovered that the contentless form of PEACE applied to many of their cases too. These external confirmations, in addition to those internal to my practice, make me less uncomfortable with the relentless marketing forces that compel acronymization and similar noetic distillations, and which often err on the side of oversimplification if not wanton dumbing-down, on the misguided premise that popularization necessitates "stupidification" as opposed to edification. I am also unopposed to having the PEACE Process represented on book-jackets as my "signature" innovation; there are many worse things with which one might be identified.

In any case, PEACE applies to organizations as well as to individuals; that is to say, it can be used as a schema for addressing individual problems manifest in the workplace. As such, it can be a meta-methodology for philosophical consultants. In case you missed *Plato Not Prozac*, the five steps are:

> Problem: correctly identifying the thing that is
> problematic.
>
> Emotion: constructively expressing one's emotional
> response to the problem.
>
> Analysis: rationally deliberating one's options in
> aid of resolving the problem.
>
> Contemplation: discovering a disposition that allows
> one to choose the best option.
>
> Equilibrium: reaching a state in which the problem
> is no longer problematic.

LEADERSHIP AND GOVERNANCE

While all the aforementioned forms of philosophical consulting are either meant to be applied, or can be applied, across the spectrum of a given organization, philosophical tools for leadership and governance appear dedicated, self-evidently, to leaders and governors. While this is *prima facie* true, the dedication is not exclusive. A leading pioneer of philosophical practice for leaders is Peter Koestenbaum, who has explored the philosophy of leadership more deeply and more keenly than any other practitioner I know. His "Leadership Diamond," which incorporates Vision, Reality, Ethics, and Courage at its vertices, in the service of eliciting inner greatness from leaders, is a philosophically rich and aesthetically textured model.[17] It is not accidental that Koestenbaum has enjoyed great success modeling greatness; he is gifted with a wonderful combination of analytical expertise, creative insight, and practical wisdom. However, insofar as all enlightened individuals strive to lead their lives authentically and usefully, and to govern their affairs sagaciously and optimally, regardless of their particular occupations or stations, it follows that philosophical tools for leadership and governance can be utilized by a great many thoughtful people. One need not be a leader or a governor to derive significant benefits from Koestenbaum' s model.

ARTISTRY

Having briefly treated the substance and some of the more prevalent forms of philosophical consulting, it is germane to say a few words about artistry. In the performing arts—which include politics, acting, music, and philosophical practice—there is no substitute for artistry. The components of artistry include charisma, confidence, credibility, charm, energy, flair, perceptiveness, reactivity, spontaneity, style, technical mastery, improvisational skill, showmanship, and the right balance of gravity and levity. Some of these qualities (e.g., technical mastery, perceptiveness, style) can be developed by direct practice; others (e.g., confidence, spontaneity, energy) can be enhanced by indirect practice; others still (e.g., allure, intensity, humor) appear to be gifts of nature, which can be diminished by adverse circumstance but cannot be greatly augmented by exercise.

These qualities are more important to the organizational consultant than to the group facilitator, and more important to the group facilitator than to the client counselor. The reason for this is not difficult to ascertain, if we consider that the distinction between theoretical philosophy and philosophical practice resembles the distinction between teaching in a classroom and performing on a stage. Classroom teaching, from K–12 through university, ranges from inspiring to appalling. There are great teachers and terrible teachers, and all kinds of teachers in between, but this makes little difference to a student who knows what he wants to learn, and knows how to wend his way through the system. Some students, however, will mistake an interesting teacher for an interesting subject. They will value (or devalue) a given subject according to the interest (or disinterest) the teacher stirs in them. They will fondly remember spirited courses, and simply toil through or sleep through the remainder.[18] Memories of some professor or other may inspire them or discourage them for a lifetime, but the point is that they *have* a lifetime aside from and beyond their formal schooling. Working adults, locked into careers that in turn sustain other possibilities and responsibilities, careers whose rewards are often tempered with conflicts, are much more in need of fresh inspiration than are students. If their organization brings in a motivational speaker who puts them to sleep or bores them to tears—or worse, exacerbates their problems—then motivational speaking's reputation will suffer, and the speaker will be looking for other work soon. And if their organization brings in a philosophical consultant who is long on substance, deep on methodology, but short on style, philosophical consulting's reputation will suffer, and the philosopher will be looking for other work soon. Consulting to an organization is about performance, as well as content and method. It entails artistry and entertainment, as well as professionalism and education. Organizations hire consultants to improve aspects of performance; and the consultant also has to perform. That means delivering a service that has not only substance and form, but also style.

By contrast, philosophical counseling more closely resembles classroom teaching, in that the counselor, like the teacher, can be competent without being charismatic. In fact, there are many effective counselors and teachers alike whose effectiveness reposes precisely on a placid, cautious, or studious demeanor. These qualities can be very desirable in one-on-one counseling, as well as in classroom teaching, but they are not so desirable on Broadway stages, on Hollywood sets, or in high-energy corporate arenas.

While I believe that most philosophers can master contents and methods of organizational consulting, I do not believe that most can master performance in quite the same way. It seems to me that a performer can learn to improve performance more easily than a non-performer can learn to perform. I believe this to be true of politics, acting, music, sports, and philosophical practice. This is not a strictly a credo; my belief is founded on my experience with politics, acting, music, sports, and philosophical practice.

7.4. THE SUMMIT OF PRACTICE

From this brief excursion into philosophy qua organizational consulting, it should be clear that the opportunities in this area represent the summit of philosophical practice. Philosophy for organizations not only entails a modular application of counseling, facilitation, and consulting techniques; it also has potentially far-reaching ramifications in terms of *realpolitik* in the twenty-first century. To recapitulate the overarching thesis of this chapter: from the ancient to the early modern world, philosophers and their writings were the tutors of choice to monarchs, crown princes, and popes, and thus exerted seminal influence on those who governed the political (and hence, at that time, every other) estate of man. Politics was the noblest art, as Aristotle conceived it, and it persisted as such until the very successes of the Enlightenment and the Industrial Revolution renormalized it, for both good and ill. *Homo politicus* remained the same in substance, but he metamorphosed too often from a statesman to a politician, on average from a ruler to a lawyer, in the main from an aristocrat to a bureaucrat, and at worst from an autocrat to a sociopath. The relentless flow of political power from theocrats to ruling classes to democratic mobs to ideocratic revolutionaries potentiated egalitarian reforms, but by the same token depotentiated statesmanship, permitted the resources of unstable states to be monopolized by sadistic mass-murderers and squandered by egregious doctrines, and debased elected political office in stable states to the extent that politics became just unimportant enough to be left in the hands of politicians. Bereft of teleology, hamstrung with expediency, prostrate from electioneering, profligate through whoring after votes, flesh bought and paid for by campaign contributors, and soul mortgaged to spin doctors, a less noble creature than the twentieth-century politician can scarcely be conceived. In the course of a typical day, or incumbency, he no more needed philosophical guidance than a worm needs a backbone or a pig needs wings.

The denobilization of political office and the concomitant atrophy of political purpose produced a dearth of statesmanship. This, combined with the unsurpassed and uncontained destructiveness of modern warfare, the dramatic shift of primary targets from military to nonmilitary installations, and the ultimate conscription of civilian women, children and other noncombatants into front-line "troops" of nuclear war, long-term hostages of cold war, and immediate targets of terrorism, convinced the would-be developers and sustainers of economic prosperity that their interests were far better served if political machination became subordinate to economic growth. In sum, the failures of nationalism sired the successes of multinationalism, which speedily paved the way for globalization. So politics is finally relegated to a sport, more intricate but less entertaining than football, and sponsored (like all sports) by large corporations. And warfare is finally relegated to international business, mainly in conventional weapons, smaller only than the petroleum industry, and an order of magnitude larger than microelectronics. If two tribes or two states wish to indulge in mutual slaughter, dozens of developed nations will sell them arms, on the conditions that no nukes are deployed, that no oil supplies are compromised, and that the conflict is locally contained. If they tire of fighting, the developers can show them how to elect politicians, franchise fast-food chains, warehouse toxic waste, open sweatshops, unionize labor, use contraceptives, get divorces, build tennis courts, and host an ATP event. The populace can be lured by the real promise of a more commodious life—rather than be dragged kicking and screaming—from whatever century they've been inhabiting, into the twenty-first. It's not utopia, but it beats dystopia hands down.

Unlike politicians, corporations need philosophical guidance, and moreover know they need it. Like Renaissance monarchs, corporations control the resources and have the vision to patronize the finest arts—poetry, literature, music, dance, painting, sculpting, acting, play-writing, film-making—and, of course, philosophy. Corporations could even resuscitate politics, if some philosopher showed them how. Much of their artistic patronage is conspicuously consigned to advertising, which is why some ads embody far better artistry than many arts sold as art. Although some corporations have begun to appreciate aesthetics, they could benefit from philosophical guidance in that area too.

Plato was wrong about philosophers in one key respect: on the whole, they do not make good kings. But they do make superlative tutors to kings, queens, princes, princesses, and their courts; which is to say, superlative consultants to corporate directors, officers, and their organizations.

NOTES

1. E.g., see my *Fair New World*, of which reviewer D. Smith wrote: "To the casual reader some of these excursions may appear too bizarre to be taken seriously. The truth, however, is more disturbing. *Fair New World* satirizes the actual daily life in a growing number of North American universities." David Smith, Review of *Fair New World*, in *Newsletter of the Society for Academic Freedom and Scholarship*, July 1995, p. 14.

2. H. Bergson, *The Meaning of the War (Life and Matter in Conflict)* (London: T. Fisher Unwin 1915), pp. 35–36: "What would happen if the mechanical forces, which science had brought to a state of readiness for the service of mankind, should themselves take possession of man in order to make his nature material as their own? What kind of a world would it be if this mechanism should seize the human race entire, and if the peoples, instead of raising themselves to a richer and more harmonious diversity, as *persons* may do, were to fall into the uniformity of *things*? ... What would happen, in short, if the moral effort of humanity should turn in its tracks at the moment of attaining its goal, and if some diabolical contrivance should cause it to produce the mechanization of spirit instead of the spiritualization of matter?" Later, Mumford called human servitude to machines and concomitant attenuation of consciousness "mechanically engineered coma": see L. Mumford, *The Transformations of Man* (New York: Harper & Brothers, 1956), p. 174 *et passim*.

3. For the usual reason, a kind of reverse Berry Paradox: the Tao that can be named is not the true Tao. (See Lao Tzu, chap. 1.) Hence the consultant with "Taoist" on his business card is not a true Taoist.

4. See S. Mintz, *The Hunting of the Leviathan* (Cambridge: Cambridge University Press, 1962), p. 62. See also *Journal of the* [House of] *Commons*, 17 October 1666: "that the Committee to which the Bill against Atheism and Profaneness is committed to be empowered to receive information touching such books as tend to atheism, blasphemy and profaneness, or against the essence and attributes of God, and in particular ... the book of Mr. Hobbes called the 'Leviathan,' and to report the matter with their opinion to the House." Among many similar occurrences, Daniel Scargill, Fellow of Corpus Christi College, Cambridge, was expelled from the University in 1668, which accepted the third draft of his recantation: "professing that I gloried to be an Hobbsist and an Atheist ... I have lived in great licentiousness, swearing rashly, drinking intemperately, boasting myself insolently, corrupting others by my pernicious principles and examples, to the Dishonour of God, the Reproach of the University, the Scandal of Christianity, and the just offence of mankind." Cited by Mintz, pp. 50–51.

5. J. von Neumann and O. Morgenstern, *Theory of Games and Economic Behaviour* (New York: Wiley, 1964), pp. 10–11 (original work published 1946): "A particularly striking expression of the popular misunderstanding about this pseudo-maximum problem is the famous statement according to which the purpose of social effort is the 'greatest possible good for the greatest possible number.' A guiding

principle cannot be formulated by the requirement of maximizing two (or more) functions at once." Although near-universally ignored or uncomprehended by moralists, this is the kernel of the refutation of utilitarianism as a workable ethic.

6. See M. Cranston's *Introduction* to J. J. Rousseau, *The Social Contract* (Harmondsworth: Penguin, 1968), p. 27 (original work published 1762): "Indeed the *Social Contract* may be read as an answer to Hobbes by an author whose mind was stimulated by the brilliance of Hobbes's reasoning, but who could not stomach Hobbes's conclusions."

7. J. J. Rousseau, *The Social Contract*, Book 1, chap. 1. If you prefer, "Man was born free, and he is everywhere in chains."

8. Cited by B. Inglis, *The Opium War* (London: Hodder & Stoughton, 1976), p. 41.

9. Ibid., p. 126.

10. Ibid., p. 204.

11. Ibid., pp. 198–199.

12. P. T. de Chardin, *The Phenomenon of Man* (Glasgow: William Collins & Sons, 1982) (original work published 1955). The nöosphere is a sphere of consciousness "outside and above the biosphere" (pp. 201–202). Chardin imagined that a Martian observer of earth would, through unspecified instrumentation, be able to detect "the phosphorescence of thought" (p. 203).

13. There is no better illustration of this tendency than the recent book by J. Schiro, ed., *Memos to the President—Management Advice from the Nation's Top CEOs* (New York: Wiley, 2000). In his *Introduction*, editor James Schiro, who is the CEO of PriceWaterhouseCoopers, states the book's premise: "The management challenges facing government, business, and the non-profit sectors today are more similar than they are different. The CEOs who participated in this project believe that the insights they have gained in managing large organizations are transferrable to other organizations" (pp. xi–xii).

14. See B. Russell, "The Fate of Thomas Paine," in *Why I Am Not a Christian* (New York: Simon & Schuster, 1957), pp. 133–147.

15. I have touched on this in Chapter 5. I have not yet published the work—*On Human Conflict*—that more fully deconflates biology and culture.

16. This was on prime-time television, which is the only citation it merits.

17. See P. Koestenbaum, *Leadership: The Inner Side of Greatness* (San Francisco: Jossey-Bass, 1991).

18. A *sine qua non* of entertaining professors was Stephen Leacock, the great Canadian satirist (and serious drinker), whose sense of humor was so profound that he packed lecture halls as an economist—hardly an intrinsically entertaining subject. People flocked to hear his hilarious lectures without bothering to register for the course.

PART III

Professionalization of Philosophical Practice

CHAPTER 8

Pioneering Versus Pedagogy

*A*merica is a place wherein professionalism is not only pioneered—it is also respected. This follows from the *raison d'être* of America: it is the definitive place where money is made. Consider some great empires past and their respective legacies. The primary legacy of the temporal Athenian empire is the power of rational inquiry, as embodied in Plato's Academy. This is the near-ubiquitous model for higher education. The primary legacy of the temporal Roman Empire is the spiritual Roman Church. The latter has proved incomparably further-reaching and enduring. The primary legacy of the temporal British Empire is the universal English language, the international language of business and science alike. Again, the latter has proved more far-reaching and enduring. What will be the primary legacy of the American Empire? I submit that it is already plain: the American dollar is the global unit of currency. While not everyone accepts America's liberties, or is prepared to pay the price that Americans pay to maintain them, I have never seen anyone decline American dollars. And as regards the aforementioned legacies, we all know people who repudiate rational inquiry, or reject Roman Catholicism, or refuse to learn English—but I know no one who declines American dollars. The dollar self-asserts its status: it proclaims "*Novus Ordo Seclorum,*" or New World Order.

If we ask Americans themselves what they expect to purchase with their dollars, they usually reply: reliable goods and reputable services. People who manufacture reliable goods or deliver reputable services also tend to make more money themselves, so they can afford to purchase luxuriously reliable goods and elegantly reputable services. What is given away freely in America falls into one of two classes: real things for which consumers don't pay, because these things are either prizes or *pro bono* services, but are otherwise worth their market price; and unreal things for which consumers do pay, because these unreal things are come-ons for various kinds of confidence artistry, but are otherwise worth less than their asking price.

Americans are quite good at distinguishing professionalism from amateurism, although just as likely as anyone to be cheated by unscrupulous professionals or swindled by impostors posing as professionals. Nonetheless, professionalism is a virtue in America, because it implies expertise and experience, which are usually worth paying for. One of the cornerstones of professionalism is pedagogy: a profession implies a corpus of specialized knowledge, which although nonproprietary is not usually acquired autodidactically. The knowledge possessed by doctors, lawyers, engineers, and other professionals is public knowledge, in the sense that anyone can go to a decent library and read what they read. Their experience is less nonproprietary, for that is mostly acquired after graduating from an accredited degree program of specialized higher education, which entitles one to the privilege of serving an internship, a residency, an apprenticeship, or the equivalent transitional period during which one learns, under supervision from seasoned professionals, how to apply the knowledge.

Even at this early stage of characterizing professions, we have invoked a political dimension, for a professional is not an isolated individual practicing in a vacuum; rather, a member of a professional association that (among other things) liaises with governments to recognize and regulate the criteria of a given professional practice. This is a peripatetic teleological phenomenon, in that the structure of a given professional practice is largely determined by its function. Its end determines its means and, since the ends of all professions are conditioned explicitly or implicitly by a normative as opposed to a technical precept—"First do no harm"—the State has an obligation to abet the enforcement of this ethical principle in law, in due consultation with the body of professionals in question; for the first (and some say only) business of any just state is to protect its citizens from harms they do not seek to incur.

The means of satisfying non-maleficence changes with knowledge, and knowledge—where not throttled by dogma, preempted by superstition or banned by ideology—is bound to grow more reliable over time. Thus Hippocrates practiced non-maleficence by refusing to operate on patients; whereas after the antiseptic reforms of Lister and Semmelweis, procedures previously proscribed by their expected outcomes (infection, gangrene, and death) became routine and routinely survivable. It is now malpractice *not* to perform some surgeries. It is not medicine that needs to be learned and practiced; rather, the state of the art and science of medicine. Those who best understand the state of that art and science best represent its professional interests, and liaise appropriately with governments to ensure that no unqualified persons practice that art and science, in order to protect patents from harms they do not seek to incur. Note that this professional edifice, erected and elaborated primarily to satisfy the precept of non-maleficence, has the secondary fiduciary effect of bringing repute to the profession, by instilling public trust.

In order to protect the public from harms they do not seek to incur, only doctors are lawfully permitted to perform or supervise surgeries, and only engineers are lawfully permitted to erect or supervise erection of edifices. Not all professions, however, are regulated in this way. While only lawyers can join a bar association, anyone may choose to represent himself, or to be represented by a non-lawyer, in a court of law. Although the adage "anyone who acts as his own attorney has a fool for a client" is indubitable, this libertarian privilege persists in a nation increasingly manipulated by lawyers, controlled by judicial activists, and whose constitution is undermined by both.[1] The salient distinction in this matter, as reflected (or not) in laws regulating the practice of medicine or engineering on the one hand, and law itself on the other, is between harms to one's physical person versus harms to one's collateral interests. Most criminal law does not allow a victim's consent, even if informed, to be a ground of exculpation for murder or other harms done to that person.[2] Thus the state will not permit an unlicensed physician to prescribe medications or perform operations, or an unlicensed engineer to build bridges or wire buildings, because of the obvious physical harms that can ensue, from which the state is obliged to shield its citizens. Inappropriate legal counsel, however, is not construed in the same light. While physical harms can follow from receiving inappropriate iatrogenic attentions, and injury or death can follow from using or inhabiting hazardous structures, the potential harms that ensue from legal misrepresentation are not direct injuries to one's person; rather, are partly self-inflicted injuries to one's collateral interests—e.g., liberty, property, opportunity, and the like. Civil law permits an individual to seek or to consent to incur such harms, just as it permits one to drink too much or marry badly. Criminal lawyers, however, can be chastened by the courts, disciplined by law societies, or even disbarred for inadequately representing their clients' interests, and ill-advised pleas can be questioned by judges—all this for the sake of not harming the client, and avoiding disrepute to the profession.

Since psychological and philosophical counseling are also professions, and are likewise governed by the precept of non-maleficence, one is bound to ask what kind of harms they can do. In so far as inappropriate talk-therapy can harm one's person, it should be regulated. In so far as it can harm only one's collateral interests, it should not. In the cases of both psychological and philosophical counseling, the potential harm to a client's person is real but indirect; it issues hypothetically from mistaking a physical problem for a psychological or a philosophical one. Talk-therapy alone cannot heal a broken arm, but it can and should provide a referral to a physician. Talk-therapy alone cannot stop a manic-depressive from being manic or depressed, but it can help deliberate the benefits and detriments of medication. Talk-therapy alone cannot stop a suicidal person from committing suicide, but neither can any other form of treatment (save, in the short run, extreme restraint). Persons who are nonfunctional because of physical illness or injury, or acute or debilitating emotional distress, are not good candidates for talk-therapy in the first instance, although they may become excellent candidates once their physical or emotional state is medically stable. Failure to recognize the kinds of dysfunctionalities that make people poor candidates for talk-therapy is professionally maleficent, and is therefore the main justification for regulating its practice. In so far as injury to one's collateral interests is concerned, just as in the matter of legal representation, the state has no business regulating the provision of verbal advice purely to prevent such nonphysical harms. Thus professional talk-therapists of psychological or philosophical stripe occupy a ground somewhere between the medical and the legal professions. We shall return to this comparison when we deal directly with political and legislative issues, in Chapters 9 and 10.

Second in rank after the precept of non-maleficence, and often foremost in the consumer's mind, is beneficence. While the professional seeks first to do no harm, and second to do what good he can, most consumers seek some benefit in the first instance, and may thus be unwary or incognizant of harms disguised as goods, or may be surprised when good intentions, accompanied by unintended errors, occasion harmful results. The latter is what malpractice insurance covers. But when it becomes clear that a given profession accomplishes, on balance, conspicuously more good than harm, then it becomes desirable that the profession be recognized by governments. Such recognition is not restrictive; rather, probative. Most professions are licensed or certified because of the enormous good they can do: their legislative recognition goes toward acknowledgment and enhancement of repute, and not solely toward prevention of harm.

Consistently, where non-maleficence is not a factor, one also finds professions recognized solely on the basis of beneficence. One example is accounting, whose practice is unrestricted. Anyone may call himself a public accountant (PA), hang out a shingle, and render professional services. Companies like H&R Block render this service annually, and undoubtedly most of their seasonally recruited "tax-consultants" know only how to fill in the required fields in the income-tax software—if they know that much. But since they can harm only one's collateral interests in sheltering income, governments have no business interfering with their provision of services.

Caveat emptor. By the same token, some public accounts have demonstrated professional expertise and ongoing familiarity with increasingly complex regimens of taxation, to the extent that they merit probative recognition for the beneficent services they render: thus they may become certified public accountants, or CPAs. The consumer who chooses a CPA over a PA can be reasonably assured that the CPA, unlike the PA, has surpassed a certain threshold of professionalism, in aid of rendering a beneficent service. Any PA who claims to be just as expert and experienced as a CPA thus begs a simple question: "Then why don't you become Certified, and call yourself a CPA?"

Notwithstanding the considerable differences between these aforementioned professions, and the spectrum of legislative recognitions they may or may not merit, they all have two things in common: first, they were once pioneered by innovators outside the academy; second, formal training of prospective practitioners is now undertaken pedagogically, inside the academy. America is a great place for pioneers, for it provides an ethos that pioneers crave: one that celebrates individuality, liberty, and opportunity. There still thrives a naive rough-and-readiness, a child-like (not necessarily childish) open-mindedness, a brash self-confidence, a willingness to take calculated risks, and a pride in self-sufficiency—qualities which at once impressed and depressed Tocqueville, and which are still in evidence today (still weathering sabotage by assorted enemies of individualism and its cognate liberties). In a way, America has pioneered pioneering itself.

First-generation pioneering entails arduous trailblazing, which opens new territories that get parceled into fresh fields. Second-generation pioneering entails the clearing, ploughing, and planting of these fields, which is accomplished by hard-working settlers attracted by novel prospects. If the climate is favorable, the soil fertile, the seed viable, the harvest bountiful, and the market amenable, then the pioneering venture becomes a retrospective success. This tradition is both neolithic and political: it consists of founding and building permanent, self-sustaining settlements from the ground up, and then of confederating a network of such settlements into a polity—or in today's parlance, an industry. Philosophical practitioners are accomplishing the work of two and more generations in one and less, primarily because of the propitiousness of the times and secondarily because of the efforts of the pioneers. In the past fleeting decade, we have blazed trails, defined new territories, attracted hardy settlers, driven off hostiles, cleared and ploughed fresh fields, and kept varmints at bay. The ground having been prepared, we are now ready to sow our seed. Although the fruits of philosophical practice are to be tasted by all who sincerely desire them, the orchards that bear this fruit are best planted and tended in the academy.

Although the humanities and social science wings of the contemporary academy are in monumental disarray—deconstructed, despoiled, and debased by tyrannies of intolerance, hyperbolic politicization of race and sex, hatred of merit, denial of facticity, perversion of justice, oppression of freedom, abolition of reason—it is therefore the ideal host of the cultural revolution and renaissance that philosophical practice heralds. The hard sciences, along with engineering, have remained largely immune from despoliation by the new self-righteous barbarians, mostly because their subject matter is incomprehensible to the illiterate and innumerate idealogues spawned in their postmodern vats of vituperative but self-immolating ruction. To be sure, there are shrill feminist critiques of quantum electrodynamics and general relativity, revisionist ethnocentric claims that sub-Saharan Africans or ancient Aztecs reached the moon before NASA, and hopeful theses asserting that the Solvay Conferences were really fronts for queer studies—but the acid test of our civilization lies is its readiness to repudiate these farragoes of nonsense; for if it succumbs wholesale to them, it succumbs full stop.

MIT has recently come under fire for alleged "gender imbalance," and it remains to be seen whether that prestigious institution's administrators possess sufficient backbone to dismiss the spurious, ideologically motivated charge, and reaffirm the plain truth: that women are on average far less interested in natural science than are men, and are on average far less well-equipped by nature to solve spatio-temporal and mathematical problems. Those who can, do; those can't, don't. Canada's formerly prestigious NSERC[3] has thoroughly sullied itself in sordid sexual politics, by earmarking "girl money" to guarantee scientific funding for undeserving women (and to deprive deserving men) in order to satisfy arbitrary quota systems that fly in the face of sex difference and gender preference. One might as well assert that dwarves can't slam-dunk basketballs because of "institutional heightism," and guarantee basketball scholarships to the "vertically challenged," in order to redress "height imbalance" in the NBA.

For the record, I have been blessed with exemplary teachers, friends, and colleagues of every conceivable race, sex, and gender orientation, as well as of many and varied ethnic origins. Their respective excellences flow from individual ability, individual persistent hard work, individual accomplishment, individual merit, individual principled character, and individual unwillingness to accept either blame or credit for membership in a group—whether identified by race, sex, gender, or ethnicity. In contemporary America, almost anyone can attain a measure of personal fulfillment. Those who fail to do so, and who blame "institutional" racism, sexism, genderism, or ethnicism had better discover and remedy the true failing in themselves, rather than reify and condemn the false failing in others.

Among those who insist on blaming others for their own shortcomings, the political tactic of choice for thirty years has been to howl the refrain "institutional ... ism", and hurl the accompanying invective as loudly as possible, until craven authorities capitulate and remove objective standards. This is the fanatical anti-realist view of social justice: that every profession must reflect the demographic profile of the largest or lowest common denominatorial populace; then everything will be utopian. When such unrealistic expectations become enshrined as unchallengeable tenets of political orthodoxy, social engineering of explicit or implicit quota systems—with its attendant purge of objective merit and the replacement of pedagogy with political indoctrination—replaces open competition, meritocracy, and the transmission and development of reliable knowledge. This is not progress but regress, not egalitarianism but barbarism, not liberty and opportunity but re-enslavement and incapacitation, not social justice but vicious fraud. "Diversity" is not a virtue: racial, sexual, genderal, or ethnic variation are features that groups may or may not manifest, and are no guides to their performance. The NBA is mostly black, and it performs very well. The PGA is mostly white, and it performs very well. The Vienna Boys Choir is entirely male, and it performs very well. The Rockettes are entirely female, and they perform very well. The New York Philharmonic Orchestra is of mixed race and sex, and it performs very well. People demand good performances from professionals; that is all they demand. Professionals need pedagogic excellence as part of their formation, and that is what the universities are supposed to supply—whether in athletics, where it is called "coaching," or in the lecture-hall, where it is called "teaching," or in administration, where it is called "governance." Lack of substantive excellence in any of these areas, and the substitution of ideology, indoctrination, and other vices disguised as virtues in the place of substantive excellence leads to immediate and often precipitous decline in performance.

American university administrators who failed to hold the line of excellence in the past thirty years, and who empowered vicious ideocrats, destructive ideologues, obtuse demagogues, and politically correct despots in the academy—whether through misplaced guilt, naive expectation, craven cowardice, abysmal incompetence, or political expedience—have brought the American mind-politic to the brink of an abyss. I teach in one of the most celebrated public institutions in America: The City College of New York. In the vanguard of the widespread cultural capitulation of 1969, City College instituted an Open Admissions policy, and instantly obliterated not only its own standards, but also the standards of the New York Public schools which furnish its students. As the Russian proverb finely says, "A fish rots from the head down." Thirty years later, the rottenness is unimaginable. I have been affiliated with some fine institutions: the University of London, the Hebrew University of

Jerusalem, and the University of British Columbia, where freshmen are very much alike. The best make it a joy to teach; the worst, a struggle; the average, a job. But aside from a few remnants of former high culture—the impecunious bodies but brilliant minds that City College elevates into productive citizens—the majority of freshmen I encounter at CCNY are so ill-prepared by their K–12 "educations" and their utter lack of ancillary acculturation that they read at high-school levels, and write and possess general knowledge at primary-school levels. This is not a university; it is a travesty. And it is not confined to City College; it is rampant throughout America.[4] On top of this, the collapse is masterminded by Education Departments, which consist of largely persons evidently unable to master any subject matter whatsoever, yet who arrogate to themselves—with the complicity of moribund and vegetative administrations—the vision to speak for the entire enterprise.

For how long does America expect to maintain itself as the world's leading power and light of liberty, when it abuses its own liberties so as produce a generation of mindless sheep? Over-attention to the body (replete with an industry of junk-food), and under-attention to the mind (replete with an industry of junk-thought) have wrought this desperate state of affairs. The decline is reversible, but at the cost of accepting some plain truths, even if they contradict sacrosanct orthodoxies. Given Americans' fondness for hamburger, they shouldn't mind butchering some sacred cows. First and foremost, the well-being of a body-politic depends primarily upon the well-being of its mind-politic. Second, the well-being of a mind-politic depends primarily upon the education its children receive. Third, the education its children receive depends primarily on who sets—or removes—the standards, from attainment of which flow professional performance, reputability, and non-maleficence to consumers; and from removal of which flow unprofessional nonperformance, disreputability, and maleficence to consumers. Thus the preeminent precept of professionalism is irrevocably linked to education: good educational programs enhance the odds of graduating good professionals; bad programs, bad professionals. Good education itself requires (among other things) good pedagogy; bad education, bad pedagogy. Thus the link between professionalism and pedagogy is forged.

And when it comes to pedagogy, America appears to harbor few Old-World prejudices. This lack of prejudice may well repose on familiar Tocquevillian ground: the absence of an *ancien régime* politically may have prefigured the absence of an *ancienne étude* pedagogically. It is somewhat paradoxical that America was founded by Renaissance men—a formidable intellectual elite—who nonetheless larded and sealed an anti-intellectualism so deep-grained that it leveled their own Renaissance, and continues to oppose every edifice that threatens to contribute to American high culture. In America, the intellectual subsists at the yahoo's pleasure. This is worse than living on borrowed time, for the postmodern yahoo cannot tell the time. Hence, America has little time for its intellectuals, unless they find a way to strike a popular chord without severely impairing the quality of their intelligence.

In keeping with lowest common denominator postmodernism, the American education system has been leveled during the past thirty years; in postmodernspeak, "deconstructed." It makes little difference whether one attends a generic State University or an Ivy League school; throngs of incoming freshman, maleficiaries of the feel-good/know-nothingism that lately passes for "education" in America, can neither read nor write nor reason. Such reading, writing, and reasoning as can be done in the humanities is largely consecrated to ideological vilification and debasement of all that is good, noble, and progressive in European civilization, and replacement of high culture with myths about aboriginal physics, primeval literature, and revisionist history. Noetic Luddites and self-righteous zealots have transformed the American academy into a gulag of miniature People's Democratic, Ethnocratic, and Femocratic Republics, rife with hatred of reason, intolerance of facticity, politicization of race, sex, and gender, infringement of individual liberties, and abrogation of due process. The American Constitution holds no more sway at Harvard or Berkeley than in Havana or Beijing.

Yet scattered survivors remain afloat in this high tide of cultural hara-kiri. The flotsam and jetsam of the scuttled Enlightenment project, there is little apparent pattern to their survival. Here a Department of Political Science; there, of Sociology; elsewhere, of Psychology; elsewhere still, of History; here again, of Philosophy—have resisted the pervasive totalitarianism, the scholarly bankruptcy, the mockery of merit, the neo-Procrustean Inn of Education, which, the better to promote its proprietors' political agenda, leaves students' feet intact and beheads them instead. A few scattered Departments still resist, however futilely, and keep the torches burning. Again, some of these are Philosophy Departments, and most of them specialize in analytic philosophy. Although analytic philosophy has very little truck with the practical world, it turns out to be an excellent preparation for that world, since it demands that students be able to read, write and reason. Unwittingly, analytic philosophy in its waning years turns out to be a bastion against barbarism, a fortress guarding the very atoms of high culture—reading, writing, reasoning—and beyond these, all the exotic molecules of civilization: the humanities, the arts, the sciences, the technologies, the interdisciplinaries.

Some analytic philosophers have been predictably hostile to applied ethics, a growth industry in its own right, which has built valuable bridges between philosophy, and business, computing, engineering, environmentalism, journalism, law and medicine. Analytic philosophy prides itself on being "hard"—that is, rigorous, logical, and complex—and often sneers at applied ethics for being "soft"—that is, lax, intuitive, and facile. This charge itself is a product of emotion, not reason. In my view, the putative distinction between "hard" and "soft" philosophy is itself "soft"—a product of internecine turf wars, ego-problems, and tunnel vision that accompany such quarrels. To be a competent philosopher today, one must know some ethical theory, among many other things. To be a more complete philosopher, one might also know something about applied ethics. If one must draw a distinction, perhaps "pure" versus "applied" or "theoretical" versus "practical" philosophy is more appropriate; after all, such nomenclature has valuable precedents in mathematics and physics alike. Then it should be noted that applied mathematicians and experimental physicists are not necessarily deficient in theory; rather, they use theory to inform practice—which may serve to reinform theory itself—rather than using theory to extend theory, as pure theoreticians do. And even the greatest of theoreticians, such as Einstein, required an equivalently great experimentalist, namely Eddington, to provide empirical confirmation, in order that his theory of general relativity be believed. As any Taoist knows, "pure" and "applied" pursuits are complementary, not competitive. One need not be hostile to the other.

Applied ethics has helped pave the way for philosophical practice, and it also overlaps aspects of philosophical practice. When biomedical ethicists counsel hospital patients and their families, they are certainly doing philosophical practice. When business ethicists consult with corporations, they too are doing philosophical practice. On the whole, applied ethics tends to be more reactive; philosophical practice, more proactive. One thing applied ethicists hold in common with philosophical practitioners is a business card; this sets both apart from theoretical philosophers of the previous generation. I often offer my business card to analytic philosophers I meet at conferences. Many of them appear never to have seen a business card before. They examine it curiously but without comprehension. Some hold it up to the light, in case that reveals a hidden explanation of what it represents. I draw from this one moral: all the symbolic logic in the world will never confer an understanding of the world. While logic helps one think, it does not help one be. Logic confers a vital understanding of valid thought-process, but in isolation from the world confers no understanding of practical life-skills, or *phronesis* itself.

As long as academic institutions retain and protect tenured faculty and provide abundant opportunities to new doctoral candidates, philosophers can afford to disdain business cards. In other words, they can no longer afford to disdain them. This brings us full-circle. The current academy is in crisis; it is experiencing neo-Reaganomic restructuring and downsizing, albeit a decade and more after Reaganomics ravaged but ultimately revitalized the corporate world. Beneath its politically correct charades and beyond its bureaucratic quagmires, the American academy is ultimately opportunistic and entrepreneurial, and will favor any program that both attracts good students and furthers their professional careers. Analytic philosophy attracts good students, but cannot further their careers. In fact, it almost guarantees not to do so. For every tenure-track job in philosophy, there are literally hundreds of applicants—roughly between two hundred and six hundred, currently. Those philosophers who do not find tenurable positions (the vast majority) will have invested six to eight arduous graduate years earning doctorates—more years than engineers or doctors or lawyers invest—but without good career prospects. While this speaks volumes about the attractiveness of philosophy to the inquiring mind, it also utters eulogies to wasted energy and expertise.

By contrast, there are hundreds of potential clients for every philosophical practitioner. A reputable university program that graduates such practitioners will not only school them in philosophical rigor, but will also afford them immediate and unlimited career prospects. What is valuable in analytic philosophy will be preserved and taught, alongside that which is valuable in applied philosophy.

So the pioneers of philosophical practice are now pioneering its pedagogy. The pedagogy of philosophical practice began modestly enough, based on another innocent American premise: if something can be done, it can be taught. And if it can be done to someone's benefit, and done profitably, then moreover it should be taught. So I had the opportunity to pioneer the first accredited graduate course in philosophical counseling in America, at Felician College in New Jersey. This was done in the usual way: as a pilot course offered through continuing education.[5] This is an excellent medium for curriculum development and refinement. It provides the instructor with a laboratory for experimentation with new pedagogic materials; it demands no long-term commitment from the institution; and it offers students an opportunity to learn something hitherto untaught, and moreover to earn credits for it. Everybody wins. Even so, the institution of a novel course, even through continuing education, can be fraught with vicious political infighting, deeply entrenched resistance, administrative duplicity, bureaucratic inefficiency—and all this in an institution heartily committed to the course! Happily, this was not the case at Felician, where both the smallness of the college and its unity of purpose went a long way toward preempting the expected hurdles, and surmounting the unexpected ones.

In order to conduct as interesting and fruitful an experiment as possible, we decided to admit three kinds of students to this course: first, those with MAs or PhDs in philosophy; second, those without graduate degrees in philosophy, but with professional counseling experience in other fields (e.g., psychology, medicine, law, social work, theology); third, those who inevitably managed to slip through the meshes of the foregoing twofold net, and qualify as exceptions under some other plausible set of criteria.

The first and most pleasurable fruit of this confluence of multidisciplinary backgrounds was an ethos of diversity in its two most significant senses; namely, variety of scholarly and professional orientation, and eclecticism of individual ability and interest. This is a far cry from the bathetic idol of diversity currently worshipped by most university administrations, which is based on the "M&M" model: to pass quality control, every pack must contain a variety of colored candies that all taste the same. Variety of color and uniformity of taste is the M&M ideal; it is also the politically correct ideal for universities: variety of race, ethnicity, and gender (called "diversity") and conformity of opinion (called "inclusiveness") is what matters to the controllers of totalitarian academic "quality." Course content is irrelevant at best and, if it encourages the challenging of received opinions, or the imparting of noetic skills necessary to mount a meaningful challenge to received opinions, is heretical. Having successfully reduced thought in the academy to a blunt instrument, the controllers of "quality" have lately discovered another Orwellian semantic transformation, by further debasing the already corrupted meaning of "diversity." A "diverse" person once meant a multi-talented person, with conspicuously divergent interests. A "diverse" person is now a euphemism for a member of an "historically disadvantaged" race or ethnicity, or "sexually oppressed" group. Hence a "diverse" student body could mean—ironically if not contradictorily—a predominantly black, Latino, or female one. On this interpretation, the NBA and the NFL have at last attained racial "diversity"—an unlooked-for egalitarian bonus, since most people suppose they merely employ the best available players. I detour frequently but necessarily into acute political commentary, precisely because (as earlier emphasized in Chapter 1) one's capacity to reason is enhanced or adumbrated by one's ability to speak, and the ongoing and agonizing Orwellization of language in postcultural America can only be seen as a sustaining cause, and not an aftereffect, of precipitous cultural decline in the face of unprecedented economic prosperity. So when I say that the graduate student body of my philosophical counseling course was diverse, I mean to say that it was composed of persons from varying academic and professional backgrounds, and of varying personal opinions and tastes. Because I am neither a racist nor a sexist, the composition of the group by race or sex was irrelevant to me. I think it had both men and women, no two of whose skins were exactly the same shade, but all of whose hearts were human and all of whose minds were inquiring. Similarly, when I say that a given individual in that graduate student body was "diverse," I mean to say that he or she was eclectic in his or her abilities and interests. Pardon me for using language meaningfully as opposed to euphemistically; it is a habit I acquired in my youth, when Orwell's grim visions were still confined to domestic novels and foreign People's Republics.

While this diversity produced a charming intellectual ambience and a rich professional matrix of exchange, it also evidenced a clear and impedimentive duality. The class divided plainly into two groups: the academically trained philosophers, who had been schooled to think deeply but also abstractly or hypothetically, and who had little or no idea how apply their considerable expertise empathetically to real problems or concrete situations in human world; and the other counseling professionals, who had very clear ideas and experience on the latter score but who lacked the formal background in academic philosophy that distinguishes philosophical counselors from all other kinds. Thus the class was almost impossible to teach in any uniform way, because one had either to acquaint the philosophers with interpersonal skills and meta-counseling considerations that the others knew all too well (i.e., "Counseling 101"), or else to acquaint the non-philosophers with fundamental philosophical concepts that the others knew all too well (i.e., "Philosophy 101"). While it appears that both constituencies benefited from the course, the course did not necessarily benefit from the two constituencies. Moreover, my experience confirms that it is far easier to familiarize philosophers with counseling than non-philosophical counselors with philosophy.

Having learned these and other valuable lessons by teaching at Felician, I concluded that this pilot course could indeed be developed into a full-fledged graduate program, offering MA and PhD degrees in Philosophical Practice, and I proceeded to design, on paper, the requirements and conditions for establishing such a program. The impetus for my design was refreshed almost weekly, as philosophical counseling continued to titillate the fancy of the press worldwide (even before the publication of *Plato Not Prozac*), as a result of whose coverage I received a steady stream of mail and e-mail from talented graduate and undergraduate philosophy students worldwide, inquiring single-mindedly about a graduate program in philosophical counseling. I told them then, as I tell them now a year or two later, that such a program is closer to being established, and will be established in a matter of time.

The second-most common question from such inquirers is "What should I study to prepare myself for a career in philosophical counseling?" Many philosophy students honestly but naively suppose that, in the absence of a graduate program in philosophical counseling, their "next-best" bet is a graduate program in psychological counseling, from which I heartily dissuade them. While philosophical counselors should be aware of common psychopathologies as indicators of poor candidacy for philosophical counseling (and my planned program entails that kind of course), psychology courses are in general as poor a preparation for an aspiring philosophical counselor as chemistry courses are for an aspiring physicist: interesting in part, but irrelevant in sum. While the DSM remains the bible for some clinical psychologists, it is also grist for the philosophical counselor's ontological mill, and contains many pages of reified disorders ideal for breaking in the philosophical counselor's paper-shredder. But from the sheer quantity and quality of inquiries, it is clear that the pioneering of this field has reached a Rubicon, which we will cross by establishing a graduate program in philosophical practice at the first university perspicacious and enterprising enough to host our moveable noetic feast.[6]

The planned graduate program is simplicity itself, and nestles comfortably enough within the ruins of the precincts of the humanities. Admission to the program would require an undergraduate major degree in philosophy, or a qualifying year for non-philosophy majors. Coursework for the MA or PhD would be compulsory, and would consist for the most part of standard graduate philosophy courses: metatheory, metaphysics and epistemology, phenomenology and existentialism, philosophy of science, Indian and Chinese philosophies, philosophy of psychology and psychiatry, philosophy of mind, ethics, applied ethics, and the like. Some courses would be required; others, elected. There would also be three streams of philosophical practice, corresponding to the three modes recognized by the APPA: client counseling, group facilitation, and organizational consulting, with a special required course for each stream. Following eighteen months to two years of coursework, and comprehensive examinations, students would undertake supervised practicums in either counseling, facilitating, or consulting, which would provide practical experience plus raw material for an MA dissertation or a PhD thesis. Graduates of the program would be certifiable by the APPA, and also eligible for state Board Certification (if and when such legislative recognition materializes: see Chapter 10). Such practicums will constitute a tremendous boon to the constituencies in which they are undertaken, as philosophical practitioners-in-training offer a full range of counseling, facilitation, and consulting services to the university community in which they are located, and to the larger community within which the university itself is situated. Students who decide that philosophical practice is not for them after all, or who show absolutely no aptitude for it, need not be disadvantaged by their studies: they would return to the mainstream of theoretical philosophy within the same institution, having been credited for their coursework, and be eligible to write more traditional dissertations or theses, if not theoretical treatments of philosophical practice itself.[7]

Once such a program is established, other such programs will proliferate throughout America, Europe, and beyond. The growth industry of applied ethics will be complemented and possibly overshadowed by its successor wave: philosophical practice. This is my pedagogic vision, and I visualize the whole functioning in place as readily as I perceive the avenue laid out before my window. There is no "if" in my mind—only a "when" and a "where." Jerusalem was a fitting place for the first Temple, Athens for the first Academy; Rome for the first Church; Washington, for the first nation conceived in liberty. When ideas are portable, methods robust, and times propitious, cultural transformations can propagate from anywhere to anywhere. The psychedelic revolution of the 1960s had three epicenters: Haight-Ashbury in San Francisco, Greenwich Village in New York, and Chelsea in London. The noetic revolution of philosophical practice could erect its first edifice of graduate studies in any of several American urban epicenters: Atlanta, Boston, Chicago, Los Angeles, New York, San Francisco, Washington—a populous hinterland being desirable for the serving of internships across the spectrum of practice—or conceivably in some less-heralded or hitherto unheralded American place, if not abroad. Build it, and they will come.

Good pedagogy is indispensable to reputable practice. In every other profession—be it medicine, law, engineering, architecture—the prestige of a given graduate program is directly linked to the repute of the practitioners who teach in it. Philosophical practice is no different, save that in America it has greater potential than in other nations; not only because of the resources and resourcefulness of Americans, and the relentless American drive to saturation marketing, but also because the academic affiliation of most leading American practitioners provides pedagogic, public, and political cachet. Consider, for example, the five founding directors of the APPA: all five had academic affiliations, four full-time, three were Chairs or former Chairs of Philosophy Departments, and three maintained full-time philosophical practices. Similarly, the majority of APPA-Certified Practitioners in America juggle academic careers and professional practices, while the majority of APPA-Certified Practitioners abroad do not maintain academic affiliations. American practitioners are not necessarily more ambitious or harder-working than our foreign colleagues, nor are we more desirous of overworking: we are simply inhabiting a different ethos, in which (as I have already said, but it bears repeating) the absence of an *ancien régime* politically implies the absence of an *ancienne étude* academically. Thus the American Academy stands wide open to programmatic innovation, to professional prospects, and to the return (from political exile) of pedagogic excellence. Philosophical practice stands for all three.

Beneath the surface of the rough-and-ready, individualistic, nonconforming, anti-elitist, and slightly boorish Tocquevillian American, with his armful of constitutional amendments, cornucopia of mail-order catalogs, plethora of pistols and projectiles, truckload of television sets, and lamentable lack of literature, there lurks an earnest and unquenchable (if also vicarious) admiration for the Academy. He does not crave much education himself, but wants some for his children. If you tell him that you profess X, practice Y, and preach Z, operating from a P.O. Box and a hotmail e-address, he will rightly look down his nose at you no matter how much money you make, to acknowledge that you are no better than he; and will envy you clandestinely only if you earn a lot more than he does, or work a lot less to make the same. But if you tell him that you profess X, practice Y, and preach Z in Yo-Yo University or Yahoo College, he will call you "Doctor" or "Professor," and respect you even though you earn a lot less than he does, and will tell his friends that he met Doctor Such-and-Thus and found him to be a "regular" guy.

This, in essence, is why there is no barrier to accredited programmatic study of philosophical practice in the American academy. As the highest-ranking intellectual authority at the state end (ergo the business end) of America's separation of church and state, the academy is bootstrapped into respectability. Even though the deconstructed (some say "Poison") Ivy League is producing grade-inflated, straight-A humanities graduates who can't spell their surnames or count their toes—or worse, who can do so but cheerfully acknowledge that this [sic] data is [sic] "socially constructed" and therefore arbitrary; or worse still, can do so but refuse on the hypersensitive grounds that their answers might "offend" someone—yet Tocquevillian Americans still spend $100,000 to send their kids to Prep U., and brag about it.

I am not jesting, but wish I were. A recent graduate of Prep U., attending one of my Philosopher's Forums, refused to answer the question "How many arms do you have?" (she had two) on the grounds that mathematics is a "social construct," from which she concluded that she might have any number of arms, or none. Moreover, even though on a good day she might be willing to concede that she appears to have two arms, she prefers to keep this opinion to herself, lest she offend someone who believes she has three. This was not Cartesian skepticism; she had not read Descartes, because celebrated dead white male philosophers are politically unfashionable, if not proscribed, at Prep U., and are in any case incomprehensible to undergraduates who read at the level of grade school. Nor had she been exposed to skepticism itself, lest she become skeptical about the viability of her deconstructed mindscape. Her father meanwhile paid $100,000 for her "education"—a nice irony, because the Registrar's Office at Prep U. was quite capable of counting every penny. Wherefore the poor girl would have received a better education working for the Registrar at minimum wage, and saved her father a pile to boot. But then he could not have boasted, "I sent my daughter to Prep U."—which, to the *cognoscenti*, means "I paid $100,000 to prepare my daughter for life as a vegetable."

Thus Americans who have not graduated from the Ivy League may be skeptical about philosophical practice when first hearing of it, but as soon as they learn that the founding president of the APPA is a Professor at City

College, they assume that philosophical practice is therefore a legitimate profession. I don't mind; on the contrary, this is a kind of poetic justice. The naive and unflagging trust that the American public perennially bestows on its Academy, which made it complicit as the groves of academe became despoiled, unpruned, blighted, and weed-choked, will also make it a partner in their restoration to fruitfulness. Philosophical practice will not be accredited in the Academy because it is good, but because it is good for business. It will not be established in the Academy because it deserves to be tried, but because everything undeserving has already been tried. Philosophical practice will not proliferate in the Academy because it is empirically successful, but because the Academy itself has failed. And philosophical practice will not be approved by the Tocquevillian American populace merely because it is sanctioned by the Academy, but because the Tocquevillian American populace desperately needs another straw at which to grasp as its very civilization implodes, or, in the redundant, blunt-instrumental postmodern Americanese that university students barely speak—"implodes in on itself."

A right thing happening for the wrong reasons is preferable to a wrong thing happening for the right ones. Thus, in one sense I care only *that* philosophical practice become an accredited graduate program; the whys and wherefores are but footnotes, fit for future historical thesis, scholarly exegesis, and rhetorical dispute.

To paraphrase T.S. Eliot (badly), between the pilot course and the graduate program falls the shadow: in our case, the lengthening shadow of the APPA's Certification Training Programs. For too long, countless philosophy graduate students have endured the rigors of the most demanding preparation for the bleakest future the Academy had to offer. Like Holy Fools, they were expected to be so enamored of their vocation that they should be willing to live in ignominy for its sake. They took no vows of poverty, yet were expected to forego employment. Versed in the noblest ratiocinations of the human mind, they endured indignities from its least mindful members. They were taught to think about everything, yet to do nothing. Not anymore. Those who once studied philosophy out of purely unrequited love of wisdom are now finding their love requited in many unexpected ways. Eliot paraphrased (badly) again: between the present opportunities in the marketplace and the near-future accreditation of practitioners in the academy lies APPA Certification Training Programs.

Offered to aspiring counselors, facilitators, and consultants, and conducted by leading counselors, facilitators, and consultants, these programs are intensive, two- or three-day professional trainings, which impart robust methodological and other tools for building from scratch or enhancing existing philosophical practices in these areas. Owing to the growing demand for these programs, both in America and abroad, the APPA has appointed a Faculty of leading practitioners, likewise from America and abroad, to conduct or supervise the trainings. In effect, the APPA now functions as a "shadow (or surrogate) university" in this capacity, and will minister to the demand as long as necessary. Even after the establishment of accredited graduate programs in philosophical practice, the international demand for training programs will persist. Philosophers already in practice in one area seek cross-training in others; philosophers practicing in a given area need to sustain professional development in that area; and graduate students in or graduates of traditional philosophy programs may wish to complement their theoretical orientations with practical applications. Hence, APPA intensive training programs will continue vitally to serve philosophical constituencies beyond the pales both of existing theoretical and envisioned practical graduate philosophy programs.

Other national and foreign national organizations are beginning to offer or may eventually offer their own trainings; this will stimulate interesting competition in an international community of national organizations whose relations are thus far characterized mostly by cooperation.[8] Individual practitioners who happen to be members of one or more national organizations for philosophical practice can and do offer their own trainings as freelance professionals, in which case the organizations to which they belong are not directly implicated, and are indirectly implicated only in so far as they maintain codes of ethics binding on practicing members. This is a charming, enlightenment-model, post-passport, open-border, EEC-style arrangement. With very few exceptions, no national organization tracks the comings and goings of philosophical practitioners fulfilling private professional contracts—nor is it their business to do so.

However, as national organizations begin to create and conduct their own training programs, there will naturally be increasing competition between organizations based in the same domestic market, increasing competition over established foreign market shares, and pseudo-colonial competition over hitherto undeveloped or newly developing markets. Local, tribal, provincial, and national interests will play correspondingly decisive roles in conditioning the birth, growth, decline, or death of a given organization for philosophical practice, and in relations between and among such organizations. Once these interests come into play, then local, tribal, provincial, or national aspects of human consciousness are also engaged—philosophers being hardly immune from these—and the result is inevitable conflict of interest. Thus the growth of organizational programs also ineluctably entails domestic and foreign politics, strategy, diplomacy, alliance, enmity, hostility, and, if all else fails, outright noetic warfare.[9] Philosophical practitioners who have not been weaned from the academy, or who have naive conceptions of professionalism and business, or who have radical political views that preempt their ability to function in a professional or business-like manner, or who suffer from debilitating psychological problems, or who are outright frauds, will be the least fit to participate in the growth of organized philosophical practice. They will either weed themselves out, or subsist on the margins, or occupy eccentric niches, or seek refuge in some other nascent enterprise, from whose primordial chaos order is not immediately forthcoming.

Good pedagogy is not only formative for aspiring professionals; its very emergence also presupposes professionalism. One hallmark of such presupposed professionalism is organization, which brings us close upon the next chapter.

Meanwhile, philosophical practice owes its current popularity, and will owe its future success, to many pioneers who have worked assiduously, patiently, perseveringly, lovingly, and often in isolation. Pioneers tend to be rugged—sometimes fragile—individualists, who chart their courses by inner stars. Heights are attained, depths plumbed, mazes mapped, labyrinths threaded, trails blazed, and territories charted by energetic pioneers, and not by inertial nay-sayers. This appears equally true regardless of the dimension of the exploration—be it artistic, scientific, geographic, technological, political, or philosophical.

In each nation where philosophical practice flourishes, the first generation of practitioners has had to find and forge its way. No one explicitly taught them how to do this, and moreover no one particularly needed to do so. For good or ill, just as ripe fruit falls from the tree, events unfold of themselves in proper time. But now that passable ways and even broad avenues have opened to philosophical practice, and now that its effectiveness, usefulness, and benefits are more commonly known, it is natural and desirable that this generation of practitioners shall more fully and mutually identify itself, and begin to train the next.

As one vouchsafed the responsibility and duty of being a torchbearer and architect of this movement, I believe our task as practitioners is not circumscribed by our practice—rather, by our influence upon the next generation of practitioners. The loop is therefore not closed between us and our clients; rather, it must remain open in a way that permits the training of new practitioners, without compromising the standard of service currently delivered. Indeed, introducing learning into philosophical practice is bound to enhance the practice itself, for the obligation to teach lends impetus to the articulation of hitherto unformulated insights, and sharpens the understanding of the teacher.

NOTES

1. See, e.g., M. Muncy, ed., *The End of Democracy?* (Dallas: Spence, 1999). Although its not-so-hidden agenda is theological, it contains cogent criticisms of judicial activism.

2. This is precisely what Dr. Kevorkian has challenged with his active euthanization, and what The Netherlands and Oregon have legalized.

3. The Natural Sciences and Engineering Research Council of Canada has fallen prey to the pernicious myth that one can measure justice and injustice via simplistic head-counts alone, and thus has adopted the purely political position—while disregarding copious objective evidence to the contrary—that smaller numbers of females than males in the natural sciences are explained by "systemic" discrimination alone, concluding therefrom that preferential measures favoring females are both warranted and justified. In a letter to NSERC's grant selection committee, SAFS President Dorothy Kimura wrote, among other things, "There are now several studies showing that in the past two decades women have been preferentially hired in Canadian universities across several disciplines, including sciences (e.g., Irvine, 1996). There is also ever-increasing evidence that the lower representation of women in the physical sciences is largely a matter of self-selection on the basis of interests and talents. Women achieve outstanding scores on math aptitude tests in much smaller numbers than men do (Benbow, 1988; Reisberg, 1998), and high mathematical ability is more critical for the physical than the biological sciences (where women have a representation approaching that of men). Even women very talented in math, however, often show strong preferences for more person-oriented occupations than men do and so do not gravitate to the physical sciences (Kleinfeld, 1999; Lubinski & Benbow, 1992). Moreover, the documented lower research productivity of women, evident in all disciplines (Cole & Zuckerman, 1987; Long, 1992; Schneider, 1998), may be especially notable in the sciences, where objective criteria such as number of refereed publications are likely to be employed." (Source: SAFS e-mail list, January 4, 2000.)

4. America's disgraceful cultural reverses are being potentially re-forwarded through important works such as E. Hirsch, J. Kett, and J. Trefil, eds., *The Dictionary of Cultural Literacy* (Boston & New York: Houghton Mifflin, 1993).

5. As far as I know, my Israeli colleague Ran Lahav taught the first-ever accredited graduate course in philosophical counseling, at the University of Haifa, also out of continuing education.

6. I will be pleased to furnish a blueprint of such a graduate program to anyone who wishes to further its establishment. As this book goes to press, the Philosophy Department at City College has voted to establish an MA Program in Applied Philosophy. This includes a stream for Philosophical Practice.

7. I have already examined or am helping supervise several theses on philosophical practice, written by graduate students in traditional programs in the U.S.A., Canada, and Europe. One of these is now commercially published: P. Raabe, *Philosophical Counseling: Theory and Practice* (Westport, CT: Praeger, 2000).

8. Potential exceptions to this rule will be discussed in Chapter 16.

9. This too will be discussed in Chapter 16.

CHAPTER 9

The Making of
a Profession

9.1. Programs of Training at Universities or Institutes
Chartered by the State and Accredited by
Professional Accrediting Bodies

9.2. Established Criteria (Including an Examination)
for Certification of Practitioners

APPA Certification Standards

Certification Standards for Client Counselors

Certification Standards for Group Facilitators

Certification Standards for Organizational Consultants

9.3. Established Body of Knowledge as Reflected in the
Publication of Reference Books and Professional
Journals and Regularly Scheduled Scientific
[sic: Read "Learned"] Meetings

9.4. Established Code of Ethics

Standards of Professional Ethical Practice

*I*n the previous chapter, we examined the relation between pioneering, pedagogy, and professionalism, ultimately with a view to justifying the establishment of accredited degree programs in philosophical practice. In this chapter, we develop a broader perspective on professionalism, by examining four criteria necessary for the legislative recognition of a profession in New York State, and by showing how philosophical practice currently satisfies three of those four. In New York, the recognition of a profession falls under the aegis of the Department of Education. The four necessary criteria certainly justify this situation:

1. Programs of training at universities or institutes chartered by the State and accredited by professional accrediting bodies.

2. Established criteria (including an examination) for certification of practitioners.

3. Established body of knowledge as reflected in the publication of reference books and professional journals and
   regularly scheduled scientific [sic: "learned"] meetings.

4. Established code of ethics.

I will discuss these in turn.

9.1. PROGRAMS OF TRAINING AT UNIVERSITIES OR INSTITUTES CHARTERED BY THE STATE AND ACCREDITED BY PROFESSIONAL ACCREDITING BODIES

The first disjunct of the first conjunct of the first criterion has been treated at
some length in the previous chapter. We have focused our treatment on the
establishment of accredited graduate programs in Philosophical Practice, as
optional streams or branches of ubiquitous programs in Philosophical Theory—to which most philosophical study is currently confined. Since an undergraduate preparation for graduate studies in philosophical theory or philosophical practice is the same in either case, there is no need to reinvent that
wheel. Moreover, since some graduate courses in philosophy would also be
common to both theoretical and practical streams, it is in principle much
simpler to expand existing graduate programs to accommodate practical
streams than it is to establish programs for philosophical practice *ex nihilo*. I
say "in principle" because neither logic nor sound judgment play any reliable
role in academic politics—a domain to be explored in Chapter 15. *Prima facie*,
however, there is no need to reinvent the wheel of graduate studies in philosophy either, only to lace a few practical spokes into the existing framework of
theoretical ones, which would considerably strengthen the wheel itself.

  The second disjunct of the first conjunct of the first criterion merits a
separate mention, but only a brief one at this stage. While founding a distinct
(i.e., stand-alone) chartered institute for the pursuit of accredited graduate
studies in Philosophical Practice remains a live possibility in America, because

it depends firstly on money and secondly on legal process, neither of which is in particularly short supply in the United States, it is also (in my view) a less desirable option than the establishment of a new branch of graduate studies within a university program extant. Again, this is not because the option cannot or should not be exercised in and of itself, but because freestanding institutes are a dime-a-dozen in America, and public perception of a given institute qua educational entity seems diminished in the first instance by a lack of attention to the key question of whether it is chartered. And even if it is chartered, more perceptive questioners will then wonder why it is not affiliated with or under the aegis of a university. Anyone in America who builds a better mousetrap envisions not only building a factory to produce better mousetraps, but also founding an Institute for Better Mouse-Trapping. The question then is whether the primary purpose of the Institute is educational, commercial, or cultural (qua cultish). Educational and therapeutic interests are epitomized by Albert Ellis's Institute for Rational Emotive Therapy. Commercial interest admixed with educational ones are attained, for example, by The Tom Morris Institute. The Ayn Rand Institute on the west coast appears to be essentially a cult, while the Objectivist Center on the East Coast is intellectual and educational. So many institutes exist purely for commercial or cultish purposes that they tend to give such entities a generally less-than-salutary reputation, that of organizations using an educational smokescreen merely to sell goods or promote ideologies. In the latter case, they are one step away from becoming churches, or contemporary universities.

The difference between an Institute and a University is also plain: the latter is an incomparably more robust entity than the former. The occidental Academy has survived the collapse of Athens, survived the dogmas of theocracy, survived the mind-numbing absurdities of Scholasticism, survived the enlightened nineteenth-century inclusion of Jews, Catholics, women, and other social pariahs of the day at University College London, and of the talented but impecunious at The City College of New York, survived the demonic twentieth-century exclusion by Nazism of "Jewish Science," survived the psychedelic revolution of the 1960s, and will survive the current feminization, ethnocentrization, affirmative action, deconstruction, admission of illiterate, innumerate, and postcultural students, and demonic exclusion of erudite "white" and "white-Jewish" males on the grounds that they have caused all the "problems" of occidental civilization (e.g., the establishment of democratic bodies-politic, the advance of science and technology, the creation of unprecedented economic opportunities, the doubling of life-expectancies) and that erudition is bad—and "diversity" good—for a University. The Academy has survived and will survive these and other absurdities, inanities, indignities, obscenities, and triumphs alike, because it is larger-looming and longer-lived than the individuals who merely serve or disserve it for a time. The institution is the culmination of a civilization's vision, ability, and energy, and as such is too powerful to be destroyed by any one culture, subculture, or cult.

Unlike institutions, institutes are lucky to outlast their founders. The institute is the culmination of one person's vision, ability, and energy. When that person expires or retires, his boots are rarely filled; rather, they are usually worn out in scuffles over their filling. So if George Soros, Jay Leno, or some other former philosophy major who went on to become a defining force of industry or entertainment sought to patronize philosophical practice, I would counsel him not to set up a freestanding Institute and hire a bevy of lawyers, lobbyists, and sophists to see it chartered. Rather, I would counsel him to endow a Chair of Philosophical Practice at a worthy University or College, and make sure it is filled by an authentic philosophical practitioner, and not by some *poseur*, anti-intellectual, or desk-jockey.

Naturally it is important to keep an open mind. Thus, if the universities continue their precipitous decline unabated, and if egregious philosophies of education—including the outrageous "outcome-oriented" initiatives touted by the late Clinton Administration—continue to destroy the K–12 system, then the aggressive and opportunistic noetic cancers currently metastasizing throughout the academy may indeed become inoperable, in which case the only choice would be to make the "patient" as comfortable as possible, and found a New Academy on the ruined foundations of the old. This putative entity would have the appearance of a freestanding institute, as Plato's Academy once did, but its mission would be to minister to the higher educational needs of the next civilization entire, namely, the global one, which is already emerging from the embers of the barely-regnant post-postmodern circus of self-immolating paradigms.

Either way, a graduate program in philosophical practice not only needs to be established at a university or chartered institute; it also needs to be accredited by a professional accrediting body. Enter the American Philosophical Practitioners Association (APPA), which is constituted precisely to fulfill this (among other) essential tasks. Note that, while a "professional accrediting body" is mentioned explicitly only at the tail end of the first of New York State's four necessary conditions, such a body is in fact implicit in all of them. Without such a body, none of the four conditions could be satisfied.

To begin with, the state recognizes professions in the same way as it charters universities or institutions: by lending its endorsement *a posteriori* to the forms of activities of the given entity, and not by dictating *a priori* what the substance of those activities should be. In a university, the administration and the faculty determine what shall be researched and taught. A state charter is an endorsement of the form of such research and teaching, not a determination of its content. All successful professions evolve, and such evolution entails development of theory, research, expertise, technique, method, modes of delivery of service, professional and pedagogic infrastructure, and so forth—all of which are primary responsibilities of the professionals themselves. When a nascent profession attains a certain critical mass, the professionals coalesce, organize, and cooperate, the better to further the interests of their common profession, and through it their individual professional interests. Thus a professional body comes into being. This body, being normally composed of the leading professionals in the field, is best qualified to articulate and update requirements for the training and credentialing of aspiring professionals. A state cannot recognize a profession unless and until a professional body exists to define and refine the profession in terms the state understands. A university course in medicine, law, or engineering counts for academic credit if offered by a chartered institution, but does not count for professional credit unless accredited by a professional body of medical, legal, or engineering practitioners. Most such programs are accredited in their entirety, which is why graduates thereof become eligible to serve internships, take credentialing examinations, and become members of respective professional organizations themselves. Without the interfacing assistance and supervision of a credible professional body, no State can determine whether a given program of study, even if academically accredited, is worthy of professional accreditation. But a professional body, if legitimately constituted, can make this determination, and can recommend to the State that graduates of a given program are suitably qualified to enter a profession at a suitable level of internship or apprenticeship, or to write credentialing examinations to demonstrate such qualifications.

But how would a government recognize a professional body itself? And why mightn't it? Experiences of organizations for philosophical practice in other countries—particularly Germany, Holland, and Israel—are quite instructive for Americans.

In Germany, Gerd Achenbach has been the predominant figure in philosophical counseling for two decades. He is generally acknowledged to have been the first European philosopher with a PhD to hang out a counseling shingle (in 1981), and move into full-time practice. Owing to the staidness, monasticism, conservatism, and assorted Old-World prejudices of the German academy, Achenbach's pioneering initiative divorced him from it. Even though Achenbach is a paragon of reputable professionalism, it is likely that some German academicians denounced him as a quack—probably owing to the puerility, vanity, and petty jealousy that pervades academic life. For Achenbach received media attention in Germany, but the academic philosophers didn't. At the same time, Achenbach maintains a neo-Feyerabendian stance against methodology in philosophical counseling, and also against its professionalization.[1]

He contends that philosophical counselors are born, not made, and that they should not seek professional credentialing or other formal recognition. Achenbach wears an aura, almost a halo, of authority, integrity, and respectability, and these are clearly the only credentials he needs.

Thus Achenbach initially disapproved of the 1998 legislative initiative in New York State, sponsored by Assemblyman Ruben Diaz Jr., to license philosophical counselors. Reported by *The New York Times*,[2] the story quickly went around the world, and caused quite a stir in both philosophical and philosophical counseling circles. But Achenbach's disapproval was quiet, discrete, reflective, diplomatic, nonjudgmental, and—above all—non-interfering. The latter is extremely important. There had been to date virtually no political interference on the international scene; each national organization for philosophical practice being left alone by the others to do its domestic business, fight its domestic wars, make its domestic treaties, and conduct its domestic affairs according to its lights. This non-interference engendered international cooperation of a very salutary kind, and allowed the succession of international conferences on philosophical practice to unfold, and the movement—being rightly perceived as diverse but unified—to gather strength in their wake.

By the summer of 1998, Achenbach would express very different sentiments toward the Diaz Bill. In a summit meeting between he and I, and our translators, conducted after hours one night during the Fourth International Conference, a comparatively lavish affair which he superbly organized and amply funded via German banking friends, he expressed the hope that the Diaz Bill would pass. This 180-degree swerve was impelled by politics, as usual. It turned out that the German establishment's escalating crusade against the Church of Scientology, also well-reported in *The New York Times* and other places, had taken a legislative turn, and that the Bundestag was actually debating a bill which would outlaw the practice of Scientology. But the bill had been drafted in such broad language that it inadvertently criminalized philosophical counseling too, and Achenbach had no friends in the Bundestag upon whom he could prevail. Thus he hoped that the Diaz Bill would pass, so that it could be used as a clarion call for the Bundestag to shape its pending charge against the Scientologists, and eliminate collateral damage to the German Society for Philosophical Practice. Membership in the German Society is open, but perhaps its openness also potentiates vulnerability.

What mildly surprised me (at the time) was the political contrast between Germany and America, and between the German and American national organizations for philosophical practice. Achenbach had been a presence in the German national news—print media, radio, television—for nearly twenty years, since 1981, and yet, by his own admission, had not one ally in the Bundestag. I became a presence in the American national news in August 1997, following the publication of Alex Kuczynski's seminal coverage of philosophical practice in the *New York Observer*. I happened to mention to her that it would be desirable if philosophical counselors were recognized by governments, and she embodied those remarks in her piece. Six months later I was holding the Diaz Bill in my hand. While holding a Bill is not the same as passing a Bill, at least it signifies involvement in the political process. "May the Government be aware of you" is an apocryphal Chinese curse, but nowadays it can be a blessing in America. At any rate, if a given organization for philosophical practice has no interest in accrediting either courses or practitioners, then it cannot fulfill the first foregoing condition of recognition of a profession.

The Dutch have a different approach. To begin with, membership in the Dutch Society is contingent upon having a graduate degree in philosophy, demonstrable experience as a practitioner, and reputable professional character. (At the same time, the Dutch Society for Philosophical Practice is governed by a council and rotating Presidency, not by one enduring authority figure.) Since membership itself entails certain credentials, the Dutch are evidently not opposed to accreditation; on the contrary. Dutch practitioners are justly proud of their professionalism, have no metaphysical biases against reliable methodology, improve almost every method they apply, and have unified three main tributaries of practice (counseling, facilitation, and consulting) into a formidable river. However, with one notable exception, Dutch practitioners also suffer consequences of divorce from the Academy, although the free and clear air of liberty in Holland is not likely to bring them into legislative peril, inadvertent or otherwise. An exception is Professor (now Emeritus) Henk van Luijk's pioneering work at Nijenrode University, where he developed a potent seven-step program for dealing with dilemmas in the workplace (detailed herein in Chapter 7). His program dovetails and overlaps with his influence and contributions in Business Ethics and the European Business Ethics community, but it has also been taught to and applied by professional philosophical consultants functioning completely outside the academy.

Most philosophical practitioners in Holland continue to function outside the academy, although they originally garnered their preparations in theoretical philosophy within it. This they hold in common with their German counterparts. But significantly, the Dutch Society did seek governmental recognition of philosophical practice. However, they were fobbed off with bureaucratic demands for statistical evidence of its efficacy. This demand itself speaks volumes about the insidious intrusion of so-called "social science" into scientific domains, by the mere naked expedient of enlisting statistics to (pretend to) measure something. When philosophical counselors show that a percentage of their clients say they "feel better" after philosophical counseling, we too will become "social scientists"—heaven forfend. Meanwhile, a grand irony perpetuates itself in The Netherlands, where philosophical practitioners work with accredited professional groups and governmental agencies of all kinds, but are not themselves officially accredited or accrediting.

Israel affords yet another interesting contrast. To begin with, it is largely owing to the formative labors and journeys of an Israeli-American philosophical counselor, Ran Lahav, that the international movement itself has taken shape. It is owing to his editorial and organizational efforts above all that the seminal collection, *Essays on Philosophical Counseling*, was published in 1995. And although Ran and I co-organized the First International Conference on Philosophical Counseling (1994), the event was his idea, and he, not I, knew exactly whom to invite, and moreover persuaded them to come. True, I raised the funds and provided the venue, through an all-important academic affiliation (in that case, the University of British Columbia); but whereas there were in principle many potential funds and venues for such an event, there was only one credible list of program presenters—and Ran knew them personally. He didn't try to run this event via his former university affiliation, in the U.S.A. at the time, because he found himself in a department full of analytic philosophers completely hostile to the idea of philosophical practice. They eventually drummed him out, and he returned to Israel. Ran has also remained aloof from the movement since then, but as I began to travel through British and European philosophical practitioner circles, I found few important pathways that were not formerly trod by Ran Lahav. Then again, Ran has withdrawn from the scene of late, and the movement misses his intellect and energy alike.

There are several other noteworthy philosophical counselors in Israel, including Lydia Amir and Ora Gruengard, and they all have PhDs in theoretical philosophy. While some of them also maintain academic affiliations, none have thus far succeeded in utilizing the Israeli academy as a platform for establishing accredited programs in philosophical practice. Ran Lahav once or twice taught a graduate course on philosophical counseling at the University of Haifa—as I later did at Felician College—through continuing education, but that initiative apparently petered out. What prevents the Israeli Society from becoming a more prominent professional body is, in my view, partly the ethos of the Middle East itself, which somehow engenders, fosters, and perpetuates conflicts of the most extreme and unmitigated variety. It is a region in which fanaticism is the norm. Three great world religions sprang from its scalding sands and biblical battlements; but for every middle-eastern poet, prophet, or prince of peace there is also an army of assassins, a legion of zealots, and a legacy of grievances—which intermittently irrigate the land with blood. Even in peacetime, such strife is often unbearable; yet anything is more bearable than a Holocaust. This is not the place either to defend the Jewish State, or to lament the vicissitudes of statehood.[3] I merely observe that Israeli philosophical counselors have made important individual contributions. It is a truism that if they could find a willing and able leader, with a mature political vision, they might accomplish more.

This cursory glance at three societies for philosophical practice, each of which illustrates important strengths and weaknesses inherent in national organizations of this kind, sets up the American arrangement, which differs considerably from the others. To begin with, and a rather fortuitous beginning it is, American philosophical practitioners had no national organization of the kind extant in Germany and Holland, nor sought to found one. The triumvirate responsible for the first organization—Elliot Cohen, Thomas Magnell, and Paul Sharkey—were all academic philosophers first, and practitioners second. That is to say, they conceived of philosophical practice as complementary to theoretical philosophy, but not therefore opposed to or removed from its precincts. Hence they founded an academic society, the American Society for Philosophy, Counseling, and Psychotherapy (ASPCP). Each of the three founders contributed something vital and unique to the organization: Elliot Cohen, considerable expertise in clinical philosophy; Paul Sharkey, long experience in health-care policy and administration, law, and philosophy of psychology and psychiatry; Thomas Magnell, knowledge of applied ethics and value theory, experience in academic politics, and political initiative sufficient to situate the ASPCP in the APA's umbrella of special-interest groups.

Thus the ASPCP was founded as an open academic society, constituted to study relations between and among philosophy, psychiatry, psychology, and psychotherapy. From its inception (in 1992), meetings of philosophers interested in the theory of philosophical counseling, increasingly populated by practitioners of philosophical counseling itself, took place in the groves of academe. Almost from the start, however, the gradually rising tide of philosophical counseling in America, or at least the perceived opportunities for its rise, tempted some careless or unethical counselors to print "Member of the ASPCP" on their business cards, as a professional "credential." Their prospective clients could not immediately penetrate this deception, but would no doubt be outraged if they discovered that for a few dollars annually they too could print "Member of the ASPCP" on their business stationery. Come to that, they could make their pet dogs members, and engrave "Member of the ASPCP" on their dog-tags. While these unsalutary developments were far from widespread, their very possibility horrified the ASPCP Board, each of whose members had some conception of integrity.

Thus, in 1994, began three years of public discussions at ASPCP meetings, which culminated in the ASPCP Certification initiative. The idea was simple: the ASPCP would remain, true to its mandate, an open academic society; but would above and beyond that recognize qualified philosophical counselors, who could then call themselves "ASPCP-Certified" without misleading the public or misrepresenting the Society. Thus the ASPCP became, in effect, the first accrediting body for philosophical counseling. Paul Sharkey formulated the certification standards, while Elliot Cohen drafted the accompanying Code of Ethics for certified counselors. I was not even a member of the ASPCP in 1994, but shared a hotel room with Ran Lahav at the 1994 Eastern Division APA meetings in Atlanta. He had come mostly to attend the ASPCP events, and was on the ASPCP Board at that time; I had come for job interviews (the "meat market," as it is affectionately known), one of which eventually landed me at City College the next autumn.

By 1996, the ASPCP had certified a dozen or so philosophical counselors. At the 1997 Third International Conference on Philosophical Practice, the watershed event which I organized in Manhattan, several more candidates sat the ASPCP certification examination as part of their application process. What the ASPCP Board had not foreseen was the infamous hue and cry that erupted at an evening plenary session, when a panel composed of Elliot Cohen, Thomas Magnell, Paul Sharkey, Kenneth Cust (then Secretary of the Society), and yours truly (then President) offered to explicate the certification initiative and associated process, and to field questions arising therefrom. Instead, this somewhat illustrious panel became the target of various forms of politically correct—and even worse—abuse. A petition was presented to us by a *nonmember* of the ASPCP, who had worked all day to gather seven signatures, demanding that we rescind the certification. A radical feminist stood up and demanded to know why the panel was constituted of five white males. (Three of us happened to be Jews, painfully aware of the irony that we were now called "white" for the purpose of being demonized by liberal fascism—whereas under Hitler we were called "non-Aryan" for the purpose of being demonized by Nazi fascism.) A gay activist stood up and similarly demonized the panel for its heterosexuality. An Israeli anarchist stood up and read us the Declaration of Independence, and actually called us Nazis. We bridled at that. I stood at the microphone and replied that the ASPCP Certification standards were intended simply to distinguish professional philosophical counselors from amateur ones—at which a handful of amateurs in the audience lustily booed and jeered. While these and kindred Boeotians clamored in the auditorium, one of them confiscated the ASPCP certification literature from the display tables, where it sat with a host of other conference literature and pamphlets publicly and freely offered by participating individuals and organizations, and disposed of it. To me, this was the most grievous insult of all. The conference was sponsored by The City College of The City University of New York, and was taking place in the CUNY Graduate Center. It was co-sponsored by the ASPCP itself. Imagine inviting some guests into your home, spending a year planning the party, offering them food and drink and open discourse, only to be soundly berated by them, and then discovering that they had surreptitiously removed from your shelves and disposed of any literature with which they disagreed.

In retrospect, as I recount this, the whole farce seems amusing enough. At the time, it was not. The tensions in the hall were palpable, and I did nothing to assuage them—on the contrary, I myself was outraged by the radical misbehaviors of this vocal but inconsequential rabble—apparently far too accustomed to getting its way in the academy, by means of usurping meetings, demonizing legitimate authority, making infantile demands for empowerment and, when all else fails, resorting to immoral and illegal tactics to further its anarchic agenda. I inadvertently roused that rabble to a greater pitch when they realized that I was no spineless university administrator with nothing better to do than cravenly capitulate to the most ludicrous set of demands they could conceive. On the contrary, they took one look at me and knew their jig was up.

Some of the Europeans in attendance were truly jarred, presumably because they prefer to confine their political disagreements to Colonial, Imperial, and World Wars. They found the no-holds-barred, in-your-face, give-and-take, rough-and-tumble of this quintessentially American "Town Hall Meeting" a bit too unnerving for their diplomatic delicacy and social sensibility. Beyond these aesthetics of style, most of them had not realized the extent to which postmodern American ethos has, by consistent abuse of its own hard-won liberties, fallen prey to vicious fanaticism in the guise of enlightened reform, and has managed to deprive itself of civility, constitutionality, and due process in the bargain. How many of these protesters had ever attended ASPCP meetings? How many had actually joined the Society? How many had sought to serve on its Board? How many were in fact philosophical counselors? The Europeans soon became cognizant that this conference had launched philosophical practice in America, precipitated further national and international media attention, resulted in the conception and publication of *Plato Not Prozac*, and enhanced the movement's profile globally. The Europeans in attendance were simply taken aback by the vituperativeness of our confrontation with the rabble, but would discover within a year or so that the emptiest vessels made the most noise that night. This was but a preliminary skirmish; we have much bigger battles to fight.[4]

The "white heterosexual patriarchal hegemonic male" panel of demons sat down later to deliberate the events of that night, and we arrived at a consensual understanding that, while the ASPCP Certification initiative has indeed solved the problem it intended to solve, it inadvertently fomented a new problem; namely, the creation of a distinction, in an otherwise open and indistinct society, that could be (and which evidently had been) perceived as invidious.

While there was nothing in the ASPCP Constitution that explicitly forbade certification, the Board now realized that in effectively protecting the Society from misrepresentation it had annexed new territory in which it was not entirely comfortable, and whose occupation left it vulnerable not only to the clamor of Boeotians but also to potentially serious legal challenges faced by certifying bodies.

There followed several months of ceaseless virtual harangues on what at that time was the sole e-mail discussion list extant for philosophical counseling, moderated by one of our disaffected enemies. Blatantly contrary to his own rules of conduct on that list, he allowed the handful of vociferous fanatics and assorted malcontents to poison its well with defamatory and libelous messages accusing the ASPCP Board of Nazism, fascism, white male heterosexual patriarchal hegemony, misrepresenting its members, failing to represent its non-members(!), hijacking philosophical counseling, and the like. Needless to say, this list rapidly became renowned for its delusional politics and daily excursions into surrealism, and thus attracted curious campers on its fringes, bemused by the ructious railings of apparent lunatics claiming to be philosophical counselors. The list provided high entertainment value, but dragged the nascent profession into low repute. It also appeared to reveal the "inside story" of the "strife-ridden inner circles" of philosophical counseling, which at the time was receiving uniformly laudatory and global media attention in the real (that is, the non-virtual) world.

The ASPCP Board eventually wearied of the ludicrous allegations daily hurled against it in cyberspace, and also learned (the hard way) what a powerful medium the internet can be for disseminating propaganda. In my last act as President of the ASPCP, I organized a plebiscite in which the Board asked the Membership whether it cared to ratify two major policy decisions: first, our certification initiative itself; second, my impending appointment as Executive Director of the ASPCP, to take effect upon the expiration of my term as President. We made it easy for members to say "No" to either or both questions. Some of our own Board members, having succumbed to the incessant and vindictive e-mail propaganda on that hostile list, to which many of our members-at-large were also subscribers, believed they would say "No" to both. More than two-thirds of ASPCP members returned their numbered ballots. Eighty-two percent ratified our certification initiative; seventy-eight percent ratified my appointment as Executive Director. When this was announced, our landslide victory penultimately silenced our detractors on that list—except for its moderator, who immediately accused the ASPCP Board of election fraud. That the mail-in ballots had been received, collected, opened, and counted by a Professor of Mathematics at City College, and their tabulation witnessed and verified by an Associate Dean of Students, both of unimpeachable character and neither having any interest or stake in the outcome, did not deter the baseless accusation. The ultimate silence ensued from our open invitation to any ASPCP member to inspect and count the ballots himself. None bothered.

At the same time, it became increasingly clear to me that the ASPCP was completely vulnerable to being hijacked by those who so wantonly accused its Founders, Directors, and Officers of being hijackers themselves. ASPCP Directors are nominated and elected at open annual business meetings, which are scarcely attended by anything like a majority of the membership. One busload of radicals could waltz in and take over. After the November plebiscite, we girded ourselves for the December business meeting in Philadelphia, and encouraged all sane members to attend. We needn't have worried: not one fanatic showed up. The new Board's first request to me, as Executive Director, was that I research and report on steps the Society would need to take to indemnify itself against undesirable legal repercussions of its certification initiative.

Even before this research was officially "commissioned," I had already learned enough to realize that, while the ASPCP was indeed the appropriate body for developing certification standards, it was not the appropriate body for conferring the certificates themselves. To be minimally indemnified in America's litigious ethos, a certifying organization needed Directors and Officers Insurance, which meant it first needed to be legally incorporated. Moreover, to be eligible for reasonably priced premiums, it should be incorporated as a nonprofit organization and obtain 501(c)(3) (i.e., tax-exempt) status from the IRS. These imperatives lay beyond the purview of the ASPCP, or at least beyond the political will of its Board.

Thus, in parallel with all these other developments, and although actively defending ASPCP certification standards during my Presidency, I managed to convince a sufficient number of key Board members that the furthering of philosophical practice in America now required not only a functional academic society—the ASPCP—but also a well-structured national association. Thus the American Philosophical Practitioners Association was born in 1998, and began accepting members in 1999. While the APPA serves the equivalent purpose in America that other national organizations serve in their respective countries, it also enjoys the unique benefits of complementing a preexisting academic society. The APPA moved swiftly to adopt and modify the ASPCP's certification standards and code of professional ethics, and by October 1999 the APPA had satisfied all the aforementioned indemnification criteria. By January 2000, the ASPCP gladly rescinded its own certification initiative, and thus eliminated the invidious distinction it had inadvertently created. Since the APPA was constituted precisely to recognize and admit various categories of members, including certified ones, this and other distinctions existed from the very inception, and could hardly be viewed as invidious. On the contrary, the creation of various categories of membership makes the APPA an *inclusive* association.

Thus Americans now enjoy a symbiotic relation of two vital organizations: an open Academic Society consecrated to exploring and developing the theoretical foundations of philosophical counseling, and an inclusive National Association which erects an edifice of philosophical practice upon those theoretical foundations. This is an ideal political arrangement, with a clear division of organizational labor, whose pragmatic value is epitomized by the ASPCP's development of standards and ethics for counselors, and their implementation by the APPA. That, in sum, explains both how the APPA came to be (partly) a professional accrediting body, and also why the older and more established European Societies for philosophical practice have yet successfully to accredit their practitioners. The linkage to the Academy is vital, and we Americans are fortunate to have it.

We have learned from the European experience that a successful national association alone is not enough to assure recognition of a profession, from the American experience that a successful academic society alone is not enough to accredit professionals. Both kinds of organizations are required. And with that, the first and most demanding of the four conditions for the recognition of a profession is on the verge of being satisfied.

9.2. ESTABLISHED CRITERIA (INCLUDING AN EXAMINATION) FOR CERTIFICATION OF PRACTITIONERS

The second condition requires the establishment of criteria (including an examination) for certification of practitioners. As we have just recounted, such criteria were developed for philosophical counselors by the ASPCP, primarily through the labors of Paul Sharkey. They were modified, extended, and adopted by the APPA, and added to them are criteria for certification of both group facilitators and organizational consultants. There are additional provisions for ongoing professional development. The ASPCP also designed an examination for candidates who hold advanced degrees in philosophy, who have experience as practitioners, and who wish to demonstrate that they merit certification. While the APPA is now conferring primary certification based on training, not examination, it is feasible and probably desirable to revise and reinstate the ASPCP examination, and to implement it both for the purposes of full APPA certification—and eventually for state Board Certification.

Meanwhile, here is the current literature on APPA Certification Standards. This literature comprises a living document, which continues to grow and mature.

APPA Certification Standards

Preamble

Adjunct Members or qualified Affiliate Members in good standing may apply for certification. There are three areas of certified practice: client counseling, group facilitation, and organizational consulting. The APPA offers two categories of certification in each area: Associate and Fellow. Within each category, there are two levels: Primary and Full Certification. An Associate or Fellow with Primary Certification may practice as a Certified Member with supervision from the APPA. An Associate or Fellow with Full Certification may practice as a Certified Member without supervision. All Certified Members are bound by the APPA Code of Professional Ethical Practice.

Certification in Multiple Areas

A Member certified in one area of practice may seek certification in another area of practice, but must fulfill respective requirements. Certification in one area of practice does not automatically confer certification in another. Members who become certified in more than one area do not pay multiple dues; they pay normal certified membership dues, independent of the number of areas in which they are certified.

Academic Credentials

The minimum academic requirement for certification as an Associate is an earned Master's Degree or ABD in Philosophy (or *Licensura* in Hispanic countries). The academic requirement for certification as a Fellow is an earned Doctoral Degree in Philosophy.

Recertification from Associate to Fellow

A Primary or Fully Certified Associate who earns a Doctorate in Philosophy from an accredited institution of higher learning may be recertified, respectively, as a Primary or Fully Certified Fellow, by submitting official proof that the Doctorate has been conferred. There will be no charge for such recertification. All other conditions of certified membership apply.

Temporal Constraints on Primary Certification (from APPA operating procedures, section 13.2)

Primary certificates will normally be valid for a period of up to two years, during which the holder may renew the primary certificate by renewing annual certified membership. However, an implied condition of primary certification is that the holder seek full certification, which is attained by advanced education and training programs. Primary certificates held by persons who do not subsequently qualify or seek to qualify for full certification will normally expire after two years, and said holders will not be eligible to renew their certified memberships until such time as they qualify for full certification. Extensions are possible on medical or compassionate grounds.

Applications

Qualified persons are invited to apply for APPA Certification. Applications should include:

- APPA Membership Application Form (if not already a member), with Adjunct or Affiliate status initially selected (whichever is most appropriate for you)
- letter stating area, category, and level of certification held (if any) and/or sought
- current curriculum vitae
- proof of advanced degree in philosophy
- graduate transcripts
- types and dates of APPA training programs completed
- summary and evidence of experience as a philosophical practitioner (include written case studies or relevant publications)
- three letters of recommendation from personal referees
- name of fully certified APPA sponsor

Please mail applications to

APPA
The City College of New York
137th Street at Convent Avenue
New York, NY 10031

CERTIFICATION STANDARDS FOR CLIENT COUNSELORS

Certification as an Associate

Primary Certification as an Associate signifies basic competency minimally required for supervised practice with individuals. The minimum academic requirement for certification as an Associate is an earned Master's Degree or ABD in Philosophy (or Licensura in Hispanic countries). Candidates must demonstrate evidence of appropriate competency in ethics (values analysis/clarification), logic (formal and informal reasoning), epistemology (belief justification), metaphysics (worldviews) and at least the major figures and themes of the history of western (and preferably also eastern) philosophy. While no particular philosophical orientation is expected or required, candidates should also be familiar with the basic principles and themes of both the analytic and existential/phenomenological traditions of recent philosophy. In addition, candidates must demonstrate practical knowledge of the principles of interpersonal psychology, psychopathology, experience, and/or training in personal counseling, familiarity with the history of philosophy as a discipline of counsel, and evidence of personal stability and good character. Evidence of satisfactory demonstration of these requisites and skills may be established by successful completion of the APPA Primary Certification Training Program for Philosophical Counselors.

Private Practice

Primary Certified Associates may practice as Certified Members of the APPA under the supervision of an APPA-approved Fully Certified Fellow in Client Counseling. Supervision is normally conducted by submission of audio cassette or written case study (with prior consent of the client) to an APPA supervisor. Recorded or written commentary on the cases will be provided by the supervisor, for which a fee will be charged. Upon the submission of a minimum of ten cases over a period of at least one year of practice, or a one-year internship under APPA supervision, Primary Certified Associates will be eligible to complete an APPA Advanced Certification Training Program for Client Counselors. Upon the successful completion of that program, candidates will be granted Full Certification in Client Counseling.

Certification as a Fellow

Primary and Full Certification as a Fellow are identical to Primary and Full Certification as an Associate, respectively, except that the minimum academic preparation for a Fellow is an earned Doctorate in Philosophy. Fully Certified Fellows are eligible, by APPA invitation, to provide training and supervision of candidates for APPA Certification.

CERTIFICATION STANDARDS FOR GROUP FACILITATORS

Certification as an Associate

Primary Certification as an Associate signifies basic competency minimally required to work with groups philosophically in both informal and formal settings. The minimum academic requirement for Certification as an Associate is an earned Master's Degree or ABD in Philosophy (or Licensura in Hispanic countries). In addition to demonstrated competency in academic philosophy, Primary Certified Facilitators must demonstrate (1) the knowledge, skills, and principles of large- and small-group facilitation, conflict resolution, and the dynamics of consensus, adversarial, and open-ended discussion formats, and (2) the application of an identifiably philosophical methodology or approach to group discussion and problem solving. The requisite skills and experience for Primary Certification as a Facilitator can be acquired through an APPA training program or by documentation of other appropriate training or experience. Evidence of satisfactory demonstration of these skills may be established by successful completion of Nelsonian Socratic Dialogue Training, or other demonstrably formal philosophically based methodologies. Full Certification will be granted to those Facilitators who can demonstrate the completion of at least one year experience as a Primary Certified Facilitator and successful completion of an APPA approved Advanced training program.

Informal Facilitation

The setting for informal group facilitation is usually a public venue, such as a bookstore, cafe, restaurant, library, shopping mall, or other public meeting place. The Facilitator is able to institute such a gathering on a regular basis and is able to facilitate and moderate a spontaneous philosophical discussion either of a preselected topic or of one selected by the group. The Facilitator does not lecture to the group but rather facilitates its philosophical interchange and maintains its philosophical character.

Formal Facilitation

The setting for formal group facilitation is usually a private venue (corporation, government organization, or other private group). The purpose of a formal gathering is to participate in a structured and focused philosophical discussion on a specific topic leading to a common resolution or outcome.

Certification as a Fellow

Primary and Full Certification as a Fellow are identical to Primary and Full Certification as an Associate, respectively, except that the minimum academic preparation for a Fellow is an earned Doctorate in Philosophy. Fully Certified Fellows are eligible, by APPA invitation, to provide training and supervision of candidates for APPA Certification.

CERTIFICATION STANDARDS FOR ORGANIZATIONAL CONSULTANTS

Certification as an Associate

Primary Certification as an Associate signifies basic competency minimally required to work with organizations philosophically. The minimum academic requirement for certification as an Associate is an earned Master's Degree or ABD in Philosophy (or Licensura in Hispanic countries). In addition to demonstrated competency in academic philosophy, Primary Certified Organizational Consultants must demonstrate (1) practical knowledge of organizational structures, missions, policy, management, and principles of strategic planning, and (2) the application of identifiably philosophical principles, knowledge, and skills to the resolution of problems and facilitation of goals in organizations and corporate entities. The requisite skills and experience for Primary Certification as an Organizational Consultant can be acquired through an APPA training program or by documentation of other appropriate training or experience. Evidence of satisfactory demonstration of these skills may be established by successful completion of an APPA Training Program for Organizational Consultants, or other demonstrably formal philosophically based methodologies. Full Certification will be granted to those Organizational Consultants who can demonstrate the completion of at least one year experience as a Primary Certified Organizational Consultant and successful completion of an APPA approved Advanced Training Program.

Relation to Counseling and Facilitation

While Certified Organizational Consultants need not be cross-certified in Group Facilitation or Client Counseling, the methods, skills, and knowledge of these other certification areas are also relevant—sometimes essential—to

Organizational Consulting. Candidates for Certification as Organizational Consultants are therefore encouraged to participate in acquiring at least the basic knowledge and skills of these other certification areas.

Certification as a Fellow

Primary and Full Certification as a Fellow are identical to Primary and Full Certification as an Associate, respectively, except that the minimum academic preparation for a Fellow is an earned Doctorate in Philosophy. Fully Certified Fellows are eligible, by APPA invitation, to provide training and supervision of candidates for APPA Certification.

These foregoing standards are stringent enough to attract applications by experienced and reputable practitioners, who are pleased and honored to be so recognized, and to attract to APPA certification training programs qualified philosophers and graduate students who aspire to be so recognized. They have also attracted an insignificant measure of detraction, predictably from persons who are not certifiable, either by reason of improper credentials (degrees in philosophy of education being the most common impostors of degrees in philosophy) or by reason of unprofessional character. In either case, the APPA does the public and the practice a service by weeding such persons out. At this writing, that is during the first eighteen months of activation of the foregoing standards, we have certified more than one hundred practitioners, in twenty states and seven foreign countries. The demand for certification training programs is growing, in America and abroad, as is the demand for philosophical services provided by their graduates.

It is conceivable that there are persons extant who are expert philosophers and proficient practitioners, yet who have had no formal academic training or have earned no advanced degrees in philosophy. The APPA is prepared to admit them as Adjunct Members—which makes them eligible to enroll in our Certification Training Programs—on two conditions. First, they must write the GRE (Graduate Record Examination), and attain a score of no less than 525 in each of its three components (verbal, quantitative, analytical). Second, they must write the APPA comprehensive philosophy examination, and demonstrate graduate-level mastery of mainstream philosophical expertise. Those who can satisfy these two conditions are acceptable as Adjunct Members.

At the same time, the APPA receives many queries from psychologists, theologians, education graduates, and others who claim either to be philosophical practitioners, or to have graduate-level philosophical expertise, but whose knowledge of philosophy and its practice is in fact minimal or nonexistent. Some psychologists are so poorly educated, if not brainwashed, that they appear incapable of distinguishing between their parent discipline (philosophy) and its offspring (psychology). They vainly suppose that a degree in psychology is itself equivalent to a degree in philosophy, and their awakening is often painful. By contrast, most theologians have actually studied philosophy, at least up to the seventeenth century, when it ceased to be an apologist for religious doctrine and an appendage of religious dogma. I myself have used Aristotle and other ancient philosophers in contemporary counseling, so can scarcely discredit Thomists for doing so. While theological philosophy is philosophical, it usually lacks a central philosophical focus and, more culpably, even a cursory awareness of the past four hundred years of seminal philosophical thought. So theologians generally need to upgrade their philosophical expertise to become eligible for APPA Adjunct Membership or Certification. Those with Education degrees are among the most troublesome, in my experience. The unvarnished truth is that education programs tend to opt out of mainstream university curricula, not because education students are ill-served by mainstream courses (as education administrators often claim), but because education students are often incapable of passing even the dumber than dumbed-down 101 courses on offer today. We have also had problems with the unprofessionalism of some education graduates, which appears all that more conspicuous when unadorned with philosophical competence.

The APPA also receives a smattering of inquiries from people with graduate degrees in comparative literature, sociology, history, and assorted other subjects, some of whom have taken a philosophy course or two, or have read a number of philosophy books, and imagine they have graduate-level philosophical expertise. My metaphoric reply is that, although I can saw wood and hammer nails, and have read some do-it-yourself carpentry books, this does not make me a professional carpenter. Hence the APPA's position is: to demonstrate the philosophical expertise of an earned MA, without having earned the MA, a candidate must do two things. First, the candidate must write the Graduate Record Examination, and attain a decent score in all three components.[5] This would demonstrate sufficient preparation to *enter* a graduate philosophy program. Second, the candidate must write the APPA Comprehensive Philosophy Examination, and attain a decent score. This would demonstrate Masters-level, mainstream expertise in philosophy. Upon fulfilling these two conditions, a candidate would be eligible for Adjunct Membership, and enrollment in APPA Certification Training Programs.

There is of course a delightful poetic justice in the APPA certification standards. (I apologize for the redundancy—what justice fails to delight?) Philosophy having temporarily succumbed to the sway of purely theoretical movements (e.g., logical positivism and the analytic school) that succeeded in divorcing it completely from the world of ordinary but pressing concerns, formal studies in philosophy tended to be avoided like the very plague by anyone desirous of making his way in the world and actually earning a living in it. Only holy fools, secular saints, or exacting intellects pursued graduate studies in philosophy, along with those few highly intelligent but otherwise normal persons who genuinely loved it, and who maintained either great faith in or complete indifference to the world's capacity to sustain authentic folly or naive idealism. Surprise of surprises, their reward is nigh. Suddenly (as it were), the vista of professional philosophical practice shimmers before them, an idyllic oasis in a parched desert. It is no mirage. And lo, the sole criterion of admission, refreshment, and sojourn in this oasis is that heretofore ill-respected, much-maligned, and under-valued scrap of paper: the graduate degree in philosophy. So it turns out that those who have apparently labored long and hard to remove themselves from the world, are now in the very thick of it. This is the Tao at work. As the Chinese Grandmaster S. M. Li used to remind his students, the ends of a string are not merely the two points furthest separated on it; they also become adjacent when the loop is closed.

9.3. ESTABLISHED BODY OF KNOWLEDGE AS REFLECTED IN THE PUBLICATION OF REFERENCE BOOKS AND PROFESSIONAL JOURNALS AND REGULARLY SCHEDULED SCIENTIFIC [SIC: READ "LEARNED"] MEETINGS

This quasi-reference book itself contributes to the satisfaction of the first conjunct's first conjunct. Other books (e.g., by Achenbach, Cohen, Grimes, Howard, Koestenbaum, Lahav, Raabe, Schuster, and others) that constitute seminal technical literature in this field, and hence form a corpus of reference literature, are listed in Appendix D. Similarly, a growing number of scholarly journals are either devoted outright to philosophical practice themselves, or have brought out special editions devoted to it. Again, a list of these is provided in Appendix E. Thus the first conjunct of condition three is satisfied. Further evidence of this satisfaction is provided by the trickle of doctoral dissertations that have begun to emerge from the academy, taking philosophical practice as their theme. Without a framework of reference literature, a scholarly thesis would be unthinkable.

The second conjunct contains this curious word: "scientific." I rather doubt that family and marriage counselors, music therapists, social workers, and other professional groups either already licensed by states or seeking state licensure would refer to themselves as "scientists." They might be willing to accept the appellation "social scientist," with or without the understanding that a gin and tonic usually contains more tonic than gin. Still, the thrust of the condition is that professional or scholarly meetings regularly take place. This has been true of the international community of philosophical practitioners since 1994, and of each national organization since its respective inception.

Hence the conjunction of condition three is already satisfied, and will become even more amply satisfied as the movement gathers strength.

9.4. ESTABLISHED CODE OF ETHICS

For a government to recognize a profession, and thereby endorse if not promote the provision of its services to the public, then the professionals who would benefit from this recognition have a duty to adopt and abide by a code of ethics. Moreover, the consumers of this service are entitled to know what ethical precepts guide and bind the professional practice in question.

Most philosophical practitioners are aware of a double-edged sword that operates in our context, which I will mention before introducing the APPA Standards of Ethical Professional Practice. First, applied or professional ethicists naturally have a hand not only in crafting codes of ethics for other professions, but also in subjecting their provisions to interpretation in scholarly case studies and professional case-work. Thus we should be expected to do for ourselves what we are often paid to do for others; namely, craft a code of ethics for philosophical practice itself. This is not as easy as it sounds, because it is not analogous merely to practicing our profession on colleagues. Doctors are routinely examined by other doctors; lawyers, routinely represented by other lawyers; philosophical counselors, routinely counseled by other philosophical counselors. In building or interpreting a code of ethics for another profession, philosophers are able intelligibly and with some consensus to frame all-important notions of virtue. But in building such a code for ourselves, we encounter a formidable second-order problem, for we must endeavor to frame virtuous ways of helping clients perforce to lead more virtuous lives. There lies some difficulty in this undertaking, for diversity of opinion among philosophers (and there is plenty) about what constitutes virtuous living may be magnified many-fold when applied to framing the virtues of a professional practice that is partly or largely concerned with explication or inculcation of virtue.

The other edge of the sword is well-known to applied ethicists: professional ethicists, for example, are often subjected to special scrutiny—those who purport to be ethics consultants for others should presumably have no chinks in their own ethical armor. Whereas doctors, lawyers, and engineers all experience and sometime succumb to ethical conflicts, professional ethicists are supposed to be immune to them. That is one view, at any rate. Another view admits that, just as dentists may suffer tooth decay and marriage counselors may get divorces, so professional ethicists may experience conflicts of interest, and sometimes make unfortunate choices. While people may reasonably expect ethicists to be ethical, ethicists are still not saints. Even so, most ethicists I know are nowhere near as profligate or dissipated as Augustine in his youth—and he was canonized eventually. By the same token, philosophical counselors who behaved as saintfully as Mother Teresa could not possibly know enough of sin to counsel their clients from experience.

Having said this much, here are the APPA Standards of Professional Ethical Practice. They were adapted from the original ASPCP Code of Ethics, which contained the twenty-five ethical standards. Some of these original standards were modified slightly, and the six Fundamental Canons added, by the APPA.

STANDARDS OF PROFESSIONAL ETHICAL PRACTICE

Preamble

While individual philosophical practitioners may differ in method and theoretical orientation, for example, analytic or existential-phenomenological, they facilitate such activities as: (1) the examination of clients' arguments and justifications; (2) the clarification, analysis, and definition of important terms and concepts; (3) the exposure and examination of underlying assumptions and logical implications; (4) the exposure of conflicts and inconsistencies; (5) the exploration of traditional philosophical theories and their significance for client issues; and (6) all other related activities that have historically been identified as philosophical.

Although several other helping professions have also incorporated some of the aforementioned ancient, philosophical activities into their therapeutic practices, they should not thereby be confused with the private practice of philosophy as defined by the performance of distinctively philosophical activities for which philosophical practitioners have uniquely been educated and trained.

As the ethical code of the American Philosophical Practitioners Association, the Standards of Ethical Practice establish principles of ethical conduct that are binding upon all member practitioners and which shall accordingly serve as the basis for addressing ethical complaints against member practitioners.

Fundamental Canons

   i. Philosophical practitioners will, above all, endeavor to do no harm.

   ii. Philosophical practitioners will render their services for the benefit of their clients.

   iii. Philosophical practitioners will refer clients for appropriate alternative care if the clients' problems are adjudged to be not primarily philosophical in origin, or not amenable to philosophical approaches.

   iv. Philosophical practitioners will respect the dignity and autonomy of their clients, and will respect their confidentiality and protect their anonymity to the extent required by law.

   v. Philosophical practitioners will conduct their consultations and deliberations with reputability and integrity, and will refrain from behaviors, practices and conflicts of interest that would bring the profession into disrepute.

   vi. Philosophical practitioners will, beyond attending to the needs of their clients, endeavor to serve the greater good of the community and society in which they reside.

Ethical Standards

1. In providing professional services, the philosophical practitioner should maintain utmost respect for client welfare, integrity, dignity, and autonomy.

2. Philosophical practitioners should facilitate maximum client participation in philosophical explorations. They should avoid dictating "correct" answers to client queries and issues, but should actively encourage the client's own engagement of reflective powers and rational determinations. In cases in which a client is seeking assistance for purposes of resolving a specific problem such as an ethical problem or other practical matter, philosophical practitioners may, in light of philosophical exploration of the matter, suggest possible courses of action. However, they should make clear to the client that the final decision rests with the client.

3. Philosophical practitioners should be sensitive to alternative "worldviews" and philosophical perspectives including those based upon cultural or gender distinctions among diverse client populations.

4. Philosophical practitioners should not engage in any form of unjust discriminatory activity. While a philosophical practitioner is not required to accept as clients all those who seek services, the refusal to render such services should be based solely upon the perceived inability to provide beneficial services, or upon other relevant issues of practice.

5. Philosophical practitioners should avoid creating dependency relations in clients and seek wherever possible to instruct clients in the methods and theories of philosophy so that clients may continue to apply these methods and theories without the assistance of the philosopher.

6. Philosophical practitioners should avoid scheduling unnecessary meetings or sessions. The services of the practitioner should be terminated when, to the client's satisfaction, the purposes for which they were sought have been fulfilled or when no further benefits are likely to accrue from their continuation.

7. The philosophical practitioner should refrain from manipulating or coercing the client, as well as any form of fraud or deceit.

8. Philosophical practitioners should be scrupulously accurate about their credentials and qualifications. They should not mislead the client about their credentials and should not hold themselves out (either implicitly or explicitly) as mental health counselors, psychologists, or authorities in any other field for which they are not otherwise qualified. No member should hold himself or herself out (either implicitly or explicitly) as a philosophical practitioner without having duly satisfied all training and degree requirements for certification as provided for by the Association.

9. Philosophical practitioners should not employ techniques or methods not associated with training in philosophy (for example, hypnosis, or other psychiatric/psychological interventions) for which they are not otherwise qualified.

10. On or prior to the first meeting, the philosophical practitioner should provide the client with clear, accurate, honest, and complete information regarding the nature of services he or she is qualified to render, and should not make any unwarranted claims about the utility or effectiveness of such services.

11. When a client's problem or reason for seeking philosophical services falls outside the purview of the practitioner's qualifications or areas of competence, then the practitioner should provide the client with an appropriate referral.

12. At all junctures in the process of providing philosophical services, the philosophical practitioner should seek to maintain the freely given and informed consent of the client.

13. The philosophical practitioner should inform the client of his or her fees prior to the commencement of services.

14. The philosophical practitioner should safeguard a client's right to privacy by treating as confidential all information obtained from the client, except where disclosure is required by law or is justified in order to prevent imminent, substantial harm to the client or to others. In all such exceptional cases, disclosure may be made provided that it is made to the appropriate party or authority and no more information than necessary is disclosed. The philosophical practitioner should inform the client of the pertinent limits to confidentiality upon initiating services.

15. The philosophical practitioner who confidentially receives information establishing that his or her client has a contagious, fatal disease is justified in disclosing (necessary) information to an identifiable third party who, by his or her relation to the client, is at high risk of contracting the disease. The philosophical practitioner should, however, first confirm that neither the client nor any other party has already disclosed the information nor intends to make the disclosure in the immediate future. Prior to disclosing the information, the practitioner should inform the client of his or her intention to disclose. In proceeding with disclosure, the practitioner should act mindfully of the welfare, integrity, dignity, and autonomy of both client and third party.

16. The philosophical practitioner should secure and treat as confidential all records and written documents obtained or produced in the course of providing services. Such documents, or the content thereof, may not be shared with other professionals without the freely given and informed consent of the client.

17. For purposes of research, training, or publication, the philosophical practitioner may use data obtained in the course of counseling provided that all identifying references are deleted or fictionalized

in order to ensure client privacy and confidentiality. Prior to initiating services, practitioners should inform their clients of such possible use of acquired data.

18. Philosophical practitioners should avoid sexual intimacy with clients or any other form of dual role relation which might compromise the integrity of the professional relationship.

19. Philosophical practitioners should not use their affiliations with colleges, universities, or other institutions or agencies as means of recruiting clients for their private practices. They may, however, use such affiliations as documentation of relevant background and/or training.

20. A philosophical practitioner who is aware of violations or intended violations of the Standards of Ethical Practice by another member practitioner should take appropriate measures to prevent the misconduct. Generally, if the misconduct can be prevented or rectified by calling the violation to the attention of the offending practitioner, then this is the preferred course of action. If such efforts fail or are not feasible, the violation should be called to the attention of the Association's Ethics Committee.

21. Philosophical practitioners should exemplify those moral qualities of character that are associated with being philosophical (for example, being open-minded, honest, rational, consistent, fair, and impartial).

22. Philosophical practitioners should keep informed about current statutes, legal precedents, social issues, etc., that are relevant to their practice and which might affect the quality of services they render. Similarly, those practicing as consultants in a specialized field, such as medical ethics, should keep informed of changes in health law and policies that may affect the quality of their services.

23. Consistent with the Standards of Ethical Practice, the philosophical practitioner should comply with existing local, state or provincial, and federal laws relevant to the private practice of philosophy and should work for change of existing laws where such laws prevent or obstruct its ethical practice.

24. Philosophical practitioners should seek to promote mutual understanding, cooperation, and respect between philosophy and other helping professions including teaching, mental health, social work, medicine, and psychology.

25. Philosophical practitioners should contribute to the advancement of the private practice of philosophy by promoting public understanding of its nature and value through such activities as research, publication, teaching, lecturing, and competent, ethical practice.

As we have seen, philosophical practitioners now satisfy three of the four criteria necessary for the recognition of a profession in New York State and, in so doing, also satisfy similar criteria elsewhere. The satisfaction of the remaining criterion, an accredited degree program in a chartered university or institute, will not be long in coming. Philosophical practice is therefore traversing political no-man's land, having emerged from the makeshift camps of the non-professions and having approached within range of the entrenched professions. We have taken minimal fire in the rear, from the amateurs, whose fire-power is negligible; and we will draw heavier fire in front, from the professionals, whose fire-power is far from negligible. But their ranks are already divided and factionalized, as we shall see in Chapter 15, and many view our approach not as an assault, rather as a liberation.

While the establishment of a profession naturally entails the making of alliances and enmities alike, if the politics of philosophical practice are played skillfully and if the prevailing ethos favors the game, then legislative recognition of philosophical counselors is inevitable. Such recognition is in any case a defining goal for all aspiring professions, and is thus mete for closer examination in the next chapter.

NOTES

1. See P. Feyerabend, *Against Method* (London: NLB, 1975), which challenges the hypothetico-deductivism and other manifestations of rational methodology in science.

2. *The New York Times*, 8 March 1998, *The World In Review*, "I Bill Therefore I Am," by Joe Sharkey.

3. My father, may he rest in peace, fought with the Haganah. See my introduction to the Hebrew edition of *Plato Not Prozac* (Tel-Aviv: Safer, 2001, in press).

4. See the Part V of this book.

5. The APPA demands a minimum raw score of 525 in each, which is relatively lenient if one studies aggregate data from across-the-board performance on these exams, as we have done. See the Educational Testing Service website: <www.ets.org>.

CHAPTER 10

Recognition Versus Regulation[1]

10.1. The Political Economy of Regulation

10.2. Licensure

10.3. Certification

10.4. Registration

10.5. Recognition qua Politics

10.1. THE POLITICAL ECONOMY OF REGULATION

I am reminded of an alleged trio of infamous Chinese curses, having to do with political life. The first one is fairly common knowledge: "May you live in interesting times." The second one circumscribes the subject matter of this chapter: "May the Government be aware of you." For completeness's sake, I have never been able to ascertain the content of the third curse; no one whom I know knows it. Perhaps its unascertainability is the clue to the curse itself: "May your knowledge of this third curse be revealed too late to avert it." We shall see. Philosophical practitioners have already fallen prey to the first two; maybe the third follows ineluctably.

The United States was founded generally on a repugnance for and rebellion against excessive governmental interference in the lives and livelihoods of private citizens. In the Old World, many citizens had no private lives to begin with; the interference of *anciens régimes* preempted privacy—if not citizenry itself—and imposed strictures of class, privilege, wealth, and the like. Americans solved the problem of nobility by replacing it wholesale with money. Even in the antebellum South, the aristocracy was one of wealth, not birth. In the

North, the Kennedy family was the nearest thing America ever had to Royalty—hence the "Camelot" metaphor of the JFK presidency. The telling difference is that, whereas European nobility inherited its wealth as a matter of legacy, American "nobility" defined its legacy as a matter of wealth. In the Old World, political power depended almost solely on birth, and the social and political connections entailed by birth. In the New World, it depends almost solely on wealth, and the connections entailed thereby.

Notwithstanding vast historical change, the American commitment to individual liberty remains essentially unchanged. The American government has little or no concern for the health, education, and welfare of its citizens, and allows them freely to sink or swim as they list. As always, the "bottom line" is money. Health care, higher education, and legal justice are merely commodities in America; you get pretty much what you can afford. The American government, and the multinational corporations which increasingly control it, are exclusively concerned with extracting as much income as possible—in the form of overt and covert taxation—from the lower and middle classes, short of bankrupting too many of them in a single year and thus fomenting economic instability or political discontent. As long as you pay your taxes in America, and do not commit violent crime, you are free to do pretty much as you please, or as you can afford.

The default state of American private affairs, and arguably its primal state, is therefore non-regulatory. American governments—be they Federal, State, or Municipal—will not step in to protect their citizens until or unless sufficient harm is done to make lack of protection politically unaffordable. It makes no difference whether one examines protracted absence of regulation of boilers on Mississippi steamboats of the nineteenth century (which resulted in hundreds of explosions and thousands of deaths); protracted absence of regulation of the tobacco industry's advertising during most of the twentieth century (which has resulted in millions of deaths); or initial absence of regulation of body-piercing parlors in Oregon (which resulted in a few hundred cases of hepatitis and other infectious diseases): the principle is the same. When enough people get hurt or killed, and when the survivors can organize a strong enough lobby, governments will take steps to protect them. Until that time, the victims appear to be governed by some variant of the putative third Chinese curse—i.e., "May the Government be unaware of you until it's too late."

More than forty professional groups, all of whom fulfill most of the criteria enumerated in the previous chapter, are currently seeking legislative recognition in New York State. These groups include Social Workers, Creative Arts Therapists, Marriage and Family Therapists, Psychoanalysts, and Philosophical Practitioners. There are three well-defined ways in which a state legislature can recognize a professional group: by licensure, by certification, or by registration.

Not all states utilize all ways; some grant one or the other, or some combination thereof. There is also a host of *ad hoc* ways, some of which also bear mention herein.

Our main question is: what form (if any) of legislative recognition is suitable for philosophical practitioners? Even that question requires preliminary clarification, for it could well be asked, even by those who support such recognition of counselors, whether facilitators and consultants should be so recognized too. *Prima facie*, it appears not. Many philosophical consultants are partly entrepreneurs, and most entrepreneurs are businesspersons but not professionals in the sense of the four criteria previously discussed at length. Does your organization wish to hire a consultant? If so, *caveat emptor*. The same is largely true of informal facilitation: there are no special professional requirements for moderating a group discussion in a coffeehouse; intellectual and social skills generally suffice. Formal facilitation is another matter, for there are indeed special requirements for conducting a Nelsonian Socratic dialogue. The question is: to what extent are these requirements professional? My answer is that they are professional in the sense that educational instruction and pedagogic methodologies are professional, and therefore that some form of recognition is appropriate. That form in this case could be indirect, subsumed under an academic credential in philosophical practice, offered by a chartered university or institution. But if Socratic dialogue becomes a mandatory component of undergraduate education in a given state, which of course it should be, then the state might see fit specifically to recognize trained facilitators of Socratic dialogue, much as it specifically recognizes other kinds of teaching specialties (e.g., special education).

The cutting edge of professional philosophical practice is of course counseling, and this is the focus of the primary initiative toward legislative recognition. When ordinary people first hear of and grasp the basic concept of philosophical counseling, they immediately understand that philosophical counselors resemble psychiatric, psychological, legal, and financial counselors in a fundamental respect; that is, they deploy special skills in a profession of personal counsel. The large question is, where does one situate philosophical counseling on the professional spectrum compassed by strict regulation of medical practice on one extreme, and non-regulation of accounting practice on the other? Let us address this question by exploring the legislative norms themselves.

10.2. LICENSURE

The most stringent form of recognition is licensure, although things licensed may themselves be utterly plebeian—such as the operation of a motor vehicle.

Moreover, there are two kinds of licensure, pertaining to two kinds of entities: license of title, and license of scope of practice. A license of title protects the actual name (or names) of a profession; for example, in New York and many other states, one cannot use the title "Psychological Counselor" unless one is licensed to do so. By the same token, one remains at liberty to use an unprotected title, such as "Psychotherapist" in New York and some other states, provided that there is no licensure on scope of practice in that state. If the scope of practice is itself defined and protected by license, then no unlicensed person may engage in that practice under any title. Driver's licenses are of exactly this kind: different gradations of license define the different types of motor vehicles that can be operated, and for what purposes, by the respective license holders. This is regulation of scope of professional driving practice. You cannot do business as a "taxi driver" or "school bus driver" in New York, unless you hold a valid license, because the respective scopes of those professional driving practices are protected by law. You can, however, call yourself a "Psychotherapist" and charge fees for psychotherapy (if you can find clients) because neither the title nor the scope of practice are protected in New York State. Similarly, I can do business legally as a philosophical counselor—neither that title nor its scope of practice are protected by law in New York.

Since licensing laws vary from state to state, one must obviously be cognizant of local laws before entering into philosophical practice, and for that matter before printing business cards. It turns out, for example, that the name "counselor" is itself protected in Texas, and thus "philosophical counselor" is also protected—so philosophical counselors cannot call themselves "philosophical counselors" in Texas unless they meet current licensing requirements. Ironically, therefore, a licensed psychological counselor in Texas *could* legally call himself a "philosophical counselor" even if he knew no philosophy. This should richly illustrate why secular laws are not graven in stone, and why legislatures need to convene regularly. Although one's ignorance of law is never a ground for exculpation in the breach (only one of possible mitigation in the penalty), irrationality, unfairness, or outmodedness of laws themselves is often a hallowed ground of civil or even criminal disobedience. The practical point is that a philosophical counselor in Texas must either seek to change the law by due political process or active floutation, or else circumvent it entirely (e.g., by calling himself a "philosophical practitioner").

Where scope of practice itself is licensed, there are different legal obstacles, as well as different ways of surmounting them. Most sensible people agree that iatrogenic (i.e., invasive) medicine should remain strictly licensed by scope of practice. Where state-of-the-art procedures for performing surgical operations exist and continue to improve, they can be universally described and their performance restricted not only by state but also by federal license. We don't want automobile mechanics performing heart transplants anymore than we want cardiac surgeons replacing car engines. But what about talk-therapy? Legislative restriction of mere conversation brushes up against, if not conflicts with, the first amendment right to freedom of speech.[2] On *prima facie* constitutional grounds, the state has no business regulating the content of conversations.

One noteworthy exception, and long-time infringer of such first amendment rights, is the State of California, which maintains blanket restrictions on both the title and scope of psychological counseling. Let us examine the California laws *verbatim*, as exemplars of badly crafted legislation.[3] First is the title law, pertaining to license of the term "psychology" and its cognates:

> 2902. (a) "Licensed psychologist" means an individual to whom a license has been issued pursuant to the provisions of this chapter, which license is in force and has not been suspended or revoked.
>
> 2902. (c) A person represents himself or herself to be a psychologist when the person holds himself or herself out to the public by any title or description of services incorporating the words "psychology," "psychological," "psychologist," "psychology consultation," "psychology consultant," "psychometry," "psychometrics" or "psychometrist," "psychotherapy," "psychotherapist," "psychoanalysis" or "psychoanalyst," or when the person holds himself or herself out to be trained, experienced, or an expert on the field of psychology.

So much for restriction of title. Unlike New York State, where you are free to call yourself a "psychotherapist" or "psychoanalyst" (but not a "psychologist"), in California you may not use the prefix "psycho" unless you are licensed, or perhaps a psychopath. Next, we come to the much more contentious restrictions on scope of practice:

> 2903. No person may engage in the practice of psychology, or represent himself to be a psychologist, without a license granted under this chapter, except as otherwise provided in this chapter. The practice of psychology is defined as rendering or offering to render for a fee to individuals, groups, organizations or the public any psychological service involving the application of psychological principles, methods, and procedures of understanding, predicting, and influencing behavior, such as the principles pertaining to learning, perception, motivation, emotions, and interpersonal relationships; and the methods and procedures for interviewing, counseling, psychotherapy, behavior modification, and hypnosis; and of constructing, administering, and interpreting tests of mental abilities, aptitudes, interests, attitudes, personality characteristics, emotions, and motivations.

The application of such principles and methods includes, but is not restricted to: diagnosis, prevention, treatment, and amelioration of psychological problems and emotional and mental disorders of individuals and groups.

Psychotherapy within the meaning of this chapter means the use of psychological methods in a professional relationship to assist a person or persons to acquire greater human effectiveness or to modify feelings, conditions, attitudes and behavior which are emotionally, intellectually, or socially ineffectual or maladjustive.

As used in this chapter, "fee" means any charge, monetary or otherwise, whether paid directly or paid on a prepaid or capitation basis by a third party, or a charge assessed by a facility, for services rendered.

So what's wrong with section 2903? An exhaustive explanation would require another book in itself, which—à la *Tristam Shandy*—I cannot begin to write before completing this one. Suffice to say, in general, that section 2903 presupposes a specialized knowledge of human emotion, perception, cognition, mentation, and socialization that psychologists simply do not possess, neither uniquely nor in any approximation of fullness, which qualifies or otherwise entitles them to monopolize the practice of professional counsel as described by that section. More specifically, psychologists are trained to know precisely nothing about intellectually maladjustive attitudes—qua unexamined philosophical positions—in the dimensions of logic, ethics, aesthetics, and axiology, whether grounded in ethos or telos. In fact, the letter of section 2903 *itself* embodies intellectually maladjustive attitudes, in that it wrongfully yet lawfully ascribes solely to psychologists the expertise (which they do not have) and the authority (which they should not have) to recognize and redress philosophical problems, in addition to psychological ones. Actually, I can write no better refutation of section 2903 than J. Michael Russell has already written, in an article entitled "The Philosopher as Personal Consultant."[4] I briefly quote some of his *Conclusions*:

> A theory is philosophical when its principal claims are predominantly justified by arguments based on the implications of concepts, rather than empirical data. Everyone does philosophy, frequently; not everyone knows what he or she is doing. The role of philosophy, and the relevance of philosophical training, has been pathetically under-rated. The contributions to an understanding of persons by the empirical disciplines ... have been vastly over-rated. The psychologists whose ideas have been really influential here—and I include the Freudians, the behaviorists, and the existential-humanistic practitioners—have been advancing theories, which were predominately philosophical in character.

Let me be more blunt. Psychology is shot through and through with conceptual muddles, which any decently trained philosopher could demonstrate, in short order, to an attentive listener, with any consecutive five pages of any psychologist's essay, picked at random. Under the guise of empirical research, psychologists are typically doing philosophy, and doing it badly. Psychology is founded on a causal perspective in its theories, in spite of the fact that in consulting practice one cannot talk about human actions in consistently causal terms. It is riddled with unclarity about the nature of explanation. It is lost in a sea of confusions about the status of mentalistic language. In short, psychology is founded on a whole way of thinking which consistently gets it into the kinds of troubles to which philosophers are sensitive. As long as theories about persons are going to be so heavily philosophical, philosophers should be playing a central rather than a peripheral role in developing theory of personal consultation....

It will come as no surprise that I am opposed to regulating or licensing the sorts of communicative activities which personal consultation and insight-oriented psychotherapy have in common, for these are part of a larger human enterprise which ought to be open to all.... There are, admittedly, dangers in not regulating these things, which can be done in ways which are stupid, inept, or wicked. There are greater dangers in regulating such communications, and a more repugnant form of audacity.

Bravissimo! So much for section 2903; now for its circumvention. Laws such as these are routinely caveated by a set of exemptions, which allow exceptions under specified conditions. Such exceptions are typically professional, academic, educational, research-oriented, or vocational in nature. Here is a relevant exemption (from section 2903) in California law:

2908. Nothing in this chapter shall be construed to prevent qualified members of other recognized professional groups licensed to practice in the State of California, such as, but not limited to, physicians, clinical social workers, educational psychologists, marriage, family and child counselors, optometrists, psychiatric technicians, or registered nurses, or attorneys admitted to the California State Bar, or persons utilizing hypnotic techniques by referral from persons licensed to practice medicine, dentistry or psychology, or persons utilizing hypnotic techniques which offer avocational or vocational self-improvement and do not offer therapy for emotional or mental disorders, or duly ordained members of the recognized clergy, or duly ordained religious practitioners from doing work of a psychological nature consistent with the laws governing their respective professions, provided they do not hold themselves out to the public by any title or description of services incorporating the words "psychological," "psychologist," "psychology," "psychometrist," "psychometrics," or "psychometry," or that they not state or imply that they are licensed to practice psychology.

If you have successfully parsed the foregoing sentence, you now realize that the scope of psychological practice has been extended to physicians, psychiatrists, dentists, lawyers, nurses, clergy, and hypnotherapists, most of whom have little or no formal training in psychological counseling, but who may nonetheless practice it under a different name. In other words, licensing by scope of practice is a hierarchical undertaking, which defines a professional pecking order, wherein a "higher" license (e.g., medicine) entails the scope of a "lower" one (e.g., psychology), but not conversely. Philosophical practitioners are still shut out, because our profession is not yet recognized. However, this exemption and others open doors more than wide enough for astute and committed philosophers to slip through. I offer three examples here: Paul Sharkey and J. Michael Russell (in California), and Alberto Hernandez (in Colorado).

Dr. Sharkey (PhD in Philosophy, Professor Emeritus, and founding Vice President of the APPA) became a certified hypnotherapist in California, which took him about one year. He is now legally able to offer philosophical counseling (in substance) under the aegis of hypnotherapy (in title) as an exemption from psychological counseling (in scope) to clients whose problems are philosophical in the first place.

J. Michael Russell (PhD in Philosophy, Professor, and APPA Faculty Member) took an alternative route. He affiliated himself with a psychoanalytic training institute, which entailed a five-year commitment, but which allowed him to register (in California) as a Research Analyst, and later as a Graduate Analyst.[5] Owing to his concomitant academic affiliation as a philosopher, he satisfied a research (rather than a professional) exemption to section 2903. To wit: persons with doctorates in academic fields not traditionally allied with mental health may, in California, train in and practice psychoanalysis in an "adjunct" capacity—meaning they can spend up to one-third of their research hours seeing clients. Since there are relatively few registered "Research Analysts," the state has not bothered to handcuff or gag them with laws; moreover, one can with good conscience and sound justification practice philosophical counseling under the rubric of eclectic psychoanalysis.

In Colorado, the legislature seems to have recognized the "repugnant form of audacity" assumed by its licensing of both title and scope of practice of psychotherapy. While the latter language appears as egregiously broad as the Californian laws,[6] the Colorado legislators explicitly intended to interpret that language as narrowly as possible. Thus they have created a "State Grievance Board" for and database of unlicensed psychotherapists, who may duly register and practice within the broader scope of psychotherapy (e.g., philosophical counseling), as long as they do not violate the associated title laws:

(10) "Unlicensed psychotherapist" means any person whose primary practice is psychotherapy or who holds himself or herself out to the public as being able to practice psychotherapy for compensation and who is not licensed under this title to practice psychotherapy ...

Alberto Hernandez (PhD in Philosophy, Instructor at Colorado College, and APPA-Certified Philosophical Counselor) was able to register with the State Grievance Board, jump through a few bureaucratic hoops, and lawfully hang out a Philosophical Counseling shingle.

One thus appreciates the practical distinction between licensing titles versus licensing scopes of practice, at least for philosophical counselors. In states where titles are licensed, even if the term "counselor" has been appropriated (as in Texas), one merely finds a convenient and unprotected synonym, prints up business cards accordingly, and practices lawfully. In states where both titles and scopes of practice are licensed, as in California and Colorado, one must find an exemption that allows one to practice philosophy under another scope, not just another name.

Some senior New York legislators, with whom I have conferred, candidly, if covertly, admit that, in retrospect, it was a great blunder to have licensed psychological counseling in either form—whether by title alone or by scope of practice. Not only did it grant psychologists a default monopoly on non-medical talk-therapy, which is now being attacked and broken by all kinds of emerging professional groups; but it was also probably unwarranted in the first place. Legislators were more easily bamboozled in the mid-twentieth century, when rapid and evident advances in the mathematical, physical, chemical, and biological sciences had encouraged extrapolation of hope of similar advances into psychological and social domains. In other words, legislators were late-comers to positivism's premature victory celebration over metaphysics; but since the bar had remained open, legislators were still becoming intoxicated when everyone else was regretting the hangover. Philosophers having aban-doned the practical field, psychologists became ersatz sovereigns over the realm of psychic dis-ease, imitating medicine's legitimate sovereignty over the realm of corporeal diseases. Counseling psychologists capitalized brilliantly on their opportunity, which is lately revealed as short-lived. Man's full noetic function is not embraced by psychology *alone*, anymore than his full physical function is embraced by hematology, endocrinology, or any -ology *alone*. Thus, in ret-rospect, the error of having licensed the scope of psychological counseling, to the exclusion of philosophy, is analogous to the hypothetical error of licensing the scope of dental surgery, to the exclusion of root canal work. But having festooned the system with one such license, legislators are now hoist with their petard. It does them no good to bemoan having recognized counseling psychology as a profession, for upon that precedent now hang the legislative aspirations of dozens of emergent talk-therapeutic and related professions. Governments will either have to deregulate psychological counseling (as, in effect, they did Colorado), or else newly regulate a host of other counselors (as the proposed Diaz Bill would do for philosophers in New York).

As even this cursory glance reveals, licensing poses many problems. Even so, the first-ever legislative bill in the U.S.A. (and probably the world) to recognize philosophical counselors, sponsored by New York State Assemblyman Ruben Diaz Jr., was a bill (A-9845) to license the title "Philosophical Counselor." It was modeled after New York's title-license for psychological counselors, and its motivation is pellucid and not particularly party-political. The Assemblyman argues that, if his constituents can be referred by their physicians to psychological counselors, who are not physicians, yet whose services can be beneficial and are subsidizable by health insurance; then likewise his constituents should be able to be referred by their physicians to philosophical counselors, who are likewise not physicians, yet whose services can also be beneficial and therefore ought to be subsidizable by health insurance.

Two objections worthy of reply have been made to this licensing Bill, and made by philosophical practitioners themselves. (Objections unworthy of reply, by reason of patent absurdity, are mentioned in Chapters 15 and 16.) The first worthy objection is that such legislation "medicalizes" philosophy, by annexing it to the health care system. The reply is twofold. First, the growing presence of medical ethicists in hospitals, whether serving on ethics committees or available on-call for cases in which medical exigencies necessitate ethical decision-making, does not "medicalize" ethics; rather, it simply and truthfully acknowledges that the responsible practice of medicine sometimes entails forays into nonmedical dimensions—ethical, legal, and social, among others. The etymology of "health" is "hale," or "whole," and as long as the goals of medicine include the maintenance or restoration of health where possible, and respect for autonomy and dignity of the patient in any case, then medicine naturally allies itself with certain nonmedical practices, e.g., ethics counseling. Occupational, physical, and other rehabilitational therapies are not administered by doctors, but by nonmedical professionals allied with medicine for the purpose of restoring health. Other allies include social workers, psychological counselors, and—lately—consulting medical ethicists and philosophical counselors. The latter are deserving of professional recognition too. The second part of my reply to this first objection is that the word "heath" itself is rapidly, if ironically, vanishing from the vocabulary of health-care. HMOs (Health

Maintenance Organizations) are being "morphed" wholesale into MCOs (Managed Care Organizations). As the conceptual locus of the system shifts, and as health issues revert to management issues, philosophical practitioners will have an even greater role to play, juxtaposed perforce to management, not to medicine.

The second objection to licensing I find more cogent, and it has been advanced by some astute philosophical practitioners. The logic of the original Diaz Bill is a normative implication ($P \supset Q$): if states should license psychological counselors, then they should license philosophical counselors too. However, a generous interpretation of the first amendment would preclude not only licensing the scope of practice of conversations, but also licensing the professional titles of conversants. Hence, it is objected that the protection even of the title "philosophical counselor" is unconstitutional—an infringement of freedom of speech—and therefore that philosophical counselors should not be licensed ($\sim Q$). The logical corollary to this objection, via *modus tollens*, is that psychological counselors should not be licensed either ($\sim P$).

These arguments of the cogent variety, as well as others too absurd for words, are all equally moot at this time, because the Diaz Bill (drafted initially as a licensure measure in February 1998) was modified to a certification measure in March 2000. On that note we move to a brief consideration of state certification.

10.3. CERTIFICATION

Certification is an alternative and less restrictive form of legislative recognition, which raises fewer constitutional hackles in any case, and which also appears authoritatively more benign. As we have seen, the profession of accounting epitomizes the certification model. In New York (and presumably most other states), anyone at all may call himself a "Public Accountant"; there is no licensure of this title. The government doesn't care who calls himself a PA; if you engage one, *caveat emptor*. However, the government does recognize PAs who demonstrate mastery of professional expertise, by virtue of passing examinations set by authorities in that profession and approved by duly constituted state boards. Passing such examinations confers a both a certificate and the privilege of calling oneself a "Certified Public Accountant" (CPA). Thus a member of the public who seeks reasonable assurance that the accountant he engages is a competent professional should preferentially hire a CPA. Certification legislation is a fair compromise in that it both allows near-complete freedom of expression by not protecting the generic title "Public Accountant," yet also grants a professional distinction by recognizing—without compelling—the attainment of certain standards. This arrangement also preempts most objections by amateurs, and even by professional PAs. A Public Accountant who has practiced competently for years and who claims to be as good as any CPA merely begs the question: "Then why don't you get certified?" At the other end of the spectrum, people who don't want or need to engage a CPA, but who do want or need inexpensive help preparing their income-tax returns come March or April, can go to an accounting version of a fast-food chain, and probably be served by someone moonlighting from a fast-food chain. *Caveat emptor*.

Thus certification permits the coexistence of egalitarianism and professionalism. It is therefore a workable compromise. Most reputable philosophical counselors with whom I have conferred remain queasy about licensure but enthusiastic about certification. Only the radicals and anarchists oppose it—but since they are predisposed to oppose anything that emanates from legitimate authority (hoping thereby to legitimate themselves as anti-authorities), they are often averse to any manifestation of professionalism. Such people also tend to auto-diagnose and self-medicate instead of consulting a physician, to represent themselves in lawsuits instead of hiring a lawyer, and to condemn democratic political systems instead of supporting a candidate of their choosing or running for office themselves. By discrediting everything, they discredit themselves.

The original Diaz Bill was framed in terms of licensure of title, and it served several worthwhile catalytic purposes even though it was probably destined to die perennial deaths in Committee.[7] From the public perspective, it considerably enhanced the repute of the philosophical counseling movement. From the professional perspective, it spurred philosophical practitioners to reflect more deeply on the merits and demerits of legislative recognition. From the interprofessional perspective, it helped build bridges between philosophy and other disciplines of personal counsel. From the political perspective, it placed additional pressure on the crumbling psychology monopoly. From the cultural perspective, it further illuminated the growing realization that not all personal problems are illnesses. From the philosophical perspective, it awakened awareness in many philosophers of the emergent role of philosophy itself; they could aspire to be not only academics, but also practitioners. And from the historical perspective, it was simply unprecedented. These are momentous achievements for a piece of legislation that stood little chance of being passed in its original form.

Informed by and responsive to developments, Assemblyman Diaz is sponsoring the next version of his Bill, which stands a far better chance of being passed. It would certify rather than license philosophical counselors. Thus, in New York State, anyone would be able to call himself a "Philosophical Counselor"—just as matters stand now. The use of this title would remain unrestricted by certification legislation but, as in the case of public accountants, philosophical counselors would be accorded the privilege of writing qualifying examinations for use of the title "Certified Philosophical Counselor" (CPC). If such a Bill runs the political gauntlet in New York or any other state, history would be made in spades. Floodgates of unprecedented opportunities for philosophical practitioners would be opened. I believe that this is going to happen, and happen sooner rather than later.

Once an accredited graduate program in Philosophical Practice is established, graduates should be automatically eligible for Primary Board Certification in their states and, after further practice and professional development, eligible for Full Board Certification. The APPA currently functions not only as the sole shadow university for educating practitioners, but also as the sole body for certifying them. Naturally we wish to see universities and governments shoulder and further their respective shares of this load.

10.4. REGISTRATION

Registration is a third category of legislative recognition that bears brief mention here. It is sometimes utilized by states as a kind of "catch-all" category, and also as an "escape-hatch" from over-restrictive licensing laws. One might be registered in a state for any number of reasons, not all of them probative. While a Registered Nurse (RN) has a higher rank than a Licensed Professional Nurse (LPN), a registered Research Psychoanalyst (in California) has a lower rank than a Licensed Psychologist. As we saw in Colorado, registration is a way of practicing unlicensed psychotherapy. Dieticians are often registered by states, but so are sex offenders. In some places, heroin addicts must be registered in order to obtain methadone. Nonregistered voters, even if eligible, cannot cast ballots; hence being a voter entails the property of being registered. State registration also applies to nonhuman entities, such as businesses, cars and handguns.

In my view, registration would be a somewhat idiosyncratic way of legislatively recognizing philosophical practitioners. But if it accomplishes that task in a given state, I'm probably for it. At any rate, being a "registerable" philosopher would give rise to fewer bad jokes than being a "certifiable" one.

10.5. RECOGNITION QUA POLITICS

Pending "species-specific" recognition, the practice of philosophy as a profession of personal counsel in America is indirectly prohibited in some states and tacitly sanctioned in others, but is officially unregulated in all. As even this cursory examination reveals, recognition and regulation of talk-therapy is effected by a crazy-quilt patchwork of positivistic (hence outdated) state laws, circumventable by various forms of *ad hocery*. APPA-Certified counselors necessarily become conversant with the particular legislative conditions under which they practice, and find ways opportunistically to align themselves with existing permissions or restrictions in order to render their beneficial services, both legally and ethically, to consumers.

Some cynics have charged that we seek legislative recognition purely for financial gain, to become eligible for third-party reimbursement of our services from HMOs or MCOs. This is hardly the case. We seek legislative recognition for the two usual reasons: to enhance the repute of our profession, and to distinguish between professional versus unprofessional or nonprofessional practice. Contrary to popular belief, philosophical practitioners do not require state licensure, certification or registration to be eligible for third-party reimbursement of services: that is a matter of business, not politics. If a philosophical counselor can engage in legal private practice in a given state, which is manifestly the case in at least twenty states in which APPA-Certified Practitioners currently counsel clients, then a cadre of philosophical counselors can be legally contracted by a organization, to provide the same service to designated clients. If the organization were a corporation with employees *in situ*, then philosophical counseling services could be contracted and rendered in-house, with the obvious proviso that the counselors not violate applicable title or scope of practice laws pertaining to psychology. Similarly, if a health maintenance organization wished to add philosophical counseling to its menu of services, it could legally subcontract counselors in any state, subject to the same proviso. As our profession is nascent, we are probably too thin on the ground to see our services integrated efficiently into the menus of large MCOs. But as philosophical counselors become more numerous, and as MCOs seek more ways of cutting costs (e.g., of reducing their subsidies for endless and possibly pointless psychotherapy), our paths may yet cross. Even so, I am confident that not all philosophical practitioners would accept third-party reimbursement for their services, at least such as those offered to psychologists under current guidelines. Those of us who detest the soul-destroying paperwork that bureaucracy inevitably generates, and those of us who resist having our professional affairs micromanaged by the bureaucrats that bureaucracy inevitably generates, will not fare particularly well with MCOs.[8]

In any case, I have explained how philosophical counseling services may be offered in accordance with existing counseling laws. These examples are meant to be instructive, but are hardly exhaustive. Since we all have implied contracts with our respective states, it behooves us to learn their laws, particularly with respect to professional practice. The goal from our perspective will be to practice neither under the umbrella of another profession's law, nor in the interstices between several other professions' laws; rather, under the aegis of laws written expressly for our own profession. That end will be achieved necessarily but not sufficiently by satisfying the requirements set forth in the previous chapter; necessarily but not sufficiently by seeing legislation appropriate to the ethos of a given state, sponsored and debated in that state's legislature; and necessarily and ultimately sufficiently by fruition of the political art of seeing such legislation passed. This latter is a uniquely Aristotelian task for *homo politicus* and, unlike the foregoing necessary but insufficient conditions that lead up to it, there is no blueprint or algorithm for its accomplishment. Rather, there must be a recognition of political opportunity favorable to the exercise of political art toward the attainment of political end, subject (as always) to the creative volition of the innovative artist, to the auspicious confluence of governing forces extant, and to the propitiousness of those still larger forces that we call "the times." Out of these may concomitantly crystallize political sanction of our profession in America, which can have no nobler secular aspiration.

Legislative recognition obviously entails professional regulation, which is desirable if philosophical practice is to emerge fully from its primordial equivalent of a Hobbesian state of nature, and into the commodious equivalent of a Commonwealth, wherein the providers of professional philosophical services, and their clients, will be symbiotically conjoined through governmental agency, instead of unproductively dissociated through governmental ignorance, indifference, or apathy.

In our battle for recognition, philosophical practitioners will have two kinds of opponents to defeat: one from without, the other from within. Like Caesar at the epic battle of Alesia, we must contend simultaneously against both an inner expanding ring, and an outer contracting one. While this is a scenario that most strategists would seek to avoid, sometimes it is inevitable.

In our case, the inner ring consists of a non-allied admixture of intolerant academic philosophers and marginalized amateur philosophers, who dislike professionalization mostly because they are largely incapable of it, and moreover may be resentful of our publicity and success. For the unqualified but qualifiable, professional qualifications represent a summit to be attained; whereas for the unqualified and unqualifiable, professional qualifications represent an invidious distinction. Reactionary academic philosophers do not wish to see professionalization at all; while amateurs and worse (e.g., charlatans) can succeed only if the public cannot tell them apart from the genuine article. Of course, impostors oppose state recognition; it eventually unmasks them. But some unmask themselves more swiftly by their opposition to it.

The outer ring consists of a loose coalition of intolerant talk-therapists— typically psychologists and psychiatrists—who view philosophical practice as an encroachment on their "turf," and who may also feel especially threatened by it. Again, those who are secure in the reputability of their own practices have nothing to fear from us. Insofar as certain "syndromes" and "disorders" are objectively diagnosed and repose upon identifiable affective or biological substrates, they are medical problems and not the province of philosophy at all. But insofar as other putative "syndromes" and "disorders" are subjectively reified and float upon nothing more than the desire to manufacture "mental illness" in the absence of physical disease, philosophical counselors certainly pose a threat.[9] This outer ring is far larger than the inner one, and it harbors a great many more charlatans, some of whom are licensed by states to perpetrate what amounts to legalized fraud upon consumers.

More will be said of our opponents—from within and without—in Chapter 15. Meanwhile, in case you are wondering, Caesar did prevail at the battle of Alesia. He prevailed because the battle pitted Roman virtues against barbarian vices. The Romans were well-led, well-trained, well-equipped, well-disciplined, and well-motivated. They employed sound strategy and effective tactics. By contrast, the barbarians were ill-led, ill-trained, ill-equipped, ill-disciplined, and ill-motivated. They had no strategy and poor tactics. The barbarians enjoyed superior numbers and superior initial position, but possessed inferior understanding of the art of war. Similarly, practitioners possessing inferior understanding of the art of living, though they be more populous or otherwise well-endowed, will not prevail against the recognition of philosophy as a profession of personal counsel. While anyone can philosophize by himself, not everyone can philosophize therapeutically with others. Governments will come to acknowledge this fact. It is also implied by the APPA's motto: *Nemo Veritatem Regit* [Nobody Governs Truth].

NOTES

1. I could not have written this chapter without special help, for which I thank Paul del Duca, Lawrence Fleischer, Alberto Hernandez, J. Michael Russell, and Paul Sharkey.

2. "Congress shall make no law ... abridging the freedom of speech ... " Amendment I, The Constitution of the United States of America. (The first ten amendments were ratified on December 15, 1791.) Many individual states have in law abridged certain freedoms of speech, a few instances of which are mentioned in this chapter.

3. The California laws quoted below are contained in the *Business and Professions Code*, sections 2900–2918.

4. J. Michael Russell, "The Philosopher as Personal Consultant," chap. 5, fn. 22.

5. We will discuss Registration itself in due course.

6. The relevant Colorado statute [12-43-201-(9) *et passim*] says: " 'Psychotherapy' means the treatment, diagnosis, testing, assessment, or counseling in a professional relationship to assist individuals or groups to alleviate mental disorders, understand unconscious or conscious motivation, resolve emotional, relationship, or attitudinal conflicts, or modify behaviors which interfere with effective emotional, social, or intellectual functioning. Psychotherapy follows a planned procedure of intervention which takes place on a regular basis, over a period of time, or in the cases of testing, assessment, and brief psychotherapy, it can be a single intervention. It is the intent of the general assembly that the definition of psychotherapy as used in this part 2 be interpreted in its narrowest sense to regulate only those persons who clearly fall within the definition set forth in this subsection."

7. That is, the Higher Education Committee, through which such legislation must pass before being tabled in the Assembly. In New York State, counseling professions are regulated under the Education Act.

8. This is an ever-worsening situation for psychological counselors. A caustic satire on bureaucracy is embodied in my novel, *Fair New World*. (See the Pavilion of Parasites in Melior, the novel's utopian polity.)

9. See Marinoff (1998a, 2001).

PART IV

Marketing of Philosophical Practice

CHAPTER 11

IRB Approval of Research Programs

11.1. **Commodities and Public Service**

11.2. **Research Involving Human Subjects**

    1. Evidence that You Are a Qualified Philosophical Counselor

    2. A Description of Your Scope of Practice

    3. A Script (i.e., Advertisement) that You Will Use to Recruit Potential Subjects

    4. A Contingency Plan and Referral List to Other Counseling Professions

    5. Instrument of Informed Consent and Relevant Procedural Details

11.3. **Bridging Necessity and Sufficiency**

11.4. **Post-hoc Speculations**

11.1. COMMODITIES AND PUBLIC SERVICE

I have lived in America—God bless it—for more than six years at this writing—I am a political refugee from The People's Femocratic Republic of Canada.[1] Thus far I fail to find any good or service that Americans cannot commodify. Given that a commodity needs not only to be conceived, designed, and produced, but also to be packaged, advertised, and sold, marketing is one of the most important activities in American life. You must market your good or service to succeed in America, the quintessential and state-of-the-art marketplace of the world. Philosophical practice is no different from any other service in this singularly American respect: it needs effective marketing.

Philosophical counselors who have earned Primary Certification from the APPA, and who then seek to build up their practices, often ask what they can do to attract (more) clients. For philosophers with permanent academic affiliations, one way of doing so—and of doing much good besides—is via a *pro bono publico* research protocol. One of the virtuous things that professionals can do is donate some of their time and expertise to the public. This is not strictly speaking an act of charity; rather, a recognition of the non-proprietariness of the knowledge acquired in the process of professional formation. Doctors and lawyers are usually expected to perform a measure of public service; i.e., to treat some patients or represent some clients without charge, as a professional duty. Likewise, part of a university professor's duty (after research, teaching, and administrative work) consists in public service, which can mean many things but usually amounts to one in the case of theoreticians—namely, giving free lectures.

However, philosophical counselors who are also permanent members of a philosophy faculty may seek to unite some of their research and public service duties under the head of a *pro bono publico* research protocol in philosophical counseling. This I do at The City College of New York, and you may endeavor to do it in your institution too. Thus far I see only benefits, and no detriments, of a such a measure. This chapter suggests how to go about establishing such a measure, then presents some of its benefits as I conceive them.

11.2. RESEARCH INVOLVING HUMAN SUBJECTS

Every institution that houses, sanctions, or sponsors research on human beings, whether invasive or intrusive or not, must first constitute an Institutional Review Board (IRB) that examines all research proposals, and that must approve any nonexempt research on human beings before it is undertaken. It must also approve applications for exemptions. An IRB is bound by stringent Federal guidelines, informed largely by the NIH, and intended foremost to protect the research subjects from foreseeable harms. These guidelines are not necessarily motivated by protective benevolence or paternalism on the part of the government; they are motivated by an ardent desire to discourage lawsuits against the researchers and their institutions. This is America, after all. An IRB-approved research program is so well-indemnified in principle that even the most litigious of beings would look elsewhere to press a suit. In effect, IRB approval confers institutional protection on the researcher, who cannot therefore be sued independently (unless he violates the conditions of the approval itself, in which case the IRB would drop him like a hot potato); and moreover, the IRB acts under regulatory law which confers federal protection on the institution, which cannot therefore be sued independently (unless the IRB violates the conditions of the guidelines, in which case the Feds would drop it like a hot potato). But as long as everything remains kosher, legal exposure is negligible. In my case, The City College of the City University of New York is a public institution, funded by the State of New York. So a subject of my IRB-approved research protocol who wanted to sue me would also have to sue the City University of New York, the State of New York, and ultimately the Federal Government. One can readily appreciate the deterrent effect of IRBs on frivolous litigation.

Now what does your IRB need from you, to grant its approval? Several things are necessary; we will deal with sufficiency afterward. Necessarily, it needs the following things: first, evidence that you are a qualified philosophical counselor; second, a description of your scope of practice; third, a script (i.e. advertisement) that you will use to recruit potential subjects; fourth, a contingency plan and referral list to other counseling professions; fifth, an instrument of informed consent and relevant procedural details. Let us discuss these in sequence.

1. Evidence that You Are a Qualified Philosophical Counselor

This obviously lies at the foundation of your research proposal itself. Again, there is not necessarily any humanitarian concern here; only a fear of litigation. While the IRB sees its function as filtering research proposals in light of federal guidelines, it sees its purpose as indemnifying the institution against lawsuits stemming from harms done, either directly or collaterally, to human subjects. When I applied to my IRB, I was able to furnish incontestable evidence of my qualifications, which included a number of years experience, seminal publications in the field, a certificate (now defunct) from the ASPCP, the ASPCP's (now rescinded) certification standards and code of ethics, and testimonials from a number of clients. Yet the IRB held up my proposal for four years, because of politics. (I'll explain that shortly.) But this news should cheer you. If you are a newly certified philosophical counselor, fresh from an APPA training program, and you want to gain experience by doing *pro bono* counseling on a research protocol, then your instructional status at your institution, your Primary Certificate from the APPA, backed up by our certification standards and code of ethics, along with any related experience or relevant publications, should be more than ample to satisfy this foundational requirement—politics aside. An IRB can readily distinguish these credentials from the claim that God spoke to you in a dream, and told you to start counseling people.

2. A DESCRIPTION OF YOUR SCOPE OF PRACTICE

This is necessary for the IRB minimally to understand what philosophical counseling is, and isn't. Some IRB members will have heard of philosophical counseling by now; others won't have heard of it but will understand it as soon as they read your proposal; others will have heard of it but will refuse to understand it at all, because their ignorance or prejudice persuade them that psychology (or possibly Jesus) offers the sole acceptable means of counseling people with problems. Still, the IRB needs to know what kinds of subjects are good candidates for your research, and what kinds are not. Since we are dealing here with philosophical counseling, the IRB needs to know specifically what kinds of problems are amenable to it in the first instance, and what makes them addressable preferentially by that modality as opposed to some other (e.g., psychology or psychiatry). Here is my scope of practice statement, which my IRB approved along with the whole package:

Scope of Practice

Philosophical counseling is intended for clients who are rational, functional, and not mentally ill, but who can benefit from philosophical assistance in resolving or managing problems associated with normal life experience. The most suitable candidates for philosophical counseling are clients whose problems are centered in:
1. issues of private morality or professional ethics; or
2. issues of meaning, value, or purpose; or
3. issues of personal or professional fulfillment; or
4. issues of underdetermined or inconsistent belief systems; or
5. issues requiring any philosophical interpretation of changing circumstances.

Examples of clients helped by philosophical counseling include the following. A woman wants to feel more valued in her job. A male employee is ordered to remove a painting from his office wall because it offends a female colleague. A professional woman's marriage is spiraling toward divorce. A young man, convinced that the human race will be extinct in thirty years, sees no point in making the movie of his dreams. A successful movie-maker is unhappy with her latest script, which she wants to imbue with a moral message. A Protestant parent, whose daughter is engaged to a Jewish man and whose son is engaged to a Muslim woman, wants to anticipate and avoid religious conflicts. A woman is trying to cope with her mother's terminal cancer. A man is trying to cope with a midlife career change. A Roman Catholic priest feels insulted and deprived because he is unfairly excluded from jury duty. A woman is seeking someone to help her reconcile the joyousness of a Zen awakening with the sadness of her brother's suicide. A New Age devotee of the *Celestine Prophecy*, who has just been mugged, believes that everything is part of "God's plan" but cannot understand why God planned to have him mugged.

Note that the five criteria of most suitable candidacy are philosophical either by reference to contemporary philosophical curricula and a 2500-year-old corpus of philosophical writings (criteria 1–4), or by definition (criterion 5). The IRB cannot deny that people have such problems; nor can it deny that these problems are legitimately philosophical as described. IRB members may calmly accept these criteria and then suddenly object when they start reading the specific examples of "clients helped by philosophical counseling" (culled mostly from *Plato Not Prozac*), because they will reflexively suppose that all these clients could, would, or should have been counseled by psychologists. Such IRB members are now caught in a trap. If they have acceded to the general kinds of philosophical problems enumerated in criteria 1–5, they cannot now object to instantiations of these criteria in the specific examples. What they are really objecting to is their sudden realization that psychologists have possibly been doing the work of philosophers all along, in addition to their own psychological work. This is a rude educational awakening which not all IRB members will be pleased to experience—although some will also be delighted by it. Nonetheless, the APPA is an educational corporation, and its certified practitioners are therefore certified as educators. We are also performing an educational service by making IRBs aware of the distinction between psychological and philosophical ways of approaching ordinary problems.

Those of you with legalistic minds may observe that, notwithstanding the foregoing argument, this scope of practice statement contravenes professional practice law in California (and possibly other states), which protects psychological scope of practice and moreover defines it in hyperbolically broad terms. But relax: You are not committing a crime if you practice philosophical counseling as institutionally sanctioned research, nor is your IRB an accomplice to any crime by approving it. This potential legal conflict is resolved by the expedient of educational exemption. Educators are normally exempt from a host of licensing restrictions either of title or scope of practice, because they are not intruding on professional turf; rather, contributing to it via research in educational settings.

3. A SCRIPT (I.E., ADVERTISEMENT) THAT YOU WILL USE TO RECRUIT POTENTIAL SUBJECTS

The wording of your script must be consistent with that of your scope of practice. Since it is intended for public circulation or posting, it need not be overly detailed. In particular, it should not mislead anyone. I ended up not needing a script, because I receive more than enough calls as it is. But here's the sort of thing you could use or adapt for your purposes:

> Are you experiencing a philosophical problem? Does your problem lie outside the scope of medical, legal, psychological and pastoral counseling? If so, then you may wish to speak with a philosophical counselor. The philosophical counselor will not decide what you should or shouldn't do, but will assist you in understanding your problem and its philosophical implications. The counselor is trained and certified by the American Philosophical Practitioners Association (APPA), and offers this service without charge as part of a university-sponsored research project. Consultations are strictly confidential. To arrange a free initial consultation, phone ***–***–****.

4. A CONTINGENCY PLAN AND REFERRAL LIST TO OTHER COUNSELING PROFESSIONS

This is a vital component, as your IRB will need to know what you do with subjects who present problems that lie outside your scope of practice (again, think *potential lawsuit*). In my original proposal, I offered the following contingency plan:

> Counselees who present problems deemed to lie beyond the scope of philosophical counseling, or who manifest involuntary indications of problems lying beyond its scope, will be referred by the counselor for appropriate professional assistance.

To this I appended a referral list, consisting of two psychiatrists, two (licensed) psychologists, a pastoral counselor, and a Zen roshi.

However, my IRB found this part of the original proposal insufficient, not because they didn't respect my judgment about the appropriateness of a subject's candidacy, but because they were thinking *potential lawsuit*. In the absence of legislative recognition of philosophical counseling by the state (in this case New York), the IRB might be talking a legal risk by allowing me to make a "professional" judgment from the dubious position of a legislatively nonexistent profession. So I proposed the following countermeasure: that I make notes following an initial consultation, along with a recommendation as to the suitability or nonsuitability of the subject for admission to the research protocol, and fax these notes to a psychiatrist or licensed psychologist for a "second opinion." This is the actual wording eventually approved by the IRB:

> Prospective subjects for the research protocol are self-selecting, having heard or read about philosophical counseling and having contacted the Principal Investigator requesting a consultation. An initial consultation is conducted by the Principal Investigator, who writes notes on the consultation and makes a recommendation regarding the subject's suitability or nonsuitability for admission to the protocol. These notes and recommendation are then sent to a licensed psychiatrist (Dr. H.), who makes an assessment on the case. If the Principal Investigator recommends admission to the protocol and the psychiatrist concurs, the subject is admitted. If the psychiatrist does not concur, the subject is asked to undergo a psychiatric evaluation and/or medical examination, after which a further determination of his or her status is made. If the Principal Investigator does not recommend admission to the protocol, the subject is likewise referred for a psychiatric evaluation and/or medical examination.

I believe this to be a reasonable measure, and I certainly have no "ego-problems" in collaborating with a licensed professional for research purposes. On the contrary, I believe it to be a professionally responsible measure to seek a second opinion, and of course Dr. H. is an enlightened psychiatrist who differentiates among philosophical, psychological, and medical issues. I generally respect the legislative process whose recognition I currently seek for my own profession, and regard it as beneficial for all concerned to liaise with established helping professions. The first tenet thereof remains: do no harm. Its corollary is: the best care is the most appropriate care.

For the empirically curious, Dr. H. and I are currently batting one thousand with respect to our concurrence of opinion. Here are two samples of my notes on initial consultations, with Dr. H.'s responses appended:

Notes on Initial Consultation with A.B., xx/yy/zz

Subject: ***** male, age ***, married, student of life and lately of *****.
Referral: Self-referred, read about philosophical counseling.
Background: The subject has been a *****, *****, and has evidently led an original life. He holds an undergraduate degree in *****, and is taking qualifying courses in *****, ostensibly in preparation for graduate work in *****. He is also employed part-time.

Issues: He feels alienated from society in general, and from his family (unsophisticated *****) in particular. Studies in ***** led him to study *****, which he clearly wants to enlist to help him make sense of life. He has never been accepted by a peer group and understands that this has hardly hindered—and may even have helped—his intellectual development. He feels both contemptuous of superficial socializing, yet desirous of social adequacy. He is very knowledgeable, well-read, and articulate, but apparently too opinionated for some people's tastes.

History: He once saw a psychological counselor, who "diagnosed" him as "mildly anxious." He found psychological counseling unproductive, and discontinued it. He has some allergies, for which he takes medication.

Assessment: Based on this initial consultation, I consider the subject a good candidate for philosophical counseling, and would admit him to the research protocol. We would meet approximately every two weeks until further notice. Should unforeseen problems emerge that are not best managed philosophically, I would reassess the subject's appropriateness accordingly.

Dr. H.'s response was: "I agree that this individual is an appropriate candidate for philosophical counseling and that there is no indication for other forms of therapy."

Notes on Initial Consultation with P.Q., xx/yy/zz

History: The client is a **-year-old ***** female from *****. She has lived in New York for seven years, and speaks English fluently. She is a graduate student at *****, finishing her Master's thesis in *****. She was referred to me by her father, who read an ***** article on philosophical counseling.

She has no relevant medical problems, no psychiatric history, and is neither seeing any other counselor nor taking any medication.

Presentation: Primarily, the client wishes to discuss her future and reassess her goals. She describes herself as "lost." Specifically, she is not fully motivated to complete her Master's thesis because she neither wishes to qualify for a PhD program, nor desires to become a professional educator (many of her family members are teachers). She also has artistic interests and abilities, but no unique creative calling. Secondarily, she wishes to consider her relationship with her boyfriend, which is important to her but not supremely so. She seeks to fulfill herself through some yet-undiscovered avenue, and not merely via the institution of marriage. Meanwhile she needs to develop criteria for being satisfied with her achievements and identity.

Recommendation: She is highly intelligent and articulate, and is seeking a constructive interpretation for her current lack of fixed purpose. I believe

she is an excellent candidate for philosophical counseling, and would admit
her to the research protocol. As usual, should future sessions reveal serious
psychological disturbance or other dysfunctionality, I would refer her for
appropriate care.

Dr. H.'s response was: "I agree with your assessment and recommendation at
this time."

In case you are wondering, I counseled the former candidate for about a
year, and he experienced very tangible benefits from the service. I counseled
the latter candidate for a few months, and she was not greatly helped—but was
not at all harmed.

5. INSTRUMENT OF INFORMED CONSENT AND RELEVANT PROCEDURAL DETAILS

In a way, this is the most important component of the research package, because
it is the one that the subjects must sign (again, think *potential lawsuit*). This
instrument is the first line of defense in any legal battle. If it holds, the battle
is won. There are many acceptable variations on this theme, so my offering is
hardly unique.[2] However, it has undergone considerable scrutiny and refinement and, since it meets the requirements of my IRB, it may well meet those
of yours.

> **Principal Investigator**: Lou Marinoff, Associate Professor, Department of
> Philosophy, The City College of CUNY, 137th Street at Convent Avenue,
> New York, NY 10031. Phone: 212-650-7647.
>
> **Project Title**: Philosophical Counseling—Case Studies and Their Impli-
> cations

Informed Consent Form

(1) Participation in and withdrawal from this study are voluntary. I will
not be paid to participate, nor will I pay to do so. I am free to withdraw
from this study at any time.

(2) My identity as a participant in this research will remain confidential
with regard to any publications and/or oral presentations of the results of
this study. Records in this study will be kept confidential to the extent
permitted by law.

(3) As a participant, I will be asked to do the following: to discuss my
problem with the philosophical counselor, and to answer relevant questions
to the best of my ability.

(4) If the counselor adjudges that my problem is not primarily a philosophical one, and that it should not be addressed in the first place through philosophical counseling, then the counselor will refer me for alternative professional consultation.

(5) The philosophical counselor will assist me in coming to terms with my problem. The philosophical counselor will NOT determine what I should or should not do, and will make NO choices for me. Rather, the counselor will help me to clarify the implications of my possible choices.

(6) The following benefits are expected to result from the consultation:

(i) Minimally, the participant should gain a deeper understanding of his/her problem.

(ii) Maximally, the participant should feel more empowered to cope with or to resolve his/her problem.

(7) No risks are expected to result from the consultation.

(8) I am at least eighteen years of age, and I voluntarily seek philosophical counseling from Professor Lou Marinoff.

I understand the given information about the counselor's responsibilities, and about my expectations. I have had an opportunity to ask preliminary questions about my participation. All questions that I did ask were answered to my satisfaction. I have been told that if I have any further questions regarding my rights as a research subject, I may call *******, Institutional Review Board Administrator, The City College of CUNY, ***–***–****.

    _____
    Participant's Printed Name

    _____
    Participant's Signature

    _____
    Date

This instrument is shown to the prospective participant at the beginning of the first meeting, and must be read and signed before any further conversation takes place.[3] A file copy of this instrument is stamped and signed by the IRB administrative officer, and bears the seal of approval of the CUNY IRB and medical school.

Two additional procedural points are embodied in the research proposal itself. The first was part of my original submission; the second was a required addition by the IRB (again, think *lawsuit*). They are both quite straightforward:

1. A subject admitted to the protocol receives *pro bono* philosophical counseling approximately weekly or fortnightly, until such time as the subject is either discharged from the protocol by mutual agreement (having exhausted all possible benefit therefrom), or manifests problems not fore-

seen during the initial assessment and not amenable to philosophical treatment. In the latter case, the subject is referred for psychiatric evaluation
and/or medical examination (there have been no instances to date).

2. To ensure the confidentiality of the research, all subject files pertaining
to the protocol are kept in a locked file drawer, access to which is restricted
to the Principal Investigator.

11.3. BRIDGING NECESSITY AND SUFFICIENCY

While the foregoing description of the naked necessities sounds plausible
enough, the verbally retentive among you may be wondering why my IRB
approval required four years. The chasm between this kind of necessity and
sufficiency is created by politics, and must be bridged by politics. And in this
context I am speaking of academic institutional politics, which is often a
euphemism for the expression of every kind of pettiness, envy, vanity, dogmatism, egotism, obstruction, grudgefulness, vendetta, small-mindedness, mean-
spiritedness, and irrationalism that permanent inmates of academic institutions
can muster—and that is no negligible sum. Because there is famously so little
of frangible significance to be gained or lost in the academic political arena, at
least in compassion with the "real world," academic politics are often fraught
with infantile conflicts and Pyrrhic victories.

At any rate, I approached the Chair of my institutional IRB's Human Subjects
Committee with good will and a pure heart, and when my original application
went unanswered for a year I thought nothing of it. That the IRB Chair
happened to be a psychologist spawned no prejudgment in me, one way or
another. When his response finally arrived, in the form of a letter, its contents
were revealing and dismaying. The IRB could not approve my application, he
said, because of the "risks" that philosophical counseling posed as a potential
cause of psychological trauma! This assertion being too patently absurd, even
for a psychologist, I then understood his delay and reply to be motivated by
his personal opposition to my proposal. So I replied carefully to him and the
IRB, reiterating that philosophical counseling addresses philosophical problems, not psychological ones. Moreover, I explained that philosophical counseling also helps clients whose problems have been exacerbated by inappropriate therapy, such as one might obtain when seeking psychological or psychiatric
help on a matter that is primarily philosophical in nature.

To this counter-argument I received no response whatsoever. Another year
passed, and more, and the good professor lacked even the courtesy and colle-
giality to reply to repeated memos and telephone messages. So I arranged a

meeting with his Dean (Social Sciences) and mine (Humanities), and sought their advice on how best to pursue the matter. Deans are always happy to give advice, particularly of the preventive kind. They were not slow to admit that this IRB Chair was, among other things, grossly derelict in his administrative duty, and they were grateful that I had come to them in this first instance of unofficial complaint. One of the Deans defused the seriousness by remarking, jocularly, that the good professor's area of research specialization was sleep; and we all laughed heartily at the implied jest that he was using himself, with evident success, as a research subject. In sum, the Deans suggested that I "offer" to make a presentation, in person, to the IRB. They gave me to understand that this was an offer that could not be refused, and that should be made through the IRB's campus administrative officer, not the Chair of its campus Human Subjects Committee.

They were correct. A date was slated, and I prepared a comprehensive proposal package for each member of the IRB. When I went into the appointed meeting, I was met with receptivity and professionalism by the administrative officer, with friendliness by a biology professor and by the lay-member, with benevolent neutrality by three or four others, with undisguised hostility and resentment by a biophysicist, and with passive-aggressive animosity by the good professor in the Chair. I made my presentation and answered a few questions. The biophysicist glared daggers at me throughout. I have no idea why. The Chair himself finally made a remarkable disclosure, namely, that as a professional psychologist he regarded philosophical counseling as an intrusion on his territory. Had there been one professional ethicist on this committee, he or she would have immediately observed that the Chair had just disclosed a conflict of interest that impaired the impartiality of his judgment, and that justifiably disqualified him from evaluating my case. But it had not disqualified him from stonewalling me for three and a half years, and several committee members began to look embarrassed and troubled. The only professional ethicist in the room, I held my peace. He had just done enough damage to himself; no need to salt his self-inflicted wound.

Since I had satisfactorily answered all other questions and objections, the Chair then sensed the majority was for me and against him, and so he played his trump card. I sincerely hoped he had lost some sleep, or at least some sleep research, in conjuring it up. He smarmily suggested that my proposal be accepted on the condition that I conduct my philosophical counseling sessions with research subjects in the presence of a licensed psychologist or psychiatrist. Before I even had a chance to reply to this suggestion, a couple of the Board members snorted in derision of it. I politely replied that the suggestion was completely inappropriate, but counter-proposed the measure that proved acceptable to the majority; namely, that I fax my notes of an initial consultation to a licensed psychologist or psychiatrist, and observe the protocol that has been described above. No sooner did I suggest this than the professor of biology declared that he saw no further reason why my proposal should not be accepted. That concluded my participation. I thanked them, excused myself, and the ensuing majority voted indeed favored the proposal. Nor did I take further action against the good professor at that time, because the round was won.

However, he has recently reemerged from his corner, and has instigated another round. This time I shall seek to finish the fight, for he is no worthy opponent. See Chapter 17 for details.

11.4. POST-HOC SPECULATIONS

I believe there are numerous clear advantages to seeking and winning IRB approval of philosophical counseling as *pro bono publico* research. To begin with, it benefits clients who could not otherwise afford the service. Second, it recognizes the counselor's donated time as a legitimate professorial research activity. Third, it legitimates philosophical counseling itself as a *bona fide* research activity in the institution, thereby enhancing the stature of the profession. Fourth, it allows philosophical counselors to encounter and overcome, within the cloisters of their respective institutions, the kinds of personal antagonisms and political animosities they are likely to meet in the wider world as well. Fifth, and by the same token, it allows them to forge alliances crucial to the recognition and development of the profession. Sixth, it provides them with the indemnification they need to practice virtuously in a litigious ethos. Seventh, it affords them wonderful opportunities to expand their professional horizons. Of this last, I must say that some of my most interesting clients have been *pro bono* subjects of the research protocol; I still counsel approximately a third of my clients on this basis.

On a scale of one to ten, I would rate my difficulty of winning IRB approval at about five. Bureaucratic or unethical or unprofessional obstruction are paper tigers, which can be tamed with more paper of the right kind. Those of you who, by dint of permanent faculty status, are eligible to run this gauntlet, are hereby encouraged to run it at your institution. In my experience, the rewards vastly outweigh the inconveniences.

Note also that IRB approval must be renewed annually. Since IRBs are ruled by federal guidelines, and since that bureaucracy is growing, your IRB's annual appetite for fresh paper may be stimulated accordingly. For my first renewal, I had to submit a Certificate of Completion of a computer-based NIH course on IRBs and the ethics of human research, and had also to modify a couple of clauses in my Informed Consent Form. The NIH computer course took forty minutes to complete, and was a complete waste of time. I have not seen anything so puerile on a cathode ray tube since I last watched Sesame Street with my (then) three-year-old son—from which he, at least, learned something useful. The NIH on-line "course" is a farce; its "Certificate," a parody. As for the required modifications to my Informed Consent Form, they resemble a relative improvement. There is no end to such tinkering; thankfully, this kind is confined to brief annual episodes.

NOTES

1. See Marinoff (2000a).

2. Paul Sharkey has developed a very fine instrument for his practice, which we provide along with mine in APPA trainings.

3. I use a similar form for my private practice, which of course is not subject to IRB approval or conditions.

CHAPTER 12

Hanging Out a Counseling Shingle: FAQ

Key #1: Publicity
Key #2: Promotion
Key #3: Packaging

*A*lthough I have given dozens of media interviews during the past few years—for newspapers, magazines, radio, television and the worldwide web—almost all the questions have been asked from the standpoint of the consumers, or potential consumers, of this service. Potential providers, i.e., aspiring philosophical counselors, have had very little opportunity to ask their complementary questions, and I have had correspondingly little time to address them, outside of APPA Certification Training Programs. As well, curious colleagues in other counseling-dispensing professions also raise pertinent questions, which have not yet received the answers they deserve. This chapter attempts to remedy that neglect.

Suppose you've done philosophical counseling for a while on a research basis, or have given informal philosophical counseling in some other setting. You believe that you have helped your clients, and they tend to confirm your belief. Now you'd like to establish a private practice, and hang out a shingle in your town: "J. Doe, Philosophical Counselor." Many people, from America and abroad, regularly contact me, or my APPA colleagues, and ask how they should proceed. They usually have a number of specific questions. This chapter will answer some of those most frequently asked.

Q: **Is philosophical counseling regulated by law?**

A: To those who have read Chapter 10 herein, it should by now be clear that, at this writing anyway, philosophical counseling is completely unregulated in America and elsewhere. So anyone can hang out a shingle. Essentially, this is exactly what American, British, Canadian, Dutch, Finnish, French, German, Israeli, Italian, Norwegian, Slovakian, Spanish, Swedish, Turkish, and other pioneers have done. We simply started making ourselves available to prospective clients. With a modicum of guidance, others who are qualified can do so too. Note again, however, that the term "counseling" itself may be protected in a given state; thus you may need to employ a synonym to avoid being charged with violating a title restriction. And again, note that scope of practice laws can be unreasonably broadly phrased; thus you may need to apply for some kind of exemption—educational, unlicensed, or other—in order to practice philosophical counseling without breaking your state laws. Of course, sometimes the quickest way to compel legislative change is through civil or criminal disobedience in conjunction with citations of First (or other appropriate) Amendment rights; unconstitutional laws will sooner or later be struck down in America. But you must be willing to pay the price for disobedience.

Q: **What qualifications do I need to become a philosophical counselor?**

A: From the answer to the foregoing question, it follows that there are no legal requirements. One can often find a wise person, who gives excellent advice on all kinds of practical matters, among family elders, or among elders of almost any community or tribe. Friends can also be very helpful. While anyone blessed with a combination of common sense, experience, insight, and compassion can provide useful counsels, such a person is not necessarily a philosophical counselor. Nor is anyone who simply earns a PhD in Philosophy necessarily a philosophical counselor; academic degrees alone are not enough. So what qualifies you to counsel others philosophically? I believe that a philosophical counselor should have an understanding of the main philosophical traditions and schools, as well as partially articulated views of his own, which together conduce to the establishment and development of a philosophical perspective on ordinary human problems—as contrasted with, and complementary to, medical and psychological ones. Moreover, the philosophical counselor should, just like other professionals who engage in personal counsel, maintain an awareness of phenomena that obtrude on such relations (e.g., transference) and observe a professional code of ethics designed to preempt their nugatory effects, both on individual clients and on the profession itself. Thus your average professor of philosophy (at this writing) is not a philosophical counselor because, although he possesses more than enough philosophical expertise, and can apply philosophical conceptions in abstract or hypothetical contexts, he has little or no conception of how to apply them to actual human problems.[1] He knows philosophical theory, not philosophical practice. Nor is your average psychological counselor a philosophical counselor because, although she has been trained precisely to address real human beings with actual problems, and is well-aware of the professional exigencies that this entails, she has little or no philosophical understanding, and thus cannot engage her clients from a philosophical perspective. If you have a background in theoretical philosophy (MA minimum) and wish to build a practice, then the APPA Certification Training Programs can help you do so. If you believe that such qualifications are desirable or necessary, then revisit the APPA criteria.

In the short-to-medium run, we expect that the current juxtaposition of graduate degrees in philosophy plus APPA certification training will be replaced by university graduate programs in philosophical practice per se, replete with both theoretical and practical components, from which graduates will emerge practice-ready—subject to further professional development via internships, etc.—just as they do in other professions of personal counsel, such as medicine, law and psychology. Once that day dawns, the answer to this question—"What qualifications do I need to become a philosophical counselor?" will be considerably simplified: "Earn a degree in philosophical counseling."

Q: **For the purposes of Adjunct Membership in the APPA, and eligibility to enroll in Certification Training Programs, what is "equivalent" to an MA in Philosophy?**

A: The very best equivalency is identity. As Leibniz pointed out, identicals are indiscernible. It is much easier to say what is *inequivalent* to an MA in philosophy. The APPA receives requests almost every week, from people with graduate degrees in psychology, theology, education, comparative literature, social work, and other subjects, who imagine that any of these alone is equivalent to a graduate degree in philosophy. One needs to be polite, respectful but firm in disparaging such wishful thinking. While it is true that the APPA has certified some counselors with degrees in other disciplines, these form the exceptions rather than the rule: all these practitioners had demonstrably sufficient philosophical expertise to warrant the recognition. I reiterate the APPA's standards, with respect to what should be known philosophically *prior to training as a counselor*:

> The minimum academic requirement for certification as an Associate is an earned Master's Degree or ABD in Philosophy (or Licensura in Hispanic countries). Candidates must demonstrate evidence of appropriate competency in ethics (values analysis/clarification), logic (formal and informal reasoning), epistemology (belief justification), metaphysics (worldviews), and at least the major figures and themes of the history of western (and preferably also eastern) philosophy. While no particular philosophical orientation is expected or required, candidates should also be familiar with

the basic principles and themes of both the analytic and existential/pheno-
menological traditions of recent philosophy.

Such knowledge can be demonstrated via transcripts of graduate coursework,
and additionally via relevant publications or writings. Those who have not
earned graduate degrees in philosophy must write the Graduate Record Examination (GRE) and, if they attain scores of 525 or better in all three areas, may
then sit the APPA's Comprehensive Philosophy Examination. A satisfactory
performance in the latter would grant Adjunct status and eligibility for APPA
Certification Training.

If the prospect of the GRE appears terrifying, then it may settle the non-
equivalency question then and there: the GRE is used as a generic admission
criterion *to* graduate school, not as an "exit visa" from it. Good performance
on the GRE also demands superior verbal, quantitative and analytical skills,
which graduate students in philosophy possess to a greater extent than any
others in the humanities, and than most others in the sciences.[2] As I explained
in Chapter 2, this is because such skills are cognate with native intelligence
(i.e., "G"), and doing analytic philosophy at a graduate level requires plenty
of that.

Most people with integrity but without graduate degrees in philosophy, who
respect both themselves and professionalism, do not seek to finagle certificates
from the APPA. Instead, they follow Leibniz's rule and simply earn MAs in
philosophy, which can be done (even part-time) in about two or three years.
Since they aspire to be philosophical practitioners for life, they deem the
investment of a few years worthwhile. In fact, significant numbers of aspiring
philosophical counselors, currently involved in other careers, are returning to
graduate schools to earn MAs in philosophy, so as to be eligible for APPA
Certification training. Thus philosophical practice is sparking a resurgent interest in academic philosophy, as well it should. The academy, and particularly
theoretical philosophy, will someday thank us for this, instead of feigning
horror, disapproval, or, incomprehension.

Meanwhile, we remain cognizant that Socrates, Plato, Confucius, Lao Tzu,
and innumerable other philosophers, from antiquity to the present, lacked
formal degrees in the subject but were nonetheless outstanding practitioners.
If you are as good a philosopher as any of those venerable fellows, but lack
formal credentials, you should be able to attain our minimal benchmark on
the GREs, and pass the APPA Comprehensive Examination. That in turn would
entitle you to take our Certification Training.

If, on the other hand, you believe that qualifications are undesirable or
unnecessary, then try to consider the client's point of view. Most clients who
seek philosophical counseling have experienced services provided by doctors,

lawyers, psychologists, psychiatrists, pastors, and other counseling-dispensing professionals. Clients generally expect their counselors to be qualified, but many learn painfully that office walls chock-a-block with certificates, licenses, and other glorified graffiti do not guarantee the ability or integrity of the practitioner. My clients are not helped by the pieces of paper on my wall; my clients are helped, if at all, by the way in which I interact with them. An idiot savant might make a great philosophical counselor; a great philosophical counselor having a bad day might make a poor one. But most clients' expectations of a philosophical counselor seem quite reasonable: they expect the counselor to know something about philosophy, and the philosopher to know something about counseling. How such expertise are acquired is of secondary importance; that they are acquired is primary.

Q: **How do you know when a subject is not suitable for philosophical counseling, and what qualifies you to make referrals to psychiatrists or psychologists?**

A: Aspiring philosophical counselors tend to ask the first part of this question; psychiatrists, psychologists, and others the second part.

I believe that a subject is not suitable for philosophical counseling either when his or her primary problem or process lies outside the scope of my practice (as defined in Chapter 11), or not suitable in the first instance when his or her secondary problem or process lies within that scope, but the primary problem lies outside it. People whose primary problems involve moral dilemmas, ethical quandaries, questions of meaning, purpose or value, issues of duty or responsibility, conflicts of interest or belief, or general interpretation of changing circumstances, are all good candidates for philosophical counseling.

The demeanor of a subject also provides strong clues to his or her suitability, particularly when the counselor's determination of a primary problem or process is impeded or overshadowed by other behaviors. If the subject says he has a philosophical problem, but cannot describe it coherently, then perhaps his primary problem is not philosophical. If a client is not lucid or rational, or is excessively emotional, or cannot tell a coherent story, or cannot answer simple questions about himself, or cannot partake in a reasonable conversation, or appears to be grossly dysfunctional with respect to ordinary patterns of living, then that subject's primary problem probably lies outside the scope of responsible philosophical practice. In that case, a referral is most appropriate.

Note that I am not speaking the languages of medicine, or psychopathology, or the DSM, because I am not trained to speak them. I am not diagnosing subjects, because I am not a trained diagnostician. I am competent to interact with clients within the scope of practice of philosophy, and can usually determine, within one or two preliminary sessions, whether a subject's primary problem lies within that scope. If it does not, then I provide a referral to a different professional, who will make a similar determination within his or her respective scope of practice. I do not need to be a psychiatrist or a psychologist—or, for that matter, a lawyer or a priest—to refer a subject to one; I need to know only that the subject's problem does not appear to be primarily a philosophical one. I can certainly make an educated guess as to where it might lie, so as to provide the most appropriate referral, but I cannot know *a priori* whether my referral will suffice.

What qualifies me to make referrals is the same thing that qualifies me to counsel philosophically: expertise and experience within my scope of professional practice, and a recognition that not every person who walks into my office has a problem lying within that scope.

Rather than sustaining a purely defensive posture on this question, it is difficult not to succumb to the temptation of counterattack. It appears that some psychiatrists and psychologists haven't the remotest idea that people also suffer from burning philosophical questions; they seem to think that every human problem is a medical or pseudo-medical one. A psychiatrist who expressed outrage that I make referrals to psychiatrists without formal training in psychiatry could not herself, when questioned by me, give a single credible example of a moral dilemma. She thought a "moral dilemma" referred to a psychotic asking for surgery to remove an army of spiders crawling around in his abdomen. Here is an MD who has no conception even of rudimentary medical ethics! She also thought that "unhappiness" meant the same thing as depression, and would therefore treat it as a "mental illness." Some psychologists are just as culpable; they have no notion of noetic agency (e.g., volition), only of affect. Their superficial conceptions of "morality" are completely attenuated by Kohlberg or Gilligan, while their vague perceptions of the shadows of axiology connote "values" as feelings. One would say, after Browning, that "their reach has exceeded their grasp." Such licensed professionals, who through ignorance or hubris come to believe that their licenses extend over the entire domain of human problems, require extensive reeducation just to recognize their own scopes of practice, and therefore to be fully professional in the sense of knowing when a subject's problems lie outside it. Responsible referral is a two-way street.

Of course there are also psychiatrists who recognize that many subjects they encounter are philosophically troubled, not mentally ill, and are relieved to learn that philosophical counselors exist who can address such problems. Similarly, there are also clinical psychologists who are making appropriate referrals to philosophers.

Helping professionals all need daily to recite their fundamental precept: "First do no harm." Helpful treatment means appropriate treatment; appropriate treatment entails recognizing one's scope of professional practice, and making referrals when presenting problems lie outside it. Thus philosophical counselors could benefit from courses in psychopathology, not for the purpose of learning to diagnose pathological personality disorders, but for the purpose of acquaintanceship with matters lying outside their own scope of practice, with a view toward appropriate referral. Similarly, and with complementary purposes, psychiatrists and psychologists could benefit from courses in ethics and axiology.

Professions should cooperate in providing appropriate care, instead of squabbling over turf. When professions imperialistically colonize other professions' territories, or when professionalism degenerates into territorial warfare, consumers are the first casualties. At such times the underlying issues are often ideological, political, or personal, and perhaps more amenable to philosophical analyses than to any other.

Q: **Is a psychological counseling degree a good preparation for philosophical counseling? Are philosophical counselors generally cross-trained in other modalities?**

A: These related questions are very frequently asked. I'll answer the first part rhetorically. Is an undergraduate degree in psychology a good preparation for graduate work in philosophy? No, it's a poor one. Similarly, a degree in psychological counseling is a poor preparation for an aspiring philosophical counselor. To earn a degree in psychological counseling, you have to learn to "think"—and in some cases I use this word charitably—like a psychologist. To counsel clients philosophically, you have to learn to think like a philosopher; in other words, learn to think about thought itself. The best way to learn to think like a philosopher is to study philosophy, and to exercise your mind philosophically. Even so, some philosophical counselors are cross-trained, in modalities ranging from rational emotive therapy to hypnotherapy, from psychoanalysis to a variety of Buddhist practices. There is nothing wrong, and plenty right, with philosophical counselors acquiring cross-training, provided that they integrate such modalities into a philosophical perspective if they wish to continue calling themselves "philosophical" counselors.

Q: **Isn't the personality of the counselor the most important factor in counseling?**

A: Empirically, it appears well-established that a charismatic counselor is more effective than a lackluster one. The same is generally true of teachers of any subject, coaches of any sport, mentors in any capacity, as well as public speakers, trial lawyers, actors, politicians, other performers, and any persons generally from whom we learn or draw inspiration. A student often develops an affinity for a subject precisely because of a teacher's enthusiasm for it, which can indeed be "contagious." Undergraduate students often declare that a subject is "really interesting," when in fact it is the professor who sustains their interest. More perspicuous undergraduates sometimes remark that the professor "makes" it interesting, which is closer to the truth, and which also implies that some other professor could "make" it equally boring. In a corporate setting, an unmotivated or non-motivating motivational speaker is a contradiction in terms. Thus what makes a counselor (as well as a teacher or a coach) "good" is not solely nor necessarily in the first instance his or her expertise; rather, his or her enthusiastic, charismatic, empathetic, intuitive, insightful, creative, understanding, compassionate, authoritative, confident, or motivational personality.

For philosophical as well as psychological counselors, it follows that a good counseling personality with a poor counseling methodology can be more effective than a poor counseling personality with a good counseling methodology. This illustrates that counseling is unquestionably more of an art than a science. This assertion does not refute one of the main themes of this book, namely, that philosophical practitioners both possess special expertise and exercise professional virtues, but it does support the notion that personality counts toward practical efficacy too.

Perhaps even more pertinent to philosophical counseling, in many cases, is the fit between personalities. By contrast, in professions where the diagnosis of a dysfunction is presupposed, and a particular methodology or treatment pre-prescribed, personalities may become irrelevant. When your car malfunctions because of a faulty part, you expect an appropriately licensed mechanic to be able to diagnose the problem and replace the part—irrespective of his interpersonal skills. When your body malfunctions because of an illness, you expect an appropriately licensed physician to be able diagnose the problem and treat the illness—also irrespective of his interpersonal skills. While a patient might desire that his surgeon have both a good bedside manner and excellent surgical skills, the former is inessential, the latter, essential to the practice of surgery. In manufacturing technologies and physical sciences, where observables are corporeal and methodologies robust, personalities play a diminished or negligible role in professional practice. In psychoanalysis, the paradigmatic pseudo-science and primogenitive art of counseling, personality and personality fit are also of diminished importance, because the "patient" is presupposed to suffer from psycho-sexual complexes, and the methodology is designed to "diagnose" these after ten or fifteen years of therapy. There is no pretense to interpersonal dialogue; the therapist lies the patient on a couch and pries into his past, much as the mechanic puts the car on a hoist and pries into its undercarriage. But since philosophical counseling proceeds by face-to-face dialogue, with no presupposition of illness, diagnosis or treatment, and without preconceived methodology, the interaction resembles a dance of two minds. For this noetic dance to be enjoyable and fulfilling, the personalities of the dancers must mesh, not clash. Hence a client's beneficial experience of philosophical counseling depends not only on the counselor's interpersonal skills, but also on the way in which their personalities dovetail.

Q: **Philosophical counseling is sometimes called "therapy for the sane," especially by the media. How does philosophical counseling differ from psychotherapy, and can philosophy be therapeutic in any accepted or acceptable sense?**

A: As far as I know, the phrase "therapy for the sane" was coined by a Canadian practitioner named Peter March, and was first aired during an NPR broadcast in 1997. It has resonated with some laypersons, and has also caused needless furor in certain philosophical circles. The phrase belongs in quotations not only because it is mentioned and not used, but because it is figurative rather than literal. When psychiatrists used to distinguish between the figurative and the literal, a generation and more ago, they produced jokes such as this: patients who arrive early for appointments are diagnosed as "anxious"; late, "hostile"; on time, "compulsive." Owing mostly to dumbed-down culture and its concomitant reduction of language from a sharp instrument to a blunt one, the distinction between figurative and literal speech has been all but obliterated. The significance of the quotations in the foregoing joke has been all but lost.

One way to address this question is via etymology. As I pointed out earlier herein, as well as in *Plato Not Prozac*, "therapy" derives from the Greek "theraps," meaning an attendant of any kind, with no particular medical connotations. "Psyche" translates variously, from "soul" or "mind" to "character" or "breath." Thus "psychotherapy" can mean "attending to the breath," which makes one's yoga instructor or flute teacher a psychotherapist. If it means "attending to the mind," then philosophical counselors practice psychotherapy more than do most (non-cognitive) psychologists. And if "attending to one's character" refers to inculcating virtues as contrasted with wallowing in feelings, then most philosophical counselors are without doubt psychotherapists, while by the same token most psychologists are not. Etymological considerations amply demonstrate that "psychotherapy" was a far more generic term in its origins than it is today, largely because of its fairly recent appropriation by the medical establishment. Note that legislators in many states inadvertently recognize the term's genericity, by leaving the term "psychotherapy" unprotected by both title and scope of practice. Anyone, including a philosophical counselor, can call himself a "psychotherapist" in New York State. But as we have cautioned in Chapter 10, check your own state's laws before you print up business cards or hang out a shingle.

Another way to address this question is via intentional meanings of the word "therapy." In a contemporary dictionary of the English (not the American) language,[3] I find two meanings: first "treatment and cure of disease"; and second "maintenance of health." It should be obvious that the first entails the practice of medicine, whether allopathic or homeopathic, while the second entails preventive medicine as well as a host of nonmedical practices nonetheless conducive to health. The etymology of "health" itself is "hale" or "whole"—and indeed, disease is always malfunction of a part, whereas health is normal function of a whole. It appears wholly noncontroversial to me that medical practice is uniquely therapeutic in the first sense, whereas a broad range of practices—including philosophical—can be construed as therapeutic in the second. Since some philosophers enjoy committing fallacies more than they enjoy arguing rationally, these two meanings have given rise to the following equivocation:

> Smith: "Philosophy can be therapeutic, as in therapy for the sane."
> Jones: "Don't be absurd. Therapy is medical practice, and sane people aren't mentally ill. Therefore sane people don't need therapy."

Jones is committing an equivocation. Sane people, like all healthy people, require therapy of the second kind (i.e., health-sustaining measures) if they are to avoid requiring therapy of the first kind (i.e., thaumaturgic measures).

There is a third sense of the word "therapeutic," which appears to me as decisive as either the etymological root or the intentional definition. In the last analysis, and for better or worse, meanings are determined by usage, not by etymologies or dictionaries. The American public understands "therapy" most colloquially as "something good for you," which conveniently amalgamates the two intentional meanings. Hence chemotherapy and aromatherapy are clearly therapeutic; but then, as we have seen, so is a well-known brand of anti-chapping formulation made from petroleum jelly, recently advertised as "lip therapy." Similarly, an in-flight magazine offering the usual array of overpriced luxury items is called, cleverly, "Retail Therapy." Since art therapy and music therapy are on the verge of becoming recognized professions, there is scarcely anything wrong with conceiving of philosophical counseling as "thought therapy"—that is, therapy for the sane. Thus Peter March's esoteric Canadian jest defines a literal commodity in America.

Many philosophical practitioners, however, sensibly wish to eschew terms that lead to possible equivocations or other conflations with medical practice. Thus they avoid the term "psychotherapy" (sometimes like the plague) not because they are incognizant of the foregoing ratiocinations, but overly cognizant of them. Since they know that a certain percentage of people can be relied on to equivocate or otherwise confuse the issues, they prefer to minimize or possibly preempt the damages, by a judicious selection of terminology. But this laudable preference finds no sure expression in practice itself, because any term that one adopts (rather than coins) will be inevitably sullied by prior usage. The very term "practitioner" bears unwanted medical connotations for some philosophers, while others dislike "counselor" because of its abundant usage by psychologists (as well as lawyers). Those who fantasize solving this problem by calling themselves "philosophical consultants" merely transpose it into the current context of corporate and management consulting—not a solution at all, but only another opportunity for equivocation and conflation.

At every international conference on philosophical practice thus far, some newcomer has managed not only to raise this problem but moreover to imagine that no one has ever conceived it before:

> "Hey everybody, I propose that we really need a new term to distinguish us from all the other [choose one: practitioners, counselors, consultants]. So I'm calling myself a philosophical [choose one, not used above: practitioner, counselor, consultant]."

This usually precipitates a heated discussion, during which the relative merits and demerits of each term are passionately debated, and during which an individual's appetite for or aversion to a given term's connotations may trigger intense emotional responses. While all this sound and fury does not signify nothing, it usually accomplishes nothing. Practitioners, counselors, and consultants return to their respective practices utilizing precisely the same terminology as they did before, often more confirmed in the correctness of their particular choice.

Paul Sharkey has provided the best answer I have yet heard to this interminable terminological debate.[4] In fact, he reminds us, we are simply "philosophers." Throughout most of recorded history, a "philosopher" was someone deemed inherently capable of doing any of the following things, among others: interacting informally with the public (e.g., from Socrates to Sautet); founding educational institutions (e.g., from Plato to Dewey); tutoring monarchs (e.g., from Aristotle to Descartes); establishing new disciplines (e.g., from Hobbes to James); performing civil service (e.g., from Lao Tzu to Hume); engaging in civil disobedience (e.g., from Thoreau to Gandhi); winning Nobel Prizes in literature (e.g., from Russell to Sartre); holding public office (e.g., from Mill to Radhakrishnan); utilizing philosophy as a psychotherapeutic modality (e.g., from Epictetus to Jaspers). It is only in the twentieth century that the term "philosopher" came pervasively to mean someone inherently incapable of anything practical. So, somewhat ironically, if philosophical practice accomplishes its mission, and restores philosophy to its former and fuller range of applications, we could then stop employing the word "philosophical" as a modifier for several contending but unconsensual titles, and revert to calling ourselves "philosophers"—which would once again imply something useful. I look forward to a time when Paul Sharkey's prescient answer will appear obvious, via pervasive future hindsight.

To me, it is far less momentous what philosophical practitioners call themselves than what philosophical practitioners do. The success of the movement hinges not on nomenclature, but rather on the nature of the services it renders. Verbal connotations did not issue full-blown from the Big Bang or Eden; they developed in the wake of usage and circumstance. Philosophical practice will evolve existing connotations of any terms it adopts by virtue of the services rendered and the circumstances in which they are rendered, and not as a result of fruitless internal debates that can neither erase nor evade received connotations themselves.

People are evidently willing to acknowledge the phenomenon of being "driven crazy." Moreover, psychology and psychiatry can both provide therapies (qua treatment of disease) relevant to this phenomenon, whether for travellers *en route* to that destination, or returning from it, or sojourning there indefinitely. However, the same people ought to be willing to entertain the opposite phenomenon as well, namely that of being "driven sane." Philosophy can indeed provide therapies (qua maintenance of health) relevant to this phenomenon, and in this wise it is unquestionably both therapeutic, and therapy for the sane.

Q: **Should I carry insurance? If so, what kind?**

A: This is a prudent question, which needs to be taken seriously. There are basically two kinds of liability issues at stake for philosophical counselors: professional, and public. America is a notoriously litigious society, and all practicing professionals carry one form or another of professional liability coverage, or "malpractice insurance" as it is generally called. Medical practitioners of all kinds, including of course psychiatrists, as well as counseling psychologists, and lawyers, protect themselves with such insurance. This precaution is taken not only to prevent financial ruin in the case of accidental wrongdoing—after all, everyone makes mistakes, including professionals—but also to ward off disaster in case of frivolous or mendacious lawsuits that succeed in eliciting unjust verdicts and overblown compensatory awards.

Malpractice insurance represents to a counseling or consulting professional what a sidearm represents to a law enforcement professional: it provides a means of defense, a deterrent against attack, and, occasionally, an invitation to attack. During the course of their careers, most cops are never fired on; many never need to draw their guns at all; some need to draw them occasionally; fewer still ever need to fire them. Since far more professionals are sued than cops are fired on, insurance is a necessity.

At the same time, at least at this writing, I know of few philosophical counselors anywhere who carry malpractice insurance, nor do I know of a single lawsuit ever having been brought against a philosophical counselor. This may well be a matter of time; nonetheless, there are mitigating arguments to be considered.

First, note a compelling technicality. Since philosophical counseling is nowhere legally recognized as a profession, it is logically (and one hopes legally) impossible for a philosophical counselor to be guilty of malpracticing a nonexistent profession. To sue a philosophical counselor for "malpracticing a profession" that is nowhere recognized or regulated by professional practice laws is a contradiction in terms.

However, there is a potentially more serious charge that can be levied against philosophical counselors and, however absurd or unjust it may be, it must be addressed sooner or later. It is the charge that offering philosophical counseling is tantamount to practicing some other profession without a license. For example, this charge was levied publicly by a past president of the American Psychiatric Association, on a front-page story in the *L.A. Times*.[5] The psychiatrist accused me of "practicing medicine without a license" because I gave philosophical counseling—in this case ethics counseling—to clients in need.

Protected by medical and psychiatric licensure, a psychiatrist's scope of professional practice is *de facto* defined by the DSM. Thus, a psychiatrist who "diagnoses" a moral dilemma as a mental illness, and treats it as a psychiatric disorder, is lawfully entitled to do so. Moreover and ironically, any MD, psychiatrist, or licensed psychologist who chooses to dispense ethics counseling per se is also lawfully entitled to do so, because their licenses allow them this much scope in their respective professional practices—even though they may have no formal training in or systemic conception of ethics itself! In other words, the current lack of legislative recognition of philosophical counseling, and the concomitant lack of recognition of its scope of practice, allows other recognized professions to misappropriate intrinsically philosophical practices, and then to turn around and accuse philosophical counselors of practicing medicine, or psychiatry, or psychology—when of fact we are practicing philosophy itself. My standard reply to the psychiatrist is twofold. First, if he believes that people with moral dilemmas are therefore mentally ill, he himself needs philosophical counseling. Second, if he treats people with moral dilemmas by psychiatric means, then he is practicing non-medicine with a license.

The unitary remedy, both for this grotesque legalism, and for the hubris of such physicians, is clear: legislative recognition of philosophical counseling, and with it the implicit or explicit recognition that ethical quandaries are philosophical problems, not psychiatric disorders. Such recognition would preempt ridiculous yet currently lawfully legitimate accusations that philosophical counselors are "practicing medicine without a license," and are therefore guilty of malpracticing another profession; and would also ground in law the currently lawfully illegitimate but nonetheless factual countercharge that mental health professionals who "diagnose" moral dilemmas as mental illnesses are practicing philosophy without a license, and are therefore guilty of malpracticing our profession.

Meanwhile, it remains an open question whether philosophical counselors ought to indemnify themselves against the first kind of charge, malpractice of a nonexistent profession, by acquiring malpractice insurance of the sort that talk-therapists use, or whether they should content themselves with the hypothetical defense that malpractice of a nonexistent profession is impossible. The majority of philosophical counselors whom I know have implicitly or explicitly chosen the latter course, at least for now. At the same time, a viable and affordable option presents itself to philosophical counselors who wish to be indemnified. They can join the American Counseling Association, in the category of "Professional Member" (if they hold an MA or PhD). ACA membership in turn makes them eligible for professional educational counseling liability insurance from the ACA's affiliated insurer. In particular, since the APPA is an educational corporation and defines philosophical practice an educational activity, there is a natural fit between the ACA's criteria of professional membership and educational liability insurance on the one hand, and the APPA's criteria for Certified Counselors on the other. At this writing, all APPA-Certified counselors on the roster of the City College Philosophical Counseling Project are being required to become insured accordingly.[6] One can acquire a million dollars in coverage for a few hundred dollars annually.

It remains another open question whether philosophical counseling is better served by mere psychiatric sabre-rattling, or by a full charge with psychiatric sabres drawn. Personally, I would gladly take my chances before an impartial judge or jury, defending the position that moral dilemmas (and existential crises, and quests for fulfillment) are not mental illnesses, and articulating its corollary: not only that philosophical counselors are not malpracticing medicine, but also that some psychiatrists are in fact malpracticing philosophy. Such a trial might do more to advance the cause of philosophical practice than all the conscientious practitioners, satisfied clients, sincere supporters, and media advocates have done to date. Notwithstanding its nugatory outcome for the defendant, the net effect of the trial of Socrates was to legitimize and ensconce philosophical inquiry in western civilization. The time may have come for a sequel to that trial, whose comparable net effect, again independent of the verdict, would be to legitimize and ensconce philosophical practice in global civilization. This may explain why no crusading psychiatrist or psychologist has yet filed charges against a philosophical counselor, and why no ambitious or overzealous district attorney has yet prosecuted one. God knows America abounds with Meletuses, and courtrooms.

A final word here on professional liability: any philosophical counselor who is legitimately APPA-Certified and who abides strictly by our Standards of Professional Ethical Practice cannot therefore commit professional philosophical malpractice as we understand it, and therefore has little to fear from a fair hearing if indeed ever accused thereof. Naturally, this presupposes that a hearing would be fair, and also acknowledges that the costs of a hearing—fair or otherwise—may be unfairly prohibitive, and may have to be born by the practitioner himself.

The problem of public liability is much clearer, and its resolution much more obvious. If you, as a professional counselor, interview clients in your office or in your home, you are liable or potentially liable for certain kinds of harms, albeit unintended, that may befall them. The same applies to any visitor or guest—even if uninvited. Thus public liability insurance of a generic kind, akin to that which states compel you to carry if operating a motor vehicle, is a prudent acquisition for philosophical counselors. If you are seeing clients on a *pro bono* research protocol in your college or university, then your public liability is subsumed under the institution's blanket coverage—you need no personal coverage here, just as you need no personal coverage to see students during your office hours. If you are counseling out of your own home, you may already have sufficient public liability insurance as part of your mandatory homeowner's coverage, or you can acquire more at a modest cost. But if you counsel clients from a rented home or office, then there will be legal lines of demarcation between areas in which you are liable as a tenant, and your landlord is liable as a property owner, for foreseeable or preventable harms to the public. There will also be issues related to your operating a business or a quasi-professional practice from a rented property. In this case, you should consult a lawyer to determine both the extent of your liability, and the permissibility of your operations, according to municipal ordinances, state laws, and the terms of your actual lease. You should take steps to acquire the necessary business permits, adjustments to your lease, and insurance policies. The latter (i.e., the underwritten insurance policy) will almost always be contingent on the former (i.e., the business permits and leasing arrangements) being in order.

Q: **How can I establish and build my philosophical practice?**

A: This is of course a key question, which is inevitably raised by almost all aspiring practitioners. If there were a formulaic answer, I would give it. Since the profession is nascent, there is no formula; but there are plenty of guidelines, anecdotes, and examples. I will offer a few herein. This large question also entails many smaller ones, some of which will be articulated in this section. A professional practice must be either built or bought. In the established professions, building a practice from scratch (like building any other business from scratch) can involve significant startup costs. Unless you are an independently wealthy philosopher, you might want to proceed on an inexpensive model of slow but steady growth. And in the established professions, buying a thriving practice is normally far more costly than establishing one yourself. Since our profession is nascent, we needn't worry about buying anyone else's practice, and should concentrate on building our own practices.

The leaders of any new and high-profile field—that is, the pioneers and entrepreneurs who found it—eventually attract all the business they can handle, and often end up taking on partners or referring clients to colleagues. But we all get started somewhere, usually modestly and sometimes inadvertently, and our pioneering initiatives generally take precedence over the notion of professional practice qua earning one's daily bread. But aspiring practitioners prudently ask:

Q: **How many philosophical practitioners actually earn their daily bread in this way?**

A: Not as many as we will soon see, but more than you might suppose. Gerd Achenbach has been doing it in Germany since 1981, and he remains the most illustrious among a few full-time German practitioners. The Dutch have perhaps a few dozen philosophers in full-time practice, including Dries Boele, Will Heutz, Ida Jongsma, and Jos Kessels. The Dutch have been practicing since the mid-1980s, and, moreover, they tend to practice across the spectrum, as counselors, facilitators, and consultants; hence they broaden their opportunities accordingly. Jos Kessels was a full professor of theoretical philosophy, but gradually moved out of the academy and into full-time (and potentially far more lucrative) philosophical practice. American practitioners, with some noteworthy exceptions, have tended to remain in the academy, dividing their time between theoretical philosophy and philosophical practice. Those at the forefront of American practice, dating back to the late 1970s and early 1980s, still maintain academic affiliations, and that by choice. Pierre Grimes, J. Michael Russell, Paul Sharkey, and Wayne Shelton are practitioners precisely of this kind. One exception is Tom Morris, who is one of the wealthiest philosophers since Seneca. Whereas Seneca had only one client—Nero—Morris has many—but they are mostly Fortune 500 companies that pay him well for his inspiring presentations. Yet Morris also got into philosophical practice by accident. He was a full professor of theoretical philosophy at Notre Dame, and one day somehow got invited, out of the blue, to make a presentation on ethics to a used car dealership in South Bend. Having no idea what to tell them, he did it *pro bono*. Other engagements followed, and he worked his way up the pay-scale incrementally. He now commands the largest hourly fee in the philosophical practice world, but he built his practice from scratch. Eventually, like Jos Kessels did in Holland, Tom Morris left the academy to practice full-time. But they are the exceptions, not the rule. Because consulting is more entrepreneurial than is counseling (as well as being completely undisadvantaged legislatively), a greater number of philosophers with PhDs are currently in full-time practice as consultants than as counselors. Examples of these are Christopher Michaelson, an in-house consultant at PriceWaterhouse-Coopers in Manhattan; Ron Nahser, who runs his own ad agency in Chicago and utilizes pragmatism as a *modus operandi*; and Peter Koestenbaum, who taught in the academy for thirty-four years before establishing himself as an international philosophical consultant of great repute.

Most of us who practice philosophical counseling find it interesting and rewarding as an activity, but we do not seek to do it full-time, to the exclusion of all else. We enjoy engaging in other philosophical activities as well—such as reading, writing, reflecting, teaching courses, and practicing other forms of philosophy too. Hence most philosophical counselors in the U.S.A. currently lead multifaceted lives, and that by choice. It is part and parcel of being what Paul Sharkey would call "a philosopher." Depending on political, economic, and other cultural developments, which no one can accurately predict, it is conceivable that more philosophical counselors will enter the market on a full-time basis. If accredited degree programs develop in conjunction with legislative recognition of philosophical counseling, then philosophers will approach an even footing with psychologists in the counseling domain, and they will have more incentive to identify with philosophical counseling as a primary rather than ancillary activity. As for market forces, I am certain that human beings will always have problems, and will usually seek help in managing or resolving them. If philosophical help is readily available, people will access it.

Whether one counsels one client per week or twenty, one renders a potentially invaluable service. One's life is enriched by practicing philosophy, however one practices it. Thus my main concern is not whether one can earn a living as a philosophical counselor, but whether one has the capacity to build a professional counseling practice. Build it, and they (the clients) will come.

Q: **How can I market myself as a philosophical counselor?**

A: For me, this is a quintessentially American question, for Americans are past masters not only of marketing goods and services, but also of marketing markets themselves. I will briefly discuss three keys to marketing yourself successfully as a philosophical counselor: publicity, promotion, and packaging.

KEY #1: PUBLICITY

Publicity is the most effective element in the short run, because it brings you to the attention of the most people in the least time. It's like casting a very large net, albeit with wide meshes. So how do you attract publicity? There are two ways, both quite uncertain and equally unable to guarantee results: first, by not seeking it at all; second, by seeking it avidly. If you find this paradoxical, that's because it is so. I speak here from immodest experience. While Tom Morris is the wealthiest contemporary philosophical practitioner, I seem to have become the most celebrated in the media. Between us, we are rich and famous. My press kit—that is, the compilation of newspaper and magazine articles, both American and international—is voluminous. By Hollywood lights, I am a very minor (if not negligible) celebrity indeed; but by philosophical lights, I dare say that no one else has attracted so much mainstream media attention. I have also worked very hard indeed at responding to such demand. The plain truth is that I did not seek most of it; rather, it happened quite serendipitously. In a somewhat solipsistic sense, it happened because I was completely indifferent to its happening. Like all else, serendipitous events do not occur without sufficient reason; but unlike much else, they do occur without their beneficiary having strived for their occurrence in any conspicuously appetitive or persistently volitional way.

When I was very young man I desired intensely and willed protractedly to be famous. This was not because I wanted, wished, or fantasized something beyond my grasp, but because I recognized something within me capable—though not necessarily destined—of expressing itself through celebrity. Moreover, I discovered that I had been vouchsafed several precious gifts—literary, musical, dramatic, athletic, romantic, noetic—any of which could have served as "the vehicle" for manifesting my particular destiny. I cultivated all these talents during my youth—an arduous but joyous undertaking—and attained a stage of creative development in some of these arts that I knew to be more than sufficient for the purpose; yet none transported me to the station that I envisaged as fitting or proper in the circumstances. All this shows only what poor judges we can be of our own fitness, propriety or circumstance. At any rate, I sometimes allowed myself a brief wallow in irony, anger, or despair, thinking it was too bad that the world had little apparent use for me, given that I had such abundant use for it. But I resolved to carry on in any case, following my heart and asserting my will; yet I take little credit for this, because at times it seemed not so much a choice as a congenital inability to capitulate to circumstance.[7] Thus I gradually inculcated a Sartrean disposition of good faith, combined with a Hindu (rather than a Stoic) renunciation of the fruits of my labors.

Naturally, no sooner did I dispossess myself of that long and winding baggage train of judgmentalness and expectation—whose elements took years to accumulate and years more to disperse—and become rather attached if anything to delightful anonymity, then suddenly the press descended on me for no apparent reason, carried my name to the four quarters of the globe, and cast it upon the countless waves of cyberspace. This is a short and mystical account of the first way to attract massive publicity: either be so destined, or else avoid it at the right time.

The second way appears more rational, but at bottom is no more comprehensible: you can attempt to purchase it, like any other commodity. Publicity is a major industry in America, and you can hire a publicist to spin-doctor your image, to write press releases, to make cold calls to editors and producers, and via these means to draw media attention to your story. Publicists are essential in the news and entertainment worlds. They are fabricators, vendors, and wardens of public perception of culture.

Although the major cultural story that launched philosophical counseling in America, by Alex Kuczynski in *The New York Observer*, was purely serendipitous,[8] soon after that I hired a publicist, who ultimately accomplished further important work. The two biggest news stories on philosophical counseling in 1998—Joe Sharkey's "I Bill Therefore I Am" in the *New York Times*, and Amy Westfeld's piece for Associated Press, which made the front page of the *L.A. Times*—were both instigated and orchestrated by a professional publicist. While the CUNY Graduate Center's Philosophy Department (like many other philosophy departments around the country) posted the *New York Times* piece, and the professorate and students were suitably impressed, only one philosophy professor from the Graduate Center, who had friends in the film and art worlds, knew enough to ask me on the sly, "Who's your publicist?"

But this is a two-edged sword. I have also hired a professional publicist who stirred major interest but who got no results whatsoever. In the world of publicity, you sometimes get what you don't pay for, and sometimes pay for what you don't get. It's more like a lottery than a service.

So how do you, a philosophical counselor in Anytown, U.S.A., draw some local media attention to your practice? Living in New York or Los Angeles provides no guarantee: these towns are world media capitals, but the local competition for media attention is correspondingly fierce. You probably stand a better chance in Anytown to begin with. If you're an APPA-Certified philosophical counselor, you can get exposure in the following way: Anytown's daily newspaper has probably *not* reprinted national or international news on philosophical counseling, precisely because they didn't have, or didn't know they had, a philosophical counselor in Anytown on whom to "peg" the piece. The journalistic concern is compelling: if they report this national and international cultural revolution without mentioning any local revolutionary cell, then they're tacitly reporting that Anytown is a cultural backwater. By contrast, if they can identify even a single local practitioner, then Anytown immediately shares the credibility of the whole movement. It's "hip"; it's part of the "avant guard"; it's not just a one-Starbuck town where people still watch the grass grow and the paint dry.

This tactic has worked brilliantly from Cleveland to Memphis, from Fayetteville to Orange County, from Westchester to Hong Kong, from Chicago to Denver.[9] And it's still waiting to work in places even as culturally rich as Boston: just like the *Anytown Annal*, the *Boston Globe* will not print a feature on philosophical counseling until it can identify a local philosophical counselor, which, believe it or not, it cannot at this writing.

So if you're an APPA-Certified philosophical counselor in Anytown, here's what you do. First, ask the APPA office to send you a "press kit"—that is, a dossier of selected newspaper and magazine articles—on philosophical counseling. Believe me, we've got plenty. Second, you write a press release—or better, get a journalism professor or graduate student from your local college to collaborate on its writing—which spotlights you as the local exponent of this burgeoning movement. Third, assemble these materials in a glossy pocket folder, with your business card tucked into the provided flaps. Fourth, before sending the package to the editor of the *Anytown Annal*, you need to decide whether to make the approach directly yourself, or whether to use an intermediary (i.e., a publicist or publicist-in-training). If you know the editor personally, or chat with him or her regularly in the barbershop or beauty salon, you can make the approach directly. If not, it's usually better (that is, more professional) to have someone else do it, who can pitch the story and sing your praises without appearing amateurish or self-serving. So you'll need a short covering letter from whoever acts as publicist. Be sure to include a statement that the APPA will gladly corroborate your status, will tell the reporter what a great job you're doing in Anytown, what a credit you are to the movement, etc.[10]

Also, a savvy intermediary will help get your package into the right hands, just in case the *Anytown Annal* has a large editorial staff. If you target the wrong person, you might as well address your package to a paper-shredder. On top of this, a smooth operator will first make a "cold call" to the right editor, to titillate his or her fancy, to convey the nub of the story, to spin it in a useful way, and to arouse interest in receiving the package—all within about one minute, which is all the time the editor will normally spend at this stage. If she can keep him on the line for two minutes, she will probably make the sale. The cold call is therefore the most vital piece of the entire media linkage, and the most crucial component of the publicist's performing art. If she's not adept at the cold call, the editor won't be interested in your package, and the story will die then and there. If she is adept, the editor will quickly (if privately) incline toward finding a way to run the piece, and your story will fly then and there. The best publicists all started this way, and discovered they had talents for making the cold call and the quick pitch. Media editors and producers eventually become the allies of successful publicists, and grow to depend on them for regular consignments of newsworthy stories—just as editors in publishing houses depend on literary agents for manuscripts. The point is, your savvy intermediary has to make the cold call, pitch the story, send the package, and then follow it up with more calls or faxes to make sure it has been received and read, and hopefully that a feature has been assigned. Once the story is assigned, you'll get your fifteen minutes of fame; and with it, a boost to your practice. You'll also get phone calls from agencies scattered across America, offering to bronze the newspaper clipping and frame it in oak for your office wall. One industry generates another, and hustlers get hustled by other hustlers. It's the American way.

Key #2: Promotion

Publicity is a service that others procure for you and a good (i.e., information) that others disseminate about you; promotion is an activity in which, although assisted or abetted by others, you yourself engage. You can promote your philosophical practice in various ways. Two more common ways include facilitating a philosopher's cafe, and speaking about philosophical practice to various constituencies. Such constituencies include institutions of higher education, associations of other practicing professionals, and organizations which feature speakers as a regular main event.

If you want to facilitate a philosopher's cafe, you should do so for its own sake. But you can also use it—tactfully—to make people aware of your philosophical counseling practice. Most people who attend my Philosopher's Forum enjoy the cut-and-thrust of spontaneous public debate. They participate primarily because they seek to air their views, and not (or not at all) because they want or need philosophical counseling.[11] At the same time, many of them are interested in the concept of philosophical counseling, and know people who are good candidates for it themselves. So they can refer clients to you. Thus a philosopher's cafe is not to be regarded as a pool for recruiting clients; rather, as a potential referral network. It is not a good or appropriate venue for "hustling" clients—there may be no such venue—but it is a good and appropriate venue for gently disseminating information about your counseling practice. In the next chapter, I'll tell you how to start up a philosopher's cafe in Anytown, U.S.A.

A very useful way to promote your philosophical practice, along with the idea of philosophical practice itself, is by public and private lectures. If you are an effective speaker, this is one of the best ways. I speak to most groups that invite me, and do so on a sliding scale. Sometimes I get full VIP treatment as a speaker (big bucks, business class airfare, and all expenses); at other times,

I speak *pro bono* and even pay my own subway fare to engagements. Either way, I love it. Promotion isn't about making money; it's about abetting movement: literally, "pro-motion." If philosophical practice were a religion (which it isn't), we'd call promotion "preaching the gospel." However, since the APPA does have the same nonprofit tax-exempt status as a church—501(c)(3)—its members can think of philosophical practice in analogous secular terms, as "leading the examined life." In particular, APPA-Certified practitioners can and should exhort people to lead more examined lives, and this they readily accomplish by addressing groups.

You can offer your services as a speaker to your local high schools, community colleges, universities, public libraries, retirement homes, prisons; to local or regional chapters of professional associations representing physicians, psychiatrists, psychologists, social workers, other health service providers, lawyers, judges, civil servants, etc.; and to local or regional chapters of organizations like the Rotary Club and a host of similar general interest or special interest groups. Philosophical practice is completely portable, and can be applied to almost anything. Consult your Yellow Pages, surf the worldwide web, and use your imagination. If allocated propitiously and earnestly, your promotional energies will be invested and not squandered. Moreover, if you do a good job with the promotional opportunities you create or are offered, you will receive even more opportunities; if a poor job, less. The cosmos is neither blind nor deaf nor dumb in this regard.

KEY #3: PACKAGING

How you package yourself, and your service, is how you appear to prospective clients. Publicity creates your image, and promotion leaves your impression, but packaging defines the features and contours of your practice itself. If you package and comport yourself like a professional, you will be received as such. You don't necessarily need an executive suite, holographic stationery, and talking business cards: your package is about the service you provide, not about bells, whistles, and gimmicks.

If you are using an institutional office to do *pro bono* counseling, make sure that there is sufficient privacy for your clients. If your conversations with clients are likely to be overheard, even inadvertently, by colleagues and other passers-by, then put a sound screen in your anteroom.[12] If you are using a home office to do private counseling, make sure that it looks like a counseling office, and not a hastily converted playroom. If you are meeting clients in cafes or restaurants—which I occasionally do if a client specifically requests or prefers this kind of venue, and if I also deem it appropriate—then conduct your meeting professionally, not fraternally. It is also possible, and possibly desirable, to share office space with other professionals. They may be interested in having a philosophical counselor on the premises, and perhaps you can cut yourself an affordable deal on a trial basis.

Once the location component of your package is settled, you should think about the hard and soft copy components. You may want to print not only business cards and stationery, but also some literature that describes yourself and your practice. You may want to make some kind of arrangement with other local professionals—physicians, psychologists, psychiatrists, social workers, lawyers, and others on your referral list—to cross-display each other's business cards and literature. This will help advertise your service, in a low-key and professional way. How you advertise your service is also part of your package. You may also want to build a website, since your potential clients are spending more and more time in cyberspace, and this trend is increasing as virtuality continues to outpace reality as both a storehouse of information and an efficient medium for information-gathering. Your website's index page is the quintessential package for your service: if it's attractive, informative, and not overly complex, prospective clients may browse long enough to make an appointment. You don't need the financial resources of a major corporation to build an engaging website.[13] Web technologies are accessible to all, and web-designers are increasingly affordable. If you have the time and interest, you can build and maintain your own site. If you are an APPA-Certified practitioner, the APPA will link to your site, and will list you in our web-based directory of philosophical practitioners. Our website gets a lot of attention, and yours can be a beneficiary too.

Ultimately, your "total package"—publicity, promotion, packaging—is your total package. Everything you do potentially enhances, or potentially diminishes, your counseling practice. Clearly, there's a lot more to "hanging out a shingle" than hanging out a shingle.

While the academy may have prepared you expertly in theoretical philosophy, in its current state it will have ill-prepared you for the realities of the non-academic world. Unlike established professions, such as medicine, law, or engineering, there is no deeply entrenched extra-academic infrastructure waiting to absorb philosophy graduates, or aspiring philosophical practitioners. You may have to dig your own trench, and this book is one of your trenching-tools. When I studied classical music, I heard similar complaints from graduates of fine conservatories. Some were truly gifted musically, but had no conception of how to market their gifts. They knew they needed courses in business, marketing, agenting, recording, and so forth, and thought that the conservatory should provide professional preparation, in addition to musical and performance training. Whether rightly or wrongly, such responsibility fell to them as graduates, and many seemed unequal to the task.

Insofar as philosophical counselors resemble artists, we may be temperamentally ill-suited to commercial ventures; yet, insofar as we resemble artisans, we can find ways to market our services if we make the right effort. Among the consequences of right effort are: that subsequent waves or generations of philosophical practitioners will find it less arduous to negotiate professional career paths than did their trail-blazing predecessors.

NOTES

1. Psychologists who imagine they are criticizing philosophical counseling have repeatedly made this claim to the media: that professors of academic (i.e., theoretical) philosophy are not automatically trained as counselors. Any psychologist who bothers to take (and is able to pass) an elementary course in critical thinking would not commit the straw man fallacy so glibly.

2. See, for example, evidence cited at <www.yorku.ca/phil> ("Why Study Philosophy?"). As earlier cited (Chapter 3, note 6), see *The Wall Street Journal* (Tuesday, 25 October 1995, p. B1): "On just about everybody's list of hot skills for the 90s are communications and analysis. So who has these skills? How about philosophy majors? Philosophy majors who took the Graduate Record Examination between 1990 and 1993 finished first among all fields in verbal skills and third in analytical skills, the American Philosophical Association notes."

3. P. Hanks, ed., *Collins Dictionary of the English Language* (London & Glasgow: William Collins & Sons, 1979).

4. Private communication (2001).

5. Herbert Sachs, quoted in *The Los Angeles Times*, Sunday, 8 April 1998, p. A1.

6. For an account of this project, see Chapter 17.

7. A famous and fabulous woman, who had never met or heard of me, took one look at me at a party and declared "You are undefeated by life!"

8. I wrote the press release to which she alone responded. At the time (as a relative newcomer to America and Manhattan), I had never heard of *The New York Observer*, and moreover didn't know what a publicist was except in very fuzzy terms. My phone has not stopped ringing since her story appeared (A. Kuczynski, "Plato or Prozac?" *New York Observer*, 4 August 1997, p. 17).

9. Among many examples, see, e.g., *Baton Rouge Advocate* (20 December 1997), *South China Morning Post* (5 July 1998), *Memphis Flyer* (22 July 1999), *Orange County Register* (30 August 1999), and *Chicago Tribune* (1 October 2000).

10. An amusing digression: this took a funny turn in one town, when I told a reporter who had phoned me for corroboration that although the counselor in question was indeed APPA-Certified, his membership had technically lapsed owing to nonpayment of dues. I said this candidly and off the record, but the reporter printed it anyway, right in the body of his piece and virtually under the mug-shot of the counselor. Within a week after the story ran, the APPA received his dues in the mail. What a way to collect late dues: turn lapsed membership into news!

11. This is also the consistent experience of a number of facilitators other than myself.

12. This is an electronic device which emits engineered "white noise" that absorbs ambient sounds. Deployed in an anteroom, it prevents eavesdropping or overhearing of conversations taking place in an inner office.

13. See Marinoff (1999b) for thoughts on the intrinsic egalitarianism of cyberspace ("cybertarianism").

CHAPTER 13

Opportunities for Facilitators

13.1. Informal Facilitation: The Philosopher's
        Café Revisited

13.2. Formal Facilitation: Socratic Dialogue
        Revisited

13.3. Philosophy for Children

13.4. Philosophy for Undergraduates

13.5. Philosophy for Seniors

13.6. Philosophy for Felons

13.7. Philosophy for the Otherwise Challenged

*A*lthough philosophical counseling has received the lion's share of the publicity thus far directed toward philosophical practice, group facilitation and organizational consulting each possess at least as much potential, if of a quieter kind, as dimensions of practice. This chapter details some of the dormant and nascent opportunities for facilitators; the next chapter, for consultants.

13.1. INFORMAL FACILITATION: THE PHILOSOPHER'S CAFÉ REVISITED

In Chapter 6, I offered fairly detailed instructions for establishing a Philosopher's Café at your local bookstore. While facilitating this kind of informal group is much like shepherding a philosophical flock, it also provides the practitioner with a foundational understanding of social forces, cultural nuances, and group dynamics that operate in assemblies of this kind, and which do not normally emerge in a one-on-one counseling session. My Canadian colleague, Peter March, interprets his facilitations as studies in "vernacular philosophy," and regards himself as a kind of philosophical anthropologist. The philosopher's café not only furnishes empirical corroboration of ordinary human propensity to lead an examined life, but also impels us practitioners to ponder, introduce, and refine formal methodologies (e.g., Nelsonian Socratic dialogue) that conduce to more effective examination by smaller and more noetically-aligned groups.

However, the philosopher's café remains one natural departure-point for aspiring facilitators, and (except apparently in France, where it is it a terminus) it can lead to many other things. This chapter touches on some of those things. But no matter how advanced your group facilitations become, you can always moderate a philosopher's café. It is a great public service, and an enjoyable opportunity to interact with thoughtful people in an informal setting. There will be passion, but no pressure. There is a preset time-limit, but no preconceived goal. There is room for at least one philosopher's café in every town with a bookstore or a coffeehouse—all that is lacking in most of these places is a philosopher willing to step forward and take the initiative. If you join the APPA, we can help you establish your café-philo. If you want to do it on your own, I've already told you how, and you certainly don't need us. But if you aspire to practice philosophy with groups more than once per week or once per month, and if you aspire to do so not only as public service but also professionally, then read on.

13.2. FORMAL FACILITATION: SOCRATIC DIALOGUE REVISITED

Socratic Dialogue is a multipurpose philosophical tool whose range of applications is far from exhausted in Germany and The Netherlands, where it has been successfully applied for decades, and whose potential in the U.S.A. has barely been tapped. It can be implemented not only at length in groups convened for that purpose, but also in abbreviated and more directed forms, within organizations themselves. While the hourglass shape of the dialogue remains structurally robust, its temporal axis is ideally elastic: both compressible and extensible. A dialogue can last two weeks, two days, or two hours. How well it is conducted, in whatever time-frame, depends mostly on the skill of the facilitator, but also upon the composition of the group. An obstructive participant can make things difficult for everyone,[1] whereas eight or ten insightful participants do not necessarily make things easy. The topic, if too emotional, can also debilitate a dialogue.[2]

The theory, form, content, and goals of Nelsonian Socratic dialogue were introduced in Chapter 6, and there is no need to reiterate them. Herein, I want both to sketch some particular opportunities for group facilitators in America and elsewhere, and to explain how aspiring facilitators can be trained in the method of Socratic dialogue. Four obvious areas of opportunity are: the K–12 system, colleges and universities, elder care facilities, and correctional institutions.

13.3. PHILOSOPHY FOR CHILDREN

Matthew Lipman is the American pioneer of record in this area.[3] His philosophy for a children's program—which he developed around the "Harry Stottlemeir" character, other works, and allied methodologies, and implemented in the 1970s—was so successful academically that it appears ultimately to have failed. I will explain. I am an unrepentant Platonist on at least one tenet of education—although perhaps perversely I arrive at my Platonism through decades of experience as an educator. I believe that young children, of roughly primary school age, enjoy a unique period of linguistic and other cultural plasticities, during which they may acquire virtually any number of languages, as well as other useful skills and less-than-useful prejudices. Like Chomsky, I hold that their grammatical capacities are innate; like Plato, that they are in possession of intuitive logical engines. I do not mean that I am convinced by Socrates' putative demonstration, in the *Meno*, that an untutored servant could reconstitute the Pythagorean (or any other) theorem of geometry without being asked what one would charitably call "leading questions." But I do mean that most untutored children, in any class, are able to exercise primitive but precise logical intuitions, which could easily be refined and enlisted in the mode of Euclidean geometry (the perennial paradigm of deduction), or any other mode of reasoning (e.g., inductive or ampliative). In my anecdotal experience, relatively untutored children are able implicitly to recognize the validity of syllogistic forms like *modus ponens* and *modus tollens*, and either implicitly or with a little coaching able to recognize the invalidity of syllogistic fallacies (e.g., affirming the consequent or denying the antecedent), and this without explicitly being able to articulate what "validity" or "invalidity" mean. My inference is that they arrive at such judgments by means of an innate and intuitive logical engine, which functions accurately but independently of their cognizance of concepts like "validity." While the introduction of such concepts reinforces what they already know to be the case, it does not determine their ability to arrive at such knowledge. Those who have difficulties performing intuitive logic will also experience difficulties learning formal or informal logic. However, a majority of children appear vouchsafed by nature the ability to perform rudimentary logical operations without prior coaching or practice in the performance, which is tantamount to claiming that they have "logical instincts."[4]

Yet there is virtually no formal training in critical thinking offered to children, which would erect an edifice on these splendid foundations. On the contrary, they are daily bombarded by barrages of uncritical pronouncements, and daily immersed in a "culture" in which even tabloid sensationalism needs dumbing-down because it is too esoteric for the mainstream. In consequence, their "logical instincts" may degenerate to a point beyond which they are unrecoverable.

Children have a taste not only for logical problems, but also for metaphysical, ontological epistemological, ethical, and axiological ones—naturally couched in suitable metaphors and sugar-coated. Yet these are rarely presented to them in the course of their K–12 educations. By the time they get to college or university, the best of them will be riddled with misunderstanding and confusion. The worst of them, in the wake of declining American civilization, debasement of merit, and eradication of standards, know absolutely nothing, and sit in the classroom like so many potted plants.

What Lipman and his cohorts found, not surprisingly, was that children who not only learn philosophy as a subject, but who also learn to think and question philosophically as a mode of meta-learning, do better in all subjects.[5] Thus Lipman's program, which turned out educators of philosophy for children, flourished for a time, and forms part of a skeletal global network of such initiatives. So why don't we see philosophy for children in every American primary school? Why do we see it in hardly *any* American primary school? Why doesn't your local public high school teach philosophy? Why don't even some of the best private high schools teach it? One macrocosmic answer readily suggests itself: the K–12 educational system as a whole went through such a precipitous decline in the past thirty years that philosophically attuned children would put it to shame. If your factory is mass-producing potted plants, you don't want any plants protesting—especially within earshot of the other plants. You don't want them asking why they're being potted, or why they're being treated as plants when in fact they're animals, particularly when the potters themselves either don't know the answers or don't even understand the questions. That's what Harry Stottlemeir does for children: he turns them into miniature philosophers, who then become a potentially giant embarrassment

for teachers—whose uncritical or ill-founded assertions are liable to be challenged—and a big pain in the posterior for parents, some of whose authoritative
but otherwise senseless pronouncements will meet exactly the same fate. In
sum, it's easier for the system to turn out a generation of potted plants than a
generation of gadflies. Thus Harry Stottlemeir took *very* early retirement. He
may have reincarnated as Sophie (of *Sophie's World*), ostensibly a child's book
of philosophy, which has international appeal to hordes of adults who never
met Harry.

When large-scale institutional politics—mainly educational bankruptcy, and
the filling of its vacuum by psychologists and pharmaceuticals—indirectly put
paid to Lipman's initiative, philosophy for children in one sense became or-
phaned, that is, ceased to be under the care of Philosophy, and was "legally"
adopted by Education interests. This is akin to placing famine victims, who
desperately need to gain weight, in the care of anorexics.

Empirically, this has had a double-edged nugatory effect. The ideal philosophical practitioner is someone with an MA or PhD in theoretical philosophy
who has subsequently acquired practical or methodological philosophical tools
and experience using them in practice. The ideal balance between knowledge
of philosophical theory and experience in philosophical practice is perhaps
50/50. Academic philosophers who are top-heavy in theory (i.e., most of them
currently) cannot practice philosophy effectively, because they simply do not
know what *practice* is; while philosophers of education who are bottom-heavy
in educational practice (i.e., most of them currently) cannot philosophize
effectively, because they simply do not know what *philosophy* is.

Anyone who holds a PhD in Education is by definition a "Doctor of Philosophy in Education"; but knowledge of philosophy per se is accidental, or
incidental, to this credential. Anyone with a PhD in Chemistry is by the same
token a "Doctor of Philosophy in Chemistry"—and, similarly, no knowledge
of philosophy is required or implied by this credential. The meaning of the
"Doctor of Philosophy in X-ology" is that the person has first mastered the
rudiments of X-ology and has then completed intensive or extensive research
in a specialized branch of X-ology, and has thus acquired some special expertise
in that branch. Having done that much, he or she should be capable of
understanding and articulating not only the findings of the particular research
and its relevance to proximate research in this branch, which is demonstrated
in the doctoral thesis, but also the metaphysical and other relevant or alternative assumptions that must be made or perforce challenged, in order to undertake and report on the research in the first place: which is demonstrated in the
defense of the thesis, and which is therefore at least implicitly philosophical.
In other words, by becoming an expert in some branch of X-ology, one necessarily but perhaps incognizantly assumes and defends a position within the

Philosophy of X-ology. It follows that the persons who best know Philosophy are PhDs in Philosophy, because of all the Doctors of X-ology they alone have made Philosophy the very object of their expertise, so that they are uniquely qualified, as Doctors of Philosophy in Philosophy, to be explicitly philosophical about their assumptions, and thus to philosophize about philosophy itself. Unfortunately, since Education is patently the most suspect of subjects-matter, and since far too many education students seem incapable of negotiating even the ruins of mainstream university curricula (including undergraduate philosophy courses), Doctors of Philosophy in Education are generally the least qualified to administer education to children, and yet they above all are charged with that task.

Of late, several of these "Doctors of Philosophy in Education" have misconceived or misrepresented themselves as philosophers (qua "Doctors of Philosophy in Philosophy"), and increasingly also as philosophical practitioners. Some of them do so as a brazen deceit; others, because they are so ill-educated or simple-minded that they do not apprehend or cannot cognize the distinction. As long as philosophy for children remains out of the hands of professional philosophers and in the hands of professional educators, it will merely trail the ongoing descent of education into the abyss of ferality, rather than lead its reascent to literacy, numeracy, culturality, functionality, utility and even nobility. This is one unsalutary edge.

Another, equally apparent and no less appalling, is the predictable and inevitable result of placing the emphasis in "Philosophy for Children" on *children*, instead of *philosophy*. By so doing one attracts not philosophers to a profession, but mothers to a vocation. Not that there is anything wrong with motherhood; it obviously has its proper place—which is not, however, the schoolroom. Yet there are people in academy who hold Doctorates in the Philosophy of Education, which they utilize primarily to mother children, yet who nonetheless advertise themselves as philosophical practitioners. I think that operating a Day-Care Center is a very good thing for some PhDs in Education to do, but I remain chary of calling it "philosophical practice."

The "Day-Care Philosopher" has her amateurish counterpart in the "Coffeehouse Philosopher," whom we have encountered in Chapter 6. The Coffeehouse Philosopher views the philosopher's café as the pinnacle of philosophical practice, whereas the professional practitioner views it as an important public service, but at the same time as only the tip of the iceberg of group facilitation. Just as Socratic Dialogue is too important to be left in the hands of Coffeehouse Philosophers, so is Philosophy for Children too important to be left in the hands of Day-Care Philosophers.

When suitably professionalized—that is, taught by persons who not only love working with children but also know something about the subject matter itself—philosophy for children will be an effective grassroots tool for reversing precipitous cultural decline. Encouraging the natural philosophicality that many if not most children possess will result in the immediate sharpening of their critical faculties, as well as the long-term improvement of their speaking, reading, and writing skills. If branched into ethical and axiological inquiry for children, it will also engender in them a sense of moral worthiness (deeper and longer-lasting than vacuous self-esteem), and thus will preempt many of the violent incidents that are so preventable if properly approached, and so inevitable when improperly approached (as by current philosophers of education and educational psychologists). If professionally practiced, philosophy for children will also have secondary and tertiary effects, such as putting to shame incompetent teachers who cannot answer questions or will not tolerate challenges by their students, and incompetent parents who cannot give good reasons for their exercise of vicarious authority over or pathological abuse of their children.

As I have elsewhere observed, philosophical practice may be the last straw at which many individual clients and organizations alike are desperately grasping, to prevent them from sliding into the abyss. It may appear as a straw, but once grasped is as secure as an oak. When such straws are grasped by the grass roots, oak forests will appear. Every single K–12 school in America could have, should have, and will have at least one properly trained philosopher for children. While the APPA is certainly capable of training and certifying such practitioners, as it does others, in the long run this mission will best be carried out by a philosophical counterpart to—and remedy for—noteworthy teachers' colleges, to reverse the incalculable damage done by some of their bankrupt philosophies of education, which have too long served as definitive beacons of degeneracy and freeways to Plato's Cave.

13.4. PHILOSOPHY FOR UNDERGRADUATES

Once K–12 children will have been exposed to the wonders and revelations of philosophy, they and it must not be abandoned in the Colleges and Universities. Here philosophical practice can learn valuable lessons from its precursor—applied ethics. While theoretical philosophy, as an administrative constituent of the Humanities (and sometimes, capriciously if not ludicrously, of Social Science) fares well or ill depending on local intellectual climate, tradition, politics and circumstance, it cannot and does not hold a proverbial candle to English or Psychology in terms of popularity among students—and therefore in terms of clout with administrations. Particularly in America, where luxury is often viewed as necessity, advertisers and marketers have fomented a false expectation that important things can be achieved without much effort. The idea is played out in endless advertisements, suggesting, for example, that buying a given club will instantly make you a better golfer; that buying a given exercise machine will straightaway cause you to become fitter; and that buying a given book will immediately make you wiser. There is almost a sense that the less time you spend working on something, the more results you will achieve. And above all—above even "sexy" and "affordable"—everything must be "easy." In contradistinction to the thermodynamic workings of the universe entire, Americans are conditioned perennially to expect something for nothing. In consequence, and in complete consonance with the thermodynamic workings of said universe, they more frequently attain "nothing for something", parting with cold cash in exchange for tepid reinforcements of hot expectations.

University students too fall prey to this way of thinking; many simply seek the most credits for the least effort. They can usually find accomplices in lazy professors, who couldn't be bothered assigning work, or worse, in zealously anti-meritocratic professors, who find "compensatory" justice and "historical" fairness in conferring the highest grades on the lowest achievers. University students who turn up for philosophy courses are often dumbfounded because they are expected to be able to read, write, and reason. Those few who can already do so then enter the portals proper of philosophy; those who cannot require remedial reasoning, and among them only some will be able to master, at great pains, the rudiments of learning how to learn, which not having been transmitted during their childhood periods of plasticity cannot without strenuous effort be acquired later in life. Remediation aside, there appear to be some bright students, in both humanities and sciences, in whom the spark of intelligence has not been doused by deconstructed and dumbed-down "education," who have either been the beneficiaries of some bastion of erudition standing miraculously fast against the barbarians—who are not at the gates but in the very keeps—or who bootstrapped themselves into positions of potential achievement by their own native intelligence and concomitant refusal to descend into savagery. At any rate, students who are least able to reason, if not read and write, can benefit from a Socratic dialogue. They need not be intimidated, as so many students are, about reading philosophical works or writing "essays" on them.[6] Moreover, the minimalistic preparation required for participating in a Socratic dialogue (i.e., choosing a universal question and thinking of an example from one's experience) happens to suit the minimalist preparation most K–12 students have had for university; save that in this case minimalism is an asset, not a liability.

In my view, no four-year University program could be remotely complete without a two-day Socratic dialogue. This is especially true for the so-called "liberal" arts, but also applies to illiberal arts, fine arts, sciences, and technologies. For many students, that one weekend will be a high point of their undergraduate educations. For many philosophy departments, hiring a faculty member who is (whatever else he is) also a trained facilitator of Socratic dialogue will be as important as hiring the ethno-specific, gender-specific, or otherwise politically correct flavor-of-the-month: that is to say, it will be unofficially mandated by university administrations (who may officially deny such mandates). In other words, universities will need to hire people who can facilitate Socratic dialogues, as opposed to tokens who can flesh out quota systems. Such facilitators will come in all sizes, shapes, colors, chromosomological configurations, and sexual orientations. (They might be lesbian dwarves, albino blacks, or even white males!) Their job will not be to advance a faddish political agenda or to be planted—like so many shrubs—by diversity landscape gardeners: their job will be to facilitate Socratic dialogues.

American students will not participate *en masse* in Socratic dialogues because such participation is good for them, because it inculcates virtues, because it encourages them to think for themselves, because it affords the ideal interface between reason and experience, or because it provides a robust method for capturing a universal: they will do so because they are obliged, as a programmatic prerequisite to graduation. If one sought to glorify the package itself, and make it appear more palatable to American youth, one would be advised to do so by calling attention to the garb in which it is already wrapped: it is *the* quintessential experience of philosophy. In other words, youth should be told the truth: that there is a world of difference between *studying* philosophy, and *being* a philosopher. Not everyone is capable of studying philosophy very deeply, and fewer still are capable of leading protractedly philosophical lives.[7] However, most are more capable of being philosophers for a weekend, by participating in a Socratic dialogue, than following even an introductory course in theoretical philosophy. If university students were taught, at minimum, Plato's doctrine of *anamnesis* (from the *Meno*), his allegory of the cave (from the *Republic*), and Nelson's theory of Socratic Dialogue (in a more palatable rendering, not Nelson's own)—perhaps ten to twelve hours of philosophical theory *in toto*—and then participated in a two-day Socratic dialogue—another twenty hours or so—they would have lifelong pleasant memories of their philosophical education, which is incomparably more than the current state of affairs produces overall. I meet (too) many young professionals today—in publishing, journalism, law, commerce, government, education—who either scrupulously avoided theoretical philosophy because it was incomprehensible by repute, or who took it but slept soundly through it, or who took it but became thoroughly disappointed when they found it utterly useless as a guide to life. Socratic dialogue will settle those scores, too.

At the very least, this thirty-hour experience in Socratic dialogue (ten of theory, twenty of practice) could count as a core philosophy requirement in a liberal arts curriculum. It would catch on, with university students, like proverbial wildfire. Consider the employment opportunities this would engender for facilitators. There are currently four of us in America who are trained in this method; thousands will eventually be needed. Those who perceive this path first, and tread it first, will lead the others. You can begin training now, if you wish. Joining the APPA, and participating in a Socratic dialogue, are your first steps. When you will have participated in two full Socratic dialogues, you will (if an Adjunct Member) be eligible to be trained as a facilitator yourself.

13.5. PHILOSOPHY FOR SENIORS

As medical science, technology, infrastructure, and general understanding of health continue to increase life-expectancy, and as the baby-boomer generation moves past middle-age and into senescence, Americans are witnessing a demographic swelling of senior citizens' ranks. As seniors will lead increasingly active lives for more years in the coming years, the question arises as to what they might do with the gift of additional time. As usual, the corporeal dimension of their existence receives some adequate attention; the noetic dimension, inadequate attention. The potential for philosophy for seniors is vast, and virtually untapped.

A typical scenario unfolds in this way: a retired schoolteacher, eighty-something years old, lives in a retirement home in Anytown, U.S.A. Although she is less than ambulatory, and needs assistance to move around, she is fully capable of walking her wits. To sustain a modicum of intellectual stimulation and aesthetic enjoyment, she runs a weekly Poetry Circle for herself and a half-dozen of her *confrères* and *consoeurs*. She has read *Plato Not Prozac*, and thinks it would be a great idea to get some philosophical stimulation too. Her daughter got in touch with the APPA, to inquire whether there is a group facilitator in or near Anytown, who would be willing to moderate a regular Philosophy Circle in her mother's home. In this case, the APPA's answer was unfortunately "Not yet—there are currently no facilitators in or near Anytown"; but just imagine the opportunities for rendering such a public service— either *pro bono* or for a small honorarium—in homes like these all across America.[8]

There is also a potentially vast virtual dimension for this service. We don't need a facilitator in or near every Anytown to bring Philosopher's Forums to their senior citizens: with the advent of the internet, facilitators can moderate virtual Forums in any location with a gateway. It turns out that more and more seniors are using computers in any case, often for keeping in touch with their families via e-mail. Such persons could obviously subscribe to an APPA Seniors Forum, a free e-mail discussion list that would sustain e-communication among seniors across the country. And for those seniors who cannot effectively operate personal computers—owing for example to problems with eyesight, fine motor skills, etc.—a chatroom could be accessed at regular intervals by a group of such people, via a technician operating a personal computer projected through a "light panel" (LCD). The technician could read aloud the ongoing chat, and could input contributions on behalf of the local participants. The benefits of a virtual forum and an accessible chatroom are obvious: they keep minds active, and they allow a vast amount of intercommunication among people who would otherwise never know of each other's existence.

This much can be done on the informal side alone. Beyond that, in given constituencies, there may be sufficient interest and ability to engage in more formal facilitations, such as Socratic dialogue adjusted to (an empirically de-termined) optimal duration—whether one hour, or one-half day. Again, the potential for seniors to get involved in philosophical practice is vast.

13.6. PHILOSOPHY FOR FELONS

There are also millions of people behind bars in America, with every indication that more prisons are being and will be built, to house yet more inmates in the future. This is a factual (i.e., phenomenological or observational) statement only, and should not be read as embodying or interpreted as implying any value-judgment. While I own a philosophy of justice that entails quite pro-nounced value-judgments concerning corrective, punitive, retributive, dis-tributive, compensatory, and other facets of justice's administration and dispen-sation, this book is hardly the proper venue for their elaboration. For now, I merely observe that millions of Americans are behind bars, and millions more are likely to be in the foreseeable future. If you prompt me, out of curiosity, for an incipient value-judgment, I will offer this minute observation: the American justice system has deprived many people of their liberty precisely because the American polity confers more individual liberty on its citizens that some can constructively manage. I have sojourned in constitutional monar-chies, social democracies, theocracies, tin-pot dictatorships, and banana repub-lics, but have never experienced more personal liberty than in the Republic of America. Where there is insufficient liberty, many will be unjustly imprisoned for want of it; but where there is abundant liberty, many will be justly imprisoned for abuse of it.

The pragmatic question is: how best can those who are behind bars serve their time—irregardless of whether they should or shouldn't be there? What are the most profitable activities (axiologically, not monetarily) in which they can engage? I have been prompted to ponder these questions primarily because *Plato Not Prozac* has penetrated the walls of many prisons, and I have subsequently received letters from a number of inmates. These letters vary drastically in their form and content. Some are from extremely articulate and thoughtful people, who write poignantly of their experiences in prison, describe what they have learned from their crimes and incarcerations, express apparently sincere hopes of leading useful and productive lives on their release, and claim that philosophies (of various schools) have already guided them a long way in their rehabilitation. I also receive other letters from inmates who appear, from their writings, to be psychopaths. If such persons came to my office for philosophical counseling, and said some of the things they had written, I would terminate the session and refer them for psychiatric help.

Some people clearly belong behind bars, for the protection of innocent citizens from their criminal predations, whether violent or nonviolent. Ironically, some of the latter predators are also lawyers. In some cases the system functions only to warehouse incorrigible recidivists between crimes, while in other cases it certainly contributes to recidivism itself. It is clear, however, that some people serve time in prison neither because it is the only life they are psychologically or vocationally fit to lead, nor because their so-called "culture" views it as a "rite of passage"—but either because they responded in socially inappropriate ways to trying or tempting circumstances and are remorsefully paying their "debt" to society, or because they were victimized by (and must triumph philosophically over) injustice itself.[9] For such people, whatever their relatively minuscule proportion among the overall inmate population, the "correction system" potentially fulfills a corrective rather than a punitive function, by affording them opportunities to be corrected, and to correct themselves. In other words, some are capable of transforming their time served into an educational experience roughly the equivalent of a graduate school: they work and learn independently, with infrequent but important episodes of intellectual supervision. Many such inmates can and do benefit greatly from direct encounters with philosophy—particularly ethics, axiology, philosophy of psychology, philosophy of law, and political philosophy. Many more could benefit from contact with philosophical practitioners themselves, who could help them apply useful ideas to their rehabilitation.

Most people behind bars who can benefit from philosophy are not at the graduate or even the undergraduate level; rather, they are people—often young people—who got into trouble because they failed to understand either that their actions would have consequences, or that their actions were harmful to their victims. Lack of prudence (i.e., anticipation of consequences) and lack of compassion (i.e., identification with another's suffering) are hallmarks of intellectual atrophy and emotional immaturity, respectively, which may be reversed by decent education and proper socialization. That the most politically civilized and technologically advanced state in the world is now producing hordes of immature savages speaks volumes about indecent education and improper socialization, which stem from such factors as the disintegration of the nuclear family, the skyrocketing birthrate of children out of wedlock, the absence of parenting in two-income families, the media's glorification of violence, the state's encouragement of all these things and its promulgation of myths of mental illness and mental health alike, and the absence of moral leadership and statesmanship in governments of lawyers, by lawyers and for lawyers. All these things, in turn, stem chiefly and ironically from abuses of liberty. While insufficient liberty may precipitate just conflicts, superabundant liberty surely precipitates undue chaos.

Far too many people behind bars simply have no idea how or why they got there. While some may be congenitally ineducable or sociopathic, others are salvageable but have clearly lacked guides or mentors at critical junctures in their lives. This is where philosophical practitioners can and do help—and could and should help much more. Among philosophical practitioners generally and APPA-Certified practitioners specifically, Vaughana Feary has done pioneering work in New Jersey correctional facilities, with both adult and juvenile offenders, to ameliorate their critical thinking skills and anticipation of consequences on the one hand, and to address their almost inevitable problems with self-worth and self-respect on the other. Another APPA member, Lawrence Jablecki, works within the corrections (parole) system in Texas, and implements Socratic methods as far as his ethos is receptive to them. I am not speaking here about large-scale prison reform, or other Quixotic crusades involving massive social engineering. I am speaking about grassroots initiatives in philosophical practice that can be taken most naturally and beneficially in the corrections system, with a view toward salvaging whatever humanity is salvageable in that increasingly populous purgatory.

13.7. PHILOSOPHY FOR THE OTHERWISE CHALLENGED

What applies to groups of the young, the elderly, and the incarcerated applies *mutatis mutandis* to groups of the blind, the deaf, the paraplegic, and the otherwise challenged—who may lack some perceptual faculty or bodily function, but who are certainly not bereft of reason. They may all engage in philosophical activities, and await only the initiative of a local practitioner. These and similar opportunities for group facilitators abound, and allow philosophical practitioners to play increasingly important roles in the lives of groups.

NOTES

1. In the worst case I have witnessed to date, an apparently rational but evidently troubled participant actually walked out of a dialogue in a huff, thereby paralyzing the whole group. He returned only after an hour of personal philosophical counseling by the experienced Dutch facilitator, who in eight years of facilitation had never seen this happen before. I have encountered difficult persons in some of my facilitations too, but an individual's functional skepticism or obstinacy can also be fruitful, by redoubling the group's efforts to attain consensus.

2. While I have facilitated a successful dialogue on the question "What is love?" notwithstanding initial skepticism of all concerned on its feasibility (owing to plurality of meanings), an experienced Dutch facilitator had a dialogue disintegrate because the question "What is hatred?" provoked intensely negative emotions in the group. Similarly, at a recent Philosopher's Forum, discussion of pain and suffering produced ill-feeling in the group.

3. Among many works, see, e.g., M. Lipman, A. Sharp, F. Oscanyan, *Philosophy in the Classroom* (Philadelphia: Temple University Press, 1986).

4. James defined instinct as the faculty of acting in such a way as to produce certain ends, without foresight of the ends, and without previous education in the performance. Cited by J. Drever, *Instinct in Man* (Cambridge: Cambridge University Press, 1917), pp. 16–17.

5. See "Philosophy for Children, A Report of Achievement," published by the Institute for the Advancement of Philosophy for Children, Montclair State University, Upper Montclair, NJ 07043.

6. A typical undergraduate "essay" at City College—as in many other institutions coast-to-coast, according to my colleagues, amounts to a few sentences of ill-conceived, syntactically challenged and semantically deprived prose. My undergraduate students find it both incomprehensible and highly amusing that a philosophical "essay" formerly meant a chapter of a book (e.g., Reid's *Essays*), or at least a self-contained booklet (e.g., Thoreau's essay on civil disobedience, or Mill's essay on liberty).

7. In the sense that Schopenhauer meant: of thinking for themselves (see Chapter 3, note 2).

8. As I revise this manuscript for publication, it comes to my attention that David Hilditch, a philosophy professor and APPA-Certified counselor, is moderating a string of "elder cafes" in the St. Louis area.

9. Some noteworthy philosophical practitioners (e.g., Socrates, Thoreau, Gandhi, King) have fallen into this latter category.

CHAPTER 14

Opportunities for Consultants

The Modularity of Practice

The General Nature of Conflict in the Workplace

Special Effects of Diversity on Conflict in
  the Workplace

Inability of Political Correctness and Other
  Oppressive Ideological Mechanisms to
  Manage Such Conflicts Equitably

The Rising Importance of Ethics Compliance,
  and the Ethical Unpreparedness of Generic
  Management Consultants

*O*pportunities for philosophical consultants to organizations may well outstrip those of client counselors and group facilitators alike. There are several reasons why. These include the modularity of philosophical practice itself, the general nature of conflict in the workplace, the special effects of diversity on conflict in the workplace, the inability of political correctness and other oppressive ideological mechanisms to manage such conflicts equitably, the rising importance of ethics compliance and the ethical unpreparedness of generic management consultants, the existential and axiological consequences of globalization and its ongoing separation of economics from politics, and the perennial value of *phronesis*. By briefly examining these reasons in turn, we reveal corresponding opportunities for organizational consultants.

THE MODULARITY OF PRACTICE

It should by now be abundantly clear that client counseling, group facilitation, and organizational consulting are not necessarily separate activities. While some practitioners do indeed specialize in one given area, whether owing to personal proclivity or undetermined factors, others practice across the spectrum. These latter practitioners, including yours truly, usually become aware of the modularity of general practice. That is, group facilitation usually entails both implicit and explicit elements of client counseling, and organizational consulting usually entails both implicit and explicit elements of group facilitation (and therefore also of client counseling). Hence, as mentioned in Chapter 7, consulting stands potentially at the summit of practice. This bodes well at least by analogy: things with summits (e.g., mountains) tend to get climbed. The idea is not merely to stand on the summit and admire the view, but to achieve the ascent itself. Some philosophical practitioners who have thus achieved can serve as guides and instructors to others who wish to achieve themselves. As with mountaineering, some climbs are relatively easy; others, more difficult. Some routes are relatively safe; others, more perilous. Experienced guides are recommended on some climbs, while a few preliminary climbing lessons allow novices to manage others. One's view of practice definitely improves as one makes the ascent.

For those leery of this argument by analogy, there are empirical confirmations of the modularity of practice. Particularly in Holland and America, we find practitioners working across the spectrum, who started with counseling, progressed to facilitation, and culminated in consulting. Those who work in all three areas, myself included, will affirm the modularity of these endeavors. At the same time, there are specialized and expert practitioners in particular modules, whose expertise in a given module does not depend upon cross-training or direct experience in another. Even so, they sometimes reconstitute the modularity itself.[1]

THE GENERAL NATURE OF CONFLICT
IN THE WORKPLACE

The places—whether real or virtual—in which we earn our daily bread are also arenas, in which we manifest two seamlessly interacting modes of human behavior: competition and cooperation. Biologists, psychologists, sociologists, anthropologists, economists, game theorists, and philosophers—among other researchers—all have vested interests in decoupling, and recoupling, aspects of this interaction. Like everything else in America, this interaction too has been politicized. Many conservatives tend to overemphasize the ostensible primacy of competition, possibly because they champion meritocracy, derive moral worthiness from winning, adore egoism, and abhor collectivization. Many liberals tend to overemphasize the ostensible primacy of cooperation, possibly because they champion egalitarianism, derive moral worthiness from gregariousness, adore altruism, and abhor individualization. This metapolitical conflict, which ineluctably prejudices and therefore preempts progressive debate on the subject, was recognizable in its current form at least as remotely as Hobbes versus Rousseau on the nature of man. It continued with Burke versus Paine on the nature of rights. After Darwin, it was rekindled by Spencer versus Kropotkin on the nature of societies. It recrudesces with E. O. Wilson versus Ashley Montagu on sociobiology and extrasomatic culture, with Thomas Sowell versus John Rawls on social justice, and with Hernnstein and Murray versus Steven Jay Gould on intelligence. Following the neo-Bolshevik revolution in the American academy, it is presently radical liberal orthodoxies that prevail as official dogmas—ironically unchallengeable in the very arena supposedly consecrated to open and reasoned inquiry. But since both the means and ends of rational inquiry are now ordained by political rectitude, reason is brain-dead. Note, however, that the death of reason in the academy and its replacement by political slogans (e.g., "committed to diversity"), whose proponents are delighted to accept illiteracy among students, political indoctrination by professors, and gross incompetence of administrators as mere transaction costs of social justice, has lately given rise to more bitter conflict than ever in the academy, conflict which percolates through society at large.

While America currently enjoys a period of economic prosperity second only to the post-World War Two boom, it is increasingly debilitated by conflicts in the workplace, many of which are ironically exacerbated, if not engendered outright, by ostensibly "cooperative" political dispositions. Psychologists, sociologists, anthropologists, economists, and game theorists can study such conflicts *ad infinitum* without contributing to their resolution. "Conflict resolution" studies themselves require conflicts as their *raison d'être*. Lawyers also require them, and make indecent fortunes on the sufferings of decent people without alleviating—and often exacerbating—their conflicts. Philosophical practitioners, however, can actually improve the human estate by addressing and either resolving or at least managing such conflicts directly. The more conflicted the workplace becomes, the more work philosophical practitioners can do. And the workplace is becoming more conflicted than ever.

We can identify two end-points, and two intermediary points, on the historical spectrum of so-called "office politics" and the conflicts to which they give rise. The earliest human societies were groups of hunter-gatherers, which maintained strict sexual division of labor. That is, the men hunted and engaged in combat; the women foraged and engaged in child-rearing. This is not surprising; rather, it is an obvious projection of human biology onto human culture. Anatomy is destiny among baboons, and similarly was destiny among any group of primates that left the shelter of trees and forests, and endeavored to thrive on open ground, in competition with and exposed to other top predators—including man himself.[2] There is no place here for philosophy, only hunting prowess and parenting skills. Thus it was for tens of thousands of years of precarious existence, which witnessed the gradual evolution of weapons, language, tradition, ritual, myth, marital strife, and rudimentary social order. The wages of social disorder were collective death.

It is the relatively recent neolithic revolution—a revolution in agriculture and animal husbandry on the one hand, and in weaponry and defense of permanent settlements on the other —that precipitated classes and castes, institutionalized division of labor, mandated accumulation of goods and chattels, necessitated laws to protect property, afforded leisure to contemplate morality and justice, and potentiated the nascent City-State in all her glory. After a few millennia of such evolution, taking root in tiny armed camps like Catal Hayuk and flowering in small civilizations like Athens, philosophy finds a place indeed; but its perch in antiquity is only as stable as political expedience, as secure as theological convenience, and as enduring as personal caprice. The great philosophical practitioners of this era were as likely to be put to death as tutor conquerors; more apt to become forest sages than civil servants; most likely to be ignored, rather than employed, by warlords. Yet permanent settlements provoked philosophical theory and practice alike. As man's cultural identity emerged *sui generis* from his biological substrate, its most primitive manifestations mimicked nature too: just as phenotype is ordained by inherited genotype, so civilized culture was from the outset dictated by received institutions—autocratic and theocratic. Biologically, might made right; culturally, tradition made justice. The chief (ab)uses of philosophy in this age were to amuse or console monarchy, and to justify or rationalize theology.

This state of affairs persisted until the Early Moderns, who formulated the theoretical cleavage of state from church and heralded the nascent deity, science. The Enlightenment carried this project through. For better or worse, it was the age of philosophy made political flesh. Democracy relentlessly sucked the vital juices of power from monarchy, until the latter became a desiccated ceremonial husk. Theology held sway only so long as fear outweighed pleasure; but the prosperity of capitalism bred hedonism, and converted religious devotion to lip-service. Philosophers have become the secular prophets of democracy. They reinvent human nature daily, willy-nilly, sagaciously, foolishly, extravagantly, parsimoniously, interminably—and man continuously remodels his social and political institutions to reflect his ever-changing self-conception, just as woman changes her garb to reflect her ever-changing mood. Whatever portrait of the human being or chart of the human voyage some philosopher commits to canvas or parchment, however inspired or demented he may be, whether vouchsafed clarity of vision and lucidity of ratiocination, or rendered blind by occupational obfuscation or dogmatic by "hardening of the categories," some group of well-intending citizens arises to emulate the portrayed figure—be it comely or contorted—and to undertake the charted journey—whether it leads to paradise or perdition. Instead of common culture being dictated by church and state, church and state are dictated by common culture. The democratic revolution, with its capitalistic fruits and modernistic flowers, employed philosophers as revolutionaries, visionaries, prophets, poets, and—occasionally and posthumously—as demigods. But by these very tokens, it had no role for them as mere consultants.

And just as partum entails postpartum, so modernism entails postmodernism. Nietzsche would singlehandedly slay God; Marx and Engels would jointly execute nobility; Sartre and his coconspirators would together assassinate human nature. Who now dictates what, and toward which end? In the world of ideas, these killings signal the twilight of modernism, and the encroaching gloom of postmodernism. In the world of ideas, this dark night of the no-soul swarms with anarchism, radicalism, and extremism masquerading as mainstream workaday doctrines. In the world of ideas, ethnocratic and femocratic people's revolutions redefine the university in the starkest and crassest political terms, engendering a grossly illiterate and incompetent "culture," while promoting an agenda that demonizes and destroys the classical liberalism that made the world of ideas accessible to ethnocrats and femocrats in the first place. In the world of ideas, liberties are coerced to the point of tyranny. In the world of ideas, potentially civilized persons are denigrated into barbarians; barbarians, into savages. Who now dictates what, and toward which end? In the world of ideas, every doctrine that has failed in *realpolitik* is enshrined in academic policy. The more fatuous the idea, and the more demonstrable its failure, the more exalted its ideology and the more inflexible its implementation. Robert Conquest describes "the permanent condition of the Soviet citizen" under Stalin as "a feverish effort by day to pretend enthusiasm for a system of lies"[3]—and this is an apt description of the condition of the classical liberal seeking tenure in the postmodern academy. In this postmodern world of ideas, philosophers are not needed. Now that privilege is utterly conflated with entitlement, students are troubled by having to read, write, and reason. Since they are now "entitled" to good grades and meaningless degrees, where their measure of entitlement is directly proportional to their "historical disadvantage," and positively correlated with their present lack of achievement, philosophers are tolerated (albeit diffidently) by administrative regimes only as far as they remain mostly incomprehensible, and as long as they hire token ethnocrats and femocrats to critique anything remotely comprehensible. This is the current state of analytic philosophy: politically isolated, socially irrelevant, administratively besieged, and graduating far more PhDs than can reasonably despair of employment within the academy's Stalinized precincts, or hope for employment outside its Irony Towers. Insofar as good analytic philosophers make poor political commissars, their talents are wasted here.

In the world of acts, as contrasted with that of ideas, human civilization has entered its newest phase, which, as I touched on in Chapter 7, is characterized above all by the removal of economics from political control. Thus the democratic and scientific revolutions of the Enlightenment have resulted not in the gradual perfection of either men or states, but in the relentless emergence of a third and unforseen agency which now governs both: global technocracy. The workplace is lately become the world, yet it lacks guiding philosophical lights. In this phase, man's evolving nature, and his conception of it, are neither ordained nor legislated by anachronistic institutions like church and state, respectively; neither is his nature redefined by enlightened philosophical revolutionaries who inverted these pyramids and sculpted democratic institutions anew and wholesale from the common clay of humankind; nor is it compassed by the deconstructions of delirious radicals who, feverishly charting imaginary courses as the foundering vessels of postmodernistic nationalism break up on the reefs surrounding the unexplored island of global technocracy, order the destruction of the lifeboats, whose very presence offends their fantasies of seaworthiness and oppresses their delusions of smooth sailing. There is much work here, on this uncharted island, for philosophical practitioners, but first we must establish a beachhead. Employees of technopolitan corporations and citizens of cyberspace now shape and are shaped by the forces of unfettered technocracy. And as human cooperation and competition alike reemerge in this technocratic world, its virtual hunters and gatherers need philosophy to negotiate its complex pathways and to realize its—and their—unprecedented potential. Technocracy does not make human conflicts vanish; rather, metamorphose.

SPECIAL EFFECTS OF DIVERSITY ON CONFLICT IN THE WORKPLACE

As we have claimed, albeit cursorily, the original hunter-gatherers needed no philosophical understanding; they relied on primatological dominance hierarchies for their survival. The later ordination of morality by religions, or its attempted dictation by the state, while necessitating expedient philosophical interpretations by agents of these institutions, usually precluded philosophical understanding by their minions. Outlooks and worldviews were essentially tribalistic and therefore largely homogeneous within tribes, and conflicts were adjudicated or mediated by received authoritative infrastructures (or "power-structures," as the unempowered seeking empowerment lately call them[4]). The acceptance of fundamentally feudal dominance hierarchies was unquestioned, even though the criteria of dominance, in the cultural sphere, were no longer simple-minded extensions of biological prowess. The lack of politically effica-cious reasoned examination of such criteria, couched in cultural and inelucta-bly philosophical terms, embodied in questions about goodness, rightness, and justness, persisted until the beginning of the Enlightenment. Even then, con-ditions in the workplace were initially worsened by myriad excesses of the industrial revolution, which begot slavery of indigenous women and children in England as well as the infamous triangular trade, which maintained the domestic working classes in appalling urban serfdom as well as dislocated Africans into colonial slavery. Conflicts in the workplace were resolved by structural or physical violence in the workplace, meted out to maintain the serfs and slaves in their respective places.

The emergence of democratic reforms, whether by revolutionary or parlia-mentary process, heralded some important changes in the workplace, such as the creation of guilds and later trade-unions, which provided countervailing forces for contending against entrenched authorities, but on the whole the power of the state increased even more, proportionately, than did the power of its constituent sub-groups. So although the enlightenment was long on elo-quent expressions of humanism, humanitarianism, and human rights, the *realpolitik* of the industrialized nations was so brutal in its worst nineteenth century manifestations that it engendered the likes of Dickens's novels and Marx's manifesto in Britain, and the Opium Wars abroad. The structural vio-lence of this period—culminating in the carnage and slaughter of World War One, a mere ritual of imperialistic squabble—was so unspeakable that it en-couraged utilitarian and socialistic thought to gain footholds in the naive hopes of the intelligentsia, which were soon after dashed by even worse excesses of collectivism in "People's Democratic" autocracies. Only in Cuba and in the American academy does undiluted Marxism still pretend to thrive, but only in Cuba do its victims long to be rid of it. Between world wars and during the Cold War, conflicts in the workplace were still settled either by coercive or judicial force, not by moral force. Only with Gandhi in India and King in America did the world witness the power of philosophical principles put into practice, and their overpowering of preventive policing and entrenched prejudice alike. However, democratic reforms were necessary but insufficient for transcending tribal politics writ large, both within and qua post-Napoleonic nation-states.

The Enlightenment also afforded rapid progress in mathematics, science, engineering, and their progeny, namely, reliable and affordable technologies. Verisimilitudinous theories and confirming experiments, along with robust products, conduced to the independence of economics from politics. As long as governments endeavored to legislate truths for political purposes, or adopt falsehoods consonant with expedient positions, they ran the risk of barbarizing their populaces, and of engendering economic and social regression through epistemic blindness. Large-scale examples have been legion, ranging from extolling Social Darwinism in Britain, which contributed to the First World War and the collapse of the British Empire; to reifying "Jewish Physics" in Nazi Germany, which contributed to Germany's failure to develop the A-bomb before America; to denying Darwinism, asserting Lamarckism and implementing Lysenkoism in the Soviet Union, which resulted in the unnecessary starvation of millions of peasants.[5] Governments that ignore good science and viable technology, or adopt bad science and inviable technology, withhold progress from or hasten harm to the governed. And while the Enlightenment brought modern science and high technology into being, it could not remove their development and application from the biased or impoverishing purviews of tribalistic governments controlling the resources entire of modern nation states.

Philosophy became a potentially refined instrument for the mathematicians, scientists, and engineers, who also discovered (as too many philosophers did not) that the Vienna Circle had been premature if not wrongheaded in its rejection of metaphysics, yet continued to function as an appendage of the defunct Hilbert program, much as nails and hair continue to grow awhile on a corpse. As the need for philosophical interpretation of scientific and techno-logical development reasserted itself, so ironically grew the self-induced mar-ginalization of mainstream academic philosophy. At the same time, philosophy became a potentially blunt instrument for modern and postmodern political and social causes, degenerating into half-baked ideologies and insipid slogans. Philosophers remained largely mute as the so-called "social sciences," suffering conspicuously from physics envy, attenuated the psyche to S–R theory, replaced steadfast moral worthiness with vapid self-esteem, reduced classical portraits of ethicity to sophomoric paintings-by-numbers, adduced natural differences in intelligence to question-begging putative nurtural lack of acculturation, attributed measurable biological sex-differences—and eventually objectivity itself—to mythological "social constructions," and substituted personal re-sponsibility for present deeds with mass victimization in past circumstances: in sum, psychologized, sociologized, historicized and politicized the human animal into a crude observable of even cruder pseudo-sciences, whose pseudo-scientists divested themselves first and foremost of fundamental philosophical skills, such as critical thinking and inductive reasoning, the better to pander to governments and universities seeking not to educate individual human beings, but to dehumanize collective constituencies.

Increased democratization in the west brought in its train increased human rights and coerced egalitarianism. Advancing science and technology, backed by *laissez-faire* capitalism, brought in its train better infrastructures, goods, and services to consumers. Along with these developments, the post–cold war military supremacy of America has thus far managed conflict management, and so has directly or indirectly fostered economic development in nations desirous and capable of emerging from tribalistic barbarism and joining the global community of trading partners. These factors in turn have led to governments being marginalized and even dwarfed by multinational corporations and sub-sequent globalization, which is motivated primarily by economic and not political concerns. The primacy of the English language in international business and science, the saturation of commercial transportation routes to the point of congestion, the instantaneity and ubiquitousness of communication, the massive scale of immigration, and the opening of vast new markets for economic development, all conduce to the transcendence of local political enclaves by global economic interests.

This transcendence has brought together and placed on an equal footing, for the first time in human history, a remarkable assortment and variety of cultures, religions, races, ethnic groups, ages, disabilities, sexes and sexual orientations—none of which, in an enlightened society, serves *a priori* as a criterion of discrimination for, or against, in the workplace. Private mores or tribal perspectives are hardly obliterated by this gathering; rather, they are subsumed under the corporate logo. Thus the corporation is a transcendentally Hegelian entity, in the sense of *aufheben*: to negate, and to preserve. Biological and cultural differences that, when accentuated by religious or secular tribal politics, made cooperation impossible and conflict inevitable, are negated by intracorporate cooperation. Yet, since individuals are not expected to deny their biological roots or cultural orientations; rather, to affirm their membership in an all-encompassing temporal (but not spiritual) entity, their differences are preserved yet disarmed.

While these transcendent structures potentiate intracorporate and inter-corporate competition, such competition—like the Olympic games—becomes a moral equivalent of war rather than a *causus belli*. The conflicts that do arise in such workplaces will tend to have their roots in philosophical misunderstandings as opposed to psychological syndromes, psychiatric disorders, religious dogmas or political doctrines, and will thus in principle be resolvable by philosophical means. This scenario affords unprecedented scope for reconciliation of hitherto irreconcilable differences, because reconciliation will be perceived as a means and not as an end. Human beings are too conflicted internally, by their general natures and not by any specific biological or cultural features, willingly to relinquish external conflict without very good reasons. Where the social pyramid is constituted under the apex of a religious or political authority, such conflicts festered in endless domestic strife and suppurated in civil or international wars. But where the social pyramid is constituted under the apex of economic authority, such conflicts can be denuded of tribal overtones, resolved internally by phronetic intervention rather than perpetuated externally by unwise action, or at worst redirected into bloodless competitions rather than projected on some demonized enemy who need be vanquished, whether by intrigue or aggression.

Philosophical consultants are able to introduce and enhance Hegelian transcendence in the workplace, thus catalyzing an invaluable, novel lived experience for workers, experience in human difference as a source of constructive competition and wholesome cooperation as viable and preferable alternatives to human difference as a source of perpetual strife and perennial conflict. These alternatives are preferable not just for their own sakes, but toward the fulfillment of explicit corporate missions and visions (as contrasted with inscrutable providence or incognizable *raison d'état*) consonant with larger interests in commodiousness. Economics is not a zero-sum game; it is not necessary that some must wither in order that others may flourish. It is culture, or lack thereof, that determines whether the biological being called "man" inhabits the leading edge of technocracy, the trailing edge of democracy, the dark age of nationalistic or theocratic tribalism, or the Stone Age itself. Moreover, one's culture is determined by one's philosophy, or lack thereof. Those who do not or cannot think for themselves merely inherit, for better or worse, the culture (or lack thereof) into which they are born. Those who can and do think for themselves can acquire the culture of their choice, or invent their own. The combination of aesthetics, ethics, rhetoric, logic, and science, which Aristotle understood as applicable toward yet subservient to the highest and noblest philosophical art, namely, politics qua statesmanship (and not qua despotism or prostitution), applies even more fruitfully and practically to the emergent global technocracy. Those who can think for themselves are already employing philosophy, and will sooner or later benefit from employing a consulting philosopher. Those who cannot think for themselves, or who are not very accomplished thinkers, must be employed by someone else's philosophy, and that employer will sooner or later benefit from employing a consulting philosopher.

Biological diversity (i.e., proliferation of species) has—in the presence of geophysical forces, climatological influences and cataclysmic events—resulted in massive extinctions.[6] Cultural diversity (i.e., proliferation of tools and symbolic structures) has—*sui generis*—potentiated massive conflicts. Under emergent global technocracy, not only guided by the generation of wealth but also informed by the modulation of philosophical transcendence, cultural evolution itself will be furthered. If interpreted under the aegis of globalization, diversity furnishes raw material for competition and cooperation, not the excuse for violent conflict. Philosophical consultants will be on hand, and on call, to abet this process of interpretation.

INABILITY OF POLITICAL CORRECTNESS AND OTHER OPPRESSIVE IDEOLOGICAL MECHANISMS TO MANAGE SUCH CONFLICTS EQUITABLY

Nature is an orderly place, in that it unfolds via lawful processes that can be modeled mathematically. Even chaos is orderly, both in the nomothetic messiness of entropy and in the complexity of its underlying patterns. Human nature and human society are disorderly, not because they are not lawful, but because the nexus of interactions between an individual's internal beliefs, volitions, and motivations and the external laws, norms, and conventions that bind individuals in groups defy other-than-crude statistical description. No gas is an ideal gas, yet the universal gas equation ($PV = NRT$) is an excellent description of a macrostate assembly of identical molecules. One critical presupposition in this model is the presumed sameness of each molecule of a given gas to every other molecule of that gas. More precisely, they are theoretically constituted as identicals, and they "behave" (i.e., are empirically observable) as if they were the same. They conform, in other words, to Leibniz's Law, which reliably asserts the indiscernibility of identicals. In vernacular, things that are alike appear alike. Note, however, that the converse does not hold: one cannot reliably assert the identity of indiscernibles. In vernacular, entities that appear alike are not necessarily alike. This holds serious implications for human laws, as we shall see.

Biologically, humans are partly identical and partly nonidentical. They are identical in that they have the same somatic imperatives—e.g., appetites for food, sex, and sleep. They are nonidentical in that their behaviors differ widely in the expression (or reexpression or nonexpression) of these appetites, ranging from gluttonousness to anorexia, from promiscuity to celibacy, from hyperactivity to sloth. Culturally, humans are also party identical and partly nonidentical. They are identical in that they all have myths of origination, beliefs about the world, political opinions, ethical precepts, tribal traditions, and social conventions. They are nonidentical in that the contents of their myths, beliefs, opinions, precepts, traditions, and conventions differ radically, from creationism to quantum fluctuation, from exploitation to conservation, from fascism to communism, from deontology to teleology, from feasts to fasts, from polygamy to polygyny. They are identical in the immature psychological predispositions that motivate and abet their attachment, habituation and commitment to different myths, beliefs, opinions, precepts, traditions, and conventions; and nonidentical in the mature philosophical post-dispositions that motivate and abet their detachment from, and de-habituation and non-commitment to, different myths, beliefs, opinions, precepts, traditions, and conventions.

The identical facets of humanity allow its variegated members to assemble in increasingly complex technocratic associations; the nonidentical facets of humanity allow both conflict and the potential for conflict to increase by virtue of such associations themselves. When members of a relatively homogeneous biological classification or cultural orientation associate and come into conflict, one can explain and endeavor to resolve such conflicts in terms of sociobiological, psychological, tribal, theological, political, or economic criteria. Where biological and cultural diversity replace homogeneity, none of the foregoing criteria suffices to explain, let alone mitigate, any conflict. Philosophical analysis, and philosophical intervention, become necessary. The brute imposition of one *zeitgeist* over another by theological authority, or the ideological inculcation of one *weltanschauung* over another by political machination, are time-honored but hopelessly outmoded forms of socioeconomic control. Society is become worldwide; economy is become global. To prosper in such circumstances, humans need a view of themselves far more mature, robust, and forward-looking than those formerly furnished by tribalism, religionism, nationalism, politicism, sexism, racism, and (perennially popular) fundamentalism. Those who wish to linger in such cultural backwaters are free to do so, but are not free to impede the relentless flow of the mainstream. While every manifestation of tribalism, religionism, nationalism, politicism, sexism, racism, and fundamentalism comes bundled with its very own philosophy, ostensibly concocted not only to assuage ubiquitous human discomforts and remedy endless human complaints, but also to enslave inevitable human herds, technocracy transcends superficial differences, supersedes obsolescent dogmas, and grinds even large bones of tribal contention into small dust-heaps of prudential cooperation. Yet technocracy has no intrinsic philosophy, and so must employ and deploy philosophical practitioners at all levels and at every turn: for mission, for vision, for value, for ethos, for cosmos, for telos. Our ancient profession—philosophy qua phronesis—gives technocracy its soul. If technocracy were a tribe, philosophers would be its shamans; if a religion, its priests; if a team, its coaches; if a government, its ministers. Since technocracy is fundamentally an association of cooperating and competing corporations, we are its meta-consultants.

THE RISING IMPORTANCE OF ETHICS COMPLIANCE, AND THE ETHICAL UNPREPAREDNESS OF GENERIC MANAGEMENT CONSULTANTS

In underdeveloped nations, governments are the main force that either promote or prevent development. While there may be some truth in the proposition that people get the governments they deserve, there is little doubt that a transition from theocracy or oligarchy or autocracy to democracy is fraught with difficulty, and that many political cultures will either never achieve it, or will achieve it only at excruciating cost. In developing nations, governments are potentially promoters of development, but dictators may turn in rapid succession from benevolent to despotic, and fundamentalistic revolutions may cause centuries' worth of cultural reversals in mere decades. A developing nation is by definition unstable, and any minor progress can become a prelude to major regress. In the developed world, where the effects of technocracy as an overarching organizational force are most strongly felt, governments are increasingly viewed as non-responsive bureaucratic impositions, which exist primarily to invent and collect taxes, but which are incapable of rendering sufficient or even necessary services in return. In America, grotesque bureaucratic intrusions of governments into the private lives of citizens and professional lives of workers represent constitutional infringements, as well as taxations without representation, as heinous as those which precipitated the American revolution against the British Crown. Militia groups in America, although camped on the fringes of civilization and civility alike—and in some cases, of sanity as well—and although somewhat paranoid in conceiving the American Federal Leviathan as their main enemy, would be nonetheless perspicuous in perceiving certain governmental agencies, or some operations of certain agencies, as inimical to the people. It is the American economic system, and the constitutional political liberties that sustain it, that make America great.

Mere government itself, when it degenerates into inertial administration and moribund bureaucracy, can make America mediocre or worse.

Meanwhile, those who struggle for life itself in economically underdeveloped nations are not in the main afflicted with ethical dilemmas, which during most of human history have been luxuries for the intelligentsia, not necessities for the ordinary citizen. Similarly, those who struggle with corruptions or against injustices induced by rapid economic growth in developing nations, which has been grafted onto preexisting political structures well-prepared to accept IMF funds but ill-equipped to extend individual liberties or equal opportunities to their citizens, have no ethical dilemmas either. They may require Declarations of Independence first, along with guns and ammunition later, to pave the way to a political ethos that makes ethics relevant.[7] However, in developed nations, citizens have learned to transmute vituperative social conflicts into media circuses, impassioned civil disputes into adversarial litigation, and irreconcilable political differences into protracted fits of mudslinging followed by brief spasms of ballot-casting. Provided that the economy remains fruitful, stable, or at least hopeful—and note America's undeniable genius in folding transmuted conflicts, disputes, and differences back into the economy by marketing them—these citizens have ethical dilemmas galore, and a surplus of other axiological problems to boot.

Theoretical philosophers have been trained since time immemorial to deal with axiology in general and ethics in particular, but not necessarily to apply systems, insights or methods to the resolution of human conflicts, to the management of human problems or to the amelioration of human estates. Philosophical practitioners are trained to do precisely these things, and moreover are trained to do them within the temporal, practical and goal-oriented constraints of the corporate world. Hitherto it has been generic management consultants for the most part, "downsized" during Reaganomics but cleverly if superficially reinventing themselves as "ethics managers," who have virtually monopolized the lucrative field of ethics compliance.

The legal purpose of ethics compliance is to reduce the liability of organizations for the actions of individual employees. The political and social philosophy that necessitates ethics compliance, as a kind of mandatory insurance policy that transmutes potentially over-punitive litigious awards into affordable if not laughable fines, is collectivism pure and simple. Where is Senator McCarthy when we really need him? Nothing could be more antithetical to the tradition of the rugged American individualist, or more repugnant to his view of liberty and autonomy, than this supersession of the group over the individual. Holding an entire organization accountable for the misdeed of an individual member is like holding an entire hive accountable for the misdirected flight of a single bee, or an entire book accountable for a single typographical error. This kind of collectivism is an affront to the foundations of moral reasoning, a detour around the assumption of personal responsibility, a barrier to the civility of social function, and—when all else is said and done— an egregious inversion of empirically effective methods of organizational motivation.

Consider the Roman practice of decimation: it meant executing literally one out of every ten men as a punishment for a legion's poor performance in battle, and as an incentive for a better performance in the next battle (*"pour encourager les autres"*). If you prefer a less sanguinary model, and accept professional sports as a moral equivalent of warfare, then you will find the counterpart of decimation in the benching or trading of a star athlete, or in the firing of a head coach, which is again intended to enhance the performance of the team. In both these cases, individuals are singled out for punishment—whether justly or unjustly—to improve the functioning of the collective. Ethics compliance utterly inverts this practice, and singles out the collective for punishment, ostensibly to improve the performance of the individual. One may as well require that a prince be punished for the misbehavior of his whipping boy, and then suppose moreover that such a measure teaches the whipping boy an invaluable moral lesson.

Theoretical philosophers can expend entire careers inveighing for or against the usurpation of individual entitlements by group rights—or in this case its mirror-image, the supersession of group accountability over individual responsibility—without appreciably ameliorating the noetically malnourished ethos that spawns such sickly babes. Philosophical practitioners, by contrast, find opportunities galore. The more that American and global corporate structures fall prey to the Screwtapian machinations of the ideological parasites they have sheltered, empowered, and financed by their very successes, the more they will need philosophical practitioners to reverse the insidious damages done and address the original problems still festering below a tourniquet of political correctness, beneath a dressing of venomous solicitude, and under a sleeve—to borrow John Furedy's phrase—of velvet totalitarianism.[8]

The modularity of philosophical practice, to which I have referred several times herein, plays out in a literal and vital way: ABC Corporation has a reserved space in its parking lot for its Resident Corporate Philosopher. This RCP is an advisor to the CEO, a consultant to the Directors, Officers, and Managers, a facilitator to other organizational teams, and a counselor to individual employees. The RCP delivers a menu of services to these constituencies. His annual salary, in five or six figures, saves them seven or eight figures annually not only by preempting ethics compliance lawsuits externally pressed, but also in preventing frivolous internal litigation based on reified allegations of sexual harassment or institutional racism. Moreover, the RCP's in-house activities enhance the morale and ethicity of the workforce, thus reducing multicolored-collar crime and increasing productivity, which saves sevens more figures annually.

The Resident Corporate Philosopher is cross-trained and cross-certified, in all areas of practice, by the APPA. Additionally, and in the near future, he or she will be a graduate of an APPA-approved and State-accredited philosophical practice program, at a university near you.

NOTES

1. Thus Henk van Luijk's seven-step "Dilemma Training," developed by philosophical consultants at Nijenrode University (the "Harvard Business School of Holland"), who have no declared interest in counseling, nonetheless includes a component of "co-counseling" in its follow-up phase.

2. And note that man and baboon thrive, while the apes (chimpanzee, gorilla, gibbon, orangutan) are all going extinct.

3. R. Conquest, *The Great Terror* (London: MacMillan, 1968), p. 278.

4. The term "power-structure" is feministic, and emanates from a primary, cerebral sex difference that gives rise to incessant gender conflict. Males tend to perceive things in the world; females tend to perceive relations between and among things in the world. Most men are interested objectively in things; most women, subjectively in relationships between and among them. These differences are almost certainly hard-wired, not "socially constructed." (The belief that they are socially constructed is socially constructed.) Thus men tend to understand social power, manifest through dominance hierarchies, as personal, objective, and active: Smith dominates Jones because Smith is more powerful than Jones. By contrast, women tend to understand social power, manifest through dominance hierarchies, as systemic, subjective, and passive: Smith dominates Jones because (allegedly) Smith is "empowered" by a "power structure" whereas Jones isn't—the implication being that Smith's power derives from a relation, and not from Smith. Hence many feminists conclude that, for the sake of "fairness," Jones should now be "empowered" to dominate Smith. A secondary sex difference is, evidently, that many feminists appear oblivious to the primary one. While equal opportunity is a laudable social policy, it mandates neither equal outcomes, nor reification of putative "institutional" prejudices to explain away unequal outcomes. I know many women who excel at various professions. They excel because they are excellent, and because they are afforded opportunities to display their excellence. But they were not "excellented" (i.e., "made excellent") by consensus or policy. While anyone can be "empowered"—man or woman alike—not everyone can wield power. Some women wield it well, and some men badly. But one cannot defy nature, and "empower" lambs to hunt lions.

5. We have seen countless instances on a smaller scale as well—such as the Scopes trial in Tennessee.

6. During the Permian period of the Paleozoic Era, there was a massive general extinction of life-forms, followed by a proliferation of insects. During the Late Cretaceous period of the Mesozoic Era, there was another massive extinction, this time of large reptiles, followed by a proliferation of mammals. We are currently witnessing a general extinction of flora and fauna on a scale at least as massive as the prior two, whose cataclysmic cause in this instance is entirely human.

7. I am reminded of the Warren Zevon lyric: "Send lawyers, guns and money."

8. John Furedy has utilized this phrase in a number of articles. See, e.g., "Velvet Totalitarianism on Canadian Campuses: Subverting Effects on the Teaching of, and Research in, the Discipline of Psychology," *Canadian Psychology Abstracts*, November 1997, *38*, 4. See also "Velvet Totalitarianism in British Academia: The Case of Chris Brand and Edinburgh University," *SAFS Newsletter*, April 2000. In the latter, Furedy writes: "After publishing a book on intelligence that argued there are race-based differences in intelligence, Chris Brand, a tenured psychology lecturer at the University of Edinburgh, was 'investigated,' and suspended for nine months. He was subsequently fired for 'disgraceful behaviour' and 'gross misconduct' after he supported an American academic accused of paedophilia in an Internet newsletter. [See *SAFS Newsletters* 14 (Sep. 1996), 16 (Mar. 1997), 17 (Aug. 1997), 18 (Feb. 1998).] ... 'What happened to me is a total suppression of academic opinion and evidence, which is comparable only to the kind of thing that used to go on in the Soviet Union,' Brand said in an interview with John O'Leary, Education Editor of *The Times* (London) (October 29, 1999). I tend to agree, while recognizing that the punishments metered out by the Soviet totalitarian regime were far more severe than the one from this distinguished British university. The Edinburgh University approach fits what I have called 'velvet totalitarianism.' One of the indicators of subtle but insidious repression is the freezing fear exhibited by faculty and their organizations when one of their colleagues is treated unfairly. In the Brand case, no British academic organization came to his aid or spoke out on the issues involved. This includes the British Council for Academic Freedom, whose president (at the time) was Lord Russell, grandson of the great philosopher and the author of a fine book on academic freedom. As far as I know, SAFS and our sister organization, the National Association of Scholars in the USA, were the only groups to speak out on the issues of academic freedom in the treatment of Chris Brand. (See *SAFS Newsletter 18*, Feb. 1998, p. 2, for our joint press release.)"

PART V

Politics of Philosophical Practice

CHAPTER 15

Friends and Foes of Philosophical Practice

15.1. **Psychiatry**

15.2. **Psychology**

15.3. **Philosophy**

    Coffeehouse Mentality

    Sophistry

    Fraud

    Ambivalence

    Concealing Personal Problems Behind Philosophical Facades

    Academic Vanity, Fear of Change or Appearance of Inadequacy

*I*nsofar as philosophical practice is a movement, and insofar as all movement meets with opposition, philosophical practice meets with opposition. At the same time, since the movement is gathering strength, philosophical practice forges important alliances as well as discovers pettifogging enmities. Interestingly enough, our friends and foes alike are generally distributed across professions and vocations; thus friends and foes are not trivially identified by profession or vocation alone. The three main professions that harbor both our best friends and our worst enemies to date are psychiatry, psychology, and—needless to say—philosophy itself. I will address each of these in turn, then move on to other potentially significant loci of cooperation and conflict.

15.1. PSYCHIATRY

Philosophy and psychiatry are potentially very close collaborators in the service of delivering appropriate care, and any conflict into which they have thus far been drawn is almost entirely instigated by mass media, which exploits consumers' interminable obsession with sensationalism and insatiable taste for scandal. Having deliberately misrepresented philosophical counseling as a substitute for psychiatry, it has been child's play for journalists to goad leading (and not-so-leading) psychiatrists into making intemperate and bellicose remarks about philosophical counseling, a subject about which—to paraphrase Ernst Mayr on speciation—their ignorance to date is nearly complete.

Since many of us philosophical practitioners are reasonably well-acquainted with the history and philosophy of medicine (including psychiatry), with biomedical and relevant legal ethics, with abuses as well as successes of medicine (including psychiatry), with many models of mind–brain reduction, adduction, and interaction, with Freudian psychoanalysis and the significant variants his disciples (e.g., Jung, Adler, Burrow, Reich, Deutsche) counter-proposed, with fundamental paradigms of behavioral science, and with salient developments in contemporary neuroscience, we understand the philosophical foundations of psychiatry better than many if not most psychiatrists. At the same time, philosophical practitioners are mostly non-physicians, and we therefore neither diagnose illness nor prescribe treatment. It is our main contention, however, that much human mentation and behavior has been overmedicalized by psychiatry (and pseudo-medicalized by psychology), whose reach into the human condition has therefore, to quote Browning yet again, exceeded its grasp. While we philosophers are not qualified to diagnose illness and prescribe medical treatment, we are well-qualified to conduct inquiries into the ontological status and causal nexus of putative "mental illnesses" (under the aegis of philosophy of psychiatry), and we are also well-qualified to recognize and address ethical, axiological, ideological, existential, and teleological problems, which cause human distress but are not necessarily psychiatric (nor at all necessarily somatic) in their origins. So a reasonable philosophical practitioner's position vis-à-vis psychiatry might be triangulated from the following three vertices.

First, some people's problems are clearly psychiatric in the first instance, and no philosophical counseling should or could be done before such people are medically stable. In more severe cases, no philosophical counseling need or can be done at all. However, in intermediate cases, there is almost always an issue about responsibility for taking one's medication—and New York state has recently passed a controversial law allowing the state to coerce an individual to take prescribed medication, just in case his or her behavior becomes harmful or threatening to others when he or she refrains from taking it. While abuses of this law will grant physicians near-totalitarian powers over non-crazed persons, the absence of such law has also allowed crazed persons to terrorize and harm innocent citizens. Moreover, abuses of other laws have allowed non-crazed persons to be acquitted of heinous crimes on the basis of "temporary insanity" claims. Philosophers have much greater understanding of ethical competency and moral agency than do lawyers or psychiatrists; hence the criminal justice system is itself collectively guilty of negligence in not enlisting philosophical inquiry in the crucial juridical process of determining sanity. "Did the defendant know the difference between right and wrong when he or she committed the crime?" is a patently philosophical question. That psychiatrists, but not philosophers, provide pivotal answers to courts is an egregious state of affairs. Nonetheless, some persons are not legally responsible for their thoughts, words, or deeds by reason of psychiatric (i.e., cerebral) illness, and these persons are neither good candidates for philosophical counseling in the first instance, nor perhaps in any instance. In sum, the first vertex asserts that psychiatry is sometimes necessary, but is not always sufficient.

Second, clear and widespread abuses of psychiatric powers run rampant through America and other polities. These abuses are so conspicuous and flagrant that the unlikeliest constellation of strange political bedfellows has aggregated to expose and repudiate them. This constellation includes psychiatrists themselves, from Thomas Szasz to Peter Breggin, parochial moralists like Beverly Eakman, and scientologists like Bruce Wiseman.[1] While scientologists have partially earned unsavory reputations as cultists, and have also been illiberally smeared by major media, the Citizens Commission on Human Rights—an organization funded by the Church of Scientology and its members but operating at arm's length from it—has done yeoman's work exposing callous and unconscionable abuses of medical license by psychiatric practitioners, and causing even State legislatures (e.g., Texas) to step in and protect their citizens from psychiatric predation, instead of sanctioning it. However justified these variegated critics of psychiatry are, they mostly tend to err on the side of fanaticism, and thereby rehearse a fallacy of overgeneralization which no philosophy major would dare to air:

> **Premise**: Some psychiatrists are guilty of gross malpractice and professional ethical misconduct. (There is unfortunately plenty of evidence to support this claim.)

> **Fallacious Conclusion**: Therefore, the entire profession of psychiatry is irremediably corrupt. (This is the fanatic's perennial overgeneralization.)

That some psychiatrists are guilty of gross malpractice and professional ethical bankruptcy does not entail that it is not the case that some people need to be medicated, constrained, and/or restrained to prevent them from harming others.

Thus I disagree with Thomas Szasz, who asserts that everyone is competent, as a Hobbesian ethical egoist, to stand trial for misdeeds.[2] And I disagree with Beverly Eakman, who clearly doesn't know the difference between Freudian analysis, Zen Buddhism, and psychedelic hallucination, but who implies that any doctrine lying beyond the pale of Christianity is automatically profane.[3] The CCHR, meanwhile, disagreed with me: after courting me because the default media distortions of my philosophical counseling practice made me appear *prima facie* fanatical enough to join the aforementioned constellation, the publication of *Plato Not Prozac* revealed that I am, for want of a more exciting word, a moderate. That I regularly consult with a (hornless, tailless, pitchforkless) psychiatrist on my *pro bono* philosophical counseling research protocol at City College, occasionally practice Zen, and fondly remember the 60s prompted the CCHR to stop inviting me to its functions. In sum, the second vertex asserts that psychiatry is sometimes unnecessary, although at other times sufficient.

These first and second vertices together imply the third; namely, that philosophers and psychiatrists have considerable potential for dialogue, cooperation, and collaboration. Determinations of both necessity and sufficiency of diagnosis versus dialogue, medication versus mentation, and mental illness versus noetic ill-conception are paramount in the scope of mutual exploration. On an individual and anecdotal level, I receive "thank-you" notes from psychiatrists who not only read *Plato Not Prozac*, but who are applying its philosophical ideas in their own practices. This suggests that joint initiatives should be taken by the APPA and the APA (American Psychiatric Association) to establish and further symbiotic professional relations. We will gladly do our part.

15.2. PSYCHOLOGY

With psychologists, we find a different set of typical reasons for their approval or opprobrium of philosophical practice. Unlike psychiatrists, psychologists once had big stakes in group facilitation and organizational consulting. "Group Therapy" was born in the 1960s, and lived a brief but interesting life, proliferating rapidly but—unable to compete with the burgeoning carriage trade in gurus and the industry of rock concerts—became almost extinct. Corporations that currently import psychologists to lead daisy-chained hand-holding and mass-emoting sessions are clearly desperate, and thirty years behind the times. They would be better off opening corporate chapels and parachuting in traveling preachers to conduct rotating denominational services. Industrial psychology, which predated group therapy, perished—like the Irish elk—of its own success. As soon as one factory-owner paid a psychologist to inform him that worker productivity and contentment would increase if he painted the walls green and piped in Muzak, other factory-owners could imitate the prescription without hiring the doctor. A conspicuous group activity in which psychologists currently engage is orgiastic grief-counseling, wherein planeloads of grief counselors stand by, along with Red Cross blood transfusions, to be flown to the site of the next high-school massacre, where they can roll up their sleeves and prolong everyone's agony. Whereas philosophical practice in the schools would prevent many such shootings, by imparting moral worthiness, civic instruction, and prudential reasoning to would-be shooters, *ad hoc* grief counseling is no more preventive of needless tragedy than embalming is preventive of sudden death.

In consequence, the aspect of philosophical practice that most concerns psychologists is counseling, and, in contrast to some psychiatrists who regard us as a complementary profession, some psychologists regard us as competitors. As we shall see, they are in a shallow sense correct to so do. Those psychologists who are more astute, more secure in themselves, in their expertise and in their professionalism, understand in a deeper sense that we are complementary to them as well as to medical practitioners (recall the triangular relation articulated in Chapter 5). They welcome us, and want to work with us and learn from us. We can learn much from them, too. Most profoundly, however, a few psychologists have long understood that practical philosophy is their parent discipline, which unfortunately lapsed into a theoretical coma some decades ago. Having an apparently irreversibly comatose parent, the adaptive child learns to fend for itself. But if the parent unexpectedly regains consciousness, the child, even if by now mature, can still benefit from the parent's regained sentience. They can renew their acquaintanceship and rekindle their relationship. This is why many psychologists, who are also intellectually astute, are joining the APPA as Affiliate Members and declaring that they have finally returned "home." We are very touched by their perceptiveness and sincerity, and will endeavor to provide a good "home" for them, as philosophers from Plato to William James have done.

In a way, it is easier to understand our psychological counseling detractors than our psychiatric ones. The former have realized independence in professional secession from their behaviorist and other academic research colleagues; have capitalized on legislative initiatives that gave them virtual monopolies on nonmedical talk-therapy subsidized by third-party medical insurers; have enjoyed positions of prominence and privilege in twentieth-century intellectual culture, as the preeminent explicators of human cognition and character; have perched precariously but deftly on a fence between art and science, leaning one way or the other as it suited their interests; removing themselves by imperceptible but relentless degrees from the rigor of their philosophical origins and harnessing themselves to a pseudo-medical model of the psyche; and ultimately inculcating a professional deformation so potentially callow that it under-represents and misrepresents mentation as a purely psychological phenomenon.

While the astutest of them have reached back to, or toward, philosophy, the current mainstream academic preparation in psychology is so unphilosophical, if not anti-philosophical, that some can reach but few can grasp the therapeutic philosophical tools they seek. Psychology is to the social sciences what physics is to the natural ones—that is, the source and wellspring to which all others respectively and putatively reduce. But the chasm between social and natural sciences has yawned unbridgeably broad, as the former have fallen prey to politicization while the latter have resisted it. The bottomless dumbing-down of humanities and social science curricula in the wake of the literacy's spiraling decline has markedly affected psychology as part of that whole, and has thus lowered the overall calibre of students whom psychology attracts and counselors whom it trains. Insofar as (analytic) philosophy has not yielded to degeneracy but has divorced itself from the world, and insofar as (social) psychology has yielded to degeneracy and has immersed itself in the world, the gap between philosophy and psychology has widened into a canyon. Thus, books such as Wallraff's (1961) *Philosophical Theory and Psychological Fact*, which brilliantly synthesizes classical epistemology and phenomenology with (then) contemporary empirical psychology of perception, has become irrelevant to philosophers and incomprehensible to psychologists. Both irrelevant and incomprehensible to far too many contemporary psychology students are seminal philosophical works that subsumed their discipline for two and half millennia, from Plato to William James. In thoroughly politicized academic settings, some psychology students who boast "A" averages in their grade-inflated departments can barely pass low-level philosophy electives. They purport to study workings of the human mind, yet cannot parse syllogisms or fathom fallacies.

Given all this, when psychological counselors see philosophical counselors on the horizon, or hear them in the news, some naturally quake in their boots. In the worst cases, their stupefying hubris leads them to make condescending pronouncements to the effect that we philosophers probably "mean well" but surely don't have "the training" to recognize homicidal maniacs or comfort lachrymating clients. Little do they realize how much anger and discomfort they themselves sometimes engender in their own clients, who then come to philosophers as refugees from psychotherapy. The human being was made to emote, but not to discount reason and wallow nostril-high in sentiment as Cape buffalo wallow in mud. The human being was made to be conditioned by external social forces during formative years, but not to abdicate volition and relinquish responsibility alike, and succumb in maturity to infantilized visions of victimhood. The human being was made to encounter and even surmount problems in life, but not to interpret every difficulty as a personality disorder and every sign of distress as a psychological syndrome. The human being was made to engage in periods of dialogue with fellow humans, then to get on with his work, not to become ensnared in endless diagnostic narratives fostered by professional co-dependency. At worst, psychologists have conspired to inculcate the latter modes; philosophers, the former. No wonder some psychologists are troubled by our reappearance in the counseling arena.

Another common "refutation" offered by adversarial psychologists goes something like this: "If we could solve our problems with logic, people wouldn't need counseling."[4] Just so. It remains to be observed that if condescending simpletons had to pass logic courses before becoming counselors, most people wouldn't get counseling. It is difficult to know exactly which fallacy the above-quoted psychologist meant to commit. It might be the fallacy of denying the antecedent in the foregoing premise, thus arguing fallaciously that since we can't solve our problems with logic, therefore people do need counseling. It might also be a fallacy of equivocation: if philosophy means the study of logic and nothing else, then clearly philosophy is insufficient for much of human problem-solving. But because philosophy means more than the study of logic, it can be both necessary for addressing some problems and insufficient for addressing others.

What I cannot here convey is the smugness, smoothness, and sugar-coated condescension with which the psychologist delivered her ostensible refutation. "I can't imagine," she implied, "how anyone can be helped by logic." And that is a fitting epitaph for thoughtless counseling psychologists. Every time one of them utters it, my voice-mail runneth over with clients tired of being treated like fools by those who are wise by default. Evidently, the public objections of our psychological detractors are almost too paltry to bear serious mention, let alone too flimsy to bear the weight of sober rebuttal.

However, growing public disenchantment with psychological pseudo-medicine, growing reluctance of third-party insurers to subsidize endless emotive narrative, growing disaffection for litanies of victimhood and abdication of reason and responsibility, growing discontent with entrenched professional inadequacies on the part of counseling psychologists themselves, growing realization of the propitiousness of the time for revisitation of psychology's philosophical roots, and growing awareness of the flowering of philosophical practice on the professional landscape—all contribute to the forging of alliances between psychological and philosophical practitioners. The ideal counseling practice would house a psychiatrist, a psychologist, and a philosopher. Until that becomes commonplace, we philosophical practitioners bear the additional onus of fostering constructive dialogue between and among all counseling professions, and that of educating other counseling professionals about philosophical practice.

Many intelligent psychologists, secure in their own competence yet unhappy about their discipline's historical bifurcation from its philosophical origins, view the emergence of our profession as an opportunity for their own professional enrichment and perhaps even personal fulfillment. While the publication of *Plato Not Prozac* did not drive a wedge between clinical and cognitive psychologists, it did oblige some of them to relocate themselves on a conceptual map. Clinical psychologists, having convinced themselves that they are physicians by virtue of their biblical faith in the DSM, are now trying to convince governments to grant them prescriptive privileges to complement their diagnostic functions. While this is a worrisome prospect, it is sadly not more preposterous than the pervasive introduction of the "physician's assistant" into medical practice. Then again, clinical psychology and philosophical counseling are not rival modalities. Their capacity to cooperate has been instantiated by Lou Matz, a philosophy professor and APPA-certified philosophical counselor at the University of the Pacific. Matz gave a talk to the clinical psychologists at UOP's Wellness Center, and they understood that his service is neither a competitor of nor a replacement for theirs. When made explicitly aware of the scope of philosophical practice, they acknowledged that some of their clients do manifest philosophical rather than psychological problems, and they began making referrals to Matz. This is the kind of example of cooperation that will best serve counseling professionals and consumers alike.

On the cognitive side, virtually every great psychologist has reached back to, or toward, philosophy for valuable insights or methods. Among the more prominent are Albert Ellis, whose rational emotive therapy (RET) was inspired by stoicism; Viktor Frankl, whose logotherapy emanated from existentialism; Carl Rogers, whose client-centered therapy was implicitly informed by Kantian respect for client autonomy and dignity; Eric Fromm, whose humanistic therapy was grounded in naturalistic ethics. In Britain, existential and phenomenological approaches to counseling provide a literal intersection of psychologists and philosophers at the Regent's College School of Psychotherapy and Counseling. Emmy van Deurzen (who founded the school) and Ernesto Spinelli (who currently directs it) are the leading exponents of this integral style.

Buddhism, in its myriad (empty) forms, also engenders opportunities for the intersection of philosophical and psychological counseling interests. While those who have put some space-time between themselves and acute suffering can benefit greatly from sitting, chanting, and other meditative practices offered across the spectrum of Buddhist schools, sects, and sanghas, many are drawn to Buddhism not just because they are suffering, but because they are suffering in ways that have been neither appropriately apprehended nor fully addressed by traditional philosophy, theology, psychiatry, or psychology. I have attended retreats with Tibetan Buddhists, with Zen Buddhists, and with followers of various celebrated eclectic gurus (e.g., Maraji and Rajneesh). My consistent experience of the general populations on such retreats is that roughly half are mature in the ways of the dharma and seek to advance their practices, while roughly the other half are suffering either acutely or chronically, and have come in hope either of escaping temporarily from their woes, or of being healed instantaneously by the presiding spiritual master, or of receiving some form of psychotherapeutic (philosophical or psychological) succor from the powers-that-be. Insofar as their problems can be accommodated or resolved by the standard practices of the community—including brief audiences with the chief guru intended for personal guidance in practice but frequently utilized as a confessional or psychotherapeutic encounter—they may remain within or on the fringes of the community. But their reasons for being there are not entirely (or not at all) consonant with the *raison d'être* of the typical Buddhist sangha. There is a salient difference between sincerely seeking and assiduously practicing means to renounce attachments, relinquish suffering and transcend sorrow (on the one hand), and striving for deeper philosophical or psychological understanding *of* one's attachments, suffering, and sorrow (on the other). Buddhism amply accommodates seekers of the former kind; philosophical or psychological counseling amply accommodates strivers of the latter kind. Since seekers and strivers often tread crisscrossing paths, and end up as frequent guests in one another's camps, it would behoove psychologists and philosophers to work together within Buddhist contexts. Such work, I am given to understand, is already well underway at places like the Naropa Institute.

Finally, I must mention that a good many professional psychologists, who are neither clinical nor cognitive therapists, maintain active philosophical interests mostly because they are intelligent people, and also because they are cognizant of psychology's debt to philosophy. How many children express gratitude to their parents? Few or none do so when immature; many do so (and many too late), when mature. Parents who expect gratitude from their children are wise to do those things that might engender such expectations, but are foolish to harbor the expectations themselves. However, philosophical practice is a beneficiary of the unanticipated but nonetheless welcome gratitude of a growing number of psychologists, epitomized in the following unsolicited review of *Plato Not Prozac*, written by Dr. Kevin Vost (PsyD) and published in *Synapse*, the newsletter of Mensa's philosophy SIG (Special Interest Group):

> As absurd and anachronistic as it may seem to some, i.e., that today's philosophers take a break from word-parsing in academic journals and actually move and function in the world (hey, what is this, Greece or Rome or something?), I personally applaud it. And I applaud it as a Doctor of Psychology (though admittedly, a teacher and researcher, and not a clinician).... I agree with Dr. Marinoff that in many cases distressed souls who seek counseling as they deal with life's problems could be better helped with ancient pearls of philosophical wisdom than with more recent scientific and pseudo-scientific practices such as self-absorbed psychoanalysis, superficial behavioral training, or assorted forms of psychological venting or navel-pondering. Philosophy should reemerge as a practical helping profession.

I quote Dr. Vost's piece to illustrate the appreciative and cooperative stance that one psychologist, representative of many, has cultivated toward philosophy in general and philosophical practice in particular. Dr. Vost's enlightened disposition, as contrasted with unenlightened sound-bytes offered by much less thoughtful and much more uninformed psychologists, serves as an ideal basis for renewed and enhanced dialogue between psychology and philosophy, and for mutual professional enrichment.

15.3. PHILOSOPHY

Philosophers themselves comprise the best of our friends, and the worst of our enemies. This is hardly surprising, and merits closer examination. If you were seeking an intelligent, informed, and interesting conversation, whether for idle speculation or serious deliberation, you could fare no better than to consult a philosopher. Then again, if you were seeking a bombastic, dogmatic or pedantic peroration, whether for auditioning the part of Lucky in *Waiting for Godot* or for illustrating the ultimate convolutions of untrammelled cogitation, you could fare no worse than to consult a philosopher.

Well-intentioned and good-hearted layfolk, perplexed and perturbed by the philosopher's perennially if not reflexively disputatious stance, fail perforce to grasp the fundamental instrument in the quintessential philosophical toolkit—namely, doubt. What an X-ray is to a physician, a precedent to a lawyer, and an article of faith to a priest, such is doubt to a philosopher. The philosopher's credo is: whatever cannot be called into question, must be called into question. A philosophical mind that ceases to inquire commences to expire. T. H. White reformulated the proposition in *The Once and Future King*: "Whatever isn't forbidden is compulsory." Thus, applied to our metier and meta-metier alike, it is compulsory that some philosophers engage in philosophical practice, equally compulsory that other philosophers doubt that this should be done, or doubt that it should be done in the ways in which it is done, and no less compulsory that still other philosophers doubt the doubters, and thereby defend philosophical practice indirectly, by repudiating its repudiators. Yet other philosophers may decline involvement in this debate altogether, and instead continue "word-parsing in academic journals."

Yet there is a salient distinction between the manner in which a philosopher doubts a received, intuitive, or sensible truth, and a brainwashed ideologue deconstructs it. Take the time-honored equation, one plus one equals two. Nearly all my philosophy 101 students believe it to be self-evidently true, and some become quite concerned when I show them how to mount a skeptical attack on ostensible truisms, let alone tautologies. Though reliablism often saves the day,[5] a healthy doubt can still linger among those with the imagination to conceive that, while some partially specifiable state of affairs may conspire to convince us wholly of the consistency of our rules of inference and hence of the veracity of our deductive methods, yet some unaccessible meta-reality may in meta-fact repudiate consistency and vitiate verity. For all we know, one plus one really equals three; the Cartesian demon is banished to the wings, but not expelled from the theater, by mere "common sense." To insist that we can "prove" that one plus one equals two begs serious questions about what constitutes a deductive "proof." Answers invariably invoke truth-preserving rules of inference, which only beg deeper and ultimately intractable questions about what constitutes "truth" itself. Here one encounters a veritable zoo of philosophical theories of truth, in which no particular specimen reigns supreme and no taxonomy establishes unequivocal primacy. There is no infallible meta-theory of truth that allows us to settle the question of which theory of truth best explains what we mean when we assert a truth. Thus, although I believe wholeheartedly and single-mindedly that one plus one equals two, and moreover know how to prove it true,[6] I also doubt fervently that I possess anything like a metaphysically adequate explanation of *why* it is true, an ontologically adequate conception of *what* is true, and an epistemically adequate account of what *makes* it true. A philosopher can balance his checkbook every month, yet spend—or squander—lifetimes pondering these questions.

Contrast this traditional classical approach with a radical postmodern one: recall (from Chapter 8) the deconstructed girl in one of my philosopher's forums who would not assert that she had two arms, and who (when pressed) would not assert that one plus one equals two. Her problem was that she had been brainwashed by the postmodern catechism that truth is a "social construct"—a convenient fiction employed solely for political purposes; and allegedly, to "oppress" various races, classes, and genders. Hence, this poor creature dared not assert that one plus one equals two, lest she become a tool of the postmodern equivalent of Running-Dog Yankee Imperialism, and offend some Stone Age tribe's cherished belief—which by its mere putative existence weighs as heavily as any other on the zero-gravity scales of postmodern epistemology—that one plus one equals three or, in case they don't count higher than one, equals infinity or is undefined. That our civilization pumps water, splits atoms, generates power, paves roads, builds bridges, erects skyscrapers, flies aircraft, launches spacecraft, and sends e-mail is not denied by this girl; but she has not been educated to understand that all of these functions depend explicitly on the soundness of the proposition that one plus one equals two, and nothing else. Although philosophers have yet to reach agreement on deeper questions concerning its truth, yet mathematicians, scientists, and engineers can do wonderful things by assuming its truth, by extending the system that produces like truths, and by applying these truths to truly magnificent endeavors. But our civilization has lately allowed its intellectual and scientific heritage to become trivialized, politicized, denigrated, demonized, and ultimately entrusted to the care of noble savages like this girl who, left to her own devices, literally could not reinvent the wheel, whose circumference must be precisely *pi* times its diameter, and everywhere equidistant from its center—and nothing else no matter who is offended—if it is to be round.

Now, if analytic philosophy cannot find out the plain truth about plain truth (which plainly it cannot), and if what precious little reliable knowledge we possess is to be extirpated in the *Fair New World*[7] of social constructivism (which clearly it is), then philosophical practice inherits the role, with civilization itself as the client, of reinstating common sense and eliminating common nonsense. I point this out to illustrate both the unrelenting perversity of the human world and the unremitting absurdity of philosophers themselves, in the service of defending my claim that philosophers are both the best friends and the worst enemies of philosophical practice. Given that Bertrand Russell coauthored a masterwork that grounded arithmetic in deductive logic (and along the way proved that one plus one equals two), but was denied employment at The City College of New York owing to his then-unpopular views on marriage;[8] and given that Richard Rorty has authored works that deny objective truth, whose social implications are a recipe for a descent into savagery, yet who is one of the most popular philosophers of our New (Stone) Age, we can appreciate that whatever philosophers might say about philosophical practice itself would have to be taken with several tons, not grains, of salt.

So how do philosophers themselves obstruct or oppose philosophical practice? Let me count the ways. These include—but are not restricted to—coffeehouse mentality, sophistry, fraud, ambivalence, concealing personal problems behind philosophical facades, academic vanity, and fear of change or appearance of inadequacy.

COFFEEHOUSE MENTALITY

As we saw in Chapter 6, the expressions "coffeehouse opening" and "coffeehouse player" refer to chess. A "coffeehouse opening" means an unorthodox but ultimately untenable opening game used successfully by an amateur player against other amateur players who succumb to its novelty, but which fails against professionals owing to its intrinsic weaknesses, which professionals know how to expose and exploit. A "coffeehouse player" is simply a good amateur player, able to ambush other amateurs by the use of coffeehouse openings and similar stratagems, but whose understanding of the game is not of a professional calibre. *Mutatis mutandis*, the term "coffeehouse philosopher" applies in the same way to amateur philosophical practitioners. Not everyone can be a mathematician, physician, or engineer, because not everyone can understand mathematics, medicine, or engineering at a professional level. Balancing your household budget does not make you a mathematician; taking two aspirins for your headache does not make you a physician; assembling a prefabricated bookshelf does not make you an engineer. However, philosophical practice is based on the premise that nonprofessional philosophers can, with some assistance from professionals, articulate and apply their own philosophies of life. To that extent, amateur philosophers are indeed philosophers. The key question is: who renders such assistance? In some coffeehouses, it is likely that amateurs will encounter nothing but other amateurs, which can result in the blind leading the blind.

While not every professionally trained philosopher is willing or able to moderate a philosopher's cafe, not everyone who moderates a philosopher's cafe is a professionally trained philosopher. This makes no difference if one attends a philosopher's cafe for pure entertainment, but if its primary purpose is diversion, recreation, or amusement, then why incorporate philosophy at all? But if a philosopher's cafe provides primarily a philosophical encounter, then the moderator should be primarily a philosopher.

Marc Sautet pioneered this form of encounter, the "café-philo," in Paris, in his celebrated *Café des Phares*. Before becoming a café proprietor, Sautet was formerly a philosophy professor, who imported some academic expertise and rigor into his informal public transactions. Although he became famous in France as a populist of philosophy, he also became infamous for the same reasons—that is, the academicians disowned him. Thus even the French Revolution, with its sanguinary elimination of the *ancien régime*, failed to kill off the idea of aristocracy. By returning philosophy to "the people," Sautet was disowned by the academic "nobility" as a traitor to "aristocratic" (i.e., institutionalized) philosophy. Note that one can betray only a group to which one once belonged. Following Sautet's example, which was well-received in the public sector,—France is after all a quintessential coffeehouse culture— hundreds of philosopher's cafés opened in Paris and throughout the country. However, there were not hundreds of Marc Sautets to be moderators and proprietors. Although one can scarcely walk into a café in France without tripping over a philosopher or interrupting an impassioned philosophical debate, not all moderators of café-philos are academically trained or even autodidactically competent philosophers. Many are simply opportunists, or political activists, capitalizing on an obvious fad. Some such opportunists from abroad "trained" with Sautet, and brought his methods to their respective homelands, including America. In both France and the United States, I have met coffeehouse philosophers from Sautet's tradition who (unlike Sautet himself) have minimalist philosophical backgrounds. Whereas French academic philosophers branded Sautet merely as a traitor, they view coffeehouse philosophers in a much dimmer light: as rabble. And some of them are indeed rabble-rousers; bawdier even than Rabelais himself. In America, where aristocrats are fashioned of money instead of nobility, where intellectual elitism is frowned on as a vice of excessive thought, where it is un-American not to be rabble or not to be immediately descended therefrom, and where rabble-rousing is a perfectly respectable occupation, such charges would be politically unpopular. So in America, we find coffeehouse philosophers as well as APPA-Certified philosophical practitioners moderating philosopher's cafes. The distinction between them is twofold. First, the APPA-Certified practitioners are schooled in academic philosophy and, increasingly, trained in Nelsonian Socratic dialogue, and hence understand not only the fundamental philosophical issues that impel the group's members, but also the dialogical forces that influence the group's dynamic. Coffeehouse philosophers take little or no cognizance of these matters. Second, the APPA-Certified practitioners understand that informal group facilitation (which is the APPA terminology for such events) is but a tip of the iceberg of philosophical practice. For coffeehouse philosophers, the café-philo is the sum total of philosophical practice.

At their worst, coffeehouse philosophers trivialize and idiosyncratize the profession of philosophical practice, just as coffeehouse openings trivialize and idiosyncratize the game of chess. Small wonder that some coffeehouse philosophers, whose graduate "Philosophy" degrees, if any, are often in Education, are unhappy about the regularization of philosophical practice. For them, APPA Certification marks an "invidious distinction" between professionals and amateurs. Most Americans, although firmly anti-elitist, are also strongly pro-professional. They care enough at least to exercise a choice between consorting with an amateur or a professional. Insofar as the APPA makes that choice plainer, the American public is grateful. By the same token, one expects and encounters a degree of animosity, if not downright hostility, from the coffeehouse philosophers. These are part of the transaction costs of professionalism.

This issue has nothing to do with money; it has to do with philosophical competence. There are professional facilitators with PhDs in philosophy but without academic affiliations, such as Gale Prawda in Paris, who earn their livings facilitating groups. I have moderated a monthly "Philosopher's Forum" in a Manhattan bookstore for four years, but because I have an income for my academic affiliation and from other modes of practice, I run the Forum as a public service. That Gale and I are both philosophically qualified to render this service is significant; that one of us accepts money for it while the other doesn't is irrelevant to the issue of competence.

SOPHISTRY

The Sophists have an undeservedly bad name. Whereas "sophistry" almost always bears pejorative connotations, "sophisticated" is almost always laudatory. Needless to say, they share a common etymology. Given that variations on the same term can be used to praise or condemn, the term itself is potentially meaningless, and must be contextualized to be understood. The word "sophist" originally connoted an "expert" in the most generic sense (just as "theraps" meant "attendant"), and, in that sense, today's *Yellow Pages* provide extensive listings of sophists. More particularly, the ancient sophists tended to be itinerant educators, and the most commonly sought-after educational expertise in the Hellenic polities of 400 BCE were rhetorical and oratorical skills. However, the marketing of such expertise eventually entailed instruction in the attack or defense of any political or ethical position whatsoever—irrespective of ethos or norms—in mere exchange for a fee. Thus, at first blush, the sophists appear guilty (if that is the appropriate word) of having trained the first generation of lawyers. Moreover, their willingness to earn money in this way was regarded as less-than-virtuous by the Socratics, for two interconnected reasons. Socrates famously accepted no money for the philosophical instruction he dispensed in the agora, ostensibly because he denied possessing explicit philosophical expertise. At the same time, he possessed sufficient implicit philosophical expertise to refute Protagoras' claims to knowledge of virtue, for which this leading sophist (at least until he encountered Socrates) derived a handsome income. Thereafter the post-Socratic mind became permanently infused with two propositions, which remain fixed in the Athenian mindscape even today, notwithstanding their repudiation by Aristotle himself: first, that virtue cannot be taught; and second, that anyone who accepts money for pretending to teach virtue is therefore vicious. Thus I am approached fairly regularly, after public lectures in America, by indignant Greeks who inform me that it is immoral to accept money for doing moral counseling or ethics consulting. I generally reply that it is also immoral for banks to be charging me compound interest on my mortgage, but since I am a better moralist than a stone-mason, I would rather be regarded as vicious in Athens than become homeless in New York. Not more to their culpability but rather less to their credit, the ancient sophists often relied unwittingly on flawed logic to further their arguments (again, in advance of Aristotle). This led to the second pejorative connotation of sophistry, namely, the employment of invalid techniques of argumentation.[9]

The first kind of charge has also been leveled at philosophical practitioners by certain philosophy professors themselves. One of them, at a foreign university, asserts that it is wicked not only to accept remuneration for philosophical counseling or consulting, but even to accept it for professing theoretical philosophy in the academy. Although he apparently earns his living in just this way, he insists that he cashes his paycheck solely on the basis of being a teacher, not a philosopher. Well and good, save that his sole "teaching" credential is his PhD in Philosophy—he is not a graduate of any teacher's college. This is the first, and regrettably not the last, example of accusations of sophistry of the first kind (i.e., accepting money for expertise in virtue) hurled at us by philosophers, who, in the act of so doing, become manifestly culpable of sophistry of the second kind (i.e., employing fallacious argumentation).

Roger Scruton is a well-known British philosopher and author who troubles very little to inform himself of facts before broadcasting half-baked opinions. Upon reading about my philosophical practice in the London papers, he immediately accused me of sophistry of the first kind, again committing in the process sophistry of the second kind. I quote his article below, and my dated but unpublished reply to it,[10] so that you can be the judge of who exactly is the sophist here.

The Times (London), 11 August 1997

Roger Scruton

The return of the sophist

... on the danger of philosophies sold from the shelf

The ancient Athenians, who roved far and wide in the Mediterranean, saw the variety and absurdity of man's religions. After centuries of successful trading, the local gods and festivals could no longer satisfy their religious need. Their spiritual hunger was exacerbated by the stress of city life, by the constant threat of destruction, and by the grim vision of totalitarian Sparta: the vision of Greeks living without light or grace or humour, as though the gods had withdrawn from their world.

Into the crowded space of Periclean Athens came the wandering teachers, selling their wisdom to the bewildered populace. Any charlatan could make a killing, if enough people believed in him. Men like Gorgias and Protagoras, who wandered from house to house demanding fees for their instruction, preyed on the gullibility of a people made anxious by war. To the young Plato, who observed their antics with outrage, these "sophists" were a threat to the very soul of Athens. One alone among them seemed worthy of attention, and that one, the great Socrates whom Plato immortalised in his dialogues, was not a sophist, but a true philosopher.

The philosopher, in Plato's characterisation, awakens the spirit of inquiry. He helps his listeners to discover the truth, and it is they who bring forth, under his catalysing influence, the answer to life's riddles. The philosopher is the midwife, and his duty is to help us to be what we are—free and rational beings, who lack nothing that is required to understand our condition. The sophist, by contrast, misleads us with cunning fallacies, takes advantage of our weakness, and offers himself as the solution to problems of which he himself is the cause.

There are many signs of the sophist, but principal among them are these: mumbo-jumbo, condescension and the taking of fees. The philosopher uses plain language, does not talk down to his audience, and never asks for payment. Such was Socrates, and in proposing him as an ideal, Plato defined the social status of the philosopher for centuries to come.

No one should doubt that sophistry is alive and well. Many of today's gurus are sophists: Derrida, Foucault, Heidegger, Lyotard, Rorty, to name but five. But those that are alive make their profits through the university system, giving lectures that pretend to be educational. The pre-Socratic practice, of offering private guidance to the bewildered and curing their troubles by squeezing their purse (a practice which creates a powerful motive to leave bewilderment behind), has been the monopoly until

recently of the psychoanalysts. But we have entered the post-modern era—
the era when beliefs and faiths are available off the shelf. More and more
people are turning to philosophy. And what is the use of guidance if it
cannot be packaged for the consumer, as the personal ointment to his
personal wound? Lou Marinoff, Professor of Philosophy at New York's City
College, has been first off the mark in exploiting the new cultural climate.
If philosophy is to be marketed successfully, then people must pay for it.
For people value goods according to the price required to obtain them, and
in a consumer culture only what is costly can console.

Professor Marinoff compares his goods favourably with those of the
psychotherapist. Discussing a recent case in which he treated a woman
haunted by her dead brother's spirit, he said: "Psychotherapists would say
she is recreating the guilt triggered by her brother's death. But it may be
possible, according to some belief systems, that there was something there.
I am there to help the client understand her belief system."

The remarks were reported in the *New York Observer*, and may not be
verbatim. But they tell us much about the professor's vision of his trade.
No longer does the philosopher guide us towards the truth, through awakening our inherent reasoning powers. He parades before us a catalogue of
"belief systems," helps us to identify our own among them, up-to-date.
And no doubt, in order to persuade the client that her money has been
well invested, the favoured "belief system" will be dressed up in suitable
mumbo-jumbo, and priced at a rate that will make it psychologically
necessary for the client to persuade herself that she is being cured.

Small wonder, then, that Professor Marinoff's wheeze is catching on, and
New York's psychotherapists are hurriedly lowering their fees in response
to the only competition they have had since the collapse of the old religions. The sophists are back with a vengeance, and are all the more to be
feared, in that they come disguised as philosophers. For, in this time of
helpless relativism and subjectivity, philosophy alone has stood against the
tide, reminding us that those crucial distinctions on which life depends—
between true and false, good and evil, right and wrong—are objective and
binding. Philosophy has until now spoken with the accents of the academy
and not with the voice of the fortune teller.

When Plato founded the first academy, and placed philosophy at the heart
of it, he did so in order to protect the precious store of knowledge from
the assaults of charlatans, to create a kind of temple to truth in the midst
of falsehood, and to marginalise the sophists who preyed on human confusion. Little did he suspect, however, that he was providing the sophist
with his ultimate disguise.

If you have actually read this far into the book, and not merely opened it
accidentally to this page, you already know how many light-years off-base are
Scruton's comments. Lest there be any doubt, here is my (heretofore unpublished) reply to Scruton:

To The Editor,

I am responding briefly but sharply to Roger Scruton's "The Return of the Sophist" (11 August), in which he libellously misrepresents my professional philosophical practice and draws utterly false inferences about my political inclinations.

On the first point: Mr. Scruton knows and is known to none of us in the international community of philosophical practitioners, has attended none of our conferences, has read none of our publications, has learned none of our history, and has talked with none of our clients. Thus, by the postmodern debasement of objective standards he rightly but ironically deplores, one might suppose him ideally qualified to pass judgment on our movement. In fact, droves of individual and corporate clients alike are finding the expertise and services of philosophical practitioners well worth the price. We have far more satisfied clients than rash critics, and far more rash critics than dissatisfied clients.

On the second point: there is no valid inference from the fact that someone markets legal, medical or psychological expertise to reliable knowledge of that person's political views. Lawyers, physicians and psychologists can be found who espouse every conceivable (and often inconceivable) political position. The same argument applies to us who market philosophical expertise. Some practitioners are social constructivists and deconstructionists; others—such as myself—their unrelenting ideological and political opponents. Were Mr. Scruton to read my third novel ("Fair New World"), which savagely satirizes political correctness and militant feminism, he would remove both feet from his mouth. "Fair New World" is so politically incorrect that no major publisher has yet shown the courage to re-issue it. I am Derrida's and Rorty's worst nightmares, not their political bed-fellows.

In sum, I stand squarely against those who stand against realism and reason. We are so few, and our foes so many, that we ought not rake one another with careless friendly fire. I do concur with Mr. Scruton's critique of sophistry. But I would counsel him to read some of my works, both philosophical and political, instead of attempting to divine my thoughts from tertiary sources. And I would counsel Her Majesty not to knight Sir Roger just yet, given his proclivity for tilting at windmills.

Sincerely, Lou Marinoff

My final example of sophistry committed by accusatory philosophers comes from a well-known anarchist within the movement, whose pronouncements are infamous for their fanaticism and surrealism alike. As we saw in Chapter 9, she publicly called the ASPCP Board "Nazis" because we instituted standards of certification. Further, she publicly claimed that the proposed Diaz Bill in New York State (then to license, now to certify philosophical practitioners) would infringe her civil liberties in the State of Israel. When it was pointed out to her that these are independent sovereign governments, she replied that she is a "citizen of the world" and that "all governments are the same." The foregoing utterances were made in Germany, whose citizens have particularly compelling reasons to assert that all governments are *not* the same. Hence the Germans within earshot simply walked away, shaking their heads in disbelief. Stridently opposed to the medical profession in its entirety, and virulently opposed to all psychiatric drugs, this philosopher seizes on the equivocation of the term "psychotherapy" and denounces all philosophers who would co-operate with the medical establishment.

By now my animating point should be clear: since philosophical practice can attract criticism from such a rainbow coalition of sophists, two of whom claim to be philosophical practitioners themselves, then it is clear both that philosophical practice has truly "arrived," and that philosophers themselves are potentially our worst enemies.

FRAUD

Several kinds of fraud have been perpetrated by people calling themselves "philosophical practitioners." While none of these frauds has apparently wrought significant harm to clients (which would have resulted in publicized lawsuits), some have nonetheless brought our nascent profession into disrepute. As we have seen, given that the profession is unregulated, some fraudulence and con-artistry may inadvertently help us politically, by making legislators and consumers disaffected with consequences of the lack of regulation.

The primary kind of fraud that one encounters is committed by persons who call themselves "philosophical counselors," usually without adequate credentials in philosophy, and occasionally without adequate counseling expertise. Since the profession is completely unregulated, and in the consequent absence even of state certification measures to distinguish "certified philosophical counselors" from the rest, there is no *prima facie* way for consumers to know precisely what the appellation "philosophical counselor" means. Again, that is why the ASPCP took pains to develop professional certification standards and a code of ethics, and why the APPA took pains to implement them. When consumers visit the APPA's website and consult its Directory of Certified Practitioners, they can be reasonably sure that those listed are at least minimally trained (if not very experienced) in both philosophy and counseling. Of practitioners not minimally trained but nonetheless free to misrepresent themselves, by far the most frequent frauds are people with education degrees—typically philosophy of education—who call themselves academically accredited "philosophers."

Again bear in mind that a PhD in X-ology means "Doctor of Philosophy in X-ology"; it does not necessarily imply any knowledge whatsoever of philosophy per se. In our unhappy experience, quite a few people have set up shop as philosophical practitioners, who rather quickly betray an acute lack of philosophical erudition and sophistication, and over time a chronic inability to conform to a code of professional ethical behavior. Such persons sometimes turn out to have degrees in education, not philosophy. Some psychologists are also jumping on this bandwagon. Licensed by states to call themselves "psychological counselors," they can quite legally call themselves "philosophical counselors" too, without necessarily knowing anything about philosophy. The fraudulence is plain. It is my contention that no member of the public should be obliged to ask someone who calls himself a "philosophical counselor" whether he actually has a degree in philosophy. Given this state of affairs, *caveat emptor* indeed.

AMBIVALENCE

A species of ambivalence has been aired publicly by a well-known British author, Alain de Botton. Botton is an intelligent and sensitive man of letters who has published acclaimed books elaborating his independent discovery that philosophical ideas have therapeutic value. He has only recently become known to Americans, after his *Consolations of Philosophy* finally came into print in the U.S.A. Botton's book was clearly a threat to the eternal downward spiral of American literary culture—its very title embodies the off-putting four-syllable word "Philosophy"—so it took Botton several years to find an American publisher willing to bring out a potential best-seller that wasn't some knocked-off trivialization of last year's knocked-off trivialization of triviality, or of knock-offery.

While Botton celebrates how philosophy can help people, he also attacks philosophical counseling. Confused? You should be. I was ambushed by Botton on BBC radio several years ago, and that ambush was knocked-off in a subsequent BBC television production. Botton's puzzling thesis is that, while philosophical ideas can definitely be helpful to people in certain kinds of situations, philosophers themselves should not be providing counsel. If one asked Botton where philosophical ideas originate, he might admit they come from philosophers. But since he apparently prefers to glean advice from dead philosophers only, he seems to think that live ones should not offer counseling services—presumably, until they are likewise deceased. I cannot say whether Botton's noetic necrophilia extends to other art-forms as well: does he attend plays only of dead playwrights, view exhibitions only of dead painters, listen to recordings only of dead musicians, and vote only for dead politicians? At any rate, Botton is both a potential friend of philosophical practice, and its actual foe; an intriguing study in contradiction.

CONCEALING PERSONAL PROBLEMS BEHIND PHILOSOPHICAL FACADES

This is a very tricky issue indeed, because it situates certain people and their problems on largely nonexistent maps. As I have pointed out, one can study philosophy of psychology and philosophy of psychiatry, but there is not yet a school of psychology of philosophy or psychiatry of philosophy.

Under existing conditions for the definition of new disorders in the DSM, namely, the "science by democracy" currently practiced by the American Psychiatric Association, it is feasible for psychiatrists to "vote in" a disorder characterized by the following signs: sedulous verbosity and verbal bellicosity, vanity bordering on egotism, habitual dogmatism, love of erudition and argumentation, ritual publication, excessive pondering of profound matters, and so forth. This would be called "philosophical personality disorder." While prophets, poets, painters, and philosophers are often quite "mad" in the sense that they inhabit worlds intangible and inconceivable to the so-called "bourgeoisie"—who require religions and DSMs alike to circumscribe behaviors compatible with the persistence of commodious society, whose immediate collective goals are to lead a comfortable life and breed the next generation of consumers—the enduring works of prophets, poets, painters, and philosophers utterly transcend bourgeois aspirations, along with their religious moral norms, psychiatric disorders, and other devices for distinguishing acceptable from unacceptable behaviors. While the foursome of Isaiah, Whitman, Gaugin, and Nietzsche would not play a particularly productive round of golf, and would not be terribly helpful around the boardroom table or especially tolerable around the office, without their transcendent works of prophecy, poetry, art, and apostasy the corporation could not function either. Why? Because between the interstices of the soullessness, tedium, drabness, and conformism that constitute the ethos of the successful institution at its worst, the best of the workers imagine that they too are prophets, poets, painters, and philosophers. Deprived of imagination, they could not work well. Deprived of art, they could not imagine well. Deprived of madmen, they could not have good art. So much for psychiatry of philosophy, among other arts. Philosophers could also return the compliment, and draw up a short list of signs for "psychiatric personality disorder," but that would hardly find a home in the DSM.

The psychology of philosophy, however, is quite another matter. As long as people can remain functional in life—or, come to that, control their dysfunctionalities—without harming or threatening harm to others, then "diagnosing" them with this or that "personality disorder" entails little or no practical consequence. Thus psychologists who passionately disagree over political or ideological issues may come to accuse one another of having psychological problems. Even if true, this may not necessarily impair their professional functions. Just as surgeons may require surgery, psychiatrists may require psychiatry, psychologists may require psychotherapy, and philosophers may require philosophical counseling. None of this is inherently stigmatic, or inimical to the professional practice of a beneficiary of co-professional services. When we start mixing and matching professional modalities, however, the question becomes more interesting. As human beings, philosophers are far from immune from medical, psychiatric, and psychological problems. Such problems do not necessarily impair, and may even enhance, their functionality as philosophers.

But what about philosophical counselors? Are philosophers with evident problems fit to counsel others? Sometimes they are. In psychotherapy, it turns out that there is no negative correlation between a counselor's personal problems and his ability to counsel others. Professional counselors can usually do their jobs, while keeping their personal problems aside. This is a virtue of professionalism. However, insofar as such problems rarely emerge in the context of counselor–client relations, they more frequently find avenues of expression intra-professional relations. Thus the field of philosophical practice can become a ground of contention for philosophers with serious psychological problems, as well as for pseudo-philosophical practitioners whose primary psychological problem is the persistent delusion that they are philosophical practitioners. It may be that the very worst enemies of philosophical practice are philosophers with psychological problems, but until the psychology of philosophy itself becomes a grounded endeavor, it will be difficult to give a satisfactory or simply other-than-anecdotal account of just what this assertion means. Thus I will eschew revisiting the anecdotes.

ACADEMIC VANITY, FEAR OF CHANGE OR APPEARANCE OF INADEQUACY

One vice encouraged by academic life is the proprietariness of ideas; another is the use of ideas to occupy and hold noetic ground—as an army would occupy and hold a fort. Thus some academic (qua purely theoretical) philosophers come to believe that they "own" philosophy, and that their corpus of like-minded (i.e., like-trained and like-biased) colleagues deservedly control and regulate the flow of ideas within the discipline. This plays out as a quasi-Darwinian struggle between dominant and emergent or competing schools of thought (or thoughtlessness) in the humanities, and between dominant and emergent or competing paradigms in the sciences.[11] As academics exercise proprietariness over their schools of thought and their paradigms, and insofar as such proprietariness feeds vanity and other human foibles, new schools of thought and novel paradigms will always meet with resistance, and even with hostility or acrimony. This is healthy in one sense, as it can lead to wholesome debate and the winnowing of inviable schools or paradigms. It is merely a passing irony that the dominant school in humanities today became dominant by pretending to repudiate dominance itself.

Analytic philosophy, which remains in the stronghold of the Anglo-American philosophical fortress, has been (unsuccessfully) fending off continental-ism for some time. The two schools were content to occupy individual departments in sometimes spiteful but mostly peaceful coexistence. Then came applied ethics and feminism, and on their heels a host of postmodern influences, which analytic philosophers (in principle) had to resist, and which continental philosophers (in principle) had to endorse. The conflict over these is ongoing in the American academy. It plays out institutionally on levels personal, departmental, divisional, and administrative; and professionally in the evolutionary and sometimes ineluctably sordid politics of the Canadian and American Philosophical Associations.

Along comes philosophical practice, which cuts across these perpetual conflicts at an entirely different angle, and in so doing identifies a novel axis along which conflicting forces can be aligned, and defines a new plane in which battles can be fought. To legitimize itself as a profession, philosophical practice must establish itself in the Academy. To accomplish this, it must successfully contend against established forces. There will be much initial resistance from purely academic philosophers, who will dislike philosophical practice basically because they know nothing about it—"I don't like it because I haven't tried it." Eventually, however, at least in America, the iron laws of economics will prevail, even in philosophy departments.

The APPA receives a steady stream of requests from philosophy students at all levels, enrolled in institutions in America and around the world. They want to earn higher degrees (MAs or PhDs) in philosophical practice. Not unreasonably, they ask "What university offers such programs?" and we are obliged to answer, "At present, none; but we are working hard to establish them." And that is the truth. At this writing, I am optimistic that a graduate program in Philosophical Practice will be soon be established in an American university. I regard the establishment of a such a program, followed by the rapid proliferation of like programs, as an inevitability. The APPA has the template, the faculty, the credibility, and the constituency to bring this off, and so we shall—notwithstanding anticipated resistance from purely academic philosophers, who will oppose the rightness of our cause for all the wrong reasons, which, behind the smoke and mirrors of committees and procedures, amount to academic vanity, fear of change or appearance of inadequacy. Our cause, however, will prevail—because at bottom America is a nation grounded in business, and we have reached a critical juncture at which, whatever else it means, philosophy means business too.

NOTES

1. Besides many books by Szasz and Breggin, see also B. Eakman, *Cloning of the American Mind: Eradicating Morality Through Education* (Lafayette, LA: Huntington House, 1998). Eakman combines a brilliantly researched expose of insidious and entrenched erosions of the American education system with an appalling ignorance of and Christian coalition-style hostility toward Freud, Zen, the 1960s, and bumper-stickers lacking the word "Jesus." See also B. Wiseman, *Psychiatry—The Ultimate Betrayal* (Los Angeles: Freedom Publishing, 1995). Although written by a scientologist for scientologists, it is well-researched, and contains many graphic examples of psychiatry's heinous excesses and abuses. Parts of it should be required reading for medical students.

2. E.g., see Szasz (1984, *passim*).

3. See Eakman (1998, *passim*).

4. This was uttered *verbatim*, on national television, by a former President of the American Psychological Association.

5. For a convincing attack on Cartesian skepticism, see, e.g., M. Levin, "Demons, Possibility and Evidence," *Nous*, 34, 2000, 422–440.

6. E.g., see B. Russell and A. Whitehead, *Principia Mathematica* (Cambridge: Cambridge University Press, 1910–13).

7. I refer again to my third novel, and will probably keep doing so until you read it.

8. We will revisit this in Chapter 17, and afford a few details and footnotes. Fifty years later, Russell's views on marriage would scarcely merit attention in America, and he would be considered a moral reactionary, not a heretic, at City College.

9. See also L. Marinoff, "Inculcating Virtue in Philosophical Practice," *Journal of Philosophy in the Contemporary World*, 7, Fall 2000b, in press.

10. I submitted but later retracted the reply, in exchange for better publicity.

11. Thomas Kuhn discussed this in his celebrated essay, *The Structure of Scientific Revolutions* (Chicago: University of Chicago Press, 1975), which unfortunately provided fodder for deconstructing science instead of merely reinterpreting its history via the meta-paradigm of paradigm shifts.

CHAPTER 16

National, International, and Inter-Professional Relations

16.1. National and International Relations
16.2. Interprofessional Relations

16.1. NATIONAL AND INTERNATIONAL RELATIONS

Most institutions (as opposed to institutes) are larger, more influential, and longer-lived than the people who found them and serve them. An institution can generally accomplish far more than an individual; even the most reclusive genius who happens to be a composer, painter, or writer needs institutions (i.e., orchestras, museums, publishers) to bring his works into the light of public awareness. I have known quite a few reclusive composers, painters, and writers, some of whom have even flirted with genius, every one of whom ardently desired to have his works performed, exhibited, or published, but not all of whom sufficiently grasped the workings of institutions to position themselves accordingly. Individuals create art; institutions proliferate it.

The same holds true of philosophical practice. While globalization is certainly making national political barriers more permeable to economic and therefore also to cultural interchange, nation-states themselves are hardly relinquishing their respective political identities. In fact, they are proliferating in order to express such identity. An obvious and natural way for philosophical practice to develop is therefore through a national organization of practitioners. Several nations have already followed this path; many more are in the process of following it. As the ethos of each nation is unique, so each one's way of organizing philosophical practice differs. We have already and briefly presented examples of such organizations, in Germany, Holland, Israel, and America.

Beyond these, other nations have formed, or are forming, national organizations; for example, in Britain, Canada, France, Finland, Israel, Italy, Norway, and Slovakia. The APPA has been happy to help facilitate contact among members of such communities of interest, as well as between new and established ones, without interfering in the internal development or organizational politics of such communities. The APPA's organizational template—including our constitution, articles of incorporation, by-laws, operating procedures, certification standards, code of professional ethics, membership categories, along with other structures and functions—is on public view on our website. The "anatomy" of the APPA is no secret. Just as we have learned from older organizations, and adapted some of their features, so newer organizations can learn from us, and adapt some of ours. It is also unproblematic for eligible practitioners in other countries to become APPA-certified; our credential need not bear upon their organizational politics.

Thus far, international relations among national groups have been characterized mostly by cooperation and respect, which themselves appear predicated on a single principle: noninterference. Since the sovereignty of each national association is mostly respected by the others, and since no national association attempts to intrude on the territory of another, there is an overall absence of noetic warfare. This makes for a highly cooperative and mutually beneficial atmosphere of cultural exchange, whose summits of expression have been attained at the International Conferences on Philosophical Practice to date. The First International (Vancouver, 1994), the Second International (Leusden, 1996), the Third International (New York, 1997), the Fourth International (Bergisch Gladbach, 1998), and the Fifth International (Oxford, 1999) have served as gathering points for the global community of practitioners, reporting points on the development of philosophical practice, and reference points for the advancement of the movement generally. The Sixth International will take place (or will have taken place, by the time you read this) in Oslo in 2001.

Since each national organization is ineluctably conditioned by the ethos of its respective nation-state, there have naturally been political tensions too, which are experienced as weak echoes of much stronger historical and political forces. For example, in 1998, the German Society for Philosophical Practice changed its name to the "International Society for Philosophical Practice." This did not happen without opposition from some of the German members themselves, who understood (correctly) that this might be perceived as a recrudescence of imperialistic ambition. As well, although several other national organizations enjoy international memberships, none had arrogated to itself that titular prerogative. In response, I co-founded (with Ernesto Spinelli, then Chair of the Society for Existential Analysis) the Anglo-American Alliance for Philosophical Practice, and lately see a new phenomenon on the international horizon; or rather, the echo of an old one—namely, a competition between European and American influence in the world of philosophical practice. Just as with politics and economics, we may reencounter rivalry between the Old and New Worlds, this time remanifesting itself in the noetic arena of philosophical practice.

But thus far the voices of all national organizations are heard in the international agora, and the APPA certainly welcomes a proliferation of such organizations. On their worst behavior, philosophers can be irascible, abrasive, antisocial, or even misanthropic individuals. Such temperaments do not conduce to a viable philosophical practice. By contrast, and on their best behavior, professional philosophical practitioners are rational, ethical, and philanthropic exemplars of mutual respect and inter-organizational cooperation.

16.2. INTERPROFESSIONAL RELATIONS

Our relations with other professions, particularly counseling and consulting professions, are potentially and similarly characterized by mutual respect and potential inter-organizational cooperation. The ongoing result of such relations is highly educational for the professionals involved, as well as highly advantageous for the beneficiaries for their (and our) services.

Now that the flames of the initial media controversy (ignited and fanned, as usual, by the media itself) have died down, and now that most sensible people realize that philosophical practitioners are not seeking to replace psychiatrists, psychologists, lawyers, or priests—rather, seeking only to provide an appropriate range of services consistent with our expertise and consumers' needs—we can get on with the important interprofessional tasks that require completion. The organizational developments, professional trainings, academic programs, and political initiatives whose planning and implementation figure largely in the day-to-day activities of myself and my colleagues in this movement are driven not solely by our understanding of what could be done and determination of what should be done; they also depend vitally upon our willingness and ability to communicate our ideas to co-professionals in established fields, to appeal to their philosophical sensibilities, to minister to their philosophical needs, and to satisfy some approximation of their philosophical ideals. By doing these things, we settle their (healthy) skepticism about what we philosophers concretely offer, and we earn their (helpful) respect as co-professionals.

I do not suppose for an instant that philosophical practitioners will be universally well-regarded or ubiquitously well-accepted by other professionals. In the first place, there is no preexisting, uniform worldview among any association of professionals, which would entail acceptance or rejection of philosophical practice across the board. Every professional association is riven by its own disputes, divided by its own schisms, conflicted by its own factions. We philosophical practitioners should expect to be championed or demonized indirectly, to fulfill the aspirations or further the ambitions of individuals, as well as the agendas of groups, already extant within a given profession.

As far as that goes is far enough. Those inclined to defame us cannot impede us, while those enlightened to embrace us can thereby advance themselves. The APPA Directors have become cognizant of enormous opportunities for alliance with other professional associations in the U.S.A., and possibly also abroad. Our mandate, as always, is educational, and we aspire to establish regular if not permanent missions to various APAs: the American Psychiatric Association, American Psychological Association, and American Philosophical Association to begin with. For now, a last word concerning each aforementioned APA is in order.

Philosophical practitioners have a natural basis for alliance with enlightened psychiatrists. Since there is a philosophy of psychiatry but no psychiatry of philosophy, they ignore us to their impoverishment and possibly detriment. (I am not speaking now of giving bioethics courses to medical students.) By entering into dialogue with psychiatrists, both by elucidating philosophical case studies and inviting psychiatric commentary, and by elucidating psychiatric case studies and inviting philosophical commentary, we will mutually enrich our respective professional practices and ultimately provide consumers with more comprehensive and more appropriate services. The APPA is currently designing professional development courses for psychiatrists. Once we begin to offer them, our main problem will be to satisfy the demand. We are also planning a panel presentation at an annual meeting of the American Psychiatric Association, but keep deferring it because we simply have too many things do so. But at least I am stating these intentions, to emphasize my sincerity and their importance.

Likewise, philosophical practitioners also have a natural basis for alliance with enlightened psychologists. *Mutatis mutandis*, I repeat the catechism: since there is a philosophy of psychology but no psychology of philosophy, they too ignore us to their impoverishment and possibly detriment. By entering into dialogue with psychologists, both by elucidating philosophical case studies and inviting psychological commentary, and by elucidating psychological case studies and inviting philosophical commentary, we will mutually enrich our respective professional practices and ultimately provide consumers with more comprehensive and more appropriate services. The APPA is likewise designing professional development courses for psychologists. Once we begin to offer them, our main problem again will be to satisfy the demand. We are also planning a panel presentation at an annual meeting of the American Psychological Association, but keep deferring it because we simply have too many things do so. But at least I am stating these intentions, to emphasize my sincerity and their importance.

There is, however, a salient distinction between our interprofessional relations with psychiatrists on the one hand, and with psychologists on the other. Aspects of this distinction were elaborated in Chapters 5 and 15 in particular, but we can summarize it here. Psychiatry is a branch of medicine, and therefore of biological (i.e., natural) science. Its neuroscientific understanding of the human being continues to improve, and that modest verisimilitude heralds an ongoing refinement of psychopharmacological interventions. While abuses of psychiatry continue owing to the perennial corruptions of power, the understanding of neurochemistry and its effect on human mood and behavior becomes increasingly sophisticated. The political and economic (as well as the professional and ethical) implications of such refinement are also matters of relevance to philosophical practitioners at the consulting level. However, the stabilization or enhancement of human mood, and the restoration or amelioration of human of functionality, via the ingestion of prescribed drugs, now confronts the successfully-treated patient with a spectrum of philosophical problems (e.g., issues of meaning, value and purpose) which he or she hitherto did not have the luxury of contemplating. Where psychiatry leaves off, philosophy can begin.

But the division of labor between psychology and philosophy is not so clean, even in tidy hypothetical form. Since philosophy originally incorporated psychology, then gave rise to it via noetic parthenogenesis, their relationship has always been intellectually incestuous. Branches of psychology not rooted in natural science are social science at best—and therefore dubious science from the outset. Much of counseling psychology is pseudoscientific reification, and amounts to no more than suspect social intervention. This is the opposite of verisimilitude; instead of gradually approaching truth, it rapidly approaches nonsense. To preserve the parallelism of our educational mission with respect to psychology, it can be asserted that in one general way philosophy does begin where psychology leaves off, and that is with the emotionally mature subject.

Peter Koestenbaum illustrates it thus, in his commendable treatise on the philosophical practice of greatness:

> Attempts to live out greatness inevitably summon resistances. The resistances to greatness ... fall into three categories. First are the *psychodynamic* resistances, the unfinished childhood business, the neurotic behavior. These are modes of coping appropriate to the different reality of an earlier age. They are atavisms, residues from long ago, encrusted in the soul's perceptions and in the body's behavior patterns. They must be shed, and not—what is usual—exaggerated. A good example is dependency, the unwillingness to take personal responsibility. Children are taken care of; adults take care of themselves.[1]

Insofar as counseling psychology is concerned with subjects who cannot help but be governed chiefly by their emotions—or subjects who have not found anyone else to talk to—and insofar as it fosters dependency of the subject on the counselor, psychology nurtures and possibly prolongs the childish aspects of man. Perforce the emotionally immature and intellectually dormant adult talks to a psychologist because he is overcome by the world, whereas the emotionally mature and intellectually active adult talks to a philosopher because he has overcome himself, and now requires precepts to govern his actions in the world—as opposed to consolation in the wake of the world's actions on him. In this sense it can be reasserted, *mutatis mutandis*, that where psychology leaves off, philosophy begins.

But there is another sense in which philosophy is not psychology's successor; rather, its scourge. Consider this from Alex Howard:

> Eventually I came to the conclusion that the psychology that could not withstand the interrogation from philosophy did not deserve to survive. Little, therefore, was left of the psychology I had learned after the philosophy I had been taught had rolled over it. A great deal of contemporary psychology seemed alarmingly ignorant of social and cultural history. It made assumptions about identity, purpose and methodology without considering the basis of these assumptions and what alternatives existed. It begged too many questions. It presupposed a body of knowledge, skill and a capacity for objectivity that it did not possess. It *professed* to a range of professional services that it could not in fact provide.[2]

Psychology in this sense requires reeducation from philosophy, and the lessons are twofold. First, many psychologists need to acquire critical thinking skills and as much logic as they can imbibe—deductive, inductive, and ampliative—in order to avoid the question-begging and circular argumentation that plagues their mentation. They also need to learn some fundamentals of ontology, epistemology and philosophy of science (especially the Duhem–Quine thesis) if they are to Occamize the facile reifications and glib assumptions with which their discipline, in its most sophomoric manifestations, is rife. Second, as Howard points out, they need large-scale historical and philosophical orientations to this being called "man," whose psyche they purport to study. Here the general noetic decline of the West, manifest technologically through supplantation of the written tradition by a visual one, and manifest pedagogically through sublime educational theories springing from ridiculous radical politics, has made psychology a torchbearer for barbarism, and an unwitting exemplar of all that is wrong with the very conception of "social science." Whereas medical science is demonstrably verisimilitudinous, too much of social science is simply egregious.

Optimistically, philosophical practitioners can help repair breaches in this social scientific dam, by offering orientation trainings to psychologists. Pessimistically, we can merely stick our philosophical fingers into a few psychological dikes, and briefly stem the inevitable flood-tide. Since I am an empiricist, I am willing to conduct the experiment, come what may. While "psychologizing" is what psychologists do *sui generis*, and do for a living, a philosophical practitioner accused of "psychologizing" is committing a fundamental affront to reason.[3] The proper education of psychologists would entail some understanding of this distinction.

Finally, philosophical practitioners also have a natural basis for alliance with enlightened academic philosophers. As I have claimed from the beginning, philosophy as construed in the contemporary academy is largely a theoretical exercise of mind, full of ideas about ideas about ideas (... *ad infinitum*) but empty of practical application to life's problems and processes. There are many virtues associated with having ideas and developing coherent systems of thought, and those who excel at leading lives consecrated to philosophical theory—or, as the case may be, at leading theoretical philosophical lives—should be trained and encouraged to do so. However, the existence of an inner academic sphere of such theoretical pursuits should not and does not negate or contradict the growth of an outer concentric sphere of philosophical practice, which has theory at its core but application on its surface. In fact, the inner potentiates the outer, and the outer reflects the inner. The two form complements of a greater whole, properly called "philosophy."

The APPA is willing to work with the APA (in this case, the American Philosophical Association) to further opportunities for professional philosophers and students of philosophy alike, who harbor interests in philosophical practice. As the demand for our services grows, not just from clients, but also from aspiring practitioners, the APPA faculty will grow, and with it the availability of professional training programs for MAs and PhDs in Philosophy, who already know more than enough theory, but who next require guidance in its applications. The APPA aims to see gainfully and constructively employed at least as many philosophers outside the academy as are currently employed—not always gainfully or constructively—within it. Notwithstanding the copious qualities that make philosophers outstanding recluses, rebels, or reprobates; notwithstanding the pettiness, vindictiveness, and myopic egotism that institutional life too often exacerbates even in its most rational charges; and notwithstanding the unrelenting ideological conflicts, vituperative social factions and unchecked descents into political folly that philosophers—as members of *homo politicus*—also fall heir or prey to, the APA has done a magnificent job of remaining intact as an umbrella organization able to concert such noetic cacophony. What the APA constructively accomplishes for theorists, the APPA aspires to accomplish for practitioners. Cooperation between the two complementary organizations will symbiotically further the respective aims of both the theoretical and the practical professions.

NOTES

1. Koestenbaum (1991, p. 55).

2. A. Howard, *Philosophy for Counseling and Psychotherapy: Pythagoras to Postmodernism* (London: Macmillan, 2000), p. viii.

3. See D. Jopling, "First Do No Harm: Over-Philosophizing and Pseudo-Philosophizing in Philosophical Counseling," *Inquiry*, 3, Spring 1998, 100–112.

CHAPTER 17

Making and Breaking News

17.1. Parting Shots

17.2. *Plato not Prozac* Goes Global

17.3. Surf and Turf at City College: Making
       Waves and Defending Territory

17.4. Philosophy and the World
       Economic Forum

17.5. Last Word

17.1. PARTING SHOTS

Philosophical practice is in its infancy, and is therefore experiencing a period of rapid growth, development, and learning. The globalizing world, which is both our parent and our client, is thus far enamored of its progeny *cum* practitioner, and thus pays increasing attentions to it. We are neither a fad nor a trend, but a movement. This book has endeavored to clarify what moves, what motivates such movement, and who moves with it. Since this is a movement of philosophers and not psychics, precisely where it is moving to is not always clear to us movers, nor need it be. Progress in our case is the journey, not the destination. As we move, we continue to gather the strength to do worthwhile yet seemingly unprecedented things, and thus (among other things) to make news. The news-making furthers our movement and increases our strength, thus enabling the doing of more worthwhile yet seemingly unprecedented things, and the consequent making of more news. This is a fortuitous instance of a positive amplification feedback loop.

As this book goes to press, I have a final opportunity to acquaint you with various items of breaking news. By the time you will have read these words, that news will naturally be old hat, and thus consigned either to history en route to oblivion, or else to oblivion straightaway. However, at this writing it's all news to me, and in that spirit I pass it on to you.

I have selected three newsworthy items for your delectation. They are: first, the growing international appetite for *Plato Not Prozac*, and what it portends for philosophical practice; second, the CCNY philosophical counseling project and the larger opportunity created by opposition to it; third, the inclusion of philosophical practice at the 2001 Annual Meeting of the World Economic Forum in Davos.

17.2. *PLATO NOT PROZAC* GOES GLOBAL

Less than two years have elapsed, at this writing, since the initial publication of *Plato Not Prozac* (August 1999). It is currently going into twenty foreign-language editions, including the major European, South American, and Asian tongues. It became an instant best-seller in Spain last August (2000), and has since become a best-seller throughout Latin America as well. I have done promotional work in Spain and Mexico, and will shortly do more such work in Argentina, Colombia, Chile, and perhaps countries too—as well as in Taiwan and Mainland China next month (April 2001). To my astonishment, *Plato Not Prozac* was the #1 best-selling book at the 2000 Latin book fair in Guadalajara, outselling Spanish-language editions of Harry Potter, Stephen King's novels, and other world-class titles. While *Plato Not Prozac* is unlikely to become a best-seller in every language or country in which it appears, it is appearing in enough languages and countries to be both indicative of a potential global market for philosophical practice, and stimulative of an actual one.

I am not, nor do I seek to be, the sole beneficiary of *Plato Not Prozac*'s success. Nor am I referring to its publisher in this regard, compared with whom I am but a minor beneficiary. The book was conceived to spearhead the philosophical practice movement itself, and it is demonstrably both a sharp and a long-handled spear. It contains four appendices, which provide resource materials that readers have evidently found useful. First, there is condensed information on five dozen or so of history's leading philosophers. Second, there are contact data for the APPA and foreign national organizations for philosophical practice. Third, there is a Directory (both national and international) of APPA-Certified Practitioners. Fourth, there is a select bibliography on philosophical practice. The APPA and its Certified Practitioners have been and continue to be significant beneficiaries of their respective "billboarding" in these appendices, which obviously offer several kinds of follow-up opportunities for readers who, having finished the book, wish to do more with philosophical practice than merely read about it.

Amazingly enough, however, a substantial proportion of foreign editors have thus far taken gross liberties with these appendices, liberties which range from omitting them altogether to mutilating them in arbitrary or capricious ways. Imagine going into a bakery and seeing a display of cakes wanting icing, or of cakes only half-iced. One would conclude that the baker was remiss in his culinary art. The first time this happened to my book, I was surprised and angered, until I realized that foreign editors need education, too—some more than others. Many had simply failed to grasp the larger cultural implications of *Plato Not Prozac*, and had therefore not understood that the book is an advertisement for a movement. They erroneously viewed its appendices as excess—rather than essential—baggage.

I quickly ascertained that any such unapproved changes to the appendices constituted breach of contract. Foreign publishers had licensed the manuscript entire, and were not legally at liberty to delete its parts. If I so insisted, the publishers in question could theoretically forfeit the right to sell these "unauthorized" editions, which we could justifiably demand that they recall from the stores and destroy. In practice, however, such a ruling from a New York State court would be difficult if not impossible to enforce worldwide, and would also be bad for business. Having understood this much, I contented myself with a sharply worded memo from my foreign rights manager, which percolated to all the foreign subagents, and through them to the foreign editors, reminding them of their legal obligations and informing them of the appendices' purposes. Whereupon most of these editors did precisely whatever they had intended to do in the first instance: some published the appendices *in toto*; others mutilated them according to caprice; others omitted them entirely.

This irritation is short-term only. Foreign readers who want to learn more about philosophical practice will surely do so, either because of or in spite of their local editions of *Plato Not Prozac*. The movement has a huge media platform and a growing presence in cyberspace. Anyone who surfs the worldwide web can swiftly find data galore.

Meanwhile, the APPA currently has members in 38 states and 20 foreign countries. This diversity of membership is steadily increasing. Driven by demand, we have just replicated our core literature in Spanish, and plan to do so in other languages as well. We are being invited to hold certification training programs in foreign countries as well, and we intend to do so wherever and whenever it is feasible.

This synopsis should persuade you at least of the potential for our movement's global growth. As a Wall Street trend-spotter and client of mine said presciently of the movement, several years ago, "This thing has legs." At that time, I hardly knew what he meant. I know slightly better now.

17.3. SURF AND TURF AT CITY COLLEGE: MAKING WAVES AND DEFENDING TERRITORY

The City College of New York recently rejuvenated its Wellness Center, and is currently offering a reasonable menu of services—that is, for an impoverished, public, inner-city university—to its students. The Vice President of Student Affairs, under whose aegis the Wellness Center operates, invited the APPA to provide philosophical counseling services as well. Subsequent meetings with the Director of the Center were fruitful in that she agreed to integrate our service into her menu, but she could not afford to offer a sufficient reimbursement to the philosophical counselors. Like me, they would gladly do some counseling for free, but not for peanuts. I was fortunate to secure a $30,000 grant from the Diana Foundation, along with matching funds from the Student Affairs Office, to subsidize the counselors' services. Merle Hoffman, the Diana Foundation's President, said in her letter of award, "On the cusp of this new century, philosophical counseling appears to offer both a theoretical and practical paradigm for expanding treatment and healing modalities. I wish you, the APPA, and CCNY the best of luck in its development and implementation." We then recruited a roster of local APPA-Certified counselors, developed an intake form and referral mechanisms, prepared a script to advertise the service, a press release to publicize it, and so forth. In the press release, the Vice President of Student Affairs said, "This will allow CCNY students to get *pro bono* philosophical counseling and, at the same time, provide an opportunity for a three-year study of the effectiveness of APPA's counselors." *The New York Times* education editor had assigned feature coverage, and the journalist was waiting to interview some beneficiaries of the service. The final hurdle—or so I thought in the early autumn of 2000—was to find office space for the sessions themselves. Office space is difficult to come by at CCNY, but not impossible.

Events soon took a different and much more interesting turn. Unknown to me, several CCNY students had already approached the Wellness Center, asking for philosophical counseling. These students had not known about our initiative, which was not yet advertised, but they knew about *Plato Not Prozac*, were aware that I was a philosophy professor on campus, and possibly found out that I had previously counseled some students *pro bono* on my research protocol. In any case, they made a reasonable if not prescient inference, namely that they could apply for philosophical counseling via the Wellness Center. This they did, and one of them apparently mentioned it to another member of CCNY Faculty. This faculty member happened to be married to a clinical psychologist at CCNY, and I am told that they were both scandalized by the idea of philosophical counseling. Apparently they complained vociferously to their Dean (Social Science), and their Dean complained to mine (Humanities). I was summoned to my Dean's office one fine November morning, and was subjected to a most unusual—or, if you like *Alice in Wonderland*, curious—tête-à-tête. Peer through the academic looking glass, and imagine a hypothetical conversation which begins like this:

Hypothetical Dean: "You act as though everyone were in favor of what you are doing. But some people are very much opposed to it."

Such a hypothetical overture would seem to imply that just because "some people" oppose what I do, therefore I shouldn't be doing it. At the same time, it would all be innuendo. Such a hypothetical accuser would neither name any specific complainant, nor state any actual ground of complaint. It would be as though he had said to me "Some people don't like that necktie you're wearing"—the implication being that I should therefore remove it at once, and never be seen wearing it again.

Hypothetically, I would entertain a number of possible replies, and would conclude that none were adequate in the circumstances. Nature gave me a very good nose for injustice, and thus far such a meeting would have reeked of it. If Socrates' defense as recorded in the *Apology* didn't get him acquitted, there was little I could have said in my defense at this hypothetical trial. But the hypothetical Dean would need a response—if only so that he could deliver his next line, which he had hypothetically prepared. So I would resort to New York-style sarcasm, which also comes quite naturally to me.

My hypothetical response: "Some people don't like what I'm doing? Excuse me. Should I ritually disembowel myself now, or later?"

Our hypothetical conversation would have deteriorated from there, and I'll spare you the hypothetical remainder. Within forty-eight hours of this hypothetical conversation, I received an actual "cease-and-desist" order, signed by the Dean, but apparently emanating from the Provost and the Dean of Faculty Relations. It forbade me to do any philosophical counseling on the CCNY campus, pending the outcome of a legal review being undertaken by the office of the University Vice Chancellor for Legal Affairs. This order itself was logically vacuous; in fact, I couldn't comply with it, because no philosophical counseling was taking place on campus. The project at the Wellness Center hadn't started up yet, and my IRB research protocol was under renewal. The IRB renewal was being delayed by the same psychologist whom we encountered in Chapter 11, for the same reasons he had espoused to delay it before: namely, that in his opinion, philosophical counseling could cause psychological problems, and therefore put subjects at risk. In other words, thinking causes mental illness.

I consulted the APPA's legal and political advisors. On their advice, I ignored the campus buffoonery and initiated a genteel correspondence with the CUNY Deputy Counsel for Legal Affairs, who had been charged with undertaking the review. Behind my back, the CCNY Administration had sent her an apparently incomplete and conceivably prejudicial dossier on my research, the APPA, the Wellness Center project, and philosophical practice in general. The CUNY Deputy Counsel wrote me a plethora of pertinent questions, and requested all manner of supporting documentation. I furnished her with a dossier of answers and supporting documents in late December 2000, and there the matter rested for the time being.

Or so I thought. I then received a further memo from the Chair of the CCNY IRB's Human Subjects Committee, the good psychologist, who had learned of the aforementioned "cease and desist" order, and had swiftly seized upon it as a pretext to suspend his committee's renewal of my IRB research protocol. In the opinions of my academic and legal advisors, his suspension is unwarranted and blatantly illegal; it both infringes fundamental academic freedoms and flouts due process. So I made a further submission to the CUNY Deputy Counsel, and asked her to enlarge the scope of her review accordingly. I have received no reply to date.

To those of you unfamiliar with the fascinating and vacillating history of City College, I highly recommend James Traub's book, *City on a Hill* (1994). It chronicles everything from the halcyon years that produced a procession of future Nobel laureates to the immense credit of the institution, to the Open Admissions period that has engendered, among other things, a succession of embarrassing lawsuits to the immense discredit of the institution.[1] Traub's book was published the year I arrived at CCNY. When I leave, it may be time for a sequel. Meanwhile, my political and legal advisors are salivating. I am sure you can imagine why.

City College has not only produced more Nobel laureates than any other public university; it has also graduated more PhDs than any other public university save Berkeley, as well as a pantheon of remarkable contributors to the sciences and humanities, to professional and political life. Jonas Salk (inventor of the polio vaccine), Andrew Grove (CEO of Intel), Daniel Goldin (Director of NASA), and Colin Powell (former Head of the Joint Chiefs of Staff and current Secretary of State) are but a few examples of its illustrious alumni. CCNY's faculty has been equally renowned, including—in the humanities alone—the likes of Morris Cohen, Alfred Tarski, Eli Wiesel, and Bertrand Russell (whose appointment was infamously nullified by the New York Supreme Court).[2] Not for nothing has CCNY earned its moniker "The Harvard of the Proletariat."

During the storm precipitated by the politically orchestrated attack on Bertrand Russell's appointment at City College, accompanied by the zealous distortion of facts and the assassination of his character, a letter signed by some of America's leading academic lights warned that if the attack succeeded, "no American college or university is safe from inquisitional control by the enemies of free inquiry."[3] It did, and they aren't. Albert Einstein remarked:

> Great spirits have always found violent opposition from mediocrities. The latter cannot understand it when a man does not thoughtlessly submit to hereditary prejudices but honestly and courageously uses his intelligence.[4]

I remain in awe of many of my contemporary colleagues at CCNY. They comprise a faculty of world-class scholars and researchers, unfortunately and lately condemned to make bricks without straw, to toil under an administration often crassly and cavalierly bent on squandering their copious talents. The CCNY "old-timers" with whom I have conferred, many of them 30- or 40-year veterans of City College, have never seen dimmer administrative lights. And the dimness produced by this power-failure spreads coast-to-coast. I have heard time and again from participants in APPA Certification Training Programs that philosophical practice holds out to them the prospect of a breath of fresh air, a way of exercising their philosophical vocations free of the stultifying miasma of myopic despotism, bureaucratic incompetence, and internecine strife that comprises the workaday norm at so many colleges and universities. Plato long ago warned those clear of the cave not to reenter it, save at their peril.[5] But even his imagination might have been beggared by the wholesale relocation of his academy into his cave. After the debacle of the Somme, where the British Army's courageous rank and file was utterly wasted on the whims of its incompetent High Command, Ludendorff sadly but aptly described the British troops as "lions led by donkeys." This is also a fitting motto for some institutions of erstwhile higher education.

17.4. PHILOSOPHY AND THE WORLD
ECONOMIC FORUM

On a happier note, I have lately returned from the Magic Mountain—that is, from the 2001 Annual Meeting of the World Economic Forum in Davos.[6] Programmers at the WEF had followed some of my recent work with interest, and had initiated contact in May of 2000. Meetings at various functions in New York, Connecticut, and London led to my participation in the Davos program. It was a privilege and a pleasure to be part of the "Davos experience"; those five days were among the most exhilarating and memorable of my life, now in its fiftieth year. I would rate the experience as highly as falling in requited romantic love, cutting a record album, having a book published, winning an athletic championship, riding a superb motorcycle on a scenic road on a perfect day, or bringing the mind to rest. In the 1960s, we would have called it a "good trip."

For those of you unclear about or incognizant of the WEF, it was founded by Professor Klaus Schwab, an extraordinary man, some thirty years ago. Its mission is "to improve the state of the world." Based in Geneva, it organizes worldwide regional summits year-round, as well as the annual meeting in Davos. These meetings are attended by global business and political leaders, as well as by a cultural fellowship of scholars, artists, scientists, and social entrepreneurs. The common purpose of the functions I have attended thus far is to identify salient issues and address key problems in the main areas of global development and planetary management. If the United Nations is an embryonic world government, then the World Economic Forum is a nascent global Chamber of Commerce.

In Davos, Forum Fellows appear to serve two simultaneous purposes: education and entertainment. In contemporary American parlance, these two have become a singular concept, united in the grotesque neologism "edutainment." Nonetheless, CEOs and senior officers of the world's most powerful corporations, as well as political leaders and their ministers of state, are no less in need of both continuing education and content-rich entertainment than anyone else. But since such persons are themselves highly accomplished, and tend to be keenly intelligent as well as extremely busy and exceptionally responsible, they demand a quality of "edutainment" normally unobtainable via tabloid media, prime-time television, and similar circuses of *Pax Americana*, on the one hand, or via Continuing Education on the other. Davos admirably satisfies their requirements.

Overall, the participants at Davos 2001 manifested a healthy appetite for philosophical practice. I had the opportunity to conduct a workshop in Dilemma Training, to moderate a Café-Philo (both firsts for Davos), and to contribute philosophically to panels of various kinds—in the company of some very astute colleagues. Both business and political leaders expressed interest in the APPA, which may portend a heightened degree of involvement of philosophical practitioners in the global village. It is clear that the world cannot be improved without constructing a moral compass suitable to the age, and philosophical practice can certainly contribute centrally to that needful project.[7]

17.5. LAST WORD

My last word to you herein is one of cordial invitation. If you have read this far, then you have also endured my Jeremiads and stomached my bromides, which means you have both a robust noetic constitution and some strong affinity for philosophical practice. In that case, I enjoin you to involve yourself in the movement. Frankly, we can use all the help we can get. If philosophical practice is to become more than a seer's pipedream or a gambler's long-shot, and really begin to stretch its legs, then it requires many persons each speaking a few words and each doing a few deeds, as opposed to a few persons each speaking many words and doing many deeds. I saw Keith Richards on television the other night, lamenting that Bob Marley's death was also the death of Reggae music, so uniquely and completely was Marley identified with the idiom, and it with him. This does not happen—or at least, not overnight—to idioms that enjoy a profusion of talented creators, players, and patrons. Pragmatism has met a similar fate to Reggae; for while the ghosts of Peirce, James, and Dewey may haunt the groves of academe, yet they are powerless to exorcise the anti-pragmatic demons who have poisoned its wells. Assisted by able and astute colleagues, I am doing all I can to help institute the idiom and further the profession of philosophical practice. I trust that eager and capable hands await the passing of its luminous torches, that light the way from Plato's cave, reason's sleep and truth's demise.

NOTES

1. For example, both Leonard Jeffries and Michael Levin—who represent very different views—have sued and won.

2. For the original account of Russell's ordeal, see Russell (1957), *Appendix* by Paul Edwards, "How Bertrand Russell Was Prevented from Teaching Philosophy at the College of the City of New York," pp. 207–259. For a broader perspective, see A. Irvine, "Bertrand Russell and Academic Freedom," *Russell: the Journal of the Bertrand Russell Archives*, 16, 1996, 255–291. See also T. Weidlich, *Appointment Denied: The Inquisition of Bertrand Russell* (Amherst, MA: Prometheus, 2000).

3. Cited by Edwards, in Russell (1957, p. 214).

4. Ibid., p. 215.

5. "If they could lay hands on the man who was trying to set them free and lead them up, they would kill him." Plato, *Republic*, chap. 25.

6. T. Mann, *The Magic Mountain*, trans. J. Woods (New York: Vintage 1996; original work published 1924).

7. L. Marinoff, "The Ethics of Business and the Business of Ethics: Building a Moral Compass for the Global Village," *WorldLink, Magazine of the World Economic Forum*, January/February 2001, pp. 117–120.

References

Adler, M. (1965). *The conditions of philosophy: Its checkered past, its present disorder, and its future promise.* New York: Atheneum.

Arendt, H. (1977). *Eichmann in Jerusalem: A report of the banality of evil.* New York: Penguin.

Ayer, A. (1984). *Philosophy in the twentieth century,* London: Unwin.

Bagehot, W. (1964). *The English constitution.* London: C.A. Watts & Co. Ltd. (Original work published 1867.)

Barrett, W. (1962). *Irrational man.* Garden City, NY: Doubleday & Co.

Benbow, C. (1988). Sex differences in mathematical reasoning ability in intellectually talented preadolescents: Their nature, effects, and possible causes. *Behavioral and Brain Sciences, 11,* 169–182.

Bergson, H. (1915). *The meaning of the war (Life and matter in conflict).* London: T. Fisher Unwin.

Bhagavad-Gita (1969). Trans. S. Purohit. London: Faber & Faber.

Boele, D. (1998). The 'benefits' of a socratic dialogue, or, which results can we promise? *Inquiry, 17,* 48–70.

Brand, C. (1996). *The G factor: General intelligence and its implications.* New York: Wiley.

Breggin, P. (1991). *Toxic psychiatry.* New York: St. Martin's.

Buber, M. (1961). *Between man and man.* Trans. R. G. Smith. London: Fontana Library.

Buddha (1899). Brahma-Gala Sutta. In *Dialogues of the Buddha.* Trans. T. Rhys Davids. London: Henry Frowde.

Buddha (1980). *Dhammapada.* Trans. H. Kaviratna. Pasadena: Theosophical University Press.

Buddha (1981). *The Word of the Buddha.* Trans. Nyantiloka. Kandy, Sri Lanka: Buddhist Publication Society, Kandy.

Burgess, A. (1963). *A clockwork orange.* New York: Norton.

Cattell, R. (1937). *The fight for our national intelligence*. London: P.S. King & Son.

Churchland, P. (1986). *Neurophilosophy: Toward a unified science of the mind/brain*. Cambridge: MIT Press.

Cole, J., & Zuckerman, H. (1987). Marriage, motherhood and research performance in science. *Scientific American*, February, pp. 119–125.

Conquest, R. (1968). *The great terror*. London: MacMillan.

Damasio, A. (1994). *Descartes' error*. New York: Avon.

Danielson, P. (1992). *Artificial morality*. London: Routledge.

Danielson, P. (Ed.) (1998). *Modeling rational and moral agents*. Vancouver Cognitive Science Series. Oxford: Oxford University Press.

de Chardin, P. T. (1982). *The phenomenon of man*. Glasgow: William Collins & Sons. (Original work published 1955.)

Dennett, D. (1991). *Consciousness explained*. Boston: Little, Brown.

Drever, J. (1917). *Instinct in man*. Cambridge: Cambridge University Press.

Dutton, D. (Ed.). *Philosophy and literature*. "Bad writing contest." Archived at <http://www.cybereditions.com/aldaily/bwc.htm>.

Eakman, B. (1998). *Cloning of the American mind: Eradicating morality through education*. Lafayette, LA: Huntington House.

Epictetus. (1944). *Discourses* and *Enchiridion*. Trans. T. Higginson. Roslyn, NY: Walter J. Black.

Erasmus. (1917). *The complaint of peace* London: Headley Brothers. (Original work published 1517.)

Feyerabend, P. (1975). *Against method*. London: NLB.

Freud, S. (1955a). *Thoughts for the times on war and death*. In J. Strachey (Ed. and Trans.), *The standard edition of the complete psychological works of Sigmund Freud*, Vol. 14. London: Hogarth. (Original work published 1914—16.)

Freud, S. (1955b). *Civilization and its discontents*. In J. Strachey (Ed. and Trans.), *The standard edition of the complete psychological works of Sigmund Freud*, Vol. 21. London: Hogarth. (Original work published 1930.)

Furedy, J. (1997). Velvet totalitarianism on canadian campuses: Subverting effects on the teaching of, and research in, the discipline of psychology. *Canadian Psychology Abstracts*, November, *38*, 4.

Furedy, J. (2000). Velvet totalitarianism in British academia: The case of Chris Brand and Edinburgh University. *SAFS Newsletter*, April.

Gairdner, W. (1992). *The war against the family*. Toronto: Stoddart.

Geach, G., & Black, M. (Trans. and eds.) (1952). *Translations from the philosophical writings of Gottlob Frege*. Oxford: Blackwell.

Gibbon, E. (1946). *The decline and fall of the Roman Empire*. New York: Heritage.

Golman, D. (1995). *Emotional intelligence*. New York: Bantam.

Gould, S. (1981). *The mismeasure of man*. New York: Norton.

Grimes, P., & Uliana, R. (1998). *Philosophical midwifery*. Costa Mesa, CA: Hyparxis.

Gross, P., & Levitt, N. (1994). *Higher superstition*. Baltimore: Johns Hopkins University Press.

Haack, S. (1998). *Manifesto of a passionate moderate*. Chicago: University of Chicago Press.

Haeckel, E. (1916). *Eternity: World-war thoughts on life and death*. Trans. T. Selzer. New York: Truth Seeker.

Hammond, D. (Ed.) (1990). *Handbook of hypnotic suggestions and metaphors*. New York: Norton.

Hanks, P. (Ed.) (1979). *Collins dictionary of the English language*. London & Glasgow: William Collins & Sons.

Held, B. (1995). *Back to reality*. New York: Norton.

Held, B. (1999). *Stop smiling, start kvetching*. Brunswick, ME: Biddle.

Herrnstein, R., & Murray, C. (1994). *The bell curve*. New York: The Free Press.

Hersh, S. (1980). The counseling philosopher. *The Humanist*, May/June, pp. 32–33.

Hirsch, E., Kett, J., & Trefil, J. (Eds.) (1993). *The dictionary of cultural literacy*. Boston & New York: Houghton Mifflin.

Hobbes, T. (1992). *Leviathan*, Ed. R. Tuck. Cambridge: Cambridge University Press. (Original work published 1651.)

Howard, A. (2000). *Philosophy for counseling and psychotherapy: Pythagoras to postmodernism*. London: MacMillan.

Humphreys, C. (1983). *Karma and rebirth*. London: Curzon.

Inglis, B. (1976). *The opium war*. London: Hodder & Stoughton.

Institute for the Advancement of Philosophy for Children (ca. 1995). *Philosophy for children: A report of achievement*. Upper Montclair, NJ: Montclair State University.

Irvine, A. (1996). Jack and Jill and employment equity. *Dialogue*, *35*, 255–291.

Irvine, A. (1996). Bertrand Russell and academic freedom. *Russell: The Journal of the Bertrand Russell Archives*, *16*, 5–36.

Itard, J. (1972). *The wild boy of Aveyron*. Trans. E. Fawcett, P. Ayrton, and J. White. London: NLB.

James, W. (1956). *The will to believe, and other essays in popular philosophy*. New York: Dover. (Original work published 1897.)

James, W. (1974). *Pragmatism*. New York: New American Library. (Original work published 1907.)

Jopling, D. (1998). First do no harm: Over-philosophizing and pseudo-philosophizing in philosophical counseling. *Inquiry*, *3*, 100–112.

Jordan, D. (1907). *The human harvest*. Boston: American Unitarian Association.

Kesey, K. (1989). *One flew over the cuckoo's nest*. New York: New American Library. (Original work published 1963.)

Kirwan-Taylor, H. (1999). No brain, no gain. *Financial Times Magazine*, March, pp. 69–70.

Kleinfeld, J. (1999). Student performance: Males versus females. *The Public Interest*, *134*, 3–20.

Koestenbaum, P. (1991). *Leadership: The inner side of greatness.* San Francisco: Jossey-Bass.

Koestler, A. (1959). *The sleepwalkers.* London: Hutchinson & Co.

Korzybski, A. (1933). *Science and sanity.* Lancaster, PA: International Non-Aristotelian Library Publishing.

Kuczynski, A. (1997). Plato or Prozac? *New York Observer*, August 4, p. 17.

Kuhn, T. (1975). *The structure of scientific revolutions.* Chicago: University of Chicago Press.

Lahav, R. (1995). A conceptual framework for philosophical counseling: Worldview interpretation. In R. Lahav and M. Tillmanns (Eds.), *Essays on philosophical counseling.* Lanham, MD: University Press of America.

Lahav, R., & Tillmanns, M. (Eds.) (1995). *Essays on philosophical counseling.* Lanham, MD: University Press of America.

Lao Tzu (1959). *Tao te ching.* Trans. Ch'u Ta-Kao. London: George Allen & Unwin.

Levin, M. (2000). Demons, possibility and evidence. *Nous, 34*, 422–440.

Lipman, M., Sharp, A., & Oscanyan, F. (1986). *Philosophy in the classroom.* Philadelphia: Temple University Press.

Long, J. (1992). Measures of sex differences in scientific productivity. *Social Forces, 71*, 159–178.

Lubinski, D., & Benbow, C. (1992). Gender differences in abilities and preferences among the gifted: Implications for the math-science pipeline. *Current Directions in Psychological Science, 1*, 61–66.

Maccoby, E., & Jacklin, C. (1975). *The psychology of sex differences.* Stanford: Stanford University Press.

MacHamer, P. (Ed.) (1998). *The Cambridge companion to Galileo.* Cambridge: Cambridge University Press.

Malson, L. (1972). *Wolf children.* Trans. E. Fawcett, P. Ayrton, & J. White. London: NLB.

Mandell, R. (1977). *The professor game.* Garden City, NY: Doubleday.

Mann, T. (1996). *The magic mountain.* Trans. J. Woods. New York: Vintage. (Original work published 1924.)

Marinoff, L. (1987–88). *On human conflict*, unpublished manuscript.

Marinoff, L. (1990). The inapplicability of evolutionarily stable strategy to the prisoner's dilemma. *The British Journal for the Philosophy of Science, 41*, 461–472.

Marinoff, L. (1992a). *Strategic interaction in the prisoner's dilemma: A game theoretic dimension of conflict research.* Unpublished doctoral dissertation, University of London.

Marinoff, L. (1992b). Maximizing expected utilities in the prisoner's dilemma. *Journal of Conflict Resolution, 36*, 183–216.

Marinoff, L. (1993). Three pseudo-paradoxes in "quantum" decision theory: Apparent effects of observation on probability and utility. *Theory and Decision, 35*, 55–73.

Marinoff, L. [a.k.a. L. Tafler] (1994a). *Fair new world.* Vancouver: Backlash.

Marinoff, L. (1994b). Hobbes, Spinoza, Kant, highway robbery and game theory. *Australasian Journal of Philosophy*, 72(4), 445–462.

Marinoff, L. (1995). On the emergence of ethical counseling: Considerations and two case studies. In R. Lahav and M. Tillmanns (Eds.), *Essays on philosophical counseling* (pp. 171–191). Lanham, MD: University Press of America.

Marinoff, L. (1996a). A reply to Rapoport. *Theory and Decision*, 41, 157–164.

Marinoff, L. (1996b). How Braess' paradox solves Newcomb's problem: Not! *International Studies in the Philosophy of Science*, 10, 217–237.

Marinoff, L. (1998a). What philosophical counseling can't do. *Journal of Philosophy in the Contemporary World*, 5, 33–41.

Marinoff, L. (1998b). The failure of success: How exploiters are exploited in the prisoner's dilemma. In P. Danielson (Ed.), *Modeling rational and moral agents* (pp. 161–185). Vancouver Cognitive Science Series. Oxford: Oxford University Press.

Marinoff, L. (1999a). *Plato not Prozac: Applying philosophy to everyday problems.* New York: HarperCollins.

Marinoff, L. (1999b). On virtual liberty: Offense, harm and censorship in cyberspace. *Inquiry: Critical Thinking Across the Disciplines*, 18, 64–76.

Marinoff, L. (1999c). The tragedy of the coffeehouse: Costly riding, and how to avert it. *Journal of Conflict Resolution*, 43, 434–450.

Marinoff, L. (2000a). Equal opportunity versus employment equity. *Sexuality and Culture*, 4, 23–44.

Marinoff, L. (2000b). Inculcating virtue in philosophical practice. *Journal of Philosophy in the Contemporary World*, 7, in press.

Marinoff, L. (2001). The ethics of business and the business of ethics: Building a moral compass for the global village. *WorldLink*, January/February, pp. 117–120.

Milgram, S. (1974). *Obedience to authority: An experimental view.* New York: Harper & Row.

Mill, J. (1956). *On liberty.* New York: Macmillan. (Original work published 1859.)

Mintz, S. (1962). *The hunting of the leviathan.* Cambridge: Cambridge University Press.

Moore, G. (1959). *Principia ethica.* Cambridge: Cambridge University Press. (Original work published 1903.)

Mumford, L. (1956). *The transformations of man.* New York: Harper & Brothers.

Muncy, M. (Ed.) (1999). *The end of democracy?.* Dallas: Spence.

Nelson, L. (1949). *Socratic method and critical philosophy.* Trans. T. Brown III. New York: Dover.

Nussbaum, M. (1996). *The therapy of desire: Theory and practice in hellenistic ethics.* Princeton: Princeton University Press. (Original work published 1994.)

Orwell, G. (1946). Politics and the english language. *Horizon*, April.

Palmer, G. (1993). *The politics of breastfeeding.* London: Pandora.

Peck, M. S. (1980). *The road less travelled.* New York: Touchstone.

Penrose, R. (1989). *The emperor's new mind.* Oxford: Oxford University Press.

Plato (1895). *Crito*. In *Dialogues of Plato*. Trans. B. Jowett. Oxford: Oxford University Press.

Plato (1941). *Republic*. Trans. F. Cornford. London: Oxford University Press.

Plato (1987). *Thaetetus*. Trans. R. Waterfield. London: Penguin.

Popper, K. (1945). *The open society and its enemies*. Vol. 1: *The spell of Plato*. London: Routledge & Kegan Paul.

Popper, K. (1945). *The open society and its enemies*. Vol. 2: *The high tide of prophecy*. London: Routledge & Kegan Paul.

Raabe, P. (2000). *Philosophical counseling: Theory and practice*. Westport, CT: Praeger, Westport.

Rachels, J. (1999). *The elements of moral philosophy*. New York: McGraw-Hill. (Original work published 1993.)

Reisberg, L. (1998). Disparities grow in SAT scores of ethnic and racial groups. *The Chronicle of Higher Education*, 11 September, p. A42.

Robertson, G. (1886). *Hobbes*. Edinburgh: William Blackwood and Sons.

Rosenhan, D. (1975). On being sane in insane places. In T. Scheff (Ed.), *Labeling madness* (pp. 54–74). Englewood Cliffs, NJ: Prentice-Hall.

Rousseau, J. J. (1968). *The social contract* Harmondsworth: Penguin. (Original work published 1762.)

Rousseau, J. J. (1993). *Émile*. Trans. B. Foxley. London: Dent, and Rutland, VT: Tuttle. (Original work published 1762.)

Roy, J. (1984). *Hobbes and Freud*. Trans. T. Osler. Toronto: Canadian Philosophical Monographs.

Russell, B. (1930). *The conquest of happiness*. New York: Horace Liveright.

Russell, B. (1957). *Why I am not a Christian*. New York: Simon & Schuster.

Russell, B. (1961). *History of western philosophy*. London: Allen & Unwin. (Original work published 1946.)

Russell, B., & Whitehead, A. (1910–13). *Principia mathematica*. Cambridge: Cambridge University Press.

Russell, J. M. The philosopher as personal consultant. Archived at <http://www.members.aol.com/jmrussell/philosas.htm>.

Sapir, E. (1949). *Selected writings*. Ed. D. Mandelbaum. Berkeley: University of California Press.

Schiro, J. (Ed.) (2000). *Memos to the president—Management advice from the nation's top CEOs*. New York: Wiley.

Schneider, A. (1998). Why don't women publish as much as men? *The Chronicle of Higher Education*, 11 September, pp. A14–A16.

Schopenhauer, A. (1985). *Essays and aphorisms*. Trans. R. Hollingdale. Middlesex: Penguin.

Searle, J. (1980). Minds, brains and programs. In *The behavioral and brain sciences*, Vol. 3. Cambridge: Cambridge University Press.

Seneca, L. (1928). *Moral essays*. Trans. J. Basore. London: William Heinemann.

Seneca, L. (1969). *Letters from a stoic*. Trans. R. Campbell. Harmondsworth: Penguin.

Sharkey, P. (1986). When?—The philosophical revolution. *Contemporary Philosophy*, *11*(3).

Shirer, W. (1985). *The rise and fall of the Third Reich*. London: Book Club Associates. (Original work published 1959.)

Smith, D. (1995). Review of *Fair New World*. *Newsletter of the Society for Academic Freedom and Scholarship*, July.

Snow, C. (1964). *Corridors of power*. New York: Scribner.

Snow, C. (1993). *The two cultures and the scientific revolution*. The Rede Lecture, 1959. Cambridge: Cambridge University Press.

Sokal, A. (1996). Transgressing the boundaries: Toward a transformative hermeneutics of quantum gravity. *Social Text*, 46/47 (Spring/Summer), 217–252.

Spencer, H. (1969). *Principles of sociology* Ed. S. Andreski. London: MacMillan. (Original work published 1893–96.)

Stotsky, S. (2000). Pedagogical advocacy. *Academic Questions*, *13*, 27–38.

Szasz, Thomas S., Cybercenter for Liberty and Responsibility (1998). <http://www.ena-bling.org/ia/szasz/>.

Szasz, T. (1984). *The myth of mental illness: Foundations of a theory of personal conduct*. New York: HarperCollins. (Original work published 1961.)

Szasz, T. (1994). *Cruel compassion: Psychiatric control of society's unwanted*. New York: Wiley.

Tauber, A. (2000). *Confessions of a medicine man—An essay in popular philosophy*. Cambridge: MIT Press.

Thucydides (1985). *History of the Peloponnesian War*. Trans. R. Warner. Harmondsworth: Penguin.

Toynbee, A. (1963). *A study of history*. Abridged by D. Somervell. London: Oxford University Press.

Traub, J. (1994). *City on a hill*. New York: Addison Wesley.

Von Bonin, G. (1955–56). Toward an anthropology of the brain. *Annals of the New York Academy of Sciences*, *63*, 505–509.

Von Neumann, J., & Morgenstern, O. (1964). *Theory of games and economic behaviour*. New York: Wiley. (Original work published 1946.)

Wallraff, C. (1961). *Philosophical theory and psychological fact*. Tucson: The University of Arizona Press.

Wall Street Journal. Tuesday, 25 October 1995, p. B1.

Walzer, M. (1978). *Just and unjust wars*. London: Allen Lane.

Weidlich, T. (2000). *Appointment denied: The inquisition of Bertrand Russell*. Amherst, MA: Prometheus.

Whorf, B. (1956/1959). *Language, thought and reality: Selected writings of Benjamin Lee Whorf*. Ed. J. Carroll. Cambridge: Technology Press of MIT, 1956. New York: Wiley, 1959.

Wiseman, B. (1995). *Psychiatry—The ultimate betrayal*. Los Angeles: Freedom Publishing.

Wood, A. (1817). *Athenae oxonienses*. Ed. Philip Bliss. London: Rivington.

APPA Membership Information

MISSION

The APPA is a nonprofit educational corporation that encourages philosophical awareness and advocates leading the examined life. Philosophy can be practiced through personal action, client counseling, group facilitation, organizational consulting, or educational programs. APPA members apply philosophical systems, insights and methods to the management of human problems and the amelioration of human estates. APPA membership is open to all.

CERTIFIED MEMBERSHIPS

Certified Memberships are offered to experienced philosophical practitioners—client counselors, group facilitators, or organizational consultants—who meet APPA requirements. Certified Members are listed in the APPA Directory of Certified Practitioners, and are eligible for referrals and other professional benefits. Certified Members are bound by the APPA Code of Ethical Professional Practice, and are committed to regular professional development.

AFFILIATE MEMBERSHIPS

Affiliate Memberships are offered to recognized counseling or consulting professionals in other fields (e.g., medicine, psychiatry, psychology, social work, law) who wish to become identified and better acquainted with philosophical practice, but who do not necessarily seek APPA certification. Affiliate Members are listed in the Affiliate Directory, and are eligible to attend special events, meetings and workshops. Qualified Affiliates may become certified.

Adjunct Memberships

Adjunct Memberships are offered to holders of an earned MA, ABD, or PhD in Philosophy (or *Licensura* in Hispanic countries). Adjunct Members are eligible to attend APPA Certification Training Programs, the completion of which enables them to become Certified Members. Adjunct Members are also eligible to attend special events, meetings and workshops.

Auxiliary Memberships

Auxiliary Memberships are offered to friends and supporters of philosophical practice. The APPA Auxiliary welcomes all who wish to join in this capacity— including students, workers, or retired persons. No special qualifications are necessary, beyond an interest in leading an examined life. Auxiliary Members are eligible to attend special events, meetings, and workshops.

Key Memberships

Key Memberships are offered to all organizations (e.g., corporations, professional associations, governments) seeking to benefit or become beneficiaries of philosophical practice. Key Members are eligible for a range of philosophical services provided personally by the APPA President, Vice Presidents, and APPA Faculty. A *Prospectus* is available on request, and is also viewable on our website <www.appa.edu>.

CRITERIA OF MEMBERSHIP

The American Philosophical Practitioners Association is a not-for-profit educational corporation. It admits Certified, Affiliate, and Adjunct Members solely on the basis of their respective qualifications. It admits Auxiliary and Key Members solely on the basis of their interest in and support of philosophical practice. The APPA does not discriminate with respect to members or clients on the basis of nationality, race, ethnicity, sex, gender, age, religious belief, political persuasion, or other professionally or philosophically irrelevant criteria.

AFFILIATE, ADJUNCT, AUXILIARY AND KEY MEMBERS ARE ENTIRELY SELF-SELECTING

- Any recognized counseling or consulting professional may apply for Affiliate Membership.
- Any MA, *Licensura*, ABD, or PhD in philosophy may apply for Adjunct Membership.
- Any student, friend, or supporter of philosophical practice may apply for Auxiliary Membership.
- Any corporation, government, institution or professional association may apply for Key Membership.

CERTIFIED MEMBERSHIP

There are three ways to become a Certified Member of the APPA: by invitation, application, or training.

Invitation

In consultation with its Boards of Professional Examiners and its National or International Advisory Boards, the APPA may invite recognized or experienced philosophical practitioners to become Certified Members. Distinguished practitioners may be invited to join the APPA Faculty.

Application

Experienced philosophical practitioners of counseling, facilitation, or consulting who satisfy APPA requirements may apply to become Certified Members. For detailed application criteria, please see "Certification Standards" herein.

Training

The APPA trains Adjunct Members who seek certification as counselors, facilitators or consultants. The APPA is working to establish accredited University programs in philosophical practice. Currently, Adjunct Members and qualified Affiliate Members may attend APPA Certification Training Programs.

All APPA Members receive our newsletter, invitations to events, and other benefits. Details and secure online memberships are available via our website: <www.appa.edu>. To request an individual membership package, or a key membership prospectus, phone 212-650-7827, fax 212-650-7409, e-mail admin@appa.edu, or write APPA, The City College of New York, 137th Street at Convent Avenue, New York, NY 10031.

Directory of APPA-Certified Practitioners

Current to April 2001. For up-to-date listings, see our website, <www.appa.edu>.

SCOPES OF PRACTICE

Certified Members have demonstrated professional competency in the following scopes of practice.

- An **APPA Certified Counselor** is able to help individual clients, through techniques and skills of philosophical analysis and dialogue, to manage or resolve personal, logical, teleological, axiological, conceptual, existential, or ethical problems adversely affecting their lives; and to recognize problems outside the scope of philosophical counseling and make referrals to appropriate professionals.

- An APPA Certified Facilitator is able to moderate public philosophical discussion groups, and is familiar with philosophical principles of small and large group facilitation, conflict resolution, and the dynamics of consensual, adversarial, and formal group discussion formats (e.g., Nelsonian Socratic dialogue).

- An APPA Certified Consultant is able to render philosophical services to organizations by virtue of familiarity with philosophical principles of corporate structure, management and strategic planning, as well as familiarity with a range of philosophical skills and methodologies applicable to organizations.

UNITED STATES BY STATE

ALABAMA

James Morrow Jr.
1055 W. Morrow St.
Elba, AL 36323
tel: 334-897-6522
counselor

ARIZONA

Richard Dance
6632 East Palm Lane
Scottsdale, AZ 85257
tel: 480-945-6525
fax: 480-429-0737
e-mail: rdance@swlink.net
counselor

Robert Nagle
8075 E. Morgan Trail
Suite #1
Scottsdale, AZ 85258
tel: 480-649-8430
tel: 480-905-7325
fax: 480-969-5322
counselor

CALIFORNIA

Peter Atterton
1566 Missouri Street
San Diego, CA 92109
tel: 858-274-2977
e-mail: atterton@rohan.sdsu.edu
counselor

Wills Borman
2477 Highway 94
Dulzura, CA 91917
tel: 619-468-9693
wborman@mindspring.com
counselor

Harriet Chamberlain
1534 Scenic Avenue
Berkeley, CA 94708
tel: 510-548-9284
e-mail: think@flash.net
counselor, facilitator

Kyle Dupen
P.O. Box 1013
Moss Beach, CA 94038
tel: 650-728-5311
e-mail: kdupen@coastside.net
counselor

Sandra Garrison
758 S. 3rd Street
San Jose, CA 95112
tel: 650-937-2983
cell: 408-893-5952
e-mail: sandrag@netscape.com
counselor

Julie Grabel
Academy of Philosophical Midwifery
1011 Brioso Dr. #109
Costa Mesa, CA 92627
tel: 949-722-2206
fax: 949-722-2204
e-mail: julieg@deltanet.com
counselor

Pierre Grimes
Academy of Philosophical Midwifery
947 Capital
Costa Mesa, CA 92627
tel: 949-722-2206
fax: 949-722-2204
e-mail: pierreg@concentric.et
counselor

Sushma Hall
315 W. Radcliffe Drive
Claremont, CA 91711
tel: 909-626-2327
e-mail: sushmahall@hotmail.com
counselor

John Hanley Jr.
34341 Aukland Ct.
Fremont, CA 94555
tel: 510-792-7346
fax: 561-679-7769
e-mail: johnhanleyjr@msn.com
facilitator

James Heffernan
Department of Philosophy
University of the Pacific
Stockton, CA 95211
tel: 209-946-3094
e-mail: jheffernan@uop.edu
counselor

Gerald Hewitt
Department of Philosophy
University of the Pacific
Stockton, CA 92511
tel: 209-946-2282
e-mail: ghewitt@uop.edu
counselor

Lou Matz
Department of Philosophy
University of the Pacific
Stockton, CA 95211
tel: 209-946-3093
e-mail: lmatz@uop.edu
counselor

Jason Mierek
8831 Hillside St. #C
Oakland, CA 94605
tel: 510-777-0923
e-mail: jmierek@msn.com
counselor

Christopher McCullough
175 Bluxome St., #125
San Francisco, CA 94107
tel: 415-357-1456
e-mail: cmccull787@aol.com
counselor, facilitator

Paul Sharkey
819 West Avenue H-5
Los Angeles, CA 93534
tel: 661-726-0102
cell: 661-435-3077
fax: 661-726-0307
e-mail: pwsharkey@email.msn.com
counselor, facilitator, consultant

Regina Uliana
16152 Beach Blvd.
#200 East
Huntington Beach, CA 92647
tel: 714-841-0663
fax: 714-847-8685
e-mail: rlu@deltanet.com
counselor

Lawrence White
1345 Arch Street
Berkeley, CA 94708
tel: 510-845-0654
fax: 510-845-0655
e-mail: LWWHITEMD@aol.com
counselor

Eleanor Wittrup
Department of Philosophy
University of the Pacific
Stockton, CA 95211
tel: 209-946-3095
counselor

Kritika Yegnashankaran
tel: 650-654-5991
e-mail: kritika@stanfordalumni.org
counselor

Martin Young
1102 S. Ross Street
Santa Ana, CA 92707
tel: 714-569-9225
e-mail: mzyoung@uci.edu
counselor

COLORADO

Jeanette Crooks
1239 S. Iris Street
Lakewood, CO 80232
tel: 303-980-8346
e-mail: myrtlemaryj@aol.com
counselor

Alberto Hernandez
1112 N. Wahsatch, Apt. A
Colorado Springs, CO 80903
tel: 719-448-0337
e-mail:
   aherandez@coloradocollege.edu
counselor

DISTRICT OF COLUMBIA

Alicia Juarrero
4432 Volta Place NW
Washington, D.C. 20007
tel: 202-342-6128
fax: 202-342-5160
e-mail: ja83@umail.umd.edu
counselor

FLORIDA

Robert Beeson
1225 Osceola Dr.
Fort Myers, FL 33901
tel: 941-332-7788
fax: 941-332-8335
e-mail: rbsun@cyberstreet.com
counselor

Carl Colavito
The Biocultural Research Institute
7131 NW 14th Avenue
Gainesville, FL 32605
tel: 904-461-8804
fax: 352-332-9931
e-mail: encc@aug.com
counselor

Maria Colavito
The Biocultural Research Institute
7131 NW 14th Avenue
Gainesville, FL 32605
tel: 352-332-9930
fax: 352-332-9931
e-mail: diotima245@aol.com
counselor

Antonio T. de Nicolas
The Biocultural Research Institute
7131 NW 14th Avenue
Gainesville, FL 32605
tel: 352-332-9930
fax: 352-332-9931
e-mail: diotima245@aol.com
counselor

GEORGIA

Mark M. du Mas
2440 Peachtree Road NW
Number 25
Atlanta, GA 30305
tel: 404-949-9113
fax: 404-846-0081
e-mail: mmdumas@msn.com
counselor, consultant

ILLINOIS

Avner Baz
5555 N. Sheridan Road
Chicago, IL 60640
tel: 773-784-4728
e-mail: abaz2@uic.edu
counselor

F. Byron (Ron) Nahser
President & CEO
The Nahser Agency, Inc.
10 South Riverside Plaza
Suite 1830
Chicago, IL 60606
tel: 312-750-9220
fax: 312-845-9075
e-mail: fbnahser@nahser.com
consultant

MARYLAND

Sidney Rainey
P.O. Box 1451
Bethesda, MD 20827
tel: 505-983-7011
e-mail:
    sidneyrainey@earthlink.com
consultant

MISSOURI

David Hilditch
7439 Wayne Avenue
St. Louis, MO 63130
tel: 314-727-1675
e-mail: hilditch@wnr.com
counselor

MONTANA

Sean O'Brien
Davidson Honors Hall
University of Montana
Missoula, MT 59812
tel: 406-243-6140
counselor

NEVADA

Claude Gratton
Philosophy Department
University of Las Vegas at Nevada
4505 Maryland Parkway, Box
455028
Las Vegas, NV 89154
tel: 702-895-4333
voice mail: 702-897-3727
e-mail: grattonc@nevada.edu
counselor

NEW JERSEY

Peter Dlugos
355 Lincoln Ave., Apt. 1C
Cliffside Park, NJ 07010
tel: 201-943-8098
e-mail: pdlugos@bergen.cc.nj.us
e-mail: pdlugos@aol.com
counselor, facilitator

Vaughana Feary
37 Parker Drive
Morris Plains, NJ 07950
tel/fax: 973-984-6692
e-mail: VFeary@aol.com
counselor, facilitator, consultant

Amy Hannon
2 River Bend Road
Clinton, NJ 08809
tel: 908-735-0728
e-mail: ardea@csnet.net
counselor

Jean Mechanic
1365 North Avenue, Apt. 9D
Elizabeth, NJ 07208
tel: 908-351-9605
e-mail: mechanicdr@aol.com
counselor

Charles Ottinger
206 Davis Station Rd., Box 98
Imlaystown, NJ 08526
tel: 609-259-4187
e-mail: cfottinger@earthlink.net
counselor

New Mexico

Jennifer Goldman
619 Don Felix St., Apt. B
Santa Fe, NM 87501
tel: 505-982-9189
counselor

New York

Barbara Cutney
782 West End Avenue, #81
New York, NY 10025
tel: 212-865-3828
counselor, consultant

Michael Davidovits
Psychiatry, Mt. Sinai Medical Center
Box 1228
New York, NY 10029
tel: 212-241-6881
e-mail: michael.davi-
dovits@mountsinai.org
counselor

Andrew Gluck
392 Central Park West, #8C
New York, NY 10025
tel: 212-316-2810
fax: 212-316-4982
e-mail: andy_gluck@msn.com
consultant

Edward Grippe
117 Lakeside Drive
Pawling, NY 12564
tel: 914-855-0992
fax: 914-855-3997
e-mail: ejgphil@aol.com
counselor

Michael Grosso
26 Little Brooklyn Road
Warwick, NY 10990
tel: 914-258-4283
e-mail: mgrosso@warwick.net
counselor

Rony Guldmann
279 E 44th St., Apt. 4J
New York, NY 10017
tel: 387-922-1393
e-mail: ronyguldmann@hotmail.com
counselor

George Hole
291 Beard Avenue
Buffalo, NY 14214
tel: 716-832-6644
e-mail: holeg@buffalostate.edu
counselor, consultant

Craig Irvine
220 Manhattan Ave., Apt. 5V
New York, NY 10025
tel: 212-305-0980
e-mail:
  irvinec@cpmc3.cpmc.columbia.edu
counselor

Lou Marinoff
Philosophy Department
The City College of New York
137th Street at Convent Avenue
New York, NY 10031
tel: 212-650-7647
fax: 212-650-7409
e-mail: marinoff@mindspring.com
counselor, facilitator, consultant

Bruce Matthews
531 West 26th Street, Loft 3R
New York, NY 10001
tel: 212-239-9223
e-mail: philobam@interport.net
counselor

Christopher Michaelson
PricewaterhouseCoopers, LLP
1177 Avenue of the Americas
New York, NY 10036
tel: 212-597-3844
fax: 212-596-8988
e-mail:
  christopher.michaelson@us.pwcglobal.com
consultant

Annselm Morpurgo
6 Union Street
Sag Harbor, NY 11963
tel: 516-725-1414
e-mail: morpurgo@msn.com
counselor

William Murnion
P.O. Box 23, Bellvale NY 10912
tel: 845-986-5406
e-mail: wmurnion@warwick.net
counselor

Elizabeth Randol
17 Mather Street, #2F
Binghamton, NY 13905
tel: 607-771-0475
e-mail: lizard2471@aol.com
consultant

Bernard Roy
396 Third Avenue, #3N
New York, NY 10016
tel: 212-686-3285
fax: 212-387-1728
e-mail:
  bernard_roy@baruch.cuny.edu
counselor, facilitator

Charles Sarnacki
199 Flat Rock Road
Lake George, NY 12845
tel: 518-668-5397
e-mail: csarnacki@hotmail.com
counselor

Mehul Shah
66 Dogwood Lane
Irvington, NY 10533
tel: 914-591-7488
e-mail: mshah1967@aol.com
counselor, facilitator, consultant

Wayne Shelton
P.O. Box 407
North Chatham, NY 12132
tel: 518-262-6423
fax: 518-262-6856
e-mail: sheltow@mail.amc.edu
counselor, consultant

Peter Simpson
College of Staten Island
2800 Victory Blvd. 2N
Staten Island, NY 10314
tel: 718-982-2902
fax: 718-982-2888
e-mail:
  simpson@postbox.csi.cuny.edu
    Manhattan address:
      425 W. 24th St. #3C
      New York, NY 10011
      tel: 212-633-9366
counselor

Nicholas Tornatore
585 Bay Ridge PKWY
Brooklyn, NY 11209
tel: 718-745-2911 or
  212-535-3939
counselor

NORTH CAROLINA

Andrew Koch
625 Lower Rush Branch Road
Sugar Grove, NC 28679
tel: 828-297-4548
e-mail: kocham@appstate.edu

OHIO

Lynn Levey
1959 Fulton Place
Cleveland, OH 44113
tel: 216-651-0009
e-mail: lynnlevey@aol.com
counselor

PENNSYLVANIA

Eric Hoffman
131 Cynwyd Road
Bala Cynwyd, PA 19004
tel: 215-419-6542
e-mail: eeworkshop@home.com
counselor, facilitator, consultant

Craig Munns
Central Penn. College
College Hill Rd.
Summerdale, PA 17025
tel: 717-728-2244
e-mail:
    craigmunns@centralpenn.edu
counselor

G. Steven Neeley
900 Powell Ave.
Cresson, PA 16630
tel: 814-472-3393
counselor

David Wolf
P.O. Box 162
Lake Como, PA 18437
tel: 570-798-2235
e-mail: socratix@epix.net
counselor

TENNESSEE

Ross Reed
3778 Friar Tuck Road
Memphis, TN 38111
tel: 901-458-8112
e-mail: doctorreed@yahoo.com
counselor

TEXAS

Amelie Benedikt
3109 Wheeler Street
Austin, TX 78705
tel: 512-695-7900
e-mail: afb@io.com
counselor

Amy McLaughlin
6811 Daugherty Street
Austin, TX 78757
tel: 512-467-8049
e-mail: episteme@swbell.net
counselor

Andrea Messineo
1418 Richmond Avenue
Houston, TX 77006
tel: 713-526-8810
e-mail: panzanella@pdq.net
counselor

VIRGINIA

Tasha Anderson
3385 Ardley Court
Falls Church, VA 22041
tel: 703-305-3919
e-mail: tashaa@wizard.net
counselor

Joseph Monast
Department of History & Philosophy
Virginia State University
Petersburg, VA 23806
tel: 804-524-5555
fax: 804-524-7802
e-mail: jmonast@erols.com
counselor

Bruce Thomas
8 Huntington Drive
Williamsburg, VA 23188
tel: 757-229-9835
e-mail: sthomas@widomaker.com
consultant

WASHINGTON

Britni Weaver
1715 W. Pacific #C
Spokane, WA 99204
tel: 509-838-4886
e-mail: britnijw@yahoo.com
counselor

CANADA

Stanley Chan
270 Old Post Road
Waterloo, Ontario
Canada N2L 5B9
tel: 519-884-5384
fax: 519-884-9120
e-mail: stanleyknchan@hotmail.com
counselor

Wanda Dawe
P.O. Box 339
Crossroads
Bay Roberts, Newfoundland
Canada A0A 1G0
tel/fax: 709-786-3166
e-mail: wanda.dawe@thezone.net
counselor, facilitator

Anthony Falikowski
Sheridan College
1430 Trafalgar Rd.
Oakville, Ontario
Canada L6L 1X7
tel: 905-845-9430 x2508
fax: 905-815-4032
e-mail:
  tony.falikowski@sheridanc.on.ca
consultant

Cheryl Nafziger-Leis
16 Meadowlark Road
Elmira, Ontario
Canada N3B 1T6
tel: 519-669-4991
fax: 519-669-5641
e-mail: Leis@sentex.net
consultant

Sean O'Connell
1806, 8920-100 St.
Edmonton, Alberta
Canada T6E 4YB
tel: 780-439-9752
e-mail: phipsibk@netscape.net
counselor

Peter Raabe
46-2560 Whitely Court
North Vancouver, BC
Canada V7J 2R5
tel: 604-986-9446
e-mail: raabe@interchange.ubc.ca
counselor

FRANCE

Anette Prins
43, Avenue Lulli
92330 Sceaux, France
e-mail: prins@aol.com
tel: 33-014-661-0032
fax: 33-014-661-0031
counselor

ISRAEL

Lydia Amir
The New School of Media Studies
The College of Management
9 Shoshana Persitz St.
Tel-Aviv, 61480 Israel
tel: 972-3-744-1086
fax: 972-3-699-0458
e-mail: lydamir55@hotmail.com
counselor

Ora Gruengard
43 Yehuda Hanasi Street
Tel-Aviv, 69391 Israel
tel: 972-3-641-4776
fax: 972-3-642-2439
e-mail: egone@mail.shenkar.ac.il
counselor

Eli Holzer
33 Halamed Heh Street
Jerusalem, 93661 Israel
tel: 972-02-567-2033
e-mail: esholzer@netvision.net.il
counselor

THE NETHERLANDS

Dries Boele
Spaarndammerplantsoen 108
1013 XT Amsterdam
tel: 31-20-686-7330
counselor, facilitator

Will Heutz
Schelsberg 308
6413 AJ Heerlen
tel: 31-45-572-0323
counselor, consultant

Ida Jongsma
Hotel de Filosoof
  (Philosopher's Hotel)
Anna Vondelstraat 6
1054 GZ Amsterdam
tel: 31-20-683-3013
fax: 31-20-685-3750
counselor, facilitator, consultant

NORWAY

Anders Lindseth
University of Tromso
N-9037 Tromso, Norway
andersl@fagmed.uit.no
counselor

TURKEY

Harun Sungurlu
P.K. 2 Emirgan
Istanbul, Turkey 80850
e-mail:
sungurludh@superonline.com
counselor

UNITED KINGDOM

Alex Howard
8 Winchester Terrace
Newcastle upon Tyne
UK, NE4 6EH
tel: 44-91-232-5530
e-mail:
consult@alexhoward.demon.co.uk
counselor, consultant

Judy Wall
The CPD Centre
51A Cecil Road
Lancing, West Sussex
United Kingdom, BN15 8HP
tel: 011-44-0193-764301
fax: 011-44-0193-765970
e-mail: lifeplan@cwcom.net
consultant

Directory of Organizations

AMERICAN ORGANIZATIONS

American Philosophical Practitioners Association (APPA)
The City College of New York
137th Street at Convent Avenue
New York, NY 10031
tel: 212-650-7827
fax: 212-650-7409
e-mail: admin@appa.edu
www.appa.edu
President: Lou Marinoff

American Society for Philosophy, Counseling
  and Psychotherapy (ASPCP)
Kenneth Cust, Co-Executive Director
Center for Applied & Professional Ethics
Central Missouri State University
Warrensburg, MO 64093

INTERNATIONAL ORGANIZATIONS

CANADA

Canadian Society for Philosophical Practice
473 Besserer Street
Ottawa, Ontario K1N 6C2
Canada
tel: 613-241-6717
fax: 613-241-9767
Stephen Hare, Interim President

FINLAND

Finnish Society for Philosophical Counseling
Tykistonkatu 11 B 30
SF-00260 Helsinki
Finland
Chair: Antti Mattila, MD

GERMANY

International Society for Philosophical Practice
(formerly, German Society for Philosophical Practice)
Hermann-Loens Strasse 56c
D-51469 Bergisch Gladbach, Germany
tel: 2202-951995
fax: 2202-951997
e-mail: Achenbach.PhilosophischePraxis@t-online.de
Gerd Achenbach, President

ISRAEL

Israel Society for Philosophical Inquiry
Horkania 23, Apt. 2
Jerusalem 93305
Israel
tel: 972-2-679-5090
e-mail: msshstar@pluto.mscc.huji.ac.il
http://www.geocities.com/Athens/Forum/5914
Chief Inquirer: Shlomit Schuster

ITALY

Italian Association for Philosophical Counseling
(Associazione Italiana Counseling Filosofico – AICF)
Corso Fiume 16, 10133 Torino, Italy
tel/fax (011) 6600015
http://utenti.tripod.it/Dr_Lodovico_E_Berra/AICF.html
http://utenti.tripod.it/AICF/homepage.html
President: Lodovico E. Berra

THE NETHERLANDS

Dutch Society for Philosophical Practice
Wim van der Vlist, Secretary
E. Schilderinkstraat 80
7002 JH Doetinchem, Netherlands
tel: 33-314-334704
e-mail: W.vanderVlist@inter.nl.net
Jos Delnoy, President
Herenstraat 52
2313 AL Leiden, Netherlands
tel: 33-71-5140964
fax 33-71-5122819
e-mail: ledice@worldonline.nl

NORWAY

Norwegian Society for Philosophical Practice
Cappelens vei 19c
1162 Oslo, Norway
tel: 47-88-00-96-69
e-mail: filosofiskpraksis@bigfoot.com
http://home.c2i.net/aholt/e-nsfp.htm
Henning Herrestad, President
e-mail: herrestad@online.no
Anders Holt, Secretary
e-mail: aholt@c2i.net
tel: 47-22-46-14-18

SLOVAKIA

Slovak Society for Philosophical Practice
Department of Social & Biological Communication
Slovak Academy of Sciences
Klemensova 19, 81364 Bratislava
Slovakia
tel: 00421-7-375683
fax: 00421-7-373442
e-mail: ksbkemvi@savba.sk
Emil Visnovsky, President

Select Bibliography on Philosophical Practice

This list is not exhaustive, but is illustrative.

Adler, M., *The Conditions of Philosophy: Its Checkered Past, Its Present Disorder, and Its Future Promise*, Atheneum, New York, 1965.

Angelett, W., "Philosophy and a career in counseling," *International Journal of Applied Philosophy*, Fall 1990, pp. 73–75.

Blass, R., "The 'person' in philosophical counseling vs. Psychotherapy and the possibility of interchange between the fields," *Journal of Applied Philosophy*, 13:279–296, 1996.

Botton, A., *The Consolations of Philosophy*, Pantheon, New York, 2000.

Cohen, E., *Philosophers at Work*, Holt, Rienhart and Winston, New York, 1989.

Grimes, P., and Uliana, R., *Philosophical Midwifery*, Hyparxis Press, Costa Mesa, 1998.

Hadot, P., *Philosophy as a Way of Life*, Blackwell, London, 1995.

Hersh, S., "The counseling philosopher," *The Humanist*, May/June, 1980, pp. 32–33.

Howard, A., *Philosophy for Counseling and Psychotherapy: Pythagoras to Postmodernism*, MacMillan, London, 2000.

Jopling, D., "Philosophical counseling: Truth and self-interpretation," *Journal of Applied Philosophy*, 13:297–310, 1996.

Koestenbaum, P., *The Inner Side of Greatness*, Jossey-Bass, San Francisco, 1991.

Lahav, R., "Applied phenomenology in philosophical counseling," *International Journal of Applied Philosophy*, 7:45–52, 1992.

Lahav, R., "Using analytic philosophy in philosophical counseling," *Journal of Applied Philosophy*, **10**:93–101, 1993.

Lahav, R., and Tillmanns M., eds., *Essays on Philosophical Counseling*, University Press of America, Lanham, 1995.

Lahav, R., "What is philosophical in philosophical counseling?" *Journal of Applied Philosophy*, **13**:197–310, 1996.

Lipman, M., Sharp, A., and Oscanyan, F., *Philosophy in the Classroom*, Temple University Press, Philadelphia, 1986.

Marinoff, L, "What philosophical counseling can't do," *Journal of Philosophy in the Contemporary World*, **5**:33–41, 1998.

Marinoff, L., *Plato Not Prozac: Applying Philosophy to Everyday Problems*, HarperCollins, New York, 1999 (currently going into twenty foreign language editions).

Morris, T., *If Aristotle Ran General Motors*, Henry Holt & Co., New York, 1997.

Nahser, F., *Learning to Read the Signs—Reclaiming Pragmatism in Business*, Butterworth-Heineman, Woburn, MA, 1997.

Nelson, L., *Socratic Method and Critical Philosophy*, trans. T. Brown III, Dover Publications Inc., New York, 1949.

Nussbaum, M., *The Therapy of Desire: Theory and Practice in Hellenistic Ethics* (1994).

Raabe, P., *Philosophical Counseling: Theory and Practice*, Praeger, Westport, 2000.

Ramsland, K., *Bliss*, Walking Stick Press, Cincinnati, 2000.

Russell, B., *The Conquest of Happiness*, Horace Liveright, New York, 1930.

Russell, J., "The philosopher as personal consultant," archived at <http://members.aol.com/jmrussell/philosas.htm>.

Sharkey, P., ed., *Philosophy, Religion and Psychotherapy: Essays in the Philosophical Foundations of Psychotherapy*, University Press of America, Washington DC, 1982.

Sharkey, P., "When?—The philosophical revolution," *Contemporary Philosophy*, **11**(3), 1986.

Sharkey, P., *A Philosophical Examination of The History and Values of Western Medicine*, The Edwin Mellen Press, Lewiston, NY, 1992.

Schuster, S., "Philosophy as if it matters: The practice of philosophical counseling," *Critical Review*, **6**:587-599, 1992.

Schuster, S., *Philosophy Practice: An Alternative to Counseling and Psychotherapy*, Praeger, Westport, 1999.

Zoe, K., "Philosophical counseling: Bridging the narrative rift," *Philosophy in the Contemporary World*, **2**:23-28, 1995.

Scholarly Journals

Zeitschrift fur Philosophische Praxis (Journal for Philosophical Practice)
Michael Schefczyk, editor
Grabengasse 27
50679 Koln, Germany
(publishes in German and English)

Filosofische Praktijk (Philosophical Practice)
edited by the Dutch Association for Philosophical Practice
(publishes in Dutch)

International Journal of Applied Philosophy
Elliot Cohen, editor
Indian River Community College
3209 Virginia Avenue
Fort Pierce, FL 33454

Journal of the Society for Existential Analysis
Hans W. Cohn and Simon du Plock, editors
Society for Existential Analysis
BM Existential
London WC1N 3XX, UK

Journal of Applied Philosophy
(Journal of the Society for Applied Philosophy)
Carfax Publishers, Abingdon, Oxfordshire

Reason in Practice
The Journal of Philosophy of Management
Nigel Laurie Editor and Publisher
74a Station Road East
Oxted, Surrey RH8 9DR

SPECIAL EDITIONS ON PHILOSOPHICAL PRACTICE

Journal of Chinese Philosophy
Chung-Ying Cheng, editor
Vol. 23, No. 3, Sept. 1996
Philosophical Counseling and Chinese Philosophy

Inquiry: Critical Thinking Across the Disciplines
Robert Esformes, editor
Vol. 27, No. 3, Spring 1998
selected papers from The Third International
   Conference on Philosophical Practice

Journal of Philosophy in the Contemporary World
Frank Joe Jones III, editor
Vol. 7, No. 4, Winter 2000, in the press
special issue on virtue in Philosophical Practice

INDEX

A

ACA. *See* American Counseling Association
Academic philosophy, 40
Academy, 201–202
Accreditation. *See also* Certification
  philosophical practice, 202
Achenbach, G., 68, 89, 90, 203–204, 278
Active meditation, 61–63
Addiction, use of term, 6–7
Adler, M., 67, 68, 105, 369
Affective-biological dyad, 100
African-American, use of term, 8
Ahimsa, 35
American Counseling Association (ACA),
  276
American Philosophical Practitioners
  Association (APPA), 348, 352, 354,
  357, 361
  certification, 61, 92
  certification standards, 212–214, 227,
    241, 339, 344
  Certification Training Program,
    193–194, 265
  directory of practitioners, 344
  founding members, 191
  press kit, 282
  standards for ethical practice, 14,
    222–227, 344

American Psychiatric Association (APA)
  ethics counseling and, 48–49, 51
American Society for Philosophy,
  Counseling, and Psychotherapy (ASPCP)
  certification of philosophical counseling,
    207–212, 344
Amir, L., 206
Analytic philosophy, 45, 144, 146–147, 157,
  185–186, 336, 348
Anglo-American Alliance for Philosophical
  Practice, 353
APPA. *See* American Philosophical
  Practitioners Association
Applied ethics, 50–51, 185, 186, 221
Arendt, H., 19, 369
Aristotle, 22, 91, 170
Artistry, 168–170
ASPCP. *See* American Society for Philosophy,
  Counseling, and Psychotherapy
Ayer, A., 5, 12–13, 18, 41, 369

B

Bagehot, W., 369
Barrett, W., 107, 369
Behavioral modification, 101
Behaviorists, 100
Benbow, C., 369, 372

Beneficence, 180
Bergson, H., 141, 172, 369
Bhagavad-Gita, 65, 81, 93, 369
Bibliotherapy, 93–94, 124
Bigotry, 157
Biological vertex, 96–97
Biomedical ethicists, 186
Black, M., 370
Boele, D., 132, 278, 369
Bohr, N., 83
Book publishing, 115, 117
Bookstore-café, 115
Bookstores, 115–119
    philosopher's café in, 115
    philosopher's forum in, 119–123
    scheduled events in, 118–119
    specialty bookstores, 116
    supermarket bookstores, 117–119
Botton, A. de, 345–346
Brand, C., 35, 321, 369
Breggin, P., 49, 53, 103, 327, 369
British pub, as philosopher's café, 115
Buber, M., 137, 369
Buddha, 24, 64, 99, 369
Buddhism, 111, 333
Building a practice, 277–286
Burgess, A., 369
Business cards, for philosophers, 186, 285
Business ethicists, 186, 205. *See also*
    Organizational consulting
Butler, J., 17

C

Café-philo, 112, 114, 125, 338
California, state licensing law, 233–234,
    236–237, 241
Capital punishment, 14
Cattell, R., 35, 370
CCHR. *See* Citizens Commission on
    Human Rights
Certification, 207–220, 239–241
    APPA certification, 61, 92, 193–194,
        212–214, 227, 241, 339
    ASPCP certification, 207–212, 344

for client counselors, 215–216
for group facilitators, 216–217
for organizational consulting, 217–220
Chamberlain, H., 88
Chan, S., 90
Chomsky, N., 291
Churchland, P., 65, 370
Cicero, 49, 60
Citizens Commission on Human Rights
    (CCHR), 327, 328
City College of New York, Wellness Center,
    362–365
Client counseling. *See* Philosophical
    counseling
"Coaching," 161
Code of ethics
    APPA standards for ethical practice,
        222–227
    organizational consulting to assist
        code-building, 161–162
    for philosophical counseling field,
        221–222, 344
Coffeehouse, 114. *See* Philosopher's café
Coffeehouse opening, 124, 337
Coffeehouse philosophy, 124, 294, 337
Cohen, E., 207, 208
Cole, J., 370
Colleges, philosophy for undergraduates,
    295–298
Colorado, state licensing law, 236–237,
    241, 245
Conflict, in workplace, 306–317
Confucius, 24
Conquest, R., 309, 370
Consulting. *See* Organizational consulting;
    Philosophical consulting
Continental schools, of philosophy, 144,
    145, 146, 348
Corporate world
    conflict in workplace, 305–317
    organizational consulting, 12, 153–159
Correctional system, philosophy for felons,
    299–301
Counseling, 67
    ethics counseling, 49
    philosophical. *See* Philosophical counseling
    as protected term, 264

Cranston, M., 145, 173
Cross-training, of philosophical counselors, 269
Cultural diversity, 315
Cultural evolution, philosophical counseling and, 72–79
Cust, K., 208

D

Damasio, A., 49, 53, 65, 370
Danielson, P., 69, 106, 370
Darwin, C., 30, 230
Day-care philosopher, 294
de Chardin, P. T., 150, 173, 370
Defendant, ethical competency and, 327
Dennett, D., 65, 370
Descartes, R., 23, 25, 61, 133, 349
Dewey, J., 30, 44
Dialogue
  between counselor and client, 81–94
  history, 126–127
  Nelsonian Socratic dialogue, 127–136, 231, 290–291
  in philosophic tradition, 81
  type A dialogue, 87–89
  type B counseling, 87, 90, 92–93
  type C counseling, 93
  worst case scenario, 302
Diaz bill, 204, 238–240
Dilemma training, 163–164, 320
Diversity, 183, 188–189, 310–315
Drever, J., 370
Durkheim, E., 30
Dutch Society for Philosophical Practice, 205
Dutton, D., 370

E

Eakman, B., 327–328, 349, 370
East India Company, 148, 150
Economy, independence of economics from politics, 148–150

Education, 30
  for philosophical counseling, 187–191
  philosophy for undergraduates, 295–298
  in United States, 185
Elder cafes, 303
Eliot, T. S., 193
Ellis, A., 103, 332
Empowerment, 320
England
  philosophical counseling in, 332
  pub as philosopher's café, 115
English history, 148
Environment, 98
Epictetus, 39, 370
Equal opportunity, 320
Erasmus, D., 40, 370
Ethics. See also Code of ethics
  APPA standards for ethical practice, 222–227, 344
  applied ethics, 50–51, 185–186, 221
  biomedical ethicists, 186
  business ethicists, 186, 205
  ethics compliance in corporate world, 159, 162–163, 317–320
  ethics counseling, 49
Ethics compliance, 159, 162–163, 317–320
Ethics counseling, 49. See also Philosophical counseling
Euclidean geometry, 142–143
Excellence, 183–184
Existentialism, 43

F

Facilitation. See Group facilitation
Feary, V., 301
Felician College (NJ), graduate course in philosophical counseling, 187–189
Felons, philosophy for, 299–301
Feyerabend, P., 227, 370
First International Conference on Philosophical Practice, 206, 352
Formal facilitation, 231, 290–291
France, café-philo, 112, 114, 124–125, 338
Frankl, V., 103, 332

Fraud, philosophical practice and, 344–345
Freud, S., 23, 106, 370
Friedman, M., 68
Fromm, E., 103, 332
Furedy, J., 321, 370
"Fuzzy speech," 8, 9

G

Gairdner, W., 18, 370
Galileo, 22, 23, 41, 81, 145
Gauss, C. F., 23, 27
Gautama, 28, 92
Geach, G., 370
Gender conflict, 320
Gender imbalance, 182, 196
Genocide, moral condemnation of, 151
Geometry, 142–143
German Society for Philosophical Prac-
    tice, 352
Germany
    Nelsonian Socratic dialogue, 129
    philosophical practice in, 203–205
    post–World War I economy, 149
"G" factor, 27
Gibbon, E., 370
Globalization, 17, 112–113, 115–116
Golman, D., 35, 370
Gould, S., 35, 370
Governance, organizational consulting
    and, 168
Government, 152
Graduate study, in philosophical counseling,
    187–191, 196–197
Great Britain
    philosophical counseling in, 332
    pub as philosopher's café, 115
Grief-counseling, 329
Grimes, P., 68, 104, 108, 125, 370
Gross, P., 371
Group facilitation, 12, 301–302
    certification for, 216–217
    in college setting, 295–298
    formal facilitation, 231, 290–291
    informal groups, 124–125, 231, 289–290
    Nelsonian Socratic dialogue, 127–136,
        231, 290–291

philosopher's café, 112–125, 283,
    289–290, 337–339
for prison population, 299–301
qualifications for facilitators, 339
for seniors, 298–299, 303
for undergraduates, 295–298
Group therapy, 328
Gruengard, O., 206

H

Haack, S., 106, 371
Haeckel, E., 35, 371
Hammond, D., 108, 371
Hanks, P., 371
Harding, S., 32
Held, B., 117, 137, 371
Herd-instinct, 90–91
Hernandez, A., 237
Herrnstein, R., 35, 371
Hersh, S., 68, 371
Heutz, W., 278
Hilditch, D., 303
Hirsch, E., 196, 371
History, 32
Hitler, A., 37, 47
Hobbes, T., 5, 7, 17–18, 22–23, 25, 34, 51,
    53, 142–143, 145–146, 371
Hoffman, M., 352
Holland
    Nelsonian Socratic dialogue, 129–130
    philosophical practice in, 154, 162,
        205–206
Homonymic, 8, 9
Hooke, R., 83
hooks, belle, 115
Howard, A., 356, 371
Hume, D., 23, 24, 25, 41, 47, 81
Humphreys, C., 371

I

I Ching, 38, 81, 93
Image of philosophical counselors, 284–286
Inactive meditation, 63–64

Incompetence, 157–158

Informal group facilitation, 124–125, 231, 289–290

Informed consent, for research subjects, 257–259

Inglis, B., 371

Inmates, philosophy for, 299–301

Institute for the Advancement of Philosophy for Children, 371

Institutes
different from universities, 201–202
for philosophical practice, 200–201

Institutionalization, 101–102

Institutional Review Board (IRB), approval of research proposal, 250–262

Insurance, for philosophical counselors, 274–277

Intelligence, 29, 35

International Conferences on Philosophical Practice, 206, 208, 352

International relations, philosophical practice and, 351–353

International Society for Philosophical Practice, 352

Interprofessional relations, philosophical counseling, 353–358

IQ, of students, 26–30, 35

IRB. See Institutional Review Board

Irvine, A., 371

Israel, philosophical practice in, 206

Itard, J., 371

J

Jablecki, L., 301

Jacklin, C., 138, 372

James, W., 30, 44, 302, 371

Jongsma, I., 278

Jopling, D., 371

Jordan, D., 35, 371

Journals, in philosophical practice, 220–221

Jung, A., 68

K

Kant, I., 51, 146

Karma, 57, 64, 65

Kennet, W., 34

Kesey, K., 371

Kessels, J., 133, 138, 278

Kett, J., 196, 371

Kierkegaard, S., 43, 137

Kimura, D., 196

King, S., 115

Kipnis, K., 162

Kirwan-Taylor, H., 107, 371

Kleinfeld, J., 371

Koestenbaum, P., 68, 168, 279, 356, 372

Koestler, A., 34, 372

Korzybski, A., 106, 372

Kuczynski, A., 205, 281, 286, 372

Kuhn, T., 34, 350, 372

L

Lahav, R., 70–71, 107, 196, 206, 208, 372

Laing, R. D., 103

Language, 79
"fuzzy speech," 8, 9
linguistic substitution, 9–11
misuse of, 6–8
Orwell on, 18
value-neutral vs. value-laden, 9–10

Language study, 4

Lao Tzu, 38, 63, 141, 372

Leacock, S., 173

Leadership, organizational consulting and, 168

Legislative recognition
Diaz bill, 204, 238–240
of philosophical counseling, 202–203, 231, 275

Leibniz, G. W., 39, 265

Levin, M., 35, 349, 372

Levitt, N., 371

Liability insurance, for philosophical counselors, 274–277

Licensing, 204, 231–239
Diaz bill, 204, 238–240
scope of practice, 232, 237
title, 232, 237

Linguistic substitution, 9–11

Lipman, M., 68, 291, 292, 293, 372
Locke, J., 23, 25, 145
Long, J., 372
Lubinski, D., 372

M

Macauley, Baron, 148
Maccoby, E., 138, 372
MacHamer, P., 34, 372
Machiavelli, N., 142
Magnell, T., 207, 208
Malpractice insurance, for philosophical
    counselors, 274–277
Malson, L., 372
Management consultants, 162
Mandelbrot, B., 143
Mandell, R., 372
Mann, T., 368, 372
March, P., 82, 271, 290
Marinoff, L., 18, 84, 106, 107, 124, 134,
    137, 208, 287, 343, 368, 372–373
Marketing, for philosophical counseling,
    279–286
Marshall Plan, 149
Marx, K., 39, 51
Mass suicide, 88
Mathematics, 142–143, 312
Matheson, J., 148
Matz, L., 332
Mayr, E., 326
McDonald, M., 69
Meditation, 57–64
Melville, H., 115
Mental illness, 17, 102–103
Michaelson, C., 279
Milgram, S., 102, 373
Mill, J., 39, 107, 373
Miller, H., 91, 114
Milton, J., 34
Mind–brain dyad, 95, 96
Mintz, S., 34, 172, 373
Modularity of practice, philosophical
    practice, 306, 319
Monarchy, 141–142, 148

Monologue, 80
Moore, G., 18, 41, 373
Moral guidance, 13
Moral self-defense, 163–164
Morgenstern, O., 172, 375
Morris, T., 278
Morrison, T., 115
Motivational speaking, 160–161
Mumford, L., 141, 172, 373
Muncy, M., 196, 373
Murray, C., 35, 371

N

Nahser, R., 279
National organizations, training programs
    of, 194
National relations, philosophical practice
    and, 351–353
Natural selection, 72
Neckar cube, 95
Nelson, L., 127–128, 134, 297, 373
Nelsonian Socratic dialogue, 127–136,
    231, 290–291
Newton, Sir Isaac, 23, 30, 32, 83
New York, licensing law, 85, 199, 232, 237
Nietzsche, F., 25, 39, 43, 146
Non-harm, 35
Non-maleficence, 178–180
Nussbaum, M., 373

O

Obsessive–compulsive disorder (OCD), 100
Office politics, 307
Opium Wars, 148, 150
Organizational consulting, 12, 153–159
    artistry, 168–170
    certification for, 217–220
    conflict in workplace, 305–317
    dilemma training, 163–164, 320
    ethics code-building, 161–162
    ethics compliance, 159, 162–163, 317–320

leadership and governance, 168
moral self-defense, 163–164
motivational speaking and, 160–161
opportunities in, 305–320
PEACE process, 167–168
Socratic dialogue and, 164–165, 290–291
Organizational mission, 155, 158
Orwell, G., 5, 9, 10, 18, 373
Oscanyan, F., 372

P

Packaging, of philosophical counselors,
284–286
Pain, 107
Paine, T., 153
Palmer, G., 373
Pauli, W., 83
PEACE process, 167–168
Peck, M. S., 103, 373
Pedagogy, 178, 195
of philosophical practice, 187–191
in United States, 184
Penrose, R., 65, 373
Personality, of philosophical counselors,
269–270
Philosophers
business cards for, 186, 285
as consultants, 141–153
Philosopher's café, 112–125, 289–290,
337–339
elder cafe, 303
selling the idea, 119–120
for seniors, 298–299, 303
types of attendees, 121–122, 283
venue for, 114–119
Philosopher's forum, 119–123
Philosophical consulting, 160, 306
artistry, 168–170
dilemma training, 163–164, 320
ethics code-building, 161–162
ethics compliance, 162–163
leadership and governance, 168
moral self-defense, 163–164
motivational speaking and, 160–161
to organizations, 12, 153–159
PEACE process, 167–168
Socratic dialogue and, 164–165, 290–291

Philosophical counseling, 12–15, 169–170
APA on, 48–49, 51
APPA standards for ethical practice,
222–227, 344
autobiographical account, 68–72
bibliotherapy, 93–94, 124
building a practice, 277–286
certification of. See Certification
code of ethics for field, 221–222, 344
cultural evolution and, 72–79
dialogue in, 81–94
different from psychotherapy, 271–274
fraud in, 344–345
freedom of speech and, 233
as full-time endeavor, 278–279
function of, 85–86
in Germany, 203–205
graduate study in, 187–191, 196–197
in Holland, 205–206
interprofessional relations, 353–358
in Israel, 206
legislative recognition, 202–203,
231, 275
licensure, 204, 231–239
malpractice insurance, 274–277
marketing for, 279–286
Nelsonian Socratic dialogue, 127–136,
231, 290–291
non-maleficence, 178–179
opportunities in, 305–320
personal problems concealed by, 346–347
philosopher's café, 112–125, 283,
289–290, 337–339
psychiatry and, 268, 286, 326–328, 354
psychology and, 268, 286, 328–334,
354–357
qualifications for, 264–268, 286, 339
regulation of, 231–244, 264
religion and, 91–92
state recognition as profession, 202–203,
231, 275
training programs for, 187–191, 196–197,
200–203, 265–267
triangular model, 94–105
type A dialogue, 87–88, 89
type B counseling, 87, 90, 92, 93
type C counseling, 93

Philosophical counselors, 318
  as advocates for clients, 81–82
  business cards for, 186, 285
  certification of. *See* Certification
  cross-training, 269
  fraud by, 344–345
  licensing of, 204, 231–239
  malpractice insurance for, 274–277
  marketing by, 279–286
  packaging, 284–286
  personality of, 269–270
  personal problems and competence,
    346–347
  press kit for, 280, 282
  promotion by, 283–284
  publicity by, 279–283
  qualifications for, 264–267, 268, 286, 339
  referrals by, 254–257, 267–269, 285
  registration of, 241
  speaking engagements by, 283–284
  training programs for, 187–191, 196–197,
    200–203, 265–267
  website for, 285
Philosophical practice, 191, 318, 359
  accreditation, 202
  ambivalence, 345–346
  APPA standards for ethical practice,
    222–227, 344
  building a practice, 277–278, 279–286
  certification. *See* Certification
  code of ethics for field, 221–222, 344
  coffeehouse mentality, 124, 337–339
  counseling. *See* Philosophical counseling
  establishing as body of knowledge,
    220–221
  fraud in, 344–345
  as full-time endeavor, 278–279
  in Germany, 203–205
  graduate training for, 187–191, 196–197
  in Holland, 205–206
  institutes for, 200–201
  international relations, 351–353
  interprofessional relations, 353–358
  in Israel, 206
  licensure, 204, 231–239
  modularity of practice, 306, 319
  national relations, 351–353

organizational consulting. *See*
    Organizational consulting
  pedagogy of, 187–191
  personal problems concealed by, 346–347
  pioneering efforts in, 195–196
  professionalism of, 199–227
  reference books and journals, 220–221
  registration process, 241
  regulation of, 231–244, 264
  research protocols, 250–262, 277
  sophistry, 339–344
  state recognition as profession, 202–203,
    231, 275
  training programs for, 187–191, 196–197,
    200–203, 265–267
Philosophy, 334–337
  academic philosophy, 40
  analytic philosophy, 45, 144, 146–147,
    157, 185–186, 336, 348
  coffeehouse philosopher, 124, 294, 337
  complementarity of religion to, 25–26
  continental schools, 144, 145, 146, 348
  current state of, 23
  as discipline, 26–34
  early 1900s, 42
  as group activity, 109–137
  history of, 21–23, 25, 38–39
  institutionalization of, 42–43
  mathematics and, 142–144
  1960s, 55
  politics and, 151–152, 311–312
  popularity of, 37–52
  published papers in, 23–24
  for seniors, 298–299, 303
  sophistry, 339–344
  students of, 26–30
  theoretical philosophy, 23, 46, 318, 319
  as therapy, 82, 94
  for undergraduates, 295–298
  as way of life, 24–25
  World Economic Forum, 366–367
Philosophy students, 26–30
Phobias, 100
Phronesis, 94, 162, 186, 305
Plato, 28, 37, 41, 51, 104, 108, 127, 138,
    141, 143, 171, 291, 297, 368, 374

Plato Not Prozac (Marinoff), 9, 38, 84, 116–117, 134, 167, 253, 271, 300, 332, 360–362
Poe, E. A., 115
Politics
    Aristotle on, 170
    independence of economics from politics, 148–150
    moral influence on, 151–152
    philosophy and, 311–312
Popper, K., 107, 374
Post–World War I economy, 149
Power-structure, use of term, 320
Pragmatism, 43, 44
Prawda, G., 339
Press kit, 280, 282
Prison population, philosophy for, 299–301
Professionalism
    of philosophical practice, 199–227
    in United States, 177–178
Professional journals, in philosophical practice, 220–221
Professional liability insurance, for philosophical counselors, 274–277
Professional organizations, 194, 352–353
Promotion, for philosophical counseling practice, 283–284
Protagoras, 156
Psychiatry, 75, 355
    philosophical counseling and, 268, 286, 326–328, 354
    scope of practice, 275
Psychoanalysts, state licensing law, 233, 236, 241
Psychologists, state licensing law, 85, 233
Psychology, 30, 75–76
    philosophical counseling and, 268, 328–334, 354–357
Psychotherapists, 85
    personal problems and competence, 346–347
    state licensing laws, 85, 232–244, 271
Psychotherapy, 67
    philosophical counseling different from, 271–274
    state licensing, 85, 232–244, 271
    use of term, 85, 271–273

Publicity, for philosophical counseling practice, 279–283
Publishing industry, 115, 117
Pythagoras, 143

R

Raabe, P., 197, 374
Rachels, J., 102, 374
Ramus, R., 22, 34
Rand, A., 52, 81
Rapoport, A., 68
Reference books, in philosophical practice, 220–221
Referrals, by philosophical counselor, 254–257, 267–269, 285
Registration, of philosophical counselor, 241
Regulation, 229–231, 264
    certification. *See* Certification
    licensure, 204, 231–239
    of philosophical practice, 231–244
    registration, 241
Reisberg, L., 374
Religion
    complementarity of philosophy to, 25–26
    philosophical counseling and, 91–92
Religious studies, 6
Research, 250, 259–262
    contingency plan and referral list, 254–257
    informed consent form, 257–259
    IRB approval, 250–253
    liability insurance, 277
    recruiting subjects, 254
Reverse Berry Paradox, 172
Richards, K., 367
Richler, M., 137
Rinpoche, S., 107
Robertson, G., 34, 374
Rogers, C., 103, 332
Rorty, R., 147, 336
Rosenhan, D., 102, 374
Rousseau, J. J., 43, 133, 138, 145–146, 374
Roy, J., 374
Russell, B., 24, 39, 41, 43, 67, 105, 336, 349, 365, 368, 374
Russell, J. M., 68, 107, 234, 236, 374

S

Salon, 123
Sapir, E., 6, 16, 374
Sapir–Whorf hypothesis. *See* Whorf–Sapir
    hypothesis
Sartre, J. P., 24, 39, 43, 81
Sautet, M., 114, 338
Scargill, D., 172
Schiro, J., 183, 374
Schneider, A., 374
Scholarly journals, in philosophical
    practice, 220–221
Schopenhauer, A., 25, 52–53, 302, 374
Schwab , K., 366
Science, 32, 312
Scientology, 327, 349
Scope of practice, 233, 252–253, 275
Scruton, R., 340–343
Searle, J., 65, 374
Self-destruction, 89
Seneca, L., 24, 39, 137, 278, 374, 375
Senior citizens, philosophy for, 298–299, 303
Sharkey, J., 281
Sharkey, P., 68, 105, 207–208, 212, 236,
    262, 273, 279, 375
Sharp, A., 372
Shirer, W., 375
Simon, P., 138
Smith, D., 172, 375
Snow, C., 29, 375
Social sciences, philosophy and, 312
Socrates, 24, 29, 39, 126, 127, 141, 276
Socratic dialogue, 130–132, 136, 290
    in college environment, 296–298
    Nelsonian, 127–136, 231, 291
    in organizational consulting, 164–165,
        290–291
    worst-case scenario, 302
Sokal, A., 17, 86, 375
Solomon, M., 36
Sophistry, 339–344
Sound-byte, use of term, 9
Speaking engagements, as philosophical
    counselor, 283–284
Specialty bookstores, 116

Spencer, H., 30, 35, 375
Spinelli, E., 103, 332, 353
Spinoza, B., 24, 39, 143
Standards
    for certification, 207–220, 344
    for ethical practice, 14, 222–227, 344
State recognition of professional group, 85,
    202–203, 230–231, 275
St. Augustine, 51
Stotsky, S., 375
Suffering, 107
Suicide, 88, 89
Supermarket bookstores, 117–119
Synonyms, 8
"Synthetic selection," 72
Szasz, T. S., 17, 82, 103, 327–328, 375

T

Talk-therapy, 180, 233
Talmud, 81
Taoism, 172
Tarski, A., 42, 143, 147
Tauber, A., 103, 375
Teamwork, 158
Texas, licensing law, 232, 237
Theoretical philosophy, 23, 46, 318, 319
Therapy, use of term, 84, 271–272
Third International Conference on
    Philosophical Practice, 208, 352
Thoreau, H., 39, 107
Thucydides, 375
Tillmanns, M., 372
Toynbee, A., 375
Training
    for philosophical counseling, 187–191,
        196–197, 200–203, 265–267
    by professional organizations, 194, 265
Traub, J., 364, 375
Trefil, J., 196, 371
Trinity, 94–95
Tutelage, 142
"Two cultures," 29
Type A dialogue, 87–88, 89
Type B counseling, 87, 90, 92, 93
Type C counseling, 93

U

Uliana, R., 108, 370
Undergraduates, philosophy for, 295–298
United States
    educational system in, 185
    ethics compliance, 162–163
    pedagogy in, 184
    philosopher's café in, 115
    philosophical practice in, 278
    professionalism in, 177–178
University
    different from Institute, 201–202
    philosophy for undergraduates, 295–298

V

van Deurzen, E., 332
van Luijk, H., 165, 205, 320
Velvet totalitarianism, 321
Von Bonin, G., 106, 375
von Morstein, P., 90
Von Neumann, J., 172, 375
Vost, K., 334

W

Wallis, J., 23, 142
Wallraff, C., 330, 375
Walzer, M., 375
War
    international business and, 171
    moral condemnation of, 151
Websites, for philosophical counselors, 285
Weidlich, T., 375
Westfeld, A., 281
Whitehead, A., 374
"White noise," 287
Whitman, W., 115
WHOA conglomerate, 5, 7, 9
Whorf, B., 5, 6, 16, 375
Whorf–Sapir hypothesis, 7, 16
Wiseman, B., 327, 349, 376
Wittgenstein, L., 39, 41–42
Wood, A., 34, 376
Workplace, conflict in, 306–317
World Economic Forum (Davos), 366–367
Writers, earning living as, 115

Z

Zuckerman, H., 370